D0858401

Why Poor People Stay Poor

A study of urban bias in
world development

Michael Lipton

Why Poor People Stay Poor

Urban Bias in World Development

HARVARD UNIVERSITY PRESS
CAMBRIDGE, MASSACHUSETTS
1977

Contents

5

III URBAN BIAS: SOME EVIDENCE

10 *Contents*

10 *Contents*

Acknowledgements

Willingness to comment on a long, difficult draft is a severe test of the loyalty of one's friends and colleagues, and of their interest in one's work. Ronald Dore, Dharma Kumar, David Newbery and Paul Streeten have saved me from many errors by their careful, detailed and unselfish help with the entire text. David Dyker, Mick Moore, Robin Murray, Guy Routh, John Thomas and David Yaffe responded most generously, from viewpoints very different from my own, to an earlier draft of chapter 4. Emanuel de Kadt commented incisively and helpfully on chapter 9, and Clive Bell on chapters 5-8.

Raphie Kaplinsky card-indexed many relevant references, some of which he also unearthed and evaluated. Kurt Hoffman, Steve Lord and David Storey performed several tabulations and computations. Anton Powell made the index.

Several secretaries, above all Esther Simmonds, have shown amazing patience with my successive and barely legible drafts. Mike Rogers, Heather Brownridge, Sheila Howard and other library staff, at the Institute of Development Studies at Sussex University, have also been much more friendly and constructive than my disorganisation justified.

I am deeply grateful to the Rockefeller Foundation, and to Mr and Mrs Olsen, for five weeks at the Villa Serbelloni in August-September 1973: a time of quiet, undistracted work when it was most needed.

Finally, the publisher, Maurice Temple Smith, has shown great patience with my frequent delays, and has provided many useful comments.

The responsibility for what follows remains entirely mine.

Note: 'Billion' is used to mean 'thousand million' throughout.

Introduction

The most important class conflict in the poor countries of the world today is not between labour and capital. Nor is it between foreign and national interests. It is between the rural classes and the urban classes. The rural sector contains most of the poverty, and most of the low-cost sources of potential advance; but the urban sector contains most of the articulateness, organisation and power. So the urban classes have been able to 'win' most of the rounds of the struggle with the countryside; but in so doing they have made the development process needlessly slow and unfair. Scarce land, which might grow millets and beansprouts for hungry villagers, instead produces a trickle of costly calories from meat and milk, which few except the urban rich (who have ample protein anyway) can afford. Scarce investment, instead of going into water-pumps to grow rice, is wasted on urban motorways. Scarce human skills design and administer, not clean village wells and agricultural extension services, but world boxing championships in showpiece stadia. Resource allocations, within the city and the village as well as between them, reflect urban priorities rather than equity or efficiency. The damage has been increased by misguided ideological imports, liberal and Marxian, and by the town's success in buying off part of the rural elite, thus transferring most of the costs of the process to the rural poor.

But is this urban bias really damaging? After all, since 1945 output per person in the poor countries has doubled; and this unprecedented growth has brought genuine development. Production has been made more scientific: in agriculture, by the irrigation of large areas, and more recently by the increasing adoption of fertilisers and of high-yielding varieties of wheat and rice; in industry, by the replacement of fatiguing and repetitive effort by rising levels of technology, specialisation and skills. Consumption has also developed, in ways that at once use and underpin the development of production; for poor countries now consume enormously expanded provisions of health and education, roads and electricity, radios and bicycles. Why, then, are so many of those involved in the development of the Third World—politicians and administrators, planners and scholars—miserable about the past and gloomy about the future? Why is the United Nations' 'Development Decade' of the 1960s, in which poor countries as a whole exceeded the growth target,[1] generally written off as a failure? Why is aid, which demonstrably contributes to a development effort apparently so promising in global terms, in accelerating decline and threatened by a 'crisis of will' in donor countries?[2]

The reason is that since 1945 growth and development, in most poor countries, have done so little to raise the living standards of the poorest people. It is scant comfort that today's mass-consumption economies, in Europe and North America, also featured near-stagnant mass welfare in the early phases of their economic modernisation. Unlike today's poor countries, they carried in their early development the seeds of mass consumption later on. They were massively installing extra capacity to supply their people with simple goods: bread, cloth and coal, not just luxury housing, poultry and airports. Also the nineteenth-century 'developing countries', including Russia, were developing not just market requirements but class structures that practically guaranteed subsequent 'trickling down' of benefits. The workers even proved able to raise their *share* of political power and economic welfare. The very preconditions for such trends are absent in most of today's developing countries (chapter 2). The sincere egalitarian rhetoric of, say, Mrs Gandhi or Julius Nyerere was — allowing for differences of style and ideology — closely paralleled in Europe during early industrial development: in Britain, for example, by Brougham and Durham in the 1830s.[3] But the rural masses of India and Tanzania, unlike the urban masses of Melbourne's Britain, lack the power to organise the pressure that alone can turn such rhetoric into distributive action against the pressure of the elite.

Some rather surprising people have taken alarm at the persistently unequal nature of recent development. Aid donors are substantially motivated by foreign-policy concerns for the stability of recipient governments; development banks, by the need to repay depositors and hence to ensure a good return on the projects they support. Both concerns coalesce in the World Bank, which raises and distributes some £ 3,000 million of aid each year. As a bank it has advocated — and financed — mostly 'bankable' (that is, commercially profitable) projects. As a channel for aid donors, it has concentrated on poor countries that are relatively 'open' to investment, trade and economic advice from those donors. Yet the effect of stagnant mass welfare in poor countries, on the well-intentioned and perceptive people who administer World Bank aid, has gradually overborne these traditional biases. Since 1971 the president of the World Bank, Robert McNamara, has in a series of speeches focused attention on the stagnant or worsening lives of the bottom 40 per cent of people in poor countries.[4] Recently this has begun to affect the World Bank's projects, though its incomplete engagement with the problem of urban bias restricts the impact (chapter 14). For instance, an urban-biased government will prepare rural projects less well than urban projects, will manipulate prices to render rural projects less apparently profitable (and hence less 'bankable') and will tend to cut down its own effort if donors step up theirs. Nevertheless, the World Bank's new concern with the 'bottom 40 per cent' is significant.

These people—between one-quarter and one-fifth of the people of the world—are overwhelmingly rural: landless labourers, or farmers with no more than an acre or two, who must supplement their income by wage labour. Most of these countryfolk rely, as hitherto, on agriculture lacking irrigation or fertilisers or even iron tools. Hence they are so badly fed that they cannot work efficiently, and in many cases are unable to feed their infants well enough to prevent physical stunting and perhaps even brain damage. Apart from the rote-learning of religious texts, few of them receive any schooling. One in four dies before the age of ten. The rest live the same overworked, underfed, ignorant and disease-ridden lives as thirty, or three hundred, or three thousand years ago. Often they borrow (at 40 per cent or more yearly interest) from the same moneylender families as their ancestors, and surrender half their crops to the same families of landlords. Yet the last thirty years have been the age of unprecedented, accelerating growth and development! Naturally men of goodwill are puzzled and alarmed.

How can accelerated growth and development, in an era of rapidly improving communications and of 'mass politics', produce so little for poor people? It is too simple to blame the familiar scapegoats—foreign exploiters and domestic capitalists (chapter 3). Poor countries where they are relatively unimportant have experienced the paradox just as much as others. Nor, apparently, do the poorest families cause their own difficulties, whether by rapid population growth or by lack of drive. Poor families do tend to have more children than rich families, but principally because their higher death rates require it, if the ageing parents are to be reasonably sure that a son will grow up, to support them if need be. And it is the structure of rewards and opportunities within poor countries that extracts, as if by force, the young man of ability and energy from his chronically stagnant rural background and lures him to serve, or even to join, the booming urban elite (chapter 11).

The disparity between urban and rural welfare is much greater in poor countries now than it was in rich countries during their early development (table 5.4). This huge welfare gap is demonstrably inefficient, as well as inequitable (chapters 5-8). It persists mainly because less than 20 per cent of investment for development has gone to the agricultural sector (table 8.1; the situation has not changed much since 1965), although over 65 per cent of the people of less-developed countries (LDCs), and over 80 per cent of the really poor who live on $1 a week each or less, depend for a living on agriculture. The proportion of skilled people who support development—doctors, bankers, engineers—going to rural areas has been lower still; and the rural-urban imbalances have in general been even greater than those between agriculture and industry. Moreover, in most LDCs, governments have taken numerous measures with the unhappy side-effect of accentuating rural-urban disparities: their own allocation of public expenditure and taxation (chapter 12); measures raising the price of industrial production relative to farm production, thus encouraging private rural saving to flow into industrial investment because the value of industrial output has been artificially boosted (chapter 13); and educational facilities encouraging bright villagers to train in cities for urban jobs (chapter 11).

Such processes have been extremely inefficient. For instance, the impact on output of $1 of carefully selected investment is in most countries two to three times as high in agriculture as elsewhere (chapter 8), yet public policy and private market power have combined to push domestic savings and foreign aid into nonagricultural uses. The process has also been inequitable. Agriculture starts with about one-third the income per head of the rest of the economy (table 5.4), so that the people who depend on it should in equity receive special attention not special mulcting. Finally, the misallocation between sectors has created a needless and acute conflict between efficiency and equity. In agriculture the poor farmer with little land is usually efficient in his use of both land and capital (pp. 97-8, 114), whereas power, construction and industry often do best in big, capital-intensive units; and rural income and power, while far from equal, are less unequal than in the cities. So concentration on urban development and neglect of agriculture have pushed resources away from activities where they can help growth *and* benefit the poor, and towards activities where they do either of these, if at all, at the expense of the other.

Urban bias also increases inefficiency and inequity *within* the sectors. Poor farmers have little land and much underused family labour. Hence they tend to complement any extra developmental resources received—pumpsets, fertilisers, virgin land—with much more extra labour than do large farmers. Poor farmers thus tend to get most output from such extra resources (as well as needing the extra income most). But rich farmers (because they sell their extra output to the cities instead of eating it themselves, and because they are likely to use much of their extra income to support urban investment) are naturally favoured by urban-biased policies; it is they, not the efficient small farmers, who get the cheap loans and the fertiliser subsidies. The patterns of allocation and distribution within the cities are damaged too. Farm inputs are produced inefficiently, instead of imported, and the farmer has to pay, even if the price is nominally 'subsidised' (chapter 13). The processing of farm outputs, notably grain milling, is shifted into big urban units and the profits are no longer reinvested in agriculture. And equalisation between classes inside the cities becomes more risky, because the investment-starved farm sector might prove unable to deliver the food that a better-off urban mass would seek to buy.

Moreover, income in poor countries is usually more equally distributed within the rural sector than within the urban sector.[5] Since income creates the power to distribute extra income, therefore, a policy that concentrates on raising income in the urban sector will worsen inequalities in two ways: by transferring not only from poor to rich, but also from more equal to less equal. Concentration on urban enrichment is triply inequitable: because countryfolk start poorer; because such concentration allots rural resources largely to the rural rich (who sell food to the cities); and because the great inequality of power *within* the towns renders urban resources especially likely to go to the resident elites.

But am I not hammering at an open door? Certainly the persiflage of allocation has changed recently, under the impact of patently damaging deficiencies in rural output. Development plans are nowadays full of 'top priority for agriculture'.[6] This is reminiscent of the pseudo-egalitarian school where, at mealtimes, Class B children get priority, while Class A children get food.[7] We can see that the new agricultural priority is dubious from the abuse of the 'green revolution' and of the oil crisis (despite its much greater impact on *industrial* costs) as pretexts for lack of emphasis on agriculture: 'We don't need it,' and 'We can't afford it,' respectively. And the 60 to 80 per cent of people dependent on agriculture are still allocated barely 20 per cent of public resources; even these small shares are seldom achieved;

and they have, if anything, tended to diminish. So long as the elite's interests, background and sympathies remain predominantly urban, the countryside may get the 'priority' but the city will get the resources. The farm sector will continue to be squeezed, both by transfers of resources from it and by prices that are turned against it. Bogus justifications of urban bias will continue to earn the sincere, prestige-conferring, but misguided support of visiting 'experts' from industrialised countries and international agencies. And development will be needlessly painful, inequitable and slow.

This book aims to prove these points: to see how, why and with what effects the squeeze happens, and to suggest remedies and alternatives. Moral indignation is irrelevant; many members of elites in poor countries struggle to generate equitable development much more unselfishly than did their nineteenth-century European predecessors. The task is to understand the political facts and constraints.

Irrelevant also to this task, but not to my own emphasis, is the fact that (to my own surprise) I first noted urban bias in my analysis of Indian development in the 1960s.[8] Here as elsewhere India 'suffers' for her virtues: relatively good data, honest and first-rate domestic scholarship, and intellectual open-mindedness and curiosity. My work for this book has convinced me that, while Indian development is seriously retarded by urban bias, matters are far worse in most other LDCs. Many of the data in this book, for example those on the allocation of doctors (table 11.3), confirm this.

Three initial objections exist to a theory that urban bias is the mainspring of 'non-disimpoverishing' development. First, does it imply that rural emphasis will solve everything?[9] Development studies have been afflicted by many a misplaced *idee fixe*. Underinvestment, undereducation, and 'underemployment' have in rapid succession been presented as the Cause of All the Trouble, each with its implicit neat cure. It is not my wish, in this book, to overstate the case for reducing urban bias. Such a reduction is not the *only* thing necessary. But a shift of resources to the rural sector, and within it to the efficient rural poor even if they do very little for urban development, is often, perhaps usually, the *overriding* developmental task.[10] I seek to marshal all the arguments because (for all the easy populist rhetoric of politicians on tour) urban bias is a tough beast: like Belloc, 'I shoot the hippopotamus with bullets made of platinum, because if I use leaden ones his hide is sure to flatten 'em.'

Secondly, does the urban bias thesis imply some conspiracy theory of history? Do people with different interests get together,

in reality or 'in effect', and decide on the numerous acts considered in this book, all tending to harm the majority of the population
— those who work the land? Do not such flimsy coalitions notoriously split as the interests of their members conflict, and will
not the pressures of increasingly articulate mass opinion in
the countryside provide natural allies — especially in democracies
— for any part of the elite that opposes urban bias? Clearly any
conspiracy among several powerful men, representing divergent
interests but all opposed to mass interests, is likely to be unstable;
and hence any theory of development alleging that *persistent*
poverty in many different countries can be explained by such
conspiracies is absurd.

However, urban bias does not rest on a conspiracy, but on con-
vergent interests. Industrialists, urban workers, even big farmers,
all benefit if agriculture gets squeezed, provided its few resources
are steered, heavily subsidised, to the big farmer, to produce
cheap food and raw materials for the cities. Nobody conspires;
all the powerful are satisfied; the labour-intensive small farmer
stays efficient, poor and powerless, and had better shut up. Meanwhile, the economist, often in the blinkers of industrial determinism, congratulates all concerned on resolutely extracting an
agricultural surplus to finance industrialisation. Conspiracy? Who
needs conspiracy?

Thirdly, how far does the urban bias thesis go towards an agricultural or rural emphasis?[11] It was noted (note 10) that there is a
rather low limit to the shifts than *can* swiftly be made in allocations of key resources like doctors or savings between huge,
structured areas of economic life like agriculture and industry.
In the longer run, if the arguments of this book are right, how
high do they push the allocations that should go to agriculture in
poor countries: from the typical 20 per cent of various sorts of
scarce resource (for the poorest two-thirds of the people, who
are also those normally using scarce resources more efficiently,
as will be shown) up to 50 per cent, or 70 per cent, or (absurdly)
100 per cent? Clearly the answer will differ according to the resource being reallocated, the length of time for the reallocation,
and the national situation under review. The optimal extra proportion of doctors for rural India, of investment for rural Peru, and
of increase in farm prices for rural Nigeria will naturally differ.
However, it remains true that pressures exist to set all these levels
far below their optima. To acquire the right to advise against
letting children go naked in winter, do I need to prescribe the
ideal designs of babies' bonnets?

Linked to the question 'Is there a limit to the share of resources agriculture ought to get?' is a more fundamental question. Does the need for a high share of rural resources last for ever? Does not development imply a move out of agriculture and away from villages? Since all developed countries have a very high proportion of resources outside agriculture, can it make sense for underdeveloped countries to push more resources *into* agriculture? And — a related question — as a poor country develops, does it not approach the British or US style of farming, where it is workers rather than machines or land that are scarce, so that the concentration of farm resources upon big labour-saving farms begins to make more sense?

The best way to look at this question is to posit four stages in the analysis of policy in a developing country towards agriculture. Stage I is to advocate leaving farming alone, allowing it few resources, taxing it heavily if possible, and getting its outputs cheaply to finance industrial development, which has top priority. This belief often rests on such comfortable assumptions as that agricultural growth is ensured by rapid technical change; does not require or cannot absorb investment; and can be directed to the poor while the rich farmers alone are squeezed to provide the surpluses. Such a squeeze on agriculture was overtly Stalin's policy, and in effect (though much more humanely) the policy of the Second Indian Plan (1956-61) as articulated by Mahalanobis, its chief architect. The bridge between the two was the economic analysis of Preobrazhensky and Feldman (chapter 4). The underlying argument, that it is better to make machines than to make consumer goods, especially if one can make machines to make machines, ignores both the possible case for international specialisation, and the decided inefficiency of using scarce resources to do the right thing at the wrong time.[12]

The second stage in policy for rural development usually arises out of the failures of Stage I. In Stage II, policy-makers argue that agriculture cannot be safely neglected if it is adequately to provide workers, materials, markets and savings to industry. Hence a lot of resources need to be put into those parts of agriculture (mainly big farms, though this is seldom stated openly) that supply industry with raw materials, and industrial workers with food. That is the stage that many poor countries have reached in their official pronouncements, and some in their actual decisions. Stage II is still permeated by urban bias, because the farm sector is allocated resources not mainly to raise economic welfare, but because, and insofar as, it uses the resources to feed urban-industrial growth. Development of the rural sector is advocated, but not for the people who live and work there.

In Stage III, the argument shifts. It is realised that, so long as resources are concentrated on big farmers to provide urban inputs, those resources will neither relieve need nor—because big farmers use little labour per acre—be used very productively. So the sequence is taken one step further back. It is recognised, not only (as in Stage II) that efficient industrialisation is unlikely without major growth in rural inputs, but also (and this is the distinctive contribution of Stage III) that such growth cannot be achieved efficiently or equitably—or maybe at all—on the basis of immediately 'extracting surplus'. Stage III therefore involves accepting the need for a transformation of the *mass* rural sector, through major resource inputs, *prior* to substantial industrialisation, except insofar as such industrialisation is a more efficient way than (say) imports of providing the mass rural sector with farm requirements or processing facilities. For development to 'march on two legs', the best foot must be put forward first.

It is at Stage III that I stop. I do not believe that poor countries should 'stay agricultural' in order to develop, let alone instead of developing. The argument that neither the carrying capacity of the land, nor the market for farm products, is such as to permit the masses in poor countries to reach high levels of living without a major shift to non-farm activities seems conclusive. The existence of a Stage IV must be recognised, however. Stage IV is the belief that industrialism degrades; that one should keep rural for ever. This is attractive to some people in poor countries because it marks a total rejection of imitativeness. Neither Western nor Soviet industrialism, but a 'national path', is advocated. Other people, notably in rich countries, argue that environmental factors preclude an industrialised world where all consume at US levels; that there would be too little of one or more key minerals, or that the use of so much energy would disastrously damage the world's air, water, climate or other aspects of the ecosystem.

The nationalist objections to industry seem to show an unwarranted lack of confidence in the capacity of a great, ancient, localised culture— the Rajasthani or the Yoruba—to preserve or develop its local character in face of changing economic styles and structures. The environmentalist objections are more serious, but most environmentalists themselves recognise that they must be pressed far more strongly on developed than on underdeveloped countries. To do the reverse is a distastefully vicarious form of asceticism (we're rich but you can't afford it). Also such objections rest on a rather static view of technology; in fact, rising mineral and energy prices are already signalling to researchers the need to find new or alternative mineral supplies and to devise ecologically improved paths to growth.[13] For paths to growth there have to be, at least for poor countries.

Growth and development have not so far *sufficed* to raise mass welfare substantially, but are certainly *needed* to provide the resources for that task. 'The wretched of the earth' now know they need no longer live in ill-health, hunger and cultural deprivation. Growth with redistribution appears to offer the only alternative. In my judgement, growth will imply ultimate industrialisation; but an incidental advantage of a 'Stage III policy' is that it can offer the ecologically sensitive a wider range of choice. Perhaps, in a few poor countries, a really efficient, egalitarian mass agriculture can offer even a long-run alternative to global industrialisation.

In most poor countries, however, the case against urban bias cannot well be made from a Stage IV position. But there is one perfectly valid Stage IV argument for concentrating future agricultural growth in the Third World (most of it has been in rich countries since 1945). Fertiliser and pesticide inputs, per ton of food output, are at much higher levels in rich countries than in poor ones.[14] The increase in food output is less than proportional to the increase in chemical inputs, but the increase in damage to humans from chemical residues is more than in proportion. So an extra ton of agro-chemicals produces *more* environmental damage, for *less* extra output, in rich countries than in poor ones. Apart from that, environmental risks—even if small—are serious enough to warrant insurance policies; and indeed if I am wrong—if the carrying capacity of the land, or the environmental (or human and political) cost of industrialisation, proves higher than I anticipate—greater attention to rural development in LDCs will at least have left their options open for a neo-populist solution.

However, the dependence of Stage IV upon such a solution—often backed by a rather idyllic vision of a return to a golden age of happy communal village life—damages it, and sometimes discredits serious advocacy of agricultural development to relieve rural poverty. The traditional village economy, society and polity are almost always internally unequal, exploitative and far from idyllic: these features are likely to reassert themselves soon after the initial enthusiasms of a communal revival have evaporated. Even the village in which Mahatma Gandhi settled for ten years lost its cohesive and egalitarian ideals soon after his charismatic leadership was removed.[15]

As we shall see in chapter 4, both Russian *narodniks* and many Western colonisers confused Stage III and Stage IV. In this book it is accepted that poor countries must grow, develop and industrialise; and that the three processes are normally locked together. But if countryfolk are to be made richer, happier and more equal by integration into the developing and industrialising national economy, they must first be given—or must take—the chance to reduce the gap in wealth, power and status that divides them from the cities. The villagers cannot help either themselves or, in the long term, national development if they are neglected (Stage I) or exploited (Stage II). Only on the basis of a tolerable level of living for a mass agriculture of small farmers can most poor countries construct, speedily and efficiently, a modern industrial society. Nor need this mean a world of polluted Tokyos; as Kautsky argued in 1899 (see chapter 4), it may well be exploitation of the countryside by the city, and not growth or development as such, which bears major blame for the damage to urban (and often rural) environment that has accompanied economic modernisation.

This book does not, impertinently, say to those who work in and on poor countries: 'Don't industrialise.' Rather it says: 'A developed mass agriculture is normally needed before you can have widespread successful development in other sectors.' Many reasons for this proposition will be given, but this introduction had better close with the most fundamental. In early development, with labour plentiful and the ability to save scarce, small farming is especially promising, because it is the part of the economy in which a given amount of scarce investible resources will be supported by the most human effort. Thus it is emphasis upon small farming that can most rapidly boost income per head to the levels at which the major sacrifices of consumption, required for heavy industrialisation, can be undertaken without intolerable hardship and repression.[16] Except for a country fortunate enough to find gold or oil, poverty is a barrier to *rapid and general* industrialisation. To attempt it willy-nilly is to attack a brick wall with one's head. Prior mass agricultural development—building a battering ram—is a quicker as well as a less painful[17] way to industrialise. The transition point, from mass rural development to industrialisation, will signal itself: as good rural projects are used up, so that urban projects begin to 'pay' best even at fair prices; as mass rural demand for urban products emphasises their new profitability; and as advancing villagers acquire urban skills and create rural labour shortages.

The learning process, needed for modern industrialisation, is sometimes long; but it is fallacious for a nation, comprising above all a promising but overwhelmingly underdeveloped agriculture, to conclude that, in order to begin the process of learning, a general attack on numerous branches of industrial activity should be initiated. A far better strategy is to concentrate first upon high-yielding mass rural development, supported (partly for learning's sake) by such selective ancillary industry as rural development makes viable. Rapid industrialisation on a broad front, doomed to self-strangulation for want of the wage goods and savings capacity that only a developed agricultural sector can provide, is likely to discredit industrialisation itself.

The arguments for rapid general industrialisation, prior to or alongside agricultural development, assume against most of the evidence that such a sequence is likely to succeed. But no national self-esteem, no learning-by-doing, no jam tomorrow, can come from a mass of false starts. If you wish for industrialisation, prepare to develop agriculture.

Part I
The Nature of the Problem

1 The coexistence of poverty and development

THE PROBLEM STATED

'In the midst of plethoric plenty, the people perish.'[1] So wrote Carlyle in 1852, addressing himself to the 'condition-of-England question'. Today the distribution of resources is seen in a world perspective. We now notice the coexistence of mass hunger in Bengal and mass obesity in Los Angeles. Many people, even in rich countries, condemn it. For various reasons — political, economic, moral — some people in rich countries have tried to develop policies to alleviate the poverty of poor countries, and in particular to help them to help themselves.

Yet even policies sincerely intended to help poor *countries* often do little for poor *people*. Leave aside insincerity — 'aid' to help British or French building companies to supply air-conditioned airports, or trade 'concessions' to one's sugar companies in the West Indies. Even policies apparently aimed directly against individual poverty, and towards self-help, often fail. For instance, when the World Food Programme of the Food and Agriculture Organisation gives food to enable workers to eat while they build a dam, the food can end up enriching speculators, or impoverishing small farmers by replacing their sales; and the dam may well enrich mainly big farmers growing vegetables for middle-class townspeople. More and more people are aware of such things. The new enthusiasm for integrating aid into a country's development plan underlines the growing understanding that a donor is unlikely to succeed in helping poor people, unless he first understands what has kept them in poverty, and then supports an attack upon its root causes ('supports' because that attack has to be mainly the responsibility of the poor countries themselves). But what are the causes?

The key observation is this. In the last thirty years, almost all the hundred-odd LDCs have enjoyed growth and even 'development' at unprecedented rates. Yet — with a few exceptions, such as China, Malaysia and Taiwan — the proportion of their populations below a fixed acceptable minimum standard of feeding, housing, clothing, and freedom from chronic illness has not fallen much.[2]

Marx wrote, 'The philosophers have only interpreted the world, in various ways; the point, however, is to change it.'[3] The economists, turned philosophers of international development,

27

have too often sought to change the world without understanding it. In poor countries, they have helped to persuade governments to tax, borrow and print money to pay for investment and education. In rich countries, they have done a good deal to increase guilt, and something to increase aid. Both aid and domestic savings have produced growth in poor *countries*. Yet the world of poor *people* remains almost the same, partly because its analysts have failed to understand the forces that keep it so.[4]

Let us begin with three facts. First, the poor countries have enjoyed a long period of unprecedented economic growth; the true value of output and income available per person in poor countries has about doubled in the last quarter-century, after many preceding centuries without any long-term upward tendency. Second, this is not 'growth without development'; on any sensible interpretation of development as modernising structural change, the poor countries have enjoyed more development in the last two decades than in the previous two millennia. Third, during this unprecedented growth and development, the condition of the really poor has undergone little improvement, except in important areas of social provision, especially health and education.

What does this add up to? The worst-off one-third of mankind comprises the village underclass of the Third World. This underclass includes landless labourers, peons, sharecroppers, owners of dwarf holdings, and even pseudo-urban (but usually jobless and temporary) migrants. This underclass has become less prone to malaria and illiteracy since 1945. It has thereby become more fit, and better fitted, to enjoy the good things of life. Yet these good things have not become available to it. Meanwhile, on a world scale, the decolonisation, growth and development of poor societies and economies have progressed quickly, smoothly, and — despite the 'cult of violence' and despite isolated horrors like the Brazilian North-East, Vietnam and Algeria — with a degree of peacefulness without historical precedent. Hence we have an astonishing contrast: rapid growth and development, yet hardly any impact on the heartland of mass poverty. Among the steel mills and airports, and despite the independent and sometimes freely elected governments, the rural masses are as hungry and ill-housed as ever.

THE FACTS OF GROWTH

One can argue endlessly, and not very fruitfully, about what counts as a less-developed country. Let us accept the UN definition: a country with output per head insufficient to buy $500 worth of resources at the prices of 1960, or about $750 worth at the higher prices of 1974. The LDCs, thus defined, increased output per head[5] by 2.6 per cent per year in the 1950s and 3.0 per cent per year in the 1960s (see table 1.1). Some of the figures are doubtful, but there is no convincing evidence of bias, up or down. The real rise in *output*-per-head certainly lies between 70 per cent and 80 per cent for non-Communist LDCs in 1950-70: say, 75 per cent. Damage done by adverse movements in their terms of trade with rich countries over this period reduces the rise of *income* per head, by about 1.5 per cent of the total 1970 level.[6] Aid, contrary to popular belief, more than compensated for this; negligible in 1950, by 1970 it was adding 1.8 per cent to the spending power of non-Communist LDCs.[7]

Hence available real income per person rose by about 75 per cent in the world's poor countries (excluding China) from 1950 to 1970. All the countries listed in table 1.1 — the 'big poor' countries, with over 70 per cent of the population of the Third World (excluding China) — share. in this improvement, though to varying degrees. Indeed Spain, Chile and a few others formally ceased to rank as LDCs by raising income per person above the UN's dividing line of $500 at 1960 prices. We know too little about growth in China — one-third of the Third World — but agricultural data suggest progress at very close to the Indian rate in this big sector.[8] Of course, movements of oil and food prices since 1973 have led to a deterioration in the prospects of most LDCs, especially the very poor ones of South Asia. Nevertheless, almost certainly, the past twenty-five years in the LDCs have seen more growth in real output per person than the previous twenty centuries. Two arithmetical arguments suggest this. First, in 1950, income per head for at least half the world's poor people (those in China, India, Pakistan, Indonesia and Nigeria) averaged below $50, and at least half of these were receiving less than $25 a year; such elemental levels can hardly have grown from a much lower base.[9] Second, even if the average Indian at the birth of Christ enjoyed only $25 worth of goods (at 1960 prices) yearly, growth at only ½% per cent per year would by 1950 have brought him to $318,000 per year. So the recency of sustained growth in India emerges from pure arithmetic. Moreover, ingenious (if sometimes strained) historical reconstructions suggest that income per person in the Indian subcontinent probably stagnated between 1600 and 1900, and perhaps fell between 1900 and 1950.[10] Yet it has risen by over one-third since 1950 — a fantastic change in economic tempo. Most poor countries have done even better.

Not only is the post-war tempo of growth in LDCs new; table

1.1 shows that it has steadily speeded up (apart from temporary surges caused by post-1945 recovery and the Korean boom in raw materials prices). The final years of the 1960s saw even faster growth.[11] The technical limits of the improved rice, wheat and maize seeds, and the damaging effects of the 1973-4 explosion in oil prices, make extrapolation dangerous. Nevertheless, this acceleration of growth is just what one should expect, once the initial thrust of national enrichment is confirmed. Such enrichment leaves a bigger share of output (after basic consumer needs are met) to provide schools, factories, fertilisers, family-planning clinics, and other sources of future advance.[12]

GROWTH AND DEVELOPMENT

Three sorts of criticism are often made of the income per head growth figures quoted in table 1.1: that they do not properly measure growth, that growth is not a good indicator of development, and that neither growth nor development brings welfare.

Growth of income is indeed imperfectly measured by national-income estimates, such as those in table 1.1, for many LDCs. Nevertheless, there is no reason to believe that such measurement problems cause the figures to overstate growth. Growth, anyway, has been recorded even in LDCs with sophisticated national accounting systems, involving estimations of the degree of error involved. Systematic attempts to correct such errors suggest that, if anything, post-war growth rates have been underestimated.[13]

Has all this been 'growth without development'? Most of the usual productivity indicators—consumption per person of telephones or cement or steel, for example—suffer from exactly the urban bias discussed in this book, but nitrogenous fertiliser consumption does not. On the welfare side, I have picked some items in principle allocable to urban or to rural people. Substantial improvement in these physical indicators appears in table 1.2.[14]

Perhaps most strikingly, the poor countries of the world have increased their productive capacity per head, through both physical capital equipment and 'human capital' in the form of skills, faster than the income-per-head growth rates shown in table 1.1. How this extra productive capacity is used—whether it is converted into genuinely rising standards of popular well-being, or diverted to increases in population growth, in foreign exploitation, or in the assets of the domestic elite[15]—is a problem not of development but of welfare: a question not of whether a country's capacity is being increased and transformed, but of how it uses the benefits of such increase and transformation. A major theme of this book is that the urban bias affecting the use of benefits reduces and ultimately strangles the increase and transformation of capacity; that to neglect equity and welfare ultimately damages efficiency and development in the circumstances of most LDCs today. At this stage, however, I wish only to show that unprecedented development (as well as growth) has taken place.

DEVELOPMENT WITHOUT DISIMPOVERISHMENT

What of our third blunt statement, that except for health and education the very poor have hardly benefited at all from this advance? Real rural income per head in East (and probably West) Pakistan was lower in 1959-64 than in 1949-54; real earnings of rural wage-earners in Brazil fell in the 1950s; the proportion of Indians below a fixed (and very modest) 'poverty line' almost certainly rose between 1950 and 1970.[16] There are also many indirect indicators: the static real wages of agricultural labourers[17] (indicating *falling* welfare because the size of their families is growing); the rising proportion of time spent unemployed and hence unrewarded; the stubbornly unchanging methods and output of the rising populations dependent on unirrigated cereal farming.

But there is one clinching piece of evidence. Food consumption in poor countries has risen much less than it would have done if the poor and hungry had shared significantly in income growth. A person with yearly income (in cash or kind) worth $100 or less, if his income rises by (say) $20, will increase his consumption of food almost as fast as his income.[18] For South and East Asia as a whole (excluding Japan), if each person's income rose by 10 per cent (we shall call this an 'equally distributed' rise) there would be a rise in daily calorie intake of at least 6.2 per cent; in West Asia and Africa, of at least 4.0 per cent; and in Latin America, of at least 3.0 per cent.

The actual improvement in nutrition has been far slower than would be expected had the income rises of table 1.1 been equally distributed. In India, from 1949-50 to 1968-9, average daily calorie consumption rose from 1,700 to 1,940, by 14 per cent, while income per person rose by about 40 per cent. If the rise in income had been equally distributed, at Indian levels of hunger, a rise in food consumption of at least 32 per cent could have been expected.[19] This sluggish growth of food consumption was due to the failure of most of the extra income to reach the poor and hungry. Prices of most major foodstuffs did not deter consumers, for they did not rise relative to other prices; and while the food needs of the average Indian did indeed fall (because more infants survived, thus temporarily raising the proportion of small children in the population) the effect was very small.

In several other populous countries, rapid growth in 'average' income and slow growth in calorie intake similarly prove the maldistribution of extra incomes. In the Philippines, daily calorie intake per person grew from 1,720 in 1953 to 1,990 in 1969, or by 15 per cent; the 45 per cent growth of income per head in this period, if equally distributed, would at Filipino income levels have led to a growth in calorie intake of about 30 per cent per person. In Mexico, daily calorie intake per person in the ten years 1955-65 grew from 2,370 to 2,620, or by 15 per cent; the 41 per cent growth of income per head in the period, at Mexican income levels, would if equally distributed imply a growth in calorie intake of at least 20 per cent.[20] The true growth in food intake available to the poor was even less than these figures suggest, because in almost all LDCs there was a rise in the proportion of calories derived from animal, dairy, fruit, vegetable and fine-grain sources. However desirable in itself, this implies that most poor people were unable to benefit from the major extra calorie sources, on account of their high price.

Broadly, available income per person in LDCs rose by about 75 per cent from 1950 to 1970; daily calorie intake per head rose by under 20 per cent, as against at least 40 per cent to be expected if growth[21] had been equally distributed; and most of those extra calories were in the more expensive forms of food. So the main gainers from growth have been those who do not need much extra simple, cheap food; not the hungry, not the poor. 'Growth in income per person' carries a subtle and misleading undertone— not quite an implication—that extra income is *distributed*, or equally distributed, to each person. In fact, the opening statement in this paragraph means only that 75 per cent extra income would have been available for each person if it were equally distributed. The calorie data show that it was not. And the poorest 10 to 20 per cent of the people, if wage and employment estimates are to be believed, have in most LDCs gained almost nothing.

A TEMPORARY PROBLEM?

The European analogy

Yet is this not a familiar and a temporary sequence of events? Carlyle's complaint that 'in the midst of plethoric plenty the people perish' and Engels's moving and tightly documented account of the sufferings of the English poor[22] date from 1852 and 1844 respectively. Like the complaints of this chapter, they reveal the fruits of thirty years of both growth and astonishing, accelerated post-war development — structural industrialising transformation — which the poor financed with their bodies and the bodies of their children, but from which they probably gained no improvement at all in their level of living.[23] Machines were scarce, and the capitalists who owned them well rewarded; labour, forced off the land, competed for urban jobs and kept down wages. Yet this was temporary; after 1850 the workers' level of living began to improve. The capitalist class, although strengthened by the fruits of past growth, was increasingly driven towards concessions as the organised urban proletariat gained political and economic strength. From 1939 to 1946, labour scarcity and the end of mass unemployment increased the share of the national product going to the workers,[24] and this higher share was subsequently kept up, though not much further increased. Although in different contexts and by different methods, a similar strengthening of working-class economic and political bargaining power followed the early phases of agricultural and industrial development in most now-rich countries.[25]

In most LDCs, modern economic growth seems to have started twenty to thirty years ago (though there is nothing automatic about its continuation!) and to have been highly unequal in benefits. In most rich countries, at a comparable stage of their development, growth had been similarly maldistributed; but political and economic pressures towards mass consumption were already being felt, and were likely to become stronger. In today's LDCs, is the coexistence of development and poverty similarly temporary? Will it cease, once the owners of scarce machines and business skills can no longer use their near-monopoly positions to exploit a still-unorganised working class temporarily weakened by a 'reserve army of unemployed'? If so, can one not safely let early development burst the feudal constraints upon productive capacity, leaving until later the question of sharing the benefits — especially since population growth will slow down, thus strengthening the bargaining power of workers as they organise?

In Pakistan in 1958-68, this parallel was in the minds of the intellectuals who guided the planning machine. Go all-out for growth, make sure that the growing incomes are mainly profits and not wages, encourage private business to save and reinvest out of profits, and deal with poverty and inequality later, when you are richer and redistribution is therefore less of a strain:[26] such was the advice of the planners, internally consistent and based (if perhaps sometimes unconsciously) on a tenable reading of Western economic history. They were perhaps naive in accepting that strong men further strengthened by growth would then voluntarily rush to share subsequent benefits; but this is a side issue. If the delaying egalitarians who steered Pakistan's planning (or that of many other poor countries today) had been correct in using the conventional categories to interpret the class struggle in such countries, they would have been correct too in drawing the conclusion that 'labour' would ultimately achieve high living standards.

How did this conversion of growth and development into a less unequal, less crisis-ridden process work, in the now affluent West? The answer will tell us how far we can extrapolate the process to poor countries today. In Britain, workers in agriculture and industry alike suffered thirty-five years of static or falling levels of living,[27] from 1815 to about 1850. Meanwhile, profits grew substantially, and were ploughed back into more and more machinery. This machinery threw men out of work, especially in farming. Neither the unemployed (whose purchasing power was tiny) nor the employed (whose wages were at best stagnant, owing to competition for their jobs from the unemployed) were in a position to buy much more of the output of all those extra machines. Rising exports and growing population helped create some demand, but not enough to save the system from recurring crises: wages and employment were just not enough to buy the output of the extra machines, so that businessmen stopped installing them, thereby throwing men out of work in the machine-building industries too, which of course reduced purchasing power still further.[28]

Yet in Britain, as in all the countries of Western Europe, this dangerous situation was somehow transformed into the mass-consumption, growing, not intolerably unequal experience of 1880-1920 and again 1935-1974 (at least).[29] How was this transformation achieved? There is no simple answer, but if we look at some partial explanations, we shall see how far extrapolation to today's developing countries is relevant. Our explanation should take account of three things: the initial condition of major socio-economic groups at the start of 'industrial revolutions', their actual and potential development during the 'revolutions', and the parallel development of class relations (exploitative and collaborative). Of course we are comparing the West's long period of modern economic growth with a much shorter recent experience in most LDCs; but the seeds of the mass-consumption era were present in the alignments of class and power even at the beginning of the process in the West. Is that true of today's South?

Labour

Most obviously, European and North American labour advanced because it began to organise, first in trade unions, later politically. The precondition was an 'organisable' working class, in the sense of a mass of non-agricultural, urbanised and substantially literate workers. There are fifteen now-rich countries with fairly reliable estimates of the commencement dates for modern, accelerated economic growth: all except one (Japan) had over 35 per cent of the labour force outside agriculture at these dates.[30]

A quite different situation prevails today in most LDCs. Not 35 to 70 per cent but 10 to 35 per cent of workers are outside agriculture. The gap between their output — and hence income — levels and those of agricultural workers is far greater than was the case in 'developing' nineteenth-century Europe or North America (table 5.4). Also the trade-union movement has developed *before* mass urbanisation. It is thus an instrument of a 'labour aristocracy', in parts of the public service and modern urban industry. Such workers seldom form more than 5 per cent of the labour force. They have much more to lose than to gain from sharing their benefits with the rural masses.[31] Hence 'organised labour' in today's LDCs is likely to fight equalising measures.[32] In yesterday's, it spearheaded them.

Business

In Europe and North America since 1850 or so, businesses (1) have been freed, as cartels replaced competition, from the need to pay very low wages if their prices were to remain competitive, and (2) have come to realise that low wages produced by high unemployment meant low demand out of wages, and thus low profits in the longer term. This largely explains the softening of business attitudes towards trade unionism. It also accounts for businessmen's acceptance after 1945, throughout the Western world, of 'Keynesian-corporate' government regulation of the levels of demand, investment, and increasingly wage and profit incomes. Essential to such acceptance is a general consensus that the major threats to prosperity are crises of monetary demand: crises caused by lack of balance between (1) the output produced by extra machinery, and (2) the extra capacity of the mass of consumers to buy that output.[33]

In LDCs today, such a consensus would be without foundation. Poverty is caused by the lack of means to create wealth, not by the super-abundance of such means and the absence of demand. A much larger proportion of workers than in nineteenth-century Western Europe comprises self-employed farmers. These are relatively unaffected by the effects of fluctuating monetary demand, and thus reduce its impact on the economy as a whole. Their problem is lack of *supply*—of fertilisers, dams, ploughs, technicians and skills.

Governments

Governments in now-rich countries became increasingly able and willing to regulate the workings, and in particular the demand crises, of capitalism—thereby in part socialising it—and, in concentrating on such crises, they attacked the main cause of mass poverty in Western Europe. This happened much earlier in the development process than many Keynesians imagine. Historians have progressively revealed the nineteenth-century origins of the welfare state—in Disraeli's Britain,[34] Louis Napoleon's France, and Bismarck's Germany. Welfare legislation, in setting 'income floors' below which the poor could not fall, not only met a clear human need; it also dampened the decline in purchasing power during slumps.

That was not all. New laws against fraud by firms seeking to borrow money; limitations of shareholders' liability to the amounts invested; the evolution of commercial banks able to expand credit, and of mechanisms for the government to control the rate of expansion; the growth of records of 'unemployment' and awareness of it as a problem—all, in different ways, reduced the danger of deepening crises, and increased the government's capacity to deal with such crises as did arise.[35] The terrible experience of 1929-35, brought about by governments that refused to reflate by what then seemed the costly and drastic method of deficit-financed public works, has blinded us to the steady growth of economic control, from the 1850s to President Nixon's introduction of price and wage controls in 1971. In most cases, crisis control and equalisation have gone hand in hand. Unemployment relief; progressive income tax; a growing public sector, that, unlike private business, does not deepen slumps by cutting investment and employment—all transfer resources from rich to poor and *in the same act* reduce the impact of slumps upon purchasing power, and hence the depth of the crisis.

Ultimately governments derive their power to do this from labour and business: from workers politically organised to press their demands for a share in growth; from businessmen who have learned, painfully, that a too-poor working class cannot buy their products.

Almost all the requirements for government equalising-cum-stabilising action are missing in most LDCs today. For a start,

their instability is caused mainly by fluctuations in climate between sowing and harvest, and in *foreign* demand for exports
like tin—fluctuations that no single government can control.
Second, the long-run causes of their poverty have far more to do
with shortage of good land, machines and human skills than with
manipulable deficiencies of home demand (because widespread
literacy, rapidly rising savings rates, and basic agricultural change
preceded industrialisation in the West, but seldom do so in today's
LDCs). Third, some governments in LDCs lack power to control
economic crises: their tax revenues and outlays affect few of their
citizens substantially; and there is no network of share markets,
banks and other capitalist financial insitutions—or their socialist
equivalents—through which governments can effectively control the circulation of money and credit. Above all, neither the
problems nor the pressures confronting today's 'developing'
governments induce them to give priority to equalising-cum-
stabilising measures. They are right to see stability and equality
as separate problems, which cannot be tackled together by social-
security measures to put a 'floor' under domestic demand, as they
could in earlier Western economic development.

Hence the slogan, 'economic equalisation for growth and stability', has little relevance to governments in today's LDCs. But why
do they seldom stress equalising measures as such, in reality
rather than rhetoric? Inequality is more severe in poor countries
than in rich ones,[36] largely because unemployment is so much
greater and labour so much less mobile. But the really poor are
mini-farmers, landless labourers, and recent immigrants to the
cities about to be forced back to the land by unemployment. They
constitute an almost voiceless, largely illiterate, dispersed, unorganised rural mass. It seldom combines, articulates its needs,
or backs them with effective political or trade-union power. The
literary intelligentsia despises it as uncouth (or so idealises it as
to deter intervention); the political ideologues dismiss it as reactionary (chapter 4). Hence most LDC governments are under
little pressure to help it. In Malcolm X's words, 'It's the door that
squeaks that gets the grease.'

Nation-states

Nation-states, reasonably homogeneous in language and culture
and with good transport and communications, had emerged in
most Western countries well before their 'industrial revolutions'
began. That not merely strengthened the governments; it helped
both workers and businessmen to move in search of higher levels
of living, and thereby created powerful equalising pressures.[37]

Jobless workers from South Wales or the Scottish Highlands could move to London and the Midlands, where the chances of finding work were better; they thereby reduced the labour surplus in their places of origin, so that the low wage rates there began to rise. At the same time, some businessmen began to move in the reverse direction, in search of cheap labour—and they thereby made it less cheap, as well as reducing unemployment. This mobility of labour (and even more of capital), like the long-standing national coherence that assists it, is weaker in most LDCs now.

Even now, we in the West often complain of this poor mobility, of the stubborn backwardness of backward regions: yet our problems are tractable compared with those of Bihar, North-East Brazil, or the impoverished and remote regions of huge countries like Ethiopia or the Sudan. Regional languages (the 2½ million people of New Guinea have about seven hundred), poor transport, huge variations in diet, all the marks of recent and often insecure nationhood reinforce the barriers that underdevelopment traditionally poses to mobility—illiteracy, bond-slavery, fragmented markets.[38] Sluices drain capital out of rural areas even where its returns could be high; but successful and lasting migration *from* impoverished regions of LDCs (chapters 9 and 11) tends to be confined to those skilled, dynamic people who might have reduced deprivation had they stayed at home.

A *false analogy*

The conditions of class structure, and of national and institutional organisation, in Europe and North America were highly special. They turned growth from a process in which the wealthy gained the power to accumulate by appropriating the economic surplus, into a process in which poor people shared. These special conditions do not exist in most poor countries today. Instead, the bargaining power of labourers is chronically weakened, because population growth roughly doubles the supply in each generation.

Several further factors suggest that most poor countries, unless there is a change of course, will not repeat the now-developed countries' transition from a period when the advances of the elite depended on keeping mass welfare from growing, to a period when they depended upon its growth. First, before modern growth started, the traditional and overwhelmingly hereditary fealties and inequalities — of feudalism and serfdom, clan and caste and chieftainship, rights in land by military conquest, interpersonal obligations resting on ascribed roles instead of achieved functions—had in most Western countries, and in Russia and Japan, been drastically reduced by violence or by edict. These rights and barriers, so damaging to growth and equality, so prone to confine the fruits of progress to traditional, now non-functional, elites, still prevail in today's Third World, reinforcing the rights and intersecting the barriers created by early capitalist development. The new wealth (and its link with the bureaucracy) reinforces the ascribed power of the leading castes of India, the top families of Pakistan's minority Moslem sects, and their counterparts among African chiefs and Spanish American absentee-landlords-turned-businessmen. Capitalism in most of the Third World has never confronted residual 'feudalism', as it did in, say, Cromwell's England; and hence 'feudal' power is normally strengthened, not replaced, by capitalist development. In the West, the new inequalities of capitalism—to some extent non-hereditary ('rags to rags in three generations') and arguably useful for capital accumulation—*replaced* the relics of an already largely destroyed 'feudalism'; in today's South, they *reinforce* still thriving 'feudalism'. Clearly today's South has worse prospects than yesterday's West of evolving a balance of forces that will direct the benefits of future development towards mass welfare because such direction represents a 'capitalist' interest.[39]

Second, almost all the high incomes from early modern economic growth in the West went to 'directly productive' businessmen, in agriculture or industry. Businessmen tend to reinvest, and when market demand falters to seek means—even equalising means—of reviving it. A much larger part of the elite incomes in today's LDCs goes to bureaucrats and traders. Their interest in mass consumption is more tenuous.[40]

The most important feature of poor countries today, tending to prolong the period during which growth and 'development' do little for the poorest people, is the imbalance between city and country. Not only is this the main single component of inequality; it weakens the poor, as compared with their situation in Northwest Europe during early modern growth.

By 1811, barely a third of British workers depended on agriculture, and rural interests (though not rural workers as such) were heavily over-represented in Parliament; in most poor countries today, with the rural-urban income gap far greater (table 5.4), rural areas are politically *under*-represented, yet still contain over two-thirds of the poor. A relatively impoverished, weak rural sector is an unpromising source of pressures towards equalisation; for how inequalities will be affected by development depends not just on the development but on the inequalities. Many ascriptive inequalities are natural to a fairly immobile, static, non-accumulating society; where there is not much scope for societal economic advance, society loses little output by rewarding not merit but old age, male sex, or ostentatious piety. Conversely, with growth, the new prospects of social gain can lead to rewards on merit, reducing the old inequalities. Mobility does that too; when men from villages near Bombay leave their farms to seek new urban opportunities, they improve the position of their sisters (who often run the farms they have left) *vis-à-vis* the traditional male gerontocracy. Unfortunately, however, urban-rural inequality, unlike inequality of age or sex, is likely to be strengthened by early development. The bourgeoisie whom capitalism enriches are also burghers — townsmen — and their new power weakens the rural interest. Therefore, if the masses are rural, while power and wealth are heavily concentrated in the cities before the early developmental upsurge, there is little prospect that such an upsurge will soon benefit the masses.

The accelerated growth of the now-rich world took place with 35 to 60 per cent of its people already outside agriculture, and averaging only one and a quarter to twice the income per person of the farming community; but today's poor countries, with only 10 to 35 per cent of their peoples outside agriculture, endow them with an advantage of three to ten times (table 5.4). Those weakened by the concentration of power in the urban centres — the rural people — though relatively more numerous, are also relatively more dispersed, poor and weak in today's South than in yesterday's West. This enormously reduces the prospects of a rapid transition to equalising growth processes. Even in the West, the outlook for mass consumption would have been bleak, had it depended on a shrinking urban-rural gap; for it took a century of growth before that gap began to shrink.[41] In today's South this gap is (1) initially much larger, (2) a much more important component of total inequality, (3) supported by a much more pro-urban balance of ideologies and political forces, (4) not shrinking, (5) not being made significantly less important by townward migration. All these factors militate against the 'automatic' conversion of development into mass welfare along the lines familiar in yesterday's West.[42]

THEN AND NOW

Hence the conditions for growth and development to become the roots of mass consumption — conditions established in most of Western Europe in the early nineteenth century, and operative around 1850-80 — are highly special. In particular, labour and capital, governments and nation-states, class structures and occupational structures, in most LDCs today do not support a reasonable expectation of replicating those conditions.

The appalling plight of the English poor in the 1840s, which stemmed from low wages and thus permitted (except during crises of underconsumption) high profits, helped to pay for high rates of capital formation. Selfish and inhumane though many capitalists were, they came increasingly to need a mass market for their products to make their machinery profitable—and an increasingly skilled and literate workforce to keep it running and improving. The wretchedness and exploitation of the English— and European and immigrant American—working class in the early and middle nineteenth century paved the way for the orga- nised, mobile, articulate working class of today: and the path of advance was not capitalist humanity but capitalist self-interest.

What a contrast is Pakistan (or Nigeria or Paraguay) today! Industry is not a mass-employment sector, or based on an already substantially urbanised workforce, or sustained by an agriculture already transformed technically, or confronting an impoverished but largely literate urban workforce. Rather, most modern in- dustry in most poor countries is an exotic, artificial, fragile plant. It is exotic in much of Latin America and West Africa, where it is largely dominated by foreigners; and in East Africa, where it is indigenous only to the extent of the African majority's tolerance of long-established, but originally Asian, business minorities. It is artificial in most poor countries—except for Hong Kong, Taiwan and perhaps Malaysia and Singapore — because it survives large- ly by compelling governments to grant it permanent and prohi- bitive protection[43] against imports, at the expense of farmers, consumers, and national efficiency and development. It is fragile, owing to its dependence—for food and inputs—on the very agri- culture whose growth it stunts by its own prodigious demands for skills, capital, incentives and enterprise.

Above all, almost everywhere in the Third World, the modern industrial sector is small. It usually produces well below 10 per cent of output. It employs a much smaller proportion of workers— usually below 5 per cent—because its power and the prevailing ideology of industrialisation enable it to persuade the govern- ment to sell it, cheaply, foreign exchange for labour-replacing capital imports. Its capacity to stimulate the rest of the domestic economy commercially is weak, though not its ability to exploit it by concessions gained politically. Its growth, in part a statistical illusion owing to protection that makes its inputs pseudo-cheap and its outputs pseudo-valuable, is slow and unstable, because farmers are too underendowed (with inputs such as fertilisers, and with techniques, and with irrigation capital to protect them from rainfall fluctuation) to supply it with sufficient raw materials, or even food for its workers.

Even in the unlikely event of the modern urban-industrial proletariat in a poor country somehow becoming the vanguard for the reduction of poverty among its poor villagers, the process will not begin from a gradual strengthening of labour in its confrontation with capital, as happened in Europe. Today, industrialists in poor countries seldom confront their workforce (or its trade-union leaders) except symbolically. That workforce is a tiny, privileged elite. Its overspecialised and hence scarce skills—required to maintain the mass of complex, overcapitalised machinery of its employers—raise the costs it can impose by strike action;[44] its small size reduces the costs of conceding wage rises (as against leaving large amounts of heavy equipment standing idle). Only over inter-union or intra-union disputes, very seldom over wages within the attainable range, would a public or private steel producer in a poor country 'confront' his workers.

The real enemies of the industrial proletarian elite in poor countries—which is a true labour aristocracy—are the rural poor. They would like to compete for urban jobs, to earn more in the village through higher food prices,[45] and to see governmental resources steered towards agriculture. The first objective would help the urban capitalist, but less than one might think; big and powerful ones, especially, have usually secured subsidies on labour-replacing machinery, so that the wage bill is a small part of total costs because of the excessive capital intensity of the production process. The other two objectives of the rural poor unite in opposition the industrial employer and the urban proletarian elite. The huge size, low literacy and poor organisation of the rural masses; the intelligentsia's oscillation between attitudes of contempt and 'idyllisation' towards them; the ideology of industrialisation: all combine to ensure that they are exploited, to 'extract a surplus' for the privileged urban sector. Domestic and foreign experts lend support to such policies. Under these circumstances, the pressures to divert the benefits of growth to the rural poor are very weak. Since they are the main group of poor people in LDCs, growth and development are unlikely to reduce mass poverty much.

Britain in 1815-1950 is not West Pakistan in 1947-2050. In Britain, inequality threatened stability: political stability as the literate poor organised, economic stability as the unemployed and underpaid proved unable to buy. Hence the dominant capitalist class tolerated a reduction in inequality as the price of stable, crisis-free growth. This involved increasing state responsibility for financing investment, education and other non-consumption expenses, as there were no longer enough very rich people to do so—and as the poor were no longer so weak as to have to accept the priorities of the rich. This process of socialisation is still going on.

In today's LDCs, inequality may also be self-destructive in the very long run. It militates against labour-intensive and efficient development paths; and it is at risk from literacy and popular political involvement (though both are generally lower than in the much more urbanised conditions of nineteenth-century North-West Europe). But in the twenty-five-year horizon, inequality assists political stability, because the articulate 'labour aristocracy' of the cities is small enough to be bought off with part of the surplus extracted from the numerous but inarticulate rural poor; and it assists economic stability, because the rest of the surplus can be used to sustain a process of capital-intensive industrialisation that, however inefficient and unjust, is thereby enabled to provide growing wages and profits to its few participants. To the biases involved in such a process we now turn.

2 What is 'Urban Bias', and is it to Blame?

'BIAS'

So growth and development in the Third World have made little impact on mass poverty. The hope that this will soon change, as it did in the West, rests on a false analogy. In today's poor and overwhelmingly agricultural societies, neither the type of conflict, nor the balance of forces emerging during growth, helps to strengthen the impoverished rural majority. Nor does it suffer merely from the sophistication and power of the urban minority; it suffers in a polity biased against it.

To speak of 'bias' is normally to speak metaphorically. It often helps us to understand a metaphor if we look at the literal sense first. In the literal sense, a 'biased' ball or die has its weight unequally distributed. The ball does not roll exactly in the direction that it is bowled; and when the die is thrown the six faces are not equally likely to show on top. In both these cases, we know what is the norm, the 'true' ball or die. A true ball, being unweighted, rolls in the direction of impulsion. A true die, being of uniform density, has an equal (one in six) chance for each face to show on top after a throw. In these literal usages, 'bias' is thus defined as deviation from the norm, the 'true'. The true refers to either a physical condition of the object (uniform density or unweightedness) or demonstrable conformity of that object to an agreed rule (that the die shall have a one-in-six chance for each face to show on top, or that a ball shall roll as bowled).[1]

Literal uses of 'bias' are easy to understand, but metaphorical uses are often obscure. Sometimes they say nothing: 'He votes for Brown because he's biased' merely adds abuse to fossilised tautology, like 'He prefers porridge to cornflakes because he's that sort of unpleasant person.' At other times, accusations of bias are merely emotive ways of rejecting a person or an opinion. I neither can nor want to remove this flavour of condemnation from the word 'bias'; but I do claim to use 'urban bias', if not antiseptically, at least with a precise and testable meaning. To do so, I must try to define a norm, a true: to show that policies are systematically shifted, in one direction, away from some 'better' or 'best' policy, unbiased[2] between urban and rural areas. Once the features of such a policy can be defined, a systematic tendency to reject it, and to prefer alternatives more favourable to a particular sector, can properly be stigmatised as bias towards that sector.

44

The two central features of any 'best' policy are efficiency and equity.[3] We shall look later at definitions of these terms. But we must first face the fact that, on any definition, the most efficient policy is seldom the fairest. There are two norms, not one. So can there be no unambiguous bias away from 'the' norm? The following diagram shows when there can and when there cannot. (Please suspend your disbelief that efficiency and equity can be measured until a little later in the chapter.)

Figure 1   Intersectoral bias and ambivalence

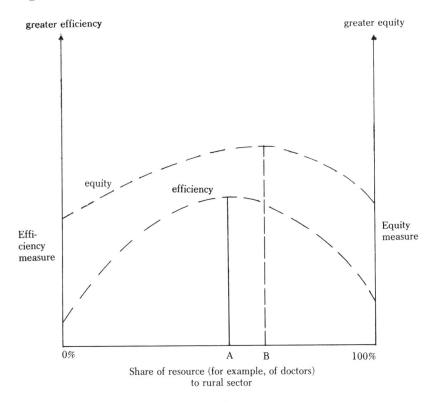

In figure 1, efficiency is at a peak at *A*, equity at *B*. Despite the existence of two norms, any systematic tendency to advocate allocations of the resource giving the rural sector less than *A* is unequivocally urban-biased; any allocation giving it more than *B* is unequivocally rural-biased. Allocations between *A* and *B* are ambivalent, being urban-biased with respect to equity but rural-biased with respect to efficiency; one's attitude towards them depends on the relative importance one attaches to efficiency and equity. Many advocates of current industrialisation policies, indeed, argue that most poor countries deliberately and rightly allocate most of their developmental resources between *A* and *B* — sacrificing immediate fairness for ultimate growth, which will eventually help rural people, and the poor, as well. The *urban bias hypothesis* is that most resources in most poor countries are systematically allocated well to the left of *A*: that 'developing' polities are so structured as to provide rural people with inefficiently *and* unfairly few resources.

It is possible (though in my judgement unlikely) that the efficiency and equity curves are not as neatly shaped, with just one peak, as in figure 1. To take efficiency alone, if one sector has too much of a particular resource, efficiency will normally continue to improve by taking that resource away from the overendowed sector until the resource is correctly distributed, and will steadily worsen if even more is then taken from the sector, as in figure 1. But if, after a certain (objectively excessive) concentration of effort in a sector is reached, economies of scale can be reaped from further allocations of resources to it — say between *C* and *D* in figure 2 — we may get situations like the following:

Figure 2   Pseudo-ambivalence

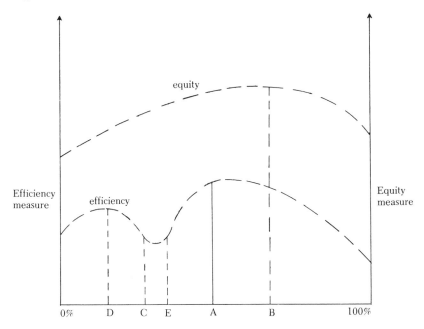

Share of resource (for example, of engineers)
to rural sector

Plainly, policies tending to push resource allocations from the range *AB* towards *C* are urban-biased, for *C* gives the rural sector too little for efficiency *(A)* or equity *(B)*. Yet a move towards even more urban bias, from *C* to *D*—because extra engineers in a sector can sometimes support each other and reap scale economies — increases efficiency; and a move from *C* towards *A* actually makes inefficiency a little worse at first, between *C* and *E*. Movements between *D* and *E* in figure 2, like movements between *A* and *B* in both figure 1 and figure 2, shift equity and efficiency in opposite directions; but while moves between *A* and *B* are genuinely ambivalent, moves from *D* to *E* *with the intention of continuing resource reallocation towards A* are 'pseudo-ambivalent'. At first, though equity improves, efficiency suffers (as urban scale economies are lost). However, if the moves are persisted with, both equity and efficiency improve, because *A* is better than *D* on both counts. We can define, as characteristics of urban bias, not only the tendency to select allocations well to the left of *A* (though this is the most important feature), but also the tendency to seek 'improving' changes away from the rural sector—to move from *C* to *D*, not from *C* to *E* to *A*, in figure 2; and the tendency to be satisfied with outcomes that are efficient only 'locally', such as *D*, although there exists a 'globally' efficient but more rural outcome over the hill at *A*.

So the metaphor of urban bias makes sense even if there are distinct 'norms' or 'trues', one for equity and one for efficiency; and even if there are misleading 'local norms' such as *D* in figure 2. There remain three definitional problems i.e. moving from literal and physical to metaphorical and socio-economic senses of 'bias'. First, 'weight' and 'density' have clear meanings and their unbiased allocation about bowls or dies is easily established; but there are lots of different sorts of 'resource' to allocate in a nation. The allocation of doctors might be urban-biased, of teachers rural-biased, and of engineers urban-biased with regard to equity but rural-biased with regard to efficiency. I shall argue that most human and physical resources are allocated in an urban-biased manner with respect to both equity and efficiency. This applies, in a different sense, even to such resources as fertilisers, which have almost wholly rural uses; for in this case allocators can permit such resources to be divided *among* farmers in ways that are inefficient and inequitable, so that city-dwellers may benefit (chapter 13). This suggests that *intrasectoral* urban bias, as against the intersectoral (and main) sense of figure 1, is also important:

Figure 3 Intrasectoral urban bias

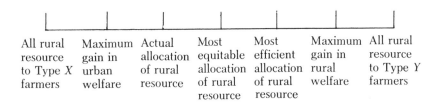

| All rural resource to Type X farmers | Maximum gain in urban welfare | Actual allocation of rural resource | Most equitable allocation of rural resource | Most efficient allocation of rural resource | Maximum gain in rural welfare | All rural resource to Type Y farmers |

Usually 'Type X farmers' are big farmers, producing for the cities, and 'Type Y farmers' are small farmers, eating most of their produce, but obtaining on each acre high output, with heavy inputs per acre of (plentiful) labour and light doses of (scarce) capital. It is likely that any intrasectoral bias imparted by central decisions to allocation of rural resources will be imparted to allocation of urban resources as well; in particular, an urban-biased allocator will not much mind that inegalitarian allocations of income among city-dwellers will mean less demand for food, and hence less income for villagers, than a more equal intra-urban allocation.[4]

The second definitional problem arises because 'to bias' is a transitive verb. The person who makes the bowl or the die (or the person who intervenes later) weights it away from true. Economies and societies are not 'made' by one agency alone, but by the interactions of their members and the influence of outside forces. To expect such interactions and influences to settle down to 'true' is naive. Even in the limited area of economic efficiency, there is no Invisible Hand, but rather several interests with enough power to get resources for themselves. In LDCs today, far more than in now-rich countries yesterday, it is urban interests that are the more concentrated, articulate and powerful. It is these interests that bias resource allocations away from efficiency, and (I shall argue) equity as well, in the direction of pushing more resources towards the cities. Governments, far from redressing the balance or even 'holding the ring', are part of — or at best tend to support — the urban interest, and thus tend to worsen the bias away from norms of efficiency and equity.

The implication, however, is not that governments should in future keep out, although it would be innocent to suppose that their general support for urban bias could be eradicated. Governmental action in poor countries can accelerate their growth in three ways. First, resources can be diverted from less productive activities to more productive ones — from luxury housebuilding to the construction of dams or factories, from banquets to the feeding of weak and hungry workers, from bookmakers' pay to teachers' pay. Second, resources can be used better, in any particular activity. Third, resources can be increased, by foreign loans or intergovernmental grants. There are numerous ways in which governmental taxing and spending, nationalising and re-distributing, borrowing and lending can help in all three tasks: and clearly some of these governmental activities contribute to development.

BIAS FROM THE EFFICIENCY NORM

The third problem concerns the definition of the 'true' or 'norm', whether of efficiency or of equity, from which I allege that most poor countries deviate through urban bias. Pareto suggested a minimum condition for efficiency: a system is efficient only if it cannot produce its present bundle of outputs with less of any of its inputs (by rearranging the way in which inputs are combined among two or more lines of production and/or by improving the technique in any line of production). Another way of expressing Pareto's condition is to say that a system is efficient only if one cannot produce more of any product, from the *same* level of inputs (by rearranging inputs among products and/or by improvements in technique in any production line), without reducing output of any other product.

That definition of efficiency — a situation where one cannot produce 'the same from less' or 'more from the same' — is both minimal and static. It is minimal because it gives only a *necessary* condition for efficient allocation of resources, and there are usual-ly many possible allocations that fulfil the condition.[5] To make Pareto's condition *sufficient* for efficiency, we strengthen it as follows: the allocation of resources is efficient if and only if it is impossible to increase total national output by shifting one or more resources among product lines, and/or by improving the tech-nique in one or more product lines. This suggests an extra way to improve efficiency. With the weak Pareto condition, we could look only for ways of raising some outputs that did not reduce other outputs. With this stronger condition, we can also look for ways to increase some outputs even if we thereby reduce other outputs, provided the value of the increase is greater than the value of the reduction.

This implies the existence of an acceptable system of valuing the outputs and comparing them. There is plenty wrong with the use of market prices as indicators of value,[6] but we shall show below (pp. 189-90) that putting these things right would normally raise the value of farm outputs and non-farm inputs, and lower the value of non-farm outputs and farm inputs. Thus, if there is urban bias even at market prices, there is far more at 'the right prices'. Yet even at market prices, most poor countries suffer from severe urban bias with respect to efficiency; shifting resources from industry to agriculture, and from city to village, could increase net national product at market prices without increasing any input.

We have dealt with the criticism that the Pareto condition for an optimum was too weak — let too many allocations through. However, the strengthened condition remains static in two senses. It makes no allowance for the fact that different allocations now may generate different amounts of resources to allocate later. And it does not tell us which of two allocations to prefer, if one gives more output this year, while the other gives *much* more output several years hence.

There is an answer to both these questions. The value of output now can be compared with the value of output later by discounting the latter, using either the market rate of discount or some other rate. If borrowers, on average, borrow at 8 per cent interest when inflation is running at about 3 per cent, that means they must value £100 today at least as highly as £105 (in today's purchasing power) in one year's time. If they find lenders at that average rate, such lenders clearly value £105 (in today's purchasing power) in one year's time at least as highly as £100 today. Hence a 'real' rate of interest of 5 per cent (a money rate of 8 per cent minus 3 per cent to cover inflation) divides society into satisfied lenders and satisfied borrowers; the lenders see the rate as at least high enough for their typical loan, the borrowers as at least low enough. 'The market' here seems to point to 5 per cent as reflecting some compromise rate of *social time-preference*, or of trade-off between income now and income next year. Certainly, at that rate, borrowers (preferring some income now) demand as much cash as lenders (preferring more income next year) lend; and both think they get good value.

Such a 'market rate', however, is at best a first shot at the true rate of social time-preference for present income over future income. First, there are lots of markets and lots of rates — what you pay to borrow depends on who you are, the length and purpose of the loan, and much else. Second, any 'average' rate ignores the preferences of the vast numbers of people — including almost all children — who do not borrow or lend at interest. Third, 'market' rates are often pushed up by the local monopoly power of, for example, village moneylenders. Fourth, and in a poor country perhaps most important, interest rates are pushed up by risks of non-repayment — due to poor harvests and the poverty of the borrowers — and by short life-expectancies and time-horizons that greatly increase personal preference for cash now over cash later.[7] It is not obvious why the high 'time-preference' of poor people today should prevent governments from raising savings and investment rates, in the certain knowledge that the consequent higher income and security will lower the time-preference of the same people in years to come. If the very high interest rates, characteristic of most poor countries, were accepted by governments as indicating preferences for, say, £100 today over £125 next year, only those few investments with over 25 per cent rates of return would be undertaken and there could be little or no development. The planner, even if ultra-democratic, should consider the preferences of people a decade hence as well as today. If development has made them richer and more secure by then, their time-preference will have fallen; if not, they will loudly complain; in either case, though for different reasons, they will reject as much too high the 'market' rates of discount of ten years ago, and excoriate those planners who took such rates as indicators of time-preference and who cut down on saving and investment accordingly.

Some writers[8] argue that planners should have *no* time-preference — that, in judging between (say) an urban and a rural investment on grounds of efficiency, income ten or even a thousand years hence should count for as much as income this year, assuming risk to be the same. But we cannot realistically assume that. Moreover, extra income *now* matters more, if we can assume that the future is luckier than the present — and, after all, the *average* life does tend to get less unhealthy, insecure, nasty, brutish and short. Technical progress will certainly enable output to be produced with less human effort,[9] and also probably increase real growth of income per person. All in all, there seems a strong case for valuing tomorrow's benefits more highly than distant, uncertain benefits to the wealthier, more leisured Earthmen of 2000 or 2500. Moreover, no government could cut consumption, in a year, to finance investment up to the point where the undiscounted net yield from any *more* extra machines and buildings, over their whole lifespan, ceased to be worth as much as the further consumption foregone by financing them. Such a policy might even starve the voters, or if persisted in, create the logical oddity of living near the bone for ever, in order to accumulate more and more capital for a beanfeast that never arrives, because it can *always* be enlarged by more than the current consumption sacrificed for enlargement!

For once, common sense and politics support economics and logic. In choosing between jam-today projects and jam-tomorrow projects, planners should give more weight to the former, but (at least in a poor country) not to such an extent as is indicated by the market rate of interest. This goes some way to removing the 'staticness' from the definition of a bias-free 'norm' for efficiency of any resource allocation. It is the allocation that maximises output from that resource together with all other available inputs. By 'output' we mean net national product (NNP), weighted by market prices, and we argue on pp. 189-90 that improved relative weightings of the components of NNP strengthen the case against urban bias. We count the output as far ahead as it is expected to be produced; but the longer the output has to be waited for, the more we discount it (although by a rate of time-preference rather less than the average interest rate in a poor country). The international borrowing rate on commercial loans has been suggested — about 4 per cent if we can exclude the part that merely compensates for expected inflation. So, if we have to choose between putting £1 million in Project A or Project B on efficiency grounds alone, we compare the following total:

Extra net output at constant prices due to[10] A in Year 1 +

$$+ \left[\text{ditto in Year 2} \times \frac{100}{100+4} \right] + \left[\text{ditto in Year 3} \times \left[\frac{100}{100+4} \right]^2 \right]$$
$$+ \left[\cdots \right] \cdots$$

with the corresponding total for Project B. Urban bias with respect to efficiency means, firstly, that urban A-projects are being chosen, even where rural B-projects have higher totals on this calculation. Secondly (see figure 3), it means that, even *within* the rural sector, A-projects that help the city substantially are being preferred to higher-yielding B-projects that do not.

There is a sense in which even the above criterion might still seem static, even shortsighted. Should we not ask (1) whether the 'extra output' in any year itself gives a further push to development, and correspondingly (2) whether the extra income paid to its producers is saved? Some of the reasons why (2) is not as appropriate or important as it seems are given in chapter 10. As for (1), its importance is reduced by the possibility of foreign trade: if *B* gives output of higher value than *A*, but *A* produces investment goods and *B* does not, it is efficient to obtain investment goods by making *B* and trading it for imported *A*. Trading brings new difficulties, and perhaps unfavourable price trends and instabilities; if all this is thought serious (or if the arguments of chapter 10 are not convincing), we can weight, more highly than the market now does, these outputs helpful to future production (or associated with high savings from people who make them).[11] An efficiency norm is definable anyway.

BIAS FROM THE EQUITY NORM

Little need be said about the 'norm' or 'true' of equity, not because such a norm is easy to define—far from it![12]—but because urban bias away from equity is fairly easy to demonstrate for *any* plausible norm. An 'efficiency norm' would imply so allocating resources as to maximise long-run output. Any 'equity norm' must imply — among other things, perhaps — distributing long-run income so as to maximise welfare. Now in most poor countries an extra £100 of income, typically distributed, will do more to raise welfare in rural than in urban areas.[13] Advocacy of high urban-industrial resource allocations usually reasons that, in the long run at least, they will create more output (in the sense of p. 52) than would more 'rural' ones; seldom that a given amount of extra income will do more good to townsmen than to villagers.

Why does income generate more welfare in rural areas? In the poor countries for which evidence is available, average personal income is substantially less in rural than in urban areas, even after allowing for higher urban living costs and for cash remissions from city workers to their rural families (chapter 9). An extra £10 makes more difference to a family of five that lives off £100 a year than to such a family enjoying £200 a year. As the family gets richer, it uses further income to satisfy wants that are less and less important to it per extra pound spent—if they were more important, they would have been satisfied first. So, under normal circumstances,[14] welfare is bound to be increased more by allocating available extra income to the poor rather than the rich. On the whole, in almost all poor countries, raising income by £10 per head per year in rural area will do more for welfare than doing so in urban areas.

Though rural people are on average worse off, might an extra £10 generated by likely state action reach poorer *individuals* in urban areas than in rural areas? Two factors make this unlikely. First, existing income is distributed even more unequally within urban areas in poor countries than within rural areas,[15] largely because involuntary idleness in the city affects the same people for long periods of time, while in the village it takes the form of some seasonal lack of farmwork for almost everybody. Extra incomes, generated by plausible government action to allocate a resource, could be distributed like existing income; or they could drift towards the better-off people in the area receiving them. On either assumption, they are likely to make more contribution to the relief of poverty if they go to rural areas, where poverty is more evenly spread. Since the rural not-so-poor are less far above their poor neighbours than the urban rich, they are (1) less likely to be politically strong enough to obtain the great bulk of the fruits of extra income, (2) even if they do, less bloated (absolutely as well as relatively to their neighbours) as a result, (3) likelier to spend a large proportion of extra income, and (because employment is distributed more equally than in the cities) to spread the benefits per unit of income spent among more people.

There is a second, administrative, reason why a given amount of extra income, generated by government action, probably gives more help to poor people in LDCs if it is concentrated in rural rather than in urban areas. Most income-generating actions by governments in poor countries, especially direct public investment and support for private investment, help people already in jobs. In big towns, much of the income is generated by forms of activity using a good deal of capital and little labour per unit of output, and this seems especially true of many of the activities where output is most likely to be raised through public action — large-scale construction, docks, modern factories. Yet urban poverty is concentrated among the unemployed, beggars, prostitutes, and unorganised service workers employed in such activities as shoe-cleaning, laundry and domestic service. These people are extremely hard to reach through government action. Even if they were not, the productive impact of such action would be remote and doubtful. (Hardly any Third World government can afford to pay unemployment relief, for example.) The fact that most of the rural poor have (expansible) work, whereas many urban poor are jobless, also means that the rural poor benefit more than the urban poor when income, received in their areas, is spent and creates a demand for more work. Hence in the cities there is a conflict between using scarce resources to alleviate need and using them to increase production. In rural areas the conflict is muted or absent, because the main cause of primary poverty is insufficient or irregular income from productive work accruing to persons *already in employment,* whether as mini-farmers or as landless labourers.

If government action to raise rural incomes productively is efficient, it will normally give the underemployed poor a better chance of getting employment, and thus raise their welfare. Government action to raise urban incomes productively, however, is likely to concentrate on lines of production with high wages, skilled workers, frequently powerful unions, and prospects of overtime — and also with high ratios of capital to labour, and therefore of profit income to wage income. It is obvious where the prospects of a major impact on poverty from a given amount of extra income would be better — even if average rural income were not below average urban income!

So, if a shift of resources from city to village improves efficiency, an equity improvement can usually be taken for granted. Suppose we shift from city to village the resources (say the investment finance) needed to generate an extra £100 of yearly rural income. Not only do we know that the welfare gain is more than the welfare loss from depriving the (richer) city-dwellers of that £100;[16] if rural resources are used more efficiently, the city-dwellers will lose *less* than £100 of yearly income by the resource transfer from which the rural population gains £100. So it looks as if we can forget about the controversial and perhaps impossible task of defining an 'equity norm'.[17] If we can show that allocations raising the rural share of various resources normally generate more total output and income, few will question that £10 of extra rural output and income normally produces more welfare than £10 of extra urban output and income.

Before we leave the equity norm, we must consider one more point. So far the term 'output and income' has been used rather glibly; but a reallocation of resources, although clearly improving on the welfare generated as a result of income yielded, may worsen the welfare position by its impact on the composition of output. Conversely, the welfare impact of changing the types of output could be favourable, but the welfare impact of the corresponding income changes unfavourable. In either case, to strike a balance, we should have to hunt the elusive equity norm after all. How would these effects work in real life, and are they likely when resources are reallocated from the cities to the countryside?

Might a reallocation of public investment (or doctors or subsidies), while increasing incomes in the rural sector at the cost of the urban sector, so change the structure of output as to harm the poor? This could happen, but it is unlikely, for three reasons.

Firstly, the reallocation of productive resources would mean more food output and fewer industrially produced consumer goods. Secondly, within food production, since poorer people receive a larger share of income because of the urban-to-rural shift, the demand and hence later the supply of foods with low costs per calorie, notably cereals,[18] will increase at the expense of rich men's foods, such as dairy products. Thirdly, quite a lot of extra farm income could, with appropriate policies for allocating the additional rural investment *among* farmers, go directly into the stomachs of the poor people that produce it, in the form of what economists repulsively call 'self-consumed produce of peasant farmers'; in this case, an equalizing change in income distribution could not produce a change in the structure of output that worsened equality.[19]

The possibility of investment in production for 'self-consumption' also reduces the other risk: that a policy to raise the rural share in output might reduce the share of poor people in income. This could happen with other forms of rural investment, however, in two ways. Firstly, the process of constructing such investment (even if it ultimately generated rural incomes) might produce incomes mainly for contractors and skilled workers. However, this would normally apply even more strongly to the construction, at the same cost, of investment to generate urban incomes.[20] Secondly, even if extra output was in the first instance redirected towards rural people, the income might be so spent that the main beneficiaries were the rural and urban rich, whereas a similar initial direction of income to urban people might lead to a spending pattern enriching mainly the poor; but this is far-fetched.

'URBAN'

It is the purpose of this chapter to define 'urban bias', and to make a *prima facie* case, amplified in later chapters, for blaming it for the persistence of poverty alongside development, and incidentally for many of the inefficiencies and inadequacies of development itself. So far we have defined 'bias', and considered two norms with respect to which we hope to demonstrate 'urban bias' in most poor countries: the efficiency norm and the equity norm. As for the former, we must give show that output (in the time-weighted sense of p. 52) would rise if a larger share of resources went to the countryside. To demonstrate urban bias with respect to equity, we have argued in the last section, it probably suffices to show that countryfolk are being enriched more slowly than townspeople, partly as a result of policy—and that countryfolk start off substantially poorer than townspeople. Subsequent chapters will establish the facts of relative rural deprivation, consider how rural resources are transferred townward beyond what is efficient or equitable, and look at the pressures causing such transfers.

First, we must scrutinise the 'urban-rural' dichotomy itself. Four criticisms are possible. (1) 'One cannot draw the line. Urban shades imperceptibly into rural, mediated by city allotments, garden suburbs and village factories.' (2) 'There is more than one line. Two sectors are too few. In particular, there exists a tertiary 'urban' sector, mainly providing services which must be considered when deciding which resource allocation is best — or whether the actual one is biased.' (3) 'The line lies elsewhere: between the capital city and the rest of the nation, not between urban and rural areas.' (4) 'The line has been drawn on the wrong map.[21] Allocations and biases are between agriculture and industry, or between consumer goods and investment goods, or between poor and rich, rather than between country and town.'

The city-country line

In poor countries, one usually can draw a fairly sharp line between city and countryside. A few exceptions spring to mind: regions where part-time farming and townward commuting are made possible by cheap and highly developed transport systems, as in the Wet Zone, Sri Lanka; semi-developed Third World city-states with considerable small-scale horticulture, such as Singapore; areas of almost continuous rural settlement with many markets and administrative centres, such as Kerala in southern India. In general, however, poor countries have townscape and countryside, and the break is sharp. Poor people can seldom afford the cash or the caloric energy for long journeys to work, and those who live in the countryside (or in the city) tend to work there.

The three main patterns of living-cum-working in the rural Third World are nomadism, homestead or hacienda farming[22] and the settled village. In the first two cases, exactly the same people, who practise open-space agriculture, also adopt the rural mode of living. This makes the boundary of the rural sector clear-cut. In the third situation, the borderline between village and town is occasionally blurred. A town normally has several characteristics (compactness, density of population, size, non-agricultural dominance) and many functions (marketing, administrative, social, educational, transportational) and some places of, say, three to seven thousand inhabitants meet some criteria but not others.[23] However, the problem is (in every sense) marginal. The great bulk of village communities in poor countries contain a few hundred people, mainly agriculturists or craft workers in support of agriculture. Most townspeople live in places of well over ten thousand[24] and few work in agriculture or in direct support of it. Thus, despite the apparently chaotic variety of national census definitions of 'urban',[25] the urban-rural dichotomy, for the great mass of places and residents, is clear and discrete. The bias diagnosed in this book stems from and benefits large towns of ten to twenty thousand people and more.[26]

An intermediate sector?

Are more divisions needed? In his great pioneering work *The Conditions of Economic Progress*, Colin Clark developed the idea (which he traced to Sir William Petty, writing in 1691!) that the rapid growth of a 'tertiary sector' of employment, neither industry nor agriculture, characterised genuine development.[27] Is there an analogous 'rurban sector', between countryside and city? Even if there is, we can still ask whether urban areas get a larger, and rural areas a smaller, share of most resources than is efficient or equitable. The analysis becomes more complicated, because we need to see whether resources, denied to (or squeezed from) rural areas, go to urban or to rurban areas — and whether excessive resources going to (or transferred to) urban areas come from rural or rurban families. But the identification of a rurban sector would cast no doubt on the *concept* of urban bias.

Anyway, it is doubtful if such a sector exists in most less-developed regions. Attempts to foster village industries, or to persuade people to locate factories in mini-towns with a substantial farm population, have seldom succeeded. Recent immigrants to the urban slums, while largely temporary, are probably best classified as rural-based persons trying to get urban jobs. Not only are rurban places hard to spot; there is no reason to believe that 'tertiary sector' workers congregate there, or are a homogeneous or smoothly growing group with a clear, single role in the development process. After all, the group includes scientific doctors, engineers and mathematics teachers; traditional herbalists, temple-builders and Koranic teachers; domestic servants, prostitutes and possibly beggars![28]

Capital-city bias?

Dudley Seers and others have suggested that while one line may do, it should be drawn elsewhere, between the capital city and everywhere else: that we are dealing not with urban bias but with capital-city bias. This is a deep point, because it asks us to explain resource misallocation by overcentralisation — *'Paris et le desert'*:

in poor countries this is made more acute by external economies in administration (if all the old government departments are in the capital city, it is costly to put new ones outside it); by the frequent reluctance of senior men to move from the scene of action in Delhi, even to empty offices and cheaper houses in other towns such as Simla or Nagpur: and by scarce, and often bad and overstretched, transport and communications systems. This last factor, together with the French tradition of highly centralised administration, lends support to 'capital-city bias' as a partial explanation of the inadequate share of resources in rural areas, above all in ministates once part of the French colonial system. In these states, however, the capital city is often the only substantial town, so that the line between it and everywhere else is also the line between urban and rural areas.

There are, however, three objections to the 'capital-city bias' analysis. Demographically, most poor countries—except for tiny, semi-developed countries—feature capitals no more swollen, by comparison with other cities, than those of rich nations.[29] Socio-economically, 'capital-city bias' obscures the link between towns *as a whole* and the urge to industrialise, modernise and 'westernise'—an urge as readily expressed in ports, tourist resorts, or company towns (and by their beneficiaries) as in capital cities, which often reflect only a long-established need for a trading and administrative centre. The newly expanded secondary cities are often the real, new centres of power. The economic power behind urban bias rests—to speak in nineteenth-century British terms—in Manchester, not in London. Politico-administratively, especially in a big federal country such as India or Nigeria, the greater strength and immediacy and sophistication of urban pressure groups is often much *less* serious in the capital city than in other towns, especially than in centres of provincial administration. To some extent, politicians and administrators in Delhi acquire distance from, and capacity to play off, the sort of urban-industrial pressures that overwhelmingly weigh upon decisions in a state capital like Patna. Closeness to a national and international milieu of academic and economic life (where decisions about resource allocation are analysed, if not always taken, on general welfare principles that do not favour any particular sector), and direct responsibility for the *national* interest insofar as it assists their political survival, also force decision-takers in the administrative capital into somewhat less urban-biased allocations than is the case in other urban centres.

Personal idealism and feelings of justice, too, are less constrained in capital cities by immediate contact with powerful urban groups, especially at the highest level of all. It is characteristic of President Kaunda of Zambia that he asks the Cabinet to enquire, 'Is it rural?' of all major project proposals. Equally, it is characteristic of poor countries that he is seldom able to make the answer influence the decision, because of the great pressures on Cabinet of urban elites, not only, perhaps not mainly, in Lusaka itself. In the capital the very top echelons in the administration sometimes find themselves in alliance with the peasants and landless against the urban sector—a modern version of King John of England's thirteenth-century attempts to squeeze the barons between the peasantry and the Crown (and seldom much more successful). Hence it is not surprising that urban bias distorts allocation least in those few poor countries with either a very powerful, pro-rural, yet development-oriented top elite in the administrative capital, or an exceptionally articulate and powerful rural mass movement. To speak of 'capital-city bias' to the exclusion of urban bias is to obscure these key economic-industrial and political considerations.[30]

Industrial bias?

The most plausible objection to an urban-rural analysis is that an industrial-agricultural division is preferable. There are five defences of the choice of an urban-rural split. First, 'urban' and 'rural' in fact divide people, workers, places and capital quite similarly to 'industrial' and 'agricultural', but avoid the difficult problem that the latter division compels us to make a more or less arbitrary decision about how to classify, say, transport workers or teachers, with their families and the equipment supporting them. Second, the urban-rural distinction is in some ways more convenient, given the available data. Third, the rural sector discriminated against is not purely agricultural. Fourth, the most wasteful and unfair parts of the city's allocation are in infrastructure rather than industry. Finally, while neither the urban-rural nor the industrial-agricultural distinction alone suffices to capture all the allocative decisions and influence here crudely characterised as 'urban bias', to speak of 'industrial bias' is to exclude more of the operative social and political processes in the interests of a neater, but less appropriate, economic classification.

First, several censuses in LDCs give the occupational distribution of urban and rural workforces separately. In India in 1961, fractionally under 80 per cent of the rural workforce earned most of its income from agriculture (as farmers, cultivators or labourers), and probably well over half the rest from providing crafts, transport or other inputs and services almost entirely to agricultural production. In urban places, barely 10 per cent of workers earned most of their income as cultivators or agricultural labourers.[31]

Second, usually it is more convenient to use the rural-urban than the (largely overlapping) agriculture-'others' distinction: 'others' are rather a ragbag; most sample-survey, census and other residence data are collected on the urban-rural basis; and (while all resources benefit either urban or rural people) it hardly makes sense to allocate doctors, for instance, between agriculture and other sectors. The world of work cannot plausibly be bifurcated into agriculture and 'industry'. We wish to show that most developmental resources not allocated to agriculture in fact benefit the modern industrial sub-sector (pp. 204-5); we are not trying to escape from the need for argument by a trick of definition. Sometimes the data compel us to contrast agriculture and 'non-agriculture'; but such general negative terms as 'non-agriculture' have serious drawbacks. They try to impose by definition a coherence that does not exist in reality; and they leave us to assume that the contrasting, positive term is clearly definable, which is often not so (consider Aquinas' 'Hell is to be deprived of God').[32]

Third, while the individuals discriminated against by urban bias are mostly engaged in farming, many have secondary incomes from various rural crafts. This probably does not mean that official data overstate the 'agrarianness' of LDCs, because, conversely, many rural craftsmen earn subsidiary incomes from farm work. It is the rural community that loses, and the urban community that gains, even by biases transferring demand away from agriculture to industry rather than directly from rural to urban sector.[33]

Fourth, evidence of agriculture's great advantages over non-agriculture in the use of capital will appear in chapter 8. However, it is probably infrastructure — mainly urban in its benefits (power, rail, tower blocks) — and not industry that shows the most unfavourable ratios of capital to output. This was clearly true in Latin America about 1950, before the build-up of inefficient heavy industries. To speak of 'industrial' rather than urban bias is to condemn, perhaps unjustly, small light manufacturing, and to excuse the inefficiencies and inequities of power grids for urban luxury dwellings.[34]

Finally, urban, rather than industrial, bias reflects political reality. The daily contacts of, and pressures on, central decision-takers in poor countries come overwhelmingly from small groups of articulate, organised or powerful people in regular contact with senior officials and politicians; but it wrong to describe such groups as 'industrial'. Though they are often influenced by the interests of industrial workers, firms or ideologists, such interests represent too few people in most poor countries to succeed frequently alone.[35] Leaders of labour, and of public and private capital and management, in construction, railways and government service; prominent academics and other intellectuals; influential editors and radio producers—these, and not just leaders of industry, are the threateners, promisers, lobbyists, dinner companions, flatterers, financiers and friends to senior administrators and politicians in all countries, rich and poor. They are almost always 'urban', but seldom just 'industrial', in their interests, preferences, friends, places of residence, and above all perceptions.

What is special, in this regard, about the poor countries commencing accelerated development since 1945 is not their possession of an urban elite. It is rather the sharp contrast between its dominance of central decision-making, and the dominance of rural people in population, work and production. In the USA or (to a lesser extent) the USSR, urban predominance in the elite is almost matched by an urban majority in the population. But how far is the emergence of an urban elite amid a rural mass a natural and necessary concomitant of industrialisation, even of centralising government itself? In most cases of early industrial development in countries now industrialised (chapter 1)—partly because of previous rapid agricultural change—the rural elite was far stronger than in most poor countries today, and the urban sector contained a larger share of the population. Hence the extent to which the urban sector dominated, during early industrialisation, was far less disproportionate to its potentials and needs in countries now developed, than it is in countries now developing.

The balance of power, then, is more accurately described as urban-rural than as industrial-agricultural. The two dichotomies interact, and emphasis on industrialisation—except insofar as it assists efficient growth that later spreads its benefits—will help the city and harm the countryside. Moreover, I shall on occasion be compelled to use statistics collected by sectors of economic activity instead of by residence. The considerable overlap of rural and agricultural populations helps here, as we can assume pretty safely that what benefits agriculture benefits rural people;[36] similarly, the mass of persons engaged in industry is urban, except for household industry, which is usually classified separately, both in measuring its workforce and in providing its (tiny) allocations of centrally controlled resources. In estimating the urban-rural division of resources or people from sectoral information about industry and agriculture, one has to decide how to treat other sectors. By preferring the political (but measurable) concept of 'urban bias' to the economic concept of 'industrial bias' one recognises 'the primacy of politics'[37] in the development process. By describing how urban bias works one hopes to alert politicians as well as economists to the harm done by unbridled political primacy.

URBAN BIAS AS A STATE OF MIND

So far, this chapter has concentrated on justifying a choice of definition of 'urban bias' that permits us to assess whether, and to what extent, resources are being allocated in an urban-biased way — what might be called *allocative* urban bias. 'Bias' in the literal sense inheres in the bowl or the die, not the maker or the user. In the metaphorical sense, however, it inheres in the allocator as well as the allocation, the politician as well as the polity: if a decision is biased (as opposed to just mistaken) so is the umpire who gives it. The biased umpire or allocator is more than simply mistaken, but less than dishonest. He is moved, not by bribery, but by a state of mind leading him to decide according to criteria other than efficiency or equity: by *dispositional* urban bias. In speaking of allocations that are urban-biased — not just 'excessively urban', and not usually 'urban-bribed' — we are asserting that people taking allocative decisions in LDCs are biased in favour of urban areas. They are not usually dishonest people — many developing countries could not match the major scandals in Britain and France, in, say, 1972[38] — but neither are they making simple errors of analysis. The analytic mistakes made by honest and intelligent people, in the course of justifying heavily urban resource allocations, suggest a prevailing disposition[39] to make and justify such allocations.

It is insufficient to *refute* such justifications, if the disposition remains; as Butler remarked, 'He that complies against his will, is of his own opinion still.' Before attempting refutation, therefore, I propose to quote, without comment, statements by leading scholars that reveal a high degree of dispositional urban bias. The quotations have been selected largely because of the high intellectual standing and integrity of the writers; they are people from whom such citations speak for themselves. A much worse catalogue of concealed *non sequiturs*, and of valuations with morally intolerable implications, could be compiled from politicians and academics of other than the first rank; but *they* might just be muddled. The authors that follow are clear and thoughtful; we can therefore be sure that what they reveal, in others or in themselves, is a disposition to support urban allocations at the cost of relaxing normally exemplary standards of reasoning.

'Saving in Pakistan, as in most underdeveloped countries, involved squeezing the peasants. Because more than half the national income was generated in agriculture, the bulk of savings had to come from that sector.' (G. Papanek, *Pakistan's Development*, Harvard, 1967, p. 207.)

'It is only the imposition of compulsory levies on the agricultural sector itself which enlarges the supply of "savings" in the required sense for economic development.' (N. Kaldor, cited in R. B. Bangs, *Financing Economic Development*, Chicago, 1968, p. 22.)

'Since most LDCs are primarily agricultural, the burden of an initial gross increase in taxation . . . will necessarily fall rather heavily on the agricultural sector.' (Bangs, *Financing Economic Development*, p. 22.)

'As the largest sector of the economy, at least in the earliest stages of development, agriculture is the source of manpower for industrial expansion, it is the source of essential supplies for maintaining a growing industrial population and of exports to be traded for industrial goods, and it is the chief potential source of savings for non-agricultural investment.' (B. F. Johnston and H. M. Southworth, 'Agricultural Development: Problems and Issues, in Southworth and Johnston, eds., *Agricultural Development and Economic Growth*, Cornell, 1967, p. 4.)

'Agriculture must supply expanded food, expanded markets and an expanded supply of loanable funds to the modern sector.' (W. W. Rostow, *The Stages of Economic Growth*, 2nd ed., Cambridge, 1969, p. 24.)

'This shuttle pattern of migration has many advantages [especially in] a dual economy in which the urban sector represents modern, industrial activities and the rural sector is still traditional agriculture. In such situations the apparently less developed side of the society can provide many of the social overhead and welfare facilities for the more developed side without the need for extensive new investments'. (L. W. Pye, 'The Political Implications of Urbanisation and the Development Process', in Breeze, ed., *The City in Newly Developing Countries*, Prentice-Hall, 1969, p. 402.)

What can cause such assumptions: that the farm sector exists to support the rest of the economy; that it is to be contrasted with the 'modern' sector; that—even if poor and efficient in its use of capital—it should transfer savings to support an industrial sector that, though wealthier, is not efficient enough to finance the re-investment it needs for growth? Anyone familiar with the civil services of most poor countries will recognise the attitudes dispos-ing them to urban bias. They want to modernise fast; they rightly observe that rich nations are non-agricultural and that their own agriculture is poor; and they wrongly conclude that rapid indus-trialisation at the expense of agriculture can produce rapid devel-opment. Often they see their farmers as politically reactionary, economically unresponsive to incentives, and reluctant to in-novate. Such unfounded stereotypes find powerful expression in such phrases as 'We do not want to be hewers of wood and drawers of water,' and psychological underpinning in their holders' success in raising their prestige and pay through almost entirely urban actions, achievements and alliances.

There are other dispositions, not explicitly pro-urban, that have the effect of generating urban-biased allocations in LDCs. Where prestige attaches to abstraction and speculation, people will downgrade activities requiring grass-roots contact for success— and rural administration is such an activity, because its milieux are at once diverse and different from that of the urban-based decision-taker. A related, but different, factor, predisposing to-wards dispositional urban bias, is reluctance to 'get one's hands dirty' by planning or running policy in sectors where success re-quires fieldwork. A third such factor—given that able people are concentrated in large organisations, including the branches of government—is the belief that it is far harder to convince, con-trol, predict, and hence successfully plan for, thousands of small private farms than a few big, often publicly owned urban firms. Yet, if there were not deeper economic or psychological factors at work, none of this need generate urban bias. Planning of rural credit, or researching nitrogen fixation, are tasks as demanding of speculative insight as any in modern industry; top-rate Foreign Ministry administrators could transform many a Ministry of Agri-culture while keeping their hands fastidiously clean; and small farmers can certainly be planned for, by price policies and other tools of 'probabilistic' planning. One suspects, therefore, that dis-positional urban bias is the cause, rather than the result, of the elite's frequent belief that abstraction and centralisation and planning have little scope for changing rural life.

In any event—and whether dispositional urban bias is cause or effect of other forms of intellectual prejudice—the citations show that it has led many experts to advocate squeezing farmers to develop urban industry. Where ideology, advice, predilections and immediate pressures all dispose towards urban bias, it is almost certain to win. When confronted with its own inconsistencies—notably the incapacity of a poor and resource-starved rural sector to generate surpluses, especially at unattractive prices—urban-biased planners talk of 'top priority for agriculture', pass another paper land reform or speak of green revolutions. Only in the last resort do they allocate scarce resources to the rural sector, and especially to the deficit farmer, who has least to offer their urban constituency.

URBAN BIAS AND CLASS STRUCTURES: THE EXAMPLE OF FOOD PRICES

A glance at the real class structure of most poor countries casts doubt on the usual analyses of classes defined by their relationship to the means of production—land, capital and labour.[40] One sees rural rentiers—big landlords—certainly, but also many thousand small farmers, tenants or proprietors. They live in no communal idyll, and are poor and exploited by local monopolists—suppliers of credit, marketing facilities or land. Nor are these peasants egalitarian; they are highly differentiated. But, on the whole, they are consumer-producers for whom the separation of capital and labour, profit and wage,[41] process of production and use of end-product, is meaningless.

Nor is the urban sector inviting to the classical Marxian analysis. One sees a mass of urban jobless, but they are often in reality *fringe villagers,* waiting until penury forces them back to the land and meanwhile living on casual work—or on their rural relatives. They hang around the city slums more in temporary hope than in expectation of work. They are kept half-employed partly by employers' preferences for machines and small workforces: preferences due to subsidised imports and high wages, both maintained in part by unions or other skilled-labour pressures. The wage levels (and less obviously the import subsidies) are paid for by villagers, who could otherwise find urban jobs (or get more imports themselves). They are enforced through naked urban power; they lead to situations where employers prefer heavy capital equipment worked well below capacity to more employment-generating strategies of production. The existing urban labour aristocracy enjoys high wages largely because it is small: it is too costly for the employer to do without their skills, cheap to pay them off, and easy to acquire capital subsidies to keep employment levels low.

.Yet if he did go for more labour-intensive methods, he would advance equality. More people would be employed at a slightly lower urban wage. Despite some vulgar *Marxisants,* the basic conflict in the Third World is not between capital and labour, but between capital and countryside, farmer and townsman, villager (including temporarily urban 'fringe villager') and urban industrial employer-cum-proletarian elite, gainers from dear food and gainers from cheap food.[42] While the urban centres of power and government remain able and willing to steer development overwhelmingly towards urban interests, development will remain unequalising.

The systematic action by most governments in poor countries to keep down food prices (chapter 13) clarifies the operation of class interests in urban bias. Town and country are polarised, yet the powerful country interests are bought off (by subsidies for inputs, such as tractors and tubewells, that they are almost alone in using). The urban employer wants food to be cheap, so that his workforce will be well fed and productive. The urban employee wants cheap food too; it makes whatever wages he can extract from the boss go further.

Less obviously, the *whole* interest of the rural community is against cheap food. This is clear enough for the farmers who sell food to the towns (largely big farmers, bought off by input subsidies); but even the 'deficit farmer' or net food buyer (who grows too little to feed himself from his land alone) often gains when food is dear, except perhaps in the very short term. Deficit farmers cannot make ends meet on their land alone, and to buy enough food must work for others.[43] Often they work on farms for a fixed share of the crop, which is worth more when food prices are high. Whether they work for crop wages or for cash, it pays the big farmer to hire more labour when food is dearer, and this bids up farm wages as well as rural employment. The rural craftsmen who serve the big farmers' production and consumption needs—carpenters, ropemakers, goldsmiths—receive more offers of work, at higher wages, when their patrons are enriched because food is dearer; and many poor agriculturists eke out their income by traditional craft activities. Moreover, the richer farmers have more cash to lend out when food is dear and their income high, so the interest rate to the poor borrower is reduced as lenders compete. Even the people on the fringe of the countryside, the recently migrant urban unemployed, find their remittances from the village increasing when their farming fathers and brothers benefit from high food prices.

There is a 'deep' reason why an issue such as the price of food polarises city and country into opposing classes, each fairly homogeneous. The reason is that within each rural community (though hardly one is nowadays completely closed) extra income generated tends to circulate. The big farmer, when he gets a good price for his output, can buy a new seed drill from the village carpenter, who goes more often to the barber and the laundryman, who place more orders with the village tailor and blacksmith. When food becomes cheap, this sort of circulation of income is transferred from the village to the city, because it is in the city that the urban worker will spend most of the money he need no longer use to buy food.

We shall see in chapter 13 how urban power, urban government in the urban interest, has made farm products artificially cheap and farmers' requirements artificially dear in most poor countries. In Pakistan, in the early 1960s, the total effect of State action and private power balances was to *triple* the number of hours the farm sector had to work to get a typical bundle of urban goods.[44] By severe restrictions on cheap imports of industrial consumer goods, by cheap imported raw materials for factory-owners but not farmers, and by many other means, the ratio of industrial prices to agricultural prices was trebled! This is by no means unusual in poor countries. It shows a degree of exploitation, of unequal dealing, next to which intra-urban conflict between capitalist and proletariat is almost negligible.

There is nothing wicked or conspiratorial about this. It is the natural play of self-interest and power, only obfuscated by moralising from outside—*cosi fan tutti*, moralisers as well. And it is only one of many ways in which the city (where most government is) screws the village (where most people are) in poor countries. In tax incidence, in investment allocation, in the provision of incentive, in education and research: everywhere it is government by the city, from the city, for the city.

In isolated moments of war or revolution, a nation may develop a sense of shared interest between landless agricultural and casual industrial labourer, or between city capitalist and village landlord; even when things are quiet, the urban elite pacifies the big farmer by allocating him most of the few resources that can be spared for agriculture. But usually the contradictions between city capitalist and city proletariat can be resolved by negotiation—are not 'antagonistic'[45]—because they can be settled at the expense of the rural interest.[46]

Poverty persists alongside development largely because poor countries are developed from, by and for people in cities: people who, acting under normal human pressures, deny the fruits of development to the pressure-less village poor. Few of these can escape the trap by joining the exploitative city elite, because high urban wages (and subsidised capital imports) deter employers from using extra labour.[47] Many villagers, once migration has failed to secure entry to the urban labour aristocracy, return to an increasingly land-scarce village: a village that is by policy denied the high food prices that would normally be linked to land scarcity, by policy starved of public investment allocations, and hence by policy prevented from sharing in development and thus from curing its own poverty.

This is one reason why, as suggested in chapter 1, we are dealing not with temporary inequality caused by a passing weakness of the impoverished proletariat, but with self-confirming inequality caused by the alliance of the urban employer and proletariat against the rural poor. Population growth, moreover, makes it unlikely that the rural poor will be sucked out, and up, by a labour shortage for a very long time. But what is the structure of power that prevents poor villagers, even in democratic countries, from calling the tune? Why is that power structure not generally recognised for what it is?

WHY URBAN BIAS IS OVERLOOKED

In almost all countries now poor, but in very few now rich, most people live on the land and off the land; but they are governed by, from and (we argue) for townsmen. This fact is so 'set up' as to obscure it from most people likely to analyse its consequences intelligently. Teachers, planners, politicians—one would imagine —can succeed only by knowing their own world. If indigenous, they *have* succeeded, so how *can* they have misdefined that world? If foreign, they find it hard to accept that an elite can effectively remove its peasant masses from its world; when I taught a final-year class of honours students of economics in Khartoum University in 1962, I was amazed to discover that many of them had never set foot in any of the villages where over 80 per cent of their compatriots lived and worked; and even now that I know how common this situation is, I can hardly believe it. In most poor countries the politician, the civil servant, the university teacher, the businessman, or the trade-union leader is selected by townsmen, caters largely to an urban audience,[48] and in pursuing his interests or his career has every incentive to spend his time almost wholly in big cities. The potential member of the elite is 'set up' to define rural life out of his world. Even if village-born, he has reason to regard his relatives as a burden, the prospect of reabsorption into rurality as the ultimate threat, and the whole rural episode as best forgotten.

The foreign observer from a rich country is even worse placed. He may virtuously stir from his air-conditioned hotel to inspect city slums. He is almost certain never to spend long enough in any village to learn what happens. If he is an egalitarian, the grossness of intra-urban inequality — worse than within most villages — leads him to 'reward' the cities for the obviousness of their poverty, with recommended resource allocations that leave the less obvious mass rural poverty untouched.

The opinions and actions of people who make and influence policy are bound to be affected by what they see, hear and fear. They hear the conversations of the city employers and city trade unionists. They see *urban* poverty, especially noticeable and squalid (and severe) because of the adjacent extremes of unconcealed wealth — it is in this sense that high allocations for housing reward the city for its inequality — and because of the glamorous prospects of modern industrial technology in an urban setting. They fear the pressures of a city elite, the riots of a unionised city proletariat. Naturally they allocate an economically indefensible share of resources to the cities. So would you or I in their place.

URBAN BIAS AND THE PERSISTENCE OF POVERTY

Even if urban bias is significant in many countries, what has it to do with the persistence of poverty? After all, we have shown that most poor countries have greatly accelerated their growth and development since 1945 — at the same time as centralising and independent governments emerged. Indeed, the earlier advocacy of agricultural primacy by colonial regimes — for the wrong reasons — has helped to produce the urban bias of their independent successors. Typically, in Burma, the planners' 'main emphasis was to shift the economy away from a pattern of primary production . . . established in colonial times'; negligible farm investment, prices turned against farmers, and a cover-up of 'repeated assurances . . . that agriculture merited priority' followed naturally.[49]

Poor countries could have raised income per person since 1945 much faster than they did, if allocative urban bias had been reduced. I shall show that many of the resources allocated by state action to city-dwellers would have earned a higher return in rural areas; that private individuals, furthermore, were indirectly induced by administrative decisions and price distortions to transfer from countryside to town their own resources, thereby reducing the social (but increasing the private) rate of return upon those as well; and that, ultimately, inadequate inputs of rural resources substantially reduced even the efficient use of urban resources. But so what? Unprecedented growth in poor countries has proved unable to make a major impact on the conditions of the poor people who live there. A reduction of urban bias might speed growth even further; but why should that help the poor any more than past accelerations of growth?

The reason is that allocations biased townwards with respect to the efficiency norm are almost certainly heavily biased townwards with respect to the equity norm. By reallocating capital, skills and administrative attention from city to countryside, we can hardly help reducing the inequality of incomes; countrymen start much poorer than townsmen, share their income somewhat more equally, and are likelier to owe their poverty to conditions curable by income from work.

By shifting resources from city to country, a poor nation almost certainly relieves poverty in the short term. If such shifts also raise output in the sense defined above, and if the present level of urban allocations is kept up by urban bias (dispositional and hence allocative), such bias is a main cause of the persistence of poverty. So far, I have merely outlined the case; before providing proof, I look at alternative explanations for the persistence of poverty. If such explanations are in some sense 'right' *as well as* explanations of urban bias, we must ask (for instance) which, of urban bias and 'imperialism', is cause and which effect; or else which maintains poverty where—and why; or else we must admit that poverty is overdetermined: remove one cause, say urban bias, and another component of the eternal pattern of exploitation, say 'imperialism', still keeps the poor down.

Need we be so gloomy?

3 Alternative explanations of biased development

'URBAN' BIAS OR OTHER FORMS OF BIAS?

Most poor countries have attained unprecedented growth in the last three decades. However, not much of this has been shared with the poor, especially the rural poor. The process is inefficient, inequitable, and systematic. However, the cause need not be 'urban bias'. Two types of alternative explanation are possible: dimensions of bias other than urban-rural, and theories of political economy providing overarching general explanations.

Bias might be against groups of people with personal, rather than residential, characteristics: children, women, the regionally remote, or the dark-skinned. Such groups have indeed done badly out of development. However, there are three reasons for seeing urban bias, not *machismo* or racism or gerontocracy, as the moving force. First, disproportionately large numbers in all these backward groups live in rural areas. Second, urban advantages create, and urban growth increases, such disproportion, because the prospects of urban life pull in the *potentially successful* from the village. Third, relative urban 'enlightenment' with regard to racial or sexual discrimination—enlightenment that is largely itself the fruit of growth—means that it is above all in rural areas which are geographically remote that the dark-skinned, the young and the female are condemned to suffer from persistent social rigidity. Let us look at region, race and demography in turn.

Regionally, in 1947-71, when Pakistan included the present Bangladesh, the Western wing became steadily richer at the expense of the Eastern wing. In 1961, about 5.2 per cent of the East Pakistanis, but 22.5 per cent of the West Pakistanis, were urban.[1] Thus East Pakistan lost and West Pakistan gained when the terms of trade were harshly turned against agriculture (chapter 13, notes 46 and 54). This central aspect of regional 'exploitation' thus owed much to urban bias, without which the tensions that eventually tore Pakistan apart might have been contained. Similarly it is the *urban* emphasis of São Paolo as against the North-east that largely explains Brazil's glaring regional inequalities.

Racial inequalities, like regional ones, often reflect urban-rural gaps as much as 'racism'. Even in South Africa, 67 per cent of blacks, but only 13 per cent of whites, lived in rural areas in 1970.

Little is known about income differentials between town and country, but in 1970 agriculturists in South Africa produced and received only 9.1 per cent of output (gross domestic product) by value, though they comprised 28.5 per cent of working people — 36.6 per cent of working blacks and only 6.5 per cent of working whites.[2] With a gap of four to one between non-farm and farm output per person (disregarding skin colour), the concentration of blacks in the countryside clearly had much to do with what is *revealed* as 'racial' inequality and exploitation. Moreover, average black income per worker in manufacturing around 1968-9 was about 4.1 times as high as for regular black workers on white farms, and black subsistence agriculturists fared even worse.[3] The *urban* black-white gap in income per person seems since 1970 to have narrowed. Racial inequality in South Africa is due not only to race discrimination, but also to the concentration of everybody's priorities — government and opposition, reformists and revolutionaries, critics and defenders of apartheid, blacks and whites — upon 'the imperatives of industrialisation', and hence on urban growth, urban need and urban attitudes. If this is true of racial inequality even in South Africa, it is certainly true of less racially oriented societies.

Adult male domination, like skin-colour preference, is indeed a major cause of inequality in many poor countries. Female subservience is formalised in such institutions as *purdah*; the inarticulateness of children means that they are often the first victims of the harsh imperatives of poverty; and the hardships combine in what is euphemistically termed 'selective child care', in which poor parents reduce the access of small girls to food and medical attention. In Asia and Africa the proportion of the dominant demographic group — adult males — is much higher in urban than in rural areas. But these urban populations contain smaller proportions who suffer from demographic dominance, *because of urban bias*. First, it is in part the opportunities, specially (but inequitably and inefficiently) directed to the city, that pull in young men. If these special opportunities are due to urban power, they are logically prior to urban 'adult-maleness' and not caused by it. Second, children are so numerous in rural areas because, as a result of poverty, bad health and malnutrition in those areas, many children die young, inducing parents to replace them, and meanwhile boosting the child/adult ratio with millions of doomed infants. Third, urban bias itself erodes adult male dominance in the cities, by providing sufficient resources to produce better educational prospects for children, and less bad life-chances for women; moreover, their numerical dominance makes adult males see each other, more than women or youthful entrants to the work-force, as the main competitors for resources. India's urban male elite does not feel threatened by a woman prime minister; but try and find a female *patil* in any of India's 550,000 villages! Urban bias pulls adult men cityward, and the city may weaken their social dominance; but the latter is not a significant independent *cause* of rural deprivation.

In general, most poor people in LDCs, despite overall growth, are kept poor by urban bias. These people indeed tend to be women, children, the illiterate, the darker-skinned, those of minority religions, or remote and depressed regions. But it is urban bias that ensures that the rural sector both retains dispro-portionate shares of such people and gives them less chance to advance.

As for overarching general explanations of mass poverty, espe-cially rural poverty, in developing countries, three types are current. They allege the systematic allocation of 'wrong' propor-tions of resources — too much or too little — into channels benefit-ing private capitalists, or linked to the foreign sector, or leading to extra population growth. Behind the identification of these dangers lie different types of social theory: respectively, Marxist or market-oriented, autarkic or integrationist, and Malthusian or adaptationist.

THREE ALTERNATIVE EXPLANATIONS

All three pairs of dangers are scapegoats. The real goat is urban bias, with which lies the main blame for the failure of develop-ment to benefit the rural poor. The data suggest that no plausible indicator of a developing country's degree of socialism or capital-ism, of external dependence or autarky, is causally linked to either the efficiency or the equity of its overall economic performance; and that poor people do not respond to extra income by so increas-ing family size as to end up no better off than before. Intuition supports statistics. The few LDCs that might plausibly be regarded as relatively successful in steering the fruits of development to-wards the poor would presumably include: in Asia, China, Israel, South Korea, Taiwan, perhaps Ceylon (Sri Lanka); in Africa, Malawi and Tanzania; in America, Guyana and Cuba. The variety of experiences and preferences, with regard to capitalism, foreign economic relations and population growth, is striking.

Statistics and intuitions alone, however, seldom displace theo-ries. Market and Marxist theories provide rival assessments of the impact upon mass welfare of capitalism in economic development; autarkic and liberal theories, of that of external economic relations; neo-Malthusian and adaptationist[4] theories, of that of population growth. Each of the three pairs of rival theories owes its power to its claim to provide an overall explanation for many apparently obscure and unorganised events. The denial of such claims cannot rest wholly on a fusillade of counter-examples; to avoid mere hit-and-run empiricism, a counter-theory is also needed.

Hence the rejection in this book of explanations other than urban bias needs to be read in the context of the attempt to present, however crudely, an *alternative* theory of class formation and resource allocation in poor developing countries. The relations there between capital and labour, between foreign and domestic interests, and between groups with rapid and slow population growth, are here seen as (1) largely formed by relations between city and countryside, and/or (2) irrelevant in their own right to the explanation of differences in the efficiency and equity of the countries' development processes, and/or (3) resting upon dichotomies inapplicable in poor countries. It is the more obvious and largely overlapping dichotomies — primarily urban-rural, but also industry-agriculture, strong-weak, and gainer-loser from cheap food — that are here treated as maldistributing the benefits from development and slowing its pace.

Rural-urban misallocation, with its damaging impact on efficiency and equity, is the main weakness of recent development processes. One naturally looks for its cause in the rural-urban power balance. But this very naturalness can verge on crudity, even tautology. We shall have to beware of arguing that countryfolk are poor because weak, and weak because poor.

It may help if we give some examples of the differences between explanations in terms of 'urban bias' and the types of explanation being rejected. Most experts now regret that a negligible proportion of foreign aid has found its way to the small farms; indeed, probably under 12 per cent has gone to agriculture at all.[5] Some would see this as mainly a matter of biases in the aid programme, or even as a basic tendency of aid to enrich (or to provide infrastructure for) (1) the public sector itself or (2) domestic private interests close to the government, which both it and the donors wish aid to underpin, or (3) foreign capitalists or exporters from the donor nation. All three policies happen to benefit urban industry. In such an analysis, the urban bias of aid allocations becomes a secondary effect of (1) 'socialism', or (2) 'capitalism', or

(3) 'foreign exploitation'. The interpretation implied by the urban bias hypothesis is that the urban elite, given the balance of pressures upon it, will 'urbanise' aid to a great extent, whatever the degree of socialism or capitalism, of foreign dependence or autarky, in the country receiving aid. Little aid will go to the rural sector, and what goes there will help big surplus farmers to deliver the food and raw materials the city needs.

Another example can be drawn from the work of Little, Scitovsky and Scott.[6] They show that the excessive level and unbalanced structure of protection in poor countries has damaged poor people, efficiency and agriculture. Their conclusion is that the level of protection should be reduced, its structure rationalised, and more stress placed on price incentives rather than *ad hoc* administrative fiat. The urban bias hypothesis suggests that this might well treat merely the symptoms of the disease and not the disease itself. While urban interests, pressures and ideologies dominate policy formation, policies will be found to allocate to urban areas shares of developmental resources that are inefficiently and inequitably large. Dam up one of the channels of such urban-biased policy — say industrial protectionism — and the flow will simply redirect itself into other channels (which can just as easily and misleadingly be labelled 'In the National Interest'). Policy-makers are disposed to direct it thus.

It can easily *seem* that the private investor, the aid donor, or the too-powerful administrator is to blame for rural deprivation. He, after all, takes the decisions regarding what projects to support. But he takes them in a framework of law, incentive and suasion provided by the State, and beyond the State by the sanction and active support of the men of power in a society. Bankers lend more readily to industrialists than to farmers, especially small farmers, not because banking as such is wicked — and it is noteworthy that state, cooperative, private domestic and private foreign bankers share this preference — but because the profitability and security of urban-industrial lending are (1) greater, or (2) believed to be greater. That, in turn, is so because it is made so, (1) largely by government intervention in price formation, (2) by elite attitudes to small farmers, and both (1) and (2) by the relative power of urban and rural interests. If it paid bankers better to lend to small farmers, they might still be held back to some extent by the dispositional (and education-reinforced?) urban bias of the elite to which they belong; but if policy, and the pressures on policy, suffered less from allocative urban bias, a banker, capitalist or socialist, private or foreign, in a densely or sparsely populated country, would respond to the true rates of return and push more of his lending into the villages.

DOMESTIC CAPITALISM, RURAL DEPRIVATION AND POVERTY

Marx paid capitalism a back-handed compliment when he praised it for enabling the villager to leave 'the idiocy of rural life'. It is not, therefore, easy to understand the struggles of some contemporary Marxists to identify, as the source of evil, a large and dynamic capitalist farm sector in, say, India.[7] Anyway, there is strong evidence against the existence of any sequence linking excessive or deficient capitalism (C or $-C$) to the failure of development to benefit the poor (F).

There can be no universal law 'C always causes F', because one or two countries such as Taiwan have achieved 'redistribution with growth' while taking a clearly capitalist development path; they have used state intervention to steer to farmers in general — and small farmers in particular — as high shares of resources as are compatible with efficiency and equity. Nor can a law 'F never happens without C' be sustained; the USSR in 1929-39 was almost an archetype of rural deprivation, heavily damaging the poor. Thus capitalism is neither necessary nor sufficient for such deprivation.

Similarly, universal laws blaming 'lack of capitalism' for F cannot exist. Some non-capitalist countries have made strenuous efforts to avoid F, and certainly Cuba and China have succeeded better than most capitalist countries; so '$-C$ always causes F' will not do. And almost every Latin American country refutes 'F never happens without $-C$'. Thus the absence of capitalism is neither necessary nor sufficient to render growth inegalitarian.

Few if any laws in social science, however, are universal: rather they are probabilist. A probabilist law in this case would assert that some definable proportion of differences among poor countries in the severity of F was associated with variations in the amount of C. A positive association would have to be established to make CF ('more C makes F likelier') plausible, and a negative association to make $-CF$ plausible; and such an association would have to be statistically significant, in the sense that the risk of its occurring by chance was small. Even this does not *suffice* to prove CF (or $-CF$). A significant correlation, if positive, might suggest FC rather than CF; if negative, $-FC$ rather than $-CF$. Or some third element may cause both F and C (or $-C$). Even if C (or $-C$)

caused F, was the causation direct, or did C cause policy changes or biases or both, which in turn produced or aggravated F? And might urban bias cause C, with a CF sequence happening afterwards? Further enquiry would be needed to sort this out; a vital clue is whether changes in the level of C precede or postdate changes in the level of F.

We can short-circuit these complications. There is no statistically significant association between the degree to which a poor country's economic management is in private hands, and the success of that country in reducing rural deprivation. Such success can be decomposed into two components: success in obtaining a high growth rate of total available output, and success in steering such increases and the resources to generate them to rural areas. For thirty-seven poor countries, the ratio of private investment to public investment was correlated for 1960-8 with the growth of real income per person. Variance in the degree of 'capitalism' is linked (positively) with only 5.6 per cent of variance in growth, and the risk of the relationship arising by chance exceeds one in ten.[8] The indicator of 'degree of capitalism' is terribly crude, and the data are of mixed quality; but these facts cannot be blamed for the low and non-significant relationship obtained.

Perhaps there is a statistical link between private/public investment ratio and the extent to which extra income benefits countryfolk? There are several possible indicators of the latter: the ratio between agricultural and non-agricultural output per person;[9] the ratio between the growth rates of agricultural and total output per head; the ratio between the growth rates of food and total output per head;[10] the ratio between agriculture's recent shares in planned total investment (or in planned public investment) and in population (or in output);[11] and (since countryfolk are invariably poorer) the degree of overall internal equality.[12] All these indicators, eight in all, were correlated with the private/public investment ratio for all the poor countries with data available. In not a single case did we obtain a relationship 'statistically significant' in the sense that we could have some confidence (nineteen chances in twenty) that the link was not an accident. Moreover, even the insignificant associations, between 'degree of capitalism' and the various measures of rural resource allocations, are positive for some measures and negative for others.

Others will refine and develop these crude statistical tests, but it now looks as if the CF and $-CF$ horses fall at the first fence. If there is no association between C and F at all, then *a fortiori* there is no one-directional causal association starting with C (or $-C$) and ending with F.

FOREIGN IMPACT AND RURAL DEPRIVATION

Too much capitalism or too much socialism? Excessive autarky or excessive integration into the world economy? So run two pairs of contradictory attempts to account for the fact that in most LDCs growth has done little to help the poor. For each pair, the apparent strength of the argument on one side ought to predispose one to reject any explanations on the other. The city mulcted the village in Stalin's Russia, in 'capitalist' Pakistan in the 1960s, in 'mixed' Mexico since 1945; sure enough, no relation between capitalism or socialism and the maldistribution of the fruits of growth can be found at a general statistical level. As for autarky and integration, an elite selected from or influenced overwhelmingly by the urban classes will be predisposed, if it seeks autarky, towards tariff structures assisting diversification by protecting industry, thus turning the terms of trade against agriculture;[13] if it seeks integration into the world economy, towards the admission of foreign capital, techniques and specialists likely (given their origin) to favour industry rather than agriculture. It is the urban elite, not its attitudes to private ownership or to autarky, that produces pro-urban policies.

Colonialism and 'neo-colonialism' are often blamed for the division of poor countries into unequal segments, and are seen as the main or only mode of international economic integration open to poor countries. 'Limited economic development of a colonial type' is blamed for ' "primate cities" . . . "parasitic" in relation to the remainder of the national economy';[14] independence (if genuine) is believed to doom urban bias, because such ' "urban preserves" of the colonial era cannot be multiplied in a welfare state'.[15] On the other hand, and no less plausibly, 'strident nationalism propagated by city elites', starting during the fight against colonialism but mobilising sufficient self-interest to survive independence, is blamed for ' "pseudo-investment" in the costly trappings of nationalism';[16] such unproductive outlays on urban show must reduce productive rural outlays. This view echoes Fanon's pointed reminder that exploitation need not come from abroad or have a white skin (chapter 4).

Is the neglect of mass rural poverty due to colonial or to independent urban policies? Certainly neo-colonialists can encourage poor countries to foster agriculture for disgracefully wrong reasons (for example, to avoid competition in manufacturing). But this impurity of motive is only too convenient an excuse for urban elites in poor countries to neglect the rural poor: 'We do not want to be hewers of wood and drawers of water.' Analogously, the colonial legacy to independent agricultures is in part one of neglect, in part one of encouragement that after independence produced reaction.

Britain's aggregate record in Indian agriculture was far inferior to independent India's,[17] and one should always remember Nehru's bitter resentment in 1956 that 'we are warned by our British friends that . . . agriculture . . . must have first place', and his belief that this was the neo-colonial heir of an effort 'continuously and persistently' to impede her industrial development. Yet the attitude of some colonial officials (hostile to their own establishment in that case) to the Indian peasant was often uncondescending and creative.[18] Some French and British colonial officers favoured agriculture for bad reasons: it kept 'the natives' out of urban politics and law, enabled metropolitan-owned plantations to make money, and downgraded the colonised into earthy activities. Unfortunately, the over-reaction against these bad reasons, and the consequent treatment of agriculture as an inferior occupation by independent governments, has been as harmful to poor countries as the views themselves. Sometimes over-reaction is avoided: the 'colonial' Tanganyika Agricultural Development Corporation and (in Kenya) the British-American Tobacco Company were largely followed by the successor states in their organisation, pay structure, fringe benefits and career patterns, and hence they proved able to retain top-class African managers and experts in agriculture. Much more typically, however, comparable bodies in Ethiopia and Malawi (after the withdrawal of Italian and British colonial influence respectively) lost many of their ablest staff to the more attractive pay and prospects of urban areas.[19]

The over-reaction extends beyond pay structures. An extreme situation is Burma's: 'The main emphasis was to shift the economy away from the pattern of primary production . . . established in colonial times. . . . [Hence] repeated government assurances to peasants that agriculture merited priority . . . have not been translated into action,' and agriculture, with 'over two-thirds of the work-force', received under 11 per cent of public capital expenditure (including irrigation) in 1952-6.[20] Not all countries have reacted against colonialism with so deep a retreat into would-be-industrialising autarky as Burma (though similar damage is done to agriculture, and to efficiency, by the excesses of 'import-substituting industrialisation' in Latin America). Nor is all such reaction absurd. The drawbacks, for domestic equity, of extremes of integration into the world economy are real; but an urban elite will so manage either integration or autarky that the urban rich gain most, the rural poor least. Nor do some rural exporters in poor countries have much to gain from integration: tea, bananas and coffee do not compete with the products of rich countries, and hence face few restrictions to be liberalised away. Manufacturing often has most to gain from mutual export liberalisation. However (chapter 13), the net impact of protectionist import-substituting policies has also been to damage the rural sector, both relatively by forcing it to buy high-cost industrial goods and absolutely by reducing total efficiency; but the current recommendation of a general switch to export promotion, if managed with the same urban emphases, will do similar damage to the rural sector.

With colonialism and anti-colonialism, autarky and integration, alike producing policies handled by an urban elite and hence un-favourable to agriculture, one would hardly expect neat correla-tions between the degree of external economic involvement and the spread of development to the poor. Such links do exist, how-ever (though they are rather weak). It is their causal interpretation that is doubtful. The relief of poverty depends on growth and on income distribution. First of all, for forty-five LDCs, I correlated the growth of real income per person for 1951-65 with two very crude indicators of economic openness: the export/income and import/income ratios.[21] Variations in the former were linked to about 20 per cent of variations in growth of real income per person ($r^2 = 0.2025$) and in the latter to about 26 per cent ($r^2 = 0.2601$). The risk that either relation could occur by chance is less than one in a thousand.

However, one certainly cannot conclude that a high degree of 'trade-mindedness' helps growth. First, the less poor Third World countries find it easier *both* to trade freely *and* to raise income per person.[22] Growth and openness are linked partly because better-off LDCs can more easily afford the transitional costs of both of them. Second, small poor countries have a better growth record than big ones (partly because internal movement and con-trol are cheaper) *and* have greater need to trade. Third, openness and growth are linked in part because growth helps a poor country to have enough in reserve to risk the move away from autarkic solutions.

Some residual part of the link between growth and openness may be causal—stemming from the impact of trade, via specialisa-tion, on efficiency—though this residual is hard to separate from urban bias itself. Balassa points out that the use of high and un-balanced protection against imports to produce 'discrimination in favour of manufacturing and against agriculture in Brazil, Chile, Pakistan and the Philippines is the result of deliberate policies aimed at providing incentives for manufacturing, with agriculture paying much of the cost'.[23] Differences in openness could perhaps account thus for 10 per cent of differences in growth rates among LDCs. However, decisions about foreign trade policy are not taken as ends in themselves, but as means to advance the interests of the groups taking and influencing such decisions. For example, if food imports are unrestricted or even subsidised to compete with domestic farmers, while similarly competitive industrial imports are severely restricted, that is probably part of a deliberate policy aimed at industrialisation at the expense of the farm sector (a policy supported by donors, who give food aid more easily than other forms of aid). Lack of economic 'openness' may well help to cause developmental inefficiency and inequity, but is itself largely an effect of urban bias, not an alternative explanation to it.

As with 'capitalism' or 'socialism', the impact of autarky or liberalism on the poor has been decomposed into the effect on growth and on its distribution. Statistical tests, however, revealed no impact of differential 'openness' on overall, or urban-rural, income distribution.

DO POOR PEOPLE STAY POOR BECAUSE THEY ARE THAT SORT OF PEOPLE?

Behind the adage 'the poor are always with us' lies the following reasoning: 'Whatever social actions are taken to help the poor, they will be kept poor by their own conduct. That conduct may be freely chosen, genetically determined, or environmentally determined. If the poor freely choose the conduct that keeps them poor (for instance by preferring leisure to work), there is no reason why society should "compensate" them for their free choices. If their case is genetically determined, it is incurable. It is not environmentally determined, or social actions to help the poor (that is, to change their social environment) would produce much more social mobility than they in fact do.'

Can the persistence of poverty in the development process be explained by poor people's conduct, chosen or genetically determined or for other reasons not socially malleable at acceptable cost? The two forms of conduct generally meant are (1) the alleged propensity of the poor (or the rural poor) to have so many children that output per person is pressed down to subsistence level in poor families; (2) the alleged lack of energy, will to work ('high leisure preference'), or innovativeness of the poor (or the rural poor). We shall argue that allegation (1) is empirically false; that the conduct alleged in (2) is neither chosen nor genetically determined, but is the result of inegalitarian policy in general and urban bias in particular; and that the rural skill drain, a specific consequence of urban bias, in general deprives the rural sector of those who could lead it out of poverty, creating a situation easily confused with (1) and (2).

Population and poverty

There are three objections to the notion that the poor breed themselves into poverty: the data, the observed behaviour and the dynamics. The data in general confirm that poor couples have more children than rich couples, though the effect is rather weak. However, the data also suggest that the number of children reaching adulthood is no larger for poor couples than for rich couples. Hence poor couples produce more children only because, to attain the same family size as rich couples, they need to make up for a much higher risk of mortality in infancy and early childhood. Differences between rich and poor families, and between urban and rural families, in the size of the completed family—five years after the birth of the youngest child—are seldom significant, except when (as in South Korea) a substantial campaign for family planning is allocated much more outlay in urban than in rural areas. Hence the poor cannot owe their poverty to a larger completed family. The poor (especially the rural poor) do carry high ratios of young non-earning dependents to adults, but this—and the associated burden on women of numerous pregnancies—is not a form of fecklessness causing poverty, but results from an effect of poverty: high child mortality. If the urban rich seek to reduce the birth rates and dependency ratios of the rural poor, they should improve rural health, so that village couples need no longer have many children to make reasonably sure that one or two sons survive to care for them in old age.[24]

Observed behaviour confirms that poverty is the cause, not the effect, of the somewhat higher fertility of rural and other poor groups. Indeed, so dominant is the parental search for security in old age, and so grinding the poverty, that many communities where girls have few earning opportunities are compelled by poverty to practise what is euphemistically called 'selective child care', reducing the attention paid to the health and feeding of girls so that only the sturdiest survive.[25] Parents driven to such desperate straits clearly lack the will towards reckless childbearing. Moreover, the lifetime pattern of income per family member does not support the Malthusian hypothesis that the family breeds its income down to subsistence level. Such a hypothesis would be suggested if income per family member were highest at marriage, fell as children were added, and were reduced by conceptions very soon after income rose, for example, just after older siblings entered the workforce. In fact, the scant evidence indicates that income per member increases fairly steadily with age, as children mature from costs into contributors to household earnings. This suggests that children are produced, in part, from the reasonable hope that they will enrich their parents, not in 'uneconomic' response to the existence of spare family cash.[26]

The third objection to the argument that poor people are poor because they have too many children is that its dynamic implications are absurd.[27] The following table is fairly typical of the situation in many poor countries.[28]

Income group	Birth rate	Death rate	Population growth rate	Growth rate of income per head (per year)
	(per thousand per year)			
Richer half	38	8	30	2½%
Poorer half	44	14	30	½%
All	41	11	30	2%

Now suppose steps were taken to redistribute the benefits of development by raising the growth rate of income per head of the poorer half of the population from ½ per cent to 1½ per cent per person per year. For 'Malthusian' effects to destroy this, it would be necessary for the birth rate of the poorer half to rise from forty-four to fifty-four and stay there. However, first, a rise of 23 per cent in the birth rate is unprecedented and almost incredible. Second, the (not untypical) initial rate of forty-four is already probably close to a biological maximum. Third, higher income per person brings the capacity to buy better food and medical care, leading to lower child mortality rates, and hence (once the parents appreciate these facts) to a reduced incentive to procreate for purposes of ensuring *surviving* children. Finally, suppose all these three arguments were to fail, so that higher income growth did durably raise the birth rate of the 'poorer half' from forty-four to fifty-four; then its counterpart, lower income growth for the 'richer half', would presumably induce them to cut their birth rate, so that yet more of the gains from development could be redistributed to the poor, without either reducing the income per head of the rich (once they adjusted their birth rate downwards) or raising the overall national birth rate.

All this assumes that people have substantial control over the number and timing of births. Owing to the maldistribution of family-planning advice, this assumption is probably not quite as safe in LDCs for poor people as for rich people, further increasing the injustice of blaming the poor for producing many children. Nevertheless, the assumption is fairly near the truth, although the methods of contraception forced on the poor once they have attained the desired number of children—*coitus interruptus*, abstinence, prolonged lactation—are (like the need first to undergo many risky pregnancies to ensure a few surviving children to keep the parents alive when old) a concealed and monstrous ill-effect of inequality.[29]

Rapid population growth in poor countries is a drain on their capacity to develop, and investment to reduce that drain is desirable. Birth prevention, especially in rural areas with scarce land, may well yield more income per head than any other investment, especially since it permits the family to save and invest, instead of using its substance to feed more children. For all that, however, poor people are not poor because of an irrational impulse to have large families. The cheapest way to reduce the number of children they have is, in fact, to reduce the risk of child mortality—for example, by rural health centres; but to blame them for family structures forced on them by poverty is neither logical nor humane.[30]

Poverty and will

Do the poor lack the will to be rich? Are they thus poor by choice or genetics? Such allegations are not entirely false; begin with a community where each person enjoys identical income and opportunities, and some members of it will work harder or more effectively, either by preference or by genes, and soon become richer than the rest. However, this is not a very important reason why poverty is so little relieved by development in LDCs. First, LDCs vary enormously in the degree of income inequality, and some of the most developmentally successful, such as Taiwan, have most dramatically shrunk it—hardly possible if the poor were useless, or the rich alone competent, in the development process. Second, a large part of poverty and wealth is 'infectious' in the family, so that the good or bad luck of a migrant, say, spreads to his brothers and children without intervention of choice or genetics; this is particularly true of LDCs, caste being only the most familiar example (the unequalising impact in South America of colour gradations and land inheritance is probably even more severe and, for the individual, even less avoidable). Third and most important, many of the disabilities of poverty, notably lethargy and probably also physical and mental weakness, are matters neither of choice nor of heredity but of inflicted environment. The teaching hospitals and luxury restaurants of Delhi, Rio and Nairobi, by their waste of scarce medical and nutritional resources, directly cause malnutrition and dysentery in the hinterland. Then the urban elite blames the rural poor for the effects of such allocations on the will to work.

Rural skill drain

Migration saddles the rural environment with one of those avoidable features that, to the casual observer, seem the marks of inherited or chosen individual poverty. First, it is the bright young men who migrate to urban jobs (chapter 11), leaving behind the less bright, the children, the elderly and the female. Second, the structure of migration reduces population growth in the cities, but if anything increases it in rural areas (chapter 9). Third, if the policy is such that skilled persons generally gain by being urban residents, any rural leadership that may emerge with the capacity to cure mass poverty — unless exceptionally unselfish — is quickly lured to urban areas to practise its skills. Hence the rural sector comes to look as if its residents have chosen leisure and poverty, and/or been condemned to them by natural selection. In reality the choice is that of the urban elite, the selection not natural but artificial, and the fact that it creates the illusion of a 'hopeless' rural population, a *lumpenbauernstand,* no more than a tragic irony. What never ceases to amaze is the resilience and regenerative capacity of the countryfolk: their ability, constantly drained of talent as they are, to farm so well under severe constraints; to innovate selectively and efficiently; to cope with bureaucrats and businessmen who (given the relative rewards available in the city) are seldom the ablest or most honest in the land. All this hardly suggests that genetics legitimises rural poverty. One understands the dangerously mystical populism of the poet Dehmel, eulogising the resistance to Napoleon by the Russian peasant: *Ewig, ewig bluht das Volk.*

Part II
Rural and Urban Sectors:
The Poverty of Ideology

4 Ideologies of rural and urban development

A crude *prima facie* case has been presented that urban bias is the root cause of the failure of 'development' to remove mass poverty. Detailed evidence will appear in chapters 5 to 14. First, though, a prior act of mental hygiene is needed. We are all too much the prisoners of the history of human thought to be convinced by evidence *alone*, on an issue as deeply 'ideological' as the role of rural and urban sectors in development. How have the scholars and the policy-makers arrived at their present positions?

To treat the answer as fundamental to the understanding of urban bias is not to commit an idealist fallacy, as Keynes did when attributing the errors of the self-styled 'practical men' to their being the 'slaves of some defunct economist';[1] people usually choose the theories to which, for reasons of self-interest or moral ease, it is convenient to be enslaved. However, the range of intellectually respectable choice among theories is largely dependent on their historical power to survive economic and social debate (however self-interested or classbound debaters may have been). From this 'natural selection' of theories, a pretty anti-rural, pro-industrial group has survived to form that range of choice. Forms of Marxism for which socialism requires (and is partly justified by its efficiency in inducing) rapid, large-scale industrialisation; 'neo-classical' economic systems assuming that 'diminishing returns' must choke off agricultural growth, and that rapid responses to wage inequalities define urban bias out of existence; idyllic populisms that discredit rural development, either by their theoretical vacuity or by implying that rural life is best left 'unspoiled': all three main paths of socio-economic thought lead readily to urban-biased destinations.

It is impossible, without writing another book,[2] to examine the ideology of rural-urban relations in development. This chapter here is confined to what is essential if we are to understand, and place in context, the misallocations and inequities to be examined in chapters 5 to 14. It is the history of the deformation of social science by that fragmentation of forms of thought and feeling known as 'the dissociation of sensibility'. Increasingly social scientists (like other people) have come to use different skills, faculties, criteria and modes of feeling according to the materials with which they deal.

Perhaps this intellectual shattering affected *poets* as early as the seventeenth century,[3] but in the late eighteenth century the founder of modern economics, Adam Smith—also a moral philosopher and

89

a historian of distinction — seems to have escaped.[4] The effect of intellectual shattering (a different matter from specialisation) upon social science after Smith, and especially on its capacity to analyse rural development, has been disastrous. The unified, but skeletal and ramshackle, structure of classical economics disintegrated into two systems and a wraith.

The systems were Marxism and neo-classicism; the wraith was populism. Marxists have stressed the struggle among great social classes, have viewed the outcome as determined, and have interpreted the peasant interest as objectively reactionary because its advancement would delay the historically inevitable victory of the industrial proletariat. Since Marxists have been relatively uninterested in productive efficiency and markets and price incentives, the wastes and delays of forced-draft industrialisation meant much less to them than did the supersession of the peasantry as a reactionary class, and the accumulation of its surplus to finance capitalist, or better socialist, industrial development.

Neo-classical economists, and their evolutionist and functionalist counterparts in sociology, have stressed the likelihood, modalities and 'social efficiency' of individual optimising behaviour within a smoothly working market structure. Since they have been relatively uninterested in class alignments, dominance and elite formation, they could see neither how the small farmer might be continuously discriminated against under a free-market system, nor why, if in distress because deprived of resources by industrialisation, he could not join the winning side by moving to the cities for work.

That is the essential, and tragic, bifurcation of classical socio-economic thought; but there was a third path, albeit somewhat tenuous. The *moral* stresses of Smith and James Mill, obviously out of place in any system where behaviour was determined (whether by markets or by classes), combined with pastoral and romantic traditions in literature and filtered into the attitudes of Ruskin, Gandhi and Julius Nyerere. This third approach, potentially a pro-rural counterweight to the others — for a moralist in economics would stress the less rich, less unequal, more efficient sector in early development — was vitiated because almost all the intellectual power, whether in theory-building or in empirical work, was absorbed into Marxism or neo-classicism.[5]

THE ROLE OF IDEOLOGY

An ideology is a set of related and fundamental beliefs about human behaviour, political relationships and moral conduct. Several characteristics normally distinguish an ideology from 'any old' set of beliefs: the view not only that the beliefs in an ideology are morally right, but that their eventual triumph is historically inevitable; the believer's commitment to accelerate the historically inevitable by *praxis*, including persuasion; his awareness of each component of the ideology as requiring defence on account of its place in a whole structure of doctrine; great scope, extending far beyond the normal coverage of one natural or social science; and initially a challenge to, or a defence of, an entire code of accepted belief or conduct.[6]

How does a man deeply influenced by an ideology — as we all are at times — conduct rural-urban debates about pricing, resource allocation or developmental role? If he abandons his ideology, he makes nonsense of many of his past actions, even life-habits. Hence his approach to new knowledge, his efforts to reconcile 'is' and 'ought' (whether through historical determinism or by interpreting everything as response to incentive) and his urge to preserve ideological structures, all render his views robust in face of evidence. New knowledge is assimilated by conventionalist[7] adjustments of belief, fact or preference. Facts, logic and values are run together. Theories of rural-urban relationships are adopted, whatever the facts, because they fit into a grander theoretical structure: equilibrium of free markets, or a workers' state, or a populism of small self-ruling communities.

An ideology usually claims to explain the past, to be confirmed by all of it, and to predict the future. It lies too deep to be reasoned away. Hence the debate about agriculture's role in economic development cannot be 'reduced' to disagreements about facts, values and the validity of inferences. Analogously nationalisers say, 'Can one leave the London-Edinburgh railway to private enterprise, competitive or monopolistic?' and anti-nationalisers say, 'Can the state run the shop on the corner?' The choice of examples for debate, and topics for research, is not really designed to settle the debates about centralisation or state action, but to permit each side to strengthen its own paradigm.[8] In its defence, the self-interest of each contestant is heavily engaged. This self-interest, whether or not economic, is almost always psychological: it lies in justifying the contestant's own past thought and action.

Because both ruralists and urbanists build up their ideologies from eclectically gathered scraps of other ideologies, the debate is often conducted at a low level. It would therefore be agreeable to ignore it, and proceed to evaluate the technical arguments for urban bias, such as the claim that it is necessary and sufficient for higher domestic savings (chapter 10). But if that straw man, or straw Hydra-head, is cut down, then two new and more subtly persuasive replacements will grow in its place. If positions in the rural-urban debate are so integrally parts of ideologies — are tenets of faiths — one must discuss the basis of the faiths.

The main ideologies bearing on rural development form a sort of family tree:

Figure 4   Ideologies and rural development

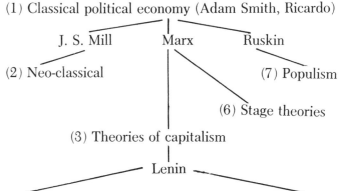

(1) Classical political economy (Adam Smith, Ricardo)

J. S. Mill   Marx   Ruskin

(2) Neo-classical   (7) Populism

(6) Stage theories

(3) Theories of capitalism

Lenin

(4) Theories of imperialism   (5) Soviet industrialisation debates

This is too unilinear; for instance 5 obviously changed 3. It leaves out too much, notably the influence of literary romanticism on 7. It neglects incest, for example between 5 and 6. And it is spuriously balanced; 1, 2, 3 and 5 contributed far more to the rural-urban debate than 4. However, our family tree gives a form to the ensuing discussion.

The seven ideologies have been used, eclectically, to justify each of four 'phases' of thinking about rural-urban and farm-industry relations (see Introduction); the first two phases basically pro-urban, the fourth rural-biased. Happily, I need not consider seven ideologies for each of four phases — twenty-eight sections in all! — but can concentrate on the issues central to the evidence of chapters 5 to 14.

CLASSICAL ECONOMICS

Most of the fallacious anti-agricultural doctrines prevalent in poor countries today can be traced to misunderstandings of, baseless extrapolations from, or (rarely) mistakes by the classical economists. Among these false doctrines are: that industry 'needs' protection more than agriculture; that high food prices benefit only landlords; that manufactured exports are better' than farm exports; that urban-industrial growth depends asymmetrically[9] on extracting a rural-agricultural surplus of food; that agriculture's 'decreasing returns' justify bleeding it of resources to help industries giving 'increasing returns'; that trade requires cities; and that city-oriented capitalist farming is 'better' than village-oriented peasant farming.

In 1776, Adam Smith published *The Wealth of Nations* as perceptions of the capitalist transformation of English agriculture were forming, and at the earliest stages of urban-industrial transformation. The two requirements of growing *capitalist industry,* for Smith, are freer trade to help *capitalists* to specialise (by enlarging a domestic into a world market) and more agricultural wage goods to feed an increasingly large *industrial* workforce. These requirements naturally culminated in the pressure from Smith's successors for the repeal of the Corn Laws; but there is no mandate from Smith for their crucially mistaken view that protection of agriculture was somehow worse than protection of industry.

Selective deprotection

How did Ricardo and McCulloch, the two classical heirs of Smith who saw most deeply into the problems of agriculture, come to argue for its deprotection without comparable measures in industry, and hence to rationalise both the exceptional industrialisation and 'de-agriculturalisation' of output and workforce[10] in Britain and urban bias as an ideology of development?

Ricardo argued that selective protection of manufacturing — removing the corn duties only — could not raise the profitability of manufacturing investment at the expense of agricultural investment. For expectations of higher profits would lead capitalists to put more and more new investment into the protected manufacturing sector instead of into agriculture; and this would go on until (because manufactures are in more ample supply, and farm products in less ample supply) the profit rates have been brought into equality.

However, first, it takes years for the process to work; meanwhile farm profits are eroded. Second, in early development, manufacturers of an industrial product can get together, more easily than the numerous and dispersed (and often ill-informed and illiterate) farmers, to eliminate or to control domestic competition; thus Ricardo's assumption, that excess profit for selectively protected manufacturers disappears because 'they are guaranteed [only] against foreign, but not against home, competition',[11] falls to the ground. Third, even if the *rate* of profit on industrial production is not raised (relative to the rate in agriculture) by selective industrial protection, the *volume* of industrial profit (the rate *times* the amount of capital) certainly is, by the very process of entry of new domestic capital that Ricardo describes as bringing down the profit rate. Unless there is implausibly large townward migration, the rising volume of industrial profit means falling profits (and hence investible funds) and wages in agriculture.[12]

Ricardo concedes that even selective protection reduces total output below the level prevailing with the higher degree of specialisation that results from totally free trade. He denies only that, 'because the costs of production, and therefore the prices of various manufactured commodities, are raised to the consumer by one error in legislation' (industrial protection), 'we should pay also an additional price for our corn and further punish ourselves by diminishing the productive power of . . . labour in the supply of raw produce'.[13] But this is to compare 'corn law plus industrial protection' and 'free entry for corn plus industrial protection'. The proper comparison is either between (1) a higher and a lower *overall* level of tariffs, or between (2) a tariff, at a given level, uniform or differentiated among products.[14] If Britain in 1846 were to have undertaken a *given* amount of deprotection,[15] British potential welfare would have been maximised by so spreading deprotection as to reduce, as much as possible, discrimination (or bogus incentives) among products. That would minimise the extent to which the tariff structure gave *special* protection to any one sector of the economy, and thus both subsidisation of that sector by others, and the distortion of investment incentives in its favour.[16] Ricardo's concern for the political priority of Corn Law repeal led him to fudge this point, to blur (1) and (2) above, and hence to advocate deprotection of corn, even alone.

The classical arguments for selective deprotection of British agriculture illuminate other *potentially* anti-agricultural features of the Great Ancestor of development theories. Moreover, agricultural deprotection through Corn Law repeal, coming as it did seventeen years before the major moves (in Gladstone's 1863 budget) towards industrial deprotection, constituted a crucial precedent for a major method of draining resources from agriculture, both in the USSR and in many development sequences since 1945.

Rural surplus, urban wages

Perhaps the main force behind 'Phase II' theory is epitomised in Smith's observation that, 'it is the surplus produce of the country only, or what is over and above the maintenance of the cultivators, that constitutes the subsistence of the town, which can therefore increase only with the increase of the surplus produce.'[17] When industry grows, so normally does the volume of its wages. That volume, however, is determined by four things: the proportion of industrial wages spent on food, the price of food and the volume of food imports, as well as Smith's target, the volume of food produced domestically and made available to non-agricultural families.[18] But does Smith's insight mean that extraction of the rural food surplus is the key requirement for industrial growth?

Simple algebra helps. In any year, if Q_I is the quantity of industrial output, and the productivity of industrial labour is m units of output per man-year, then $Q_I = mL_I$, where L_I is the number of industrial workers. If each industrial worker gets w currency units per year, then the industrial wage bill W_I is wL_I, so that $L_I = W_I/w$. Hence

$$(1) \quad Q_I = \tfrac{m}{w} W_I.$$

Now the amount industrial workers pay for food must equal two things: the price of food per unit (p) *times* the amount of food they buy (F_I); and the industrial wage bill (W_I) *times* the proportion of it spent on food (f). Thus $pF_I = fW_I$ or

$$(2) \quad W_I = \tfrac{p}{f} F_I.$$

Finally F_I equals domestic food output (F_D) *minus* food consumed by domestic non-industrial families (F_A) *minus* food exports (F_X) *plus* food imports (F_M):

$$(3) \quad F_I = F_D + F_M - F_X - F_A.$$

Combining (1), (2) and (3) we can see how industrial production is related to the availability of food:

$$(4) \quad Q_I = \tfrac{mp}{wf} (F_D + F_M - F_X - F_A).$$

All this is purely definitional — interactions among variables are ignored. But (4) indeed shows that industrial production is limited by food supply to the industrial worker. It suggests eight possible remedies. One might raise the productivity of industrial labour; the price to such labour of food;[19] domestic food output; or food imports. Or one might lower the industrial wage rate; the proportion of industrial wages spent on food; food exports; or non-industrial (primarily agricultural) food consumption. The current versions of the classical approach to development strategy concentrate almost exclusively on the last option[20] — for no good reason.

Increasing and decreasing returns

Among exports, Smith — and many modern economists and policy-makers — prefer *manufactures,* in the belief that industry benefits more than agriculture from a larger market, because it gains from the specialisation of labour.[21] Thus industry enjoys increasing returns to scale. To adapt Smith's celebrated example: if by quadrupling my output of pins I can employ specialists in several branches of pin-making, each in a special shop, instead of less-skilled generalists, then my costs of production will rise less than fourfold. But 'the nature of agriculture. . .does not admit of so many subdivisions of labour, nor of so complete a separation of one business from another, as manufactures.. . .The ploughman, the harrower, the sower of seed, and the reaper of corn, are often the same. The occasions for these different sorts of labour returning with the different seasons of the year, it is impossible that one man should be constantly employed in any one of them.'[22]

Later classical economists added that (1) because land was fixed in quantity, an increase in other factors of production — whether by growth of the population and labour force or otherwise — could not increase output proportionately; (2) good land was farmed first, so that even if cultivated land could increase as fast as other factors of production, farm output would not; (3) technical progress in agriculture could weaken, but could not be sufficiently rapid to invalidate, either (1) or (2).[23] Since the progress of industry (with or without increasing returns) is held to be constrained by the growth of the agricultural *surplus*, which will be slow indeed if *total* farm output is held back by (1) to (3) (as farm operators must still eat), the source of classical 'pessimism' is clear. Even if such pessimism is refuted by the failure of (3) — by the rapid progress of agricultural technology — little of the classical *analysis* is thereby invalidated.[24]

After all, the intellectual descendants of Ricardo accepted that agriculture suffered from diminishing returns;[25] and they could see rapid technical progress in agriculture. They nevertheless felt that diminishing returns in agriculture justified mulcting it in order to industrialise, for the following reason. Resources in agriculture command a higher reward if, due to exodus to industry, they are scarcer; farmers abandon *bad* land, and (thanks to diminishing returns) those that remain operate better land. The reverse applies to industry, where increasing scale facilitates the division of labour. Hence, Smith's heirs believed, the transfer of resources from agriculture to industry is to be encouraged, so long as the resources remaining in agriculture can supply sufficient food and raw materials for those engaged in industry. (This qualification is weakened if labour in agriculture has 'zero marginal product', or if agriculture has 'low absorptive capacity' for capital, but these twentieth-century versions of the classical argument lack its force.[26]) If the above argument applies — whatever the rate of technical progress in industry or agriculture — it *seems* to justify a wide range of measures to persuade people to transfer their labour and savings out of agriculture into industry. These range from selective deprotection to the more sophisticated measures advocated by Marshall.[27]

Agriculture probably does suffer from diminishing returns, while industry enjoys increasing returns, as the volume of output expands. But (unless actual rates of return in the two sectors start equal, as the classicals assumed) it is incorrect to conclude that resources should be transferred from agriculture to industry. Suppose you have £1,000 placed with a local authority at 7 per cent interest, whereas if you loaned them £2,000 you could earn 8 per cent interest.[25] You have another £1,000 placed with a finance house at 14 per cent and they are prepared to accept a further £1,000 but only at 12 per cent. The local-authority loan shows increasing returns, the finance-house loan decreasing returns. If you transferred any of your money from the finance house to the local authority *for that reason*,[29] you would be a mug. It is the size of the return that matters, not just the influence upon that size of the amount placed. Yet investible resources are transferred from agriculture to support 'infant industries' with increasing, but very small, returns (chapter 8).

Even if returns on an extra unit of 'resources' are greater (as well as increasing faster with the scale of output) in industry than in agriculture, in an efficient policy it is seldom resources, as a whole, that should be transferred. Normally, in early development, if (say) 20 to 25 per cent of agricultural labour resources could be shifted out of agriculture they would add more to output, whereas if 20 to 25 per cent of non-agricultural investment funds could be shifted into agriculture *they* would add more to output. To shift labour and capital together, in the direction of an 'increasing return to scale', would be a grossly inferior solution.

Capitalists or peasants?

Central to this book is the shared interest of urban worker, urban employer and big surplus farmer in ample food for the cities. Yet the big farmer wants a high price, and the townsman a low price, for the food surplus. Compromise is possible because policy decisions in the city steer such resources, subsidies and legal advantages as go to agriculture largely towards the big farmer — who alone provides a substantial surplus[30] — at the cost of the peasant and the farm labourer; and in return the big farmer supplies the city with fairly cheap food, cotton, and other raw materials and export crops. Government policy on urban-rural terms of trade forces him to accept low prices, which his cheap inputs and other artificial advantages *vis-à-vis* small farmers and labourers dispose him to bear with equanimity.

Advocacy of government encouragement to big farms, and opposition to peasant farming, dates back to the classical economists. Yet did they not believe that agriculture suffers from *diseconomies* of large scale? Yes, but only in the *dynamic* sense that growth of land, labour and capital at any particular rate called worse land into use and hence increased farm output at a slower rate. That is compatible (chapter 4, note 23) with the classical belief in *static economies* of scale, in the sense that farm output would be larger if, at any particular time, it were produced by a smaller number of farm enterprises.

Not all the classical economists' case for large farming was static. They felt that the big farmer's wish to accumulate capital counted for more than the higher levels of employment per acre on the small farm; that industry suffered from at least incipient labour and food shortages because workers produced and consumed excessively on their own peasant landholdings; and that increased transactions between agriculture and industry, consequent on a shift from small family farms to commercial agriculture, would confer general benefit. All three views were arguable in Britain in 1776-1846, but cannot be extrapolated to Asia and Africa today, either in themselves or as evidence for a policy of large farms.

Smith believed that large farmers are likelier to innovate, because they are both better informed about advances in knowledge and better able to take risks. 'The diminution of the number of cottagers and other small occupiers of land . . . has in every part of Europe been the immediate forerunner of improvement and better cultivation.'[31] Where capital is larger, a farmer 'can afford to try experiments, and is generally disposed to do so. His unsuccessful experiments occasion only a moderate loss to himself. His successful ones contribute to the improvement and better cultivation of the whole country.'[32] These beliefs, shared by Malthus and Ricardo, blind them to one implication of their central doctrine that agricultural population expansion, on a limited land area, forces wages down and rent up: that small farms, in yielding a given product,[33] use less of the increasingly scarce and costly land, and more of the increasingly plentiful labour, than do large farms. Malthus has nothing to say about this. Ricardo actually advocated larger farms, because these were judged likelier to innovate; and for him the main impact of their agricultural innovation was land-saving,[34] and outweighed their tendency to farm land with fewer workers per acre than a small family farm. Hence the main reason for improving security in Ireland was 'that small farms, and small tenancies, should be got rid of ... and an accumulation of capital would lead to all the beneficial results which everywhere follow from it'. Indeed, as 'small farms [were] laid into large, there would be an abundant demand for labour'!

Torrens saw that labour would be *displaced* if Ireland moved towards larger and hence more highly capitalised farms, even with the primitive reaping and threshing machines then available. Yet he argued that 'farms must be consolidated until the agricultural labour of Ireland can be performed by two-fifths of the labourers now [required]'. How the other three-fifths were to live is not clear. Most classical economists denied, ignored, or brushed aside the employment impact of an urban-oriented Policy of Large Farms. Despite evidence that small farms could be efficient, the few classical economists opposing scale for scale's sake — such as J. S. Mill, who advocated land redistribution to enhance employment — remained voices in the wilderness.[35] McCulloch, with perhaps the finest understanding of agriculture of all the classical economists, had a pro-capitalist, anti-peasant attitude typical of them. Understandably he felt that peasant farmers showed lower labour productivity, capacity to specialise, or motive or ability to innovate (though these deficiencies could, and can, be traced to their lack of credit, information and insurance, not to real advantages of large scale); less understandably, he shared Ricardo's strange view that small farms showed lower *land* productivity and employment per acre as well, so that 'the managerial optimum was very large. Anything which tended to reduce the size of farms, particularly the potato, was to be deplored.'[36]

In the developments and distortions of Smith's ideas,[37] we see in embryo almost all the arguments advanced for urban bias in the Third World today: the worship of intersectoral trade; the fear that the cities will get too little surplus or pay 'too much' for it; the wish to move capital along with rural workers to the cities. Then as now, all this produces a preference for big farms, selective deprotection of agriculture, cheap food, and manufactured exports. The British development experience, judging by the disparity (table 5.4), showed little urban bias; and the case for some non-agricultural emphasis (with two-thirds of the people outside agriculture by 1801) was not unreasonable, in either equity or efficiency. However, the combination of two sorts of ancestorship — Britain as the first country to attain modern development; classical economics as the first 'social science' — has given the classical conclusions from that experience an unduly general persuasive force. They pointed towards a pro-industrial policy, and their false analogues have been accepted in today's Third World, which is far more agriculture-dominated, and with much greater rural-urban inequalities and relative industrial inefficiencies, than was Britain in 1780-1850.

MARGINALIST ECONOMICS
Between 1850 and today, the problem of rural-urban balance in development has got more serious, the analytic and policy tools for dealing with it sharper — yet the analysis weaker. To understand this, we must examine the two nineteenth-century transformations of classical economics that today structure most thinking about poor countries. Marginalists have sought to identify the 'margin' of each sort of economic activity — the level to which the consumer or the producer will proceed, if each seeks to maximise individual benefit. They have thereby advanced our understanding of the logic of individual behaviour and market interaction, but have neglected the collective use of power by social classes to achieve private goals[38] — a use that alters the extent and nature of the response to price of both supply and demand. Marxists, conversely, have advanced our understanding of the struggle of classes for economic power, but have neglected the impact of individual preferences, via market forces, on the structure of production and consumption — and, thus on the commonalities of long-run interest that form and transform the borders between classes.

Since economic *institutions* cannot be explained without a theory covering both collective action and individual goal-seeking, neither marginalists nor Marxists are very good at institutional analysis. Marxists often treat institutions mainly as part of the 'super-structure' built on the basic reality of capital-labour conflict; marginalists often ignore institutions, or treat them as 'given', or as the evolved outcomes of market behaviour. Lacking analyses of institutions — rural banks, or marketing boards, or ministries allocating new roads — neither Marxists nor marginalists are likely to analyse rural-urban interactions effectively. Thus both Marxism and marginalism contain elements tending to the correct diagnosis of urban bias,[39] but each lacks necessary complementary elements and hence misses the diagnosis.

The marginal principle
Marginalism contains a major *component* of successful diagnosis. The *marginal principle of allocation* (MPA) avers that any resource should be, and since people are rational (or go under) eventually

will be, divided in a particular way to maximise the benefit to its owner. Whether the resource is housekeeping money, to be spent on eggs or fish; or sulphur, for blast furnace A or B; or engineers, for agriculture or industry—the allocator (housewife, or firm, or state) sees to it that the last or *marginal* unit of the resource, going to each use, adds the same amount to the user's benefit in each. If it does not, the user can increase satisfaction by shifting marginal units from uses where they add less to benefit, to uses where they add more. Only when no such shifts can increase the user's satisfaction is he 'optimising', or 'in equilibrium'.

MPA is violated in the numerous poor countries where agricultural investment has been associated, at the margin, with two or three times as much extra output as non-agricultural investment (table 8.2). The violation is compounded by the further transfer of agricultural savings to pay for non-agricultural investment. Marginal economics appears an ideal watchdog against such misallocations. Its practitioners dominate modern development economics. Why is the watchdog's bark muted or absent?

Why is MPA so little used to expose urban bias?
Marginalism contains (1) false as well as true prognoses of rural-urban problems, and (2) misleading claims that what is diagnosed is not sickness but health. Further, (3) neo-classical economists have tended both to neglect the specific features of agriculture and industry — to treat them as 'two lines of production, X and Y' — and to search for harmonious, equilibrium-directed and hence conflict-free analyses of social interaction. Hence (4) a series of challenges to marginalism, on grounds both of its consistency and of the correspondence of its assumptions to fact, has shaken the confidence of its best practitioners—especially in making 'macro-economic' statements about what does, or should, happen in the economy as a whole (as against 'micro-economic' statements about the behaviour of particular producers or consumers). The reluctance to apply MPA to the allocation of resources between city and country, industry and agriculture, is in part an unjustified side-effect of this justified loss of self-confidence.

FALSE PROGNOSES Marginalists tend to claim that economic systems tend automatically towards equilibrium: for instance, that the villager, if made less well off relative to the townsman by some aspect of urban bias, votes with his feet by going to live and work in the city. This would reduce the supply of labour and demand for — and hence the price of — consumer goods in the village, and raise them in the city; rural real wages would rise, and urban real wages would fall. In this and other ways most marginalists would expect urban bias to set in motion individual, market responses rendering urban life less pleasant and rural life more pleasant — and thereby destroying urban bias.[40]

No public action would then be needed to correct it; labour would move from village to city until MPA was re-enthroned. This does not happen.[41] But most marginalists' misplaced aggregation, lack of institutional theory, and emphasis on automatic equilibrium as against cumulative causation and divergence, blinds them to the ties of rural debt that keep the really poor man from moving in search of higher rewards, and to the ties of kinship and special knowledge that cause urban advantages to be self-reinforcingly transmitted among townsmen.[42]

DISEASE OR HEALTH   Some neo-classical economists claim that urban bias, if extant, is benign. They do so largely because of Pigou's revival of a classical proposition: that agriculture features decreasing returns and industry increasing returns, so that 'the market' needs to be prodded to push a larger share of investible resources into industry. This implication was rejected on p. 97; the Marshall-Pigou refinement is dealt with on pp. 96-7.

MISPLACED ABSTRACTION   These rather fleshless and independent entities, 'agriculture' and 'industry', featuring different production conditions, suggest a further feature of neo-classical economics that reduces its usefulness in evaluating urban-rural relations: its tendency towards misplaced abstraction. Smith took care not to abstract from central features of economic development in his own time, such as relations between, and the actual content of, agriculture and industry. That is why his work is so relevant to development in those poor countries of the 1970s where the relative position of a retarded agriculture is similarly central.

Early industrialisation and marginalism were rougnly simultaneous in Italy, Austria and Sweden; yet from their leading marginalists we learn little of agriculture-industry relations — or indeed of agriculture itself, save as something to put into an 'economic box' containing activities that suffer 'diminishing returns'.[43] While the peasants were mulcted so that Austria might move towards dynamic urban-biased capitalism, the Marxist Kautsky — himself no mean abstracter! — analysed the internal dynamic of that process. Meanwhile Austria's leading neo-classicists, Menger and Bohm-Bawerk, probably Kautsky's superiors as theorists, wrote almost as if the central problem of their country did not exist. To the analogous central problem of development today, marginalism has been similarly — marginal.

THE MACRO-ECONOMIC LOSS OF CONFIDENCE   Marginalists succeeded quite well in explaining the short-term behaviour of firms and consumers. However, their account of the likely behaviour of *economies* features several 'fallacies of composition'[44] — false analogies from firms or households to nations. A household cannot spend itself rich; a nation, with idle resources of most types of capital and labour and skills, often can. A firm hires until the (declining) contribution that an extra worker makes to the product falls to the (given) wage cost of hiring him; but at national level each firm's wage payments affect the demand for, and hence the wage rates payable by, other firms. A firm can find an equation that predicts the value of output from the value of equipment in use; in an economy, the value of expected output determines the valuation of the 'capital' that makes it.

For fear of such fallacies of composition, many marginalists nowadays use MPA with more discretion than valour. In particular, they seldom dare apply it to resource allocations, or interactions, between huge economic sectors like Agriculture and Industry, or Countryside and City, whose behaviour must have major macroeconomic repercussions.

DO THE SHORTCOMINGS OF MARGINALISM INVALIDATE MPA EXPOSÉS OF URBAN BIAS?   The marginalist account of the distribution of national income — between town and country, between labour and capital — looked neat. Distribution was determined entirely by the pattern of demand for products requiring different amounts of labour and capital, together with an 'aggregate production function' relating total labour and capital used to total GNP produced; workers and capital-owners earn, respectively, wage rates and profit rates equal to the marginal value-products of labour and capital. Although this theory is still kicking — to judge by the learned journals — it is no longer alive.[45] Marginalists, and not only those who feel that the state should leave such things to the market, are therefore either unwilling to pronounce on major decisions about intersectoral resource allocation, or mistrusted when they do.

The criticisms of marginal analysis were rightly directed at its capacity (1) to predict national income distribution from the conditions of production alone, (2) to construct aggregate production functions, and (3) in advanced economies with unemployment, to predict rises in the demand for employees as a consequence of falls in wage rates. None of these criticisms really vitiates the use of

MPA, in the form of social cost-benefit analysis. Yet such analysis is hardly ever intersectoral (for example, to assess the effect on GNP of alternative allocations of scarce resources between agriculture and industry). It is generally confined to the choice of projects *within* a sector for similar purposes (among schools or among airports). Rather unconvincing reasons are given for this restriction (pp. 210-11). The real reason is surely an undue extension of a justified loss of confidence in MPA as a macro-device.

Marginalists and agricultural innovation

Marshall provided an argument. much used since, for the systematic transfer of resources townwards: that agriculture features a systematically slower spread of technical progress than industry, for three reasons. First, the potentially 'enterprising agriculturists drift towards the towns', leaving behind those unlikely 'to suggest or even to follow new paths'. Second, farms vary more than factories, so that the risk of copying an innovation from one's neighbour is higher. Third, the complexity of 'joint products and . . . by-products, . . . relations of debtor and creditor between the several crops and methods of feeding' renders it very hard for farmers to assess innovations.[46] We thus have a systematic version of Smith's case for favouring manufacturers on the grounds of their more rapid innovation.

This case works only if more rapid innovation causes industry to increase its efficiency more rapidly than agriculture. Suppose the state allows 'the market' to allocate capital between agriculture and industry on the basis of expected rate of return — or does so itself on the basis of expected social returns. Suppose, further, that future innovation, not allowed for by the allocators, makes industrial capital much more efficient relative to agricultural capital. Then the static MPA, adopted by state or market, turns out after the event to have given too large a share of investment to agriculture. But this can happen only given (1) failure, by the state or the private decision-takers in 'the market', to appreciate the higher potential innovativeness of industry, (2) a genuine difference in potential of this type, and (3) the specific validity of Marshall's arguments that it is in the *adoption* of available innovations that farmers are relatively weak.

All these three requirements are unfulfilled:

(1) If one sector shows a *persistently* higher rate of effective innovation — that is, increases its total factor productivity[47] more quickly — that sector will become attractive to investors, if there is good reason to expect its innovative performance to be kept up. So why support it artificially?[48]

(2) The relative neglect of agricultural research is probably derived, not from its poor social returns, but from the difficulty of financing it—and the contradictory and weak pressures—from its many small users; from the great if often irrelevant prestige of 'Western' industrial technology; and from (probably mistaken) notions that the relatively faster growth of industrial demand renders the social profitability of industrial research higher. The only reliable long series of data, for the USA, shows that total factor productivity—the best measure of total innovation, in both machines and human skills—has risen faster in agriculture than elsewhere.[49] Probably in early development labour productivity, already higher in industry, rises faster there, while capital productivity in agriculture starts higher and pulls ahead.[50] This suggests different *types* of innovativeness in the two sectors, rather than any general conclusion that one sector should be favoured because it is *more* innovative.

(3) Marshall's fears for rural innovativeness (chapter 4, note 46) are not borne out by experience. (a) Urbanisation does select out many potential rural leaders. However, this argues against making the cities artificially attractive to the educated, not against investing in agriculture; anyway, some educated persons return to the village (sometimes with the training or the savings to improve their family farm), a process that greater research and investment in agriculture would encourage. For both reasons, the emigration of the educated is a consequence of, not an excuse for, neglect of agriculture. (b) Where innovations offer major gains and do not greatly increase risk, farmers soon learn from their neighbours — note the rapid spread of high-yielding wheats in the Punjab. (c) The complexity of farm accounting does not prevent the farmer from learning what pays, by trial and error as well as by observation, as effectively as the industrialist; if he fails to learn, it will pay him to sell out to someone more receptive.

The current crisis of marginalism
There are three main reactions, among Western economists concerned with rural development, to the 'crisis of marginalism' brought about by its inability to analyse large economic aggregates (p. 103). *Unrepentant neo-classicals* of the Chicago school have tried to reconstruct marginalism and refute (or incorporate) the attacks on it. They have been the most willing to perceive the results of urban bias as inefficient. This is because they are still prepared to make marginalist comparisions between the yields of savings in big sectors of the economy—between, say, agriculture and infrastructure—despite the 'aggregate' problems discussed on

p. 103. However, their approach, sometimes excellent for analysing events, blinds them to the frequently socio-political nature of their causes and cures. *Eclectic marginalists,* abandoning these comparisons, have constructed new and supposedly more applicable marginalist tools for macro-analysis—a method originating with Keynes, and most clearly exemplified in its bearing on agricultural development by the work of Galenson and Leibenstein (chapter 8, note 8, and chapter 10). *Marginalist classicals,* such as Rosenstein-Rodan, Lewis, Mellor and Johnston—while retaining many marginalist methods—have reverted to seeing agriculture's 'role' as the provision of wage goods for non-agricultural development; this is probably the dominant approach.

Current marginalist practice: the example of land reform
Marginalism, when used to give advice about land reform, exposes its simple analytic strength, but also its weakness (as pure, apolitical economy). Clearly, redistribution of land, from big holdings to small, improves income distribution. There are two marginalist arguments that it also raises efficiency.[51] First, for land and crops of a given type, there is normally an 'optimum level of output' that minimises cost per unit. Above this level, supervision problems grow sharply; below it, the scale of production permits neither allocation of jobs to the workers (and times) best suited for them, nor full utilisation of 'indivisible' capital items (such as ploughs). Land reform redistributes assets from farmers producing above this 'optimum level' to those below it.

Second, a farmer aiming to produce a given volume of a particular crop will, if he owns much land, generally select a method using plenty of acres, which he has; much capital equipment, for as a good credit risk he can borrow cheaply to buy it; but little labour, for (apart from rising costs of supervision) he hires on a local rural labour market, and is a sufficiently important operator to bid up the price. A small farmer usually farms mainly with family members who have little else to do, not with hired labour; he cannot acquire heavy capital investment, and hence is more prone to select 'labour-intensive' methods.[52] Since in poor countries land and capital are usually scarce and underpriced (chapter 13), and labour plentiful and underused, small farmers' techniques are socially preferable, reducing both unemployment and the drain upon scarce savings or imported capital. Moreover, they mean that small farmers — short of food and with more leisure than they want — saturate each acre (and each pound of fertilisers, and each task of removing the weeds it also fertilises) with more labour than do large farmers.

Hence land redistribution, from big farmers to small, raises farm output in two ways: through bringing both overgrown and over-small production units closer to optimum size; and through a more economical mixture of the agents of production by the typical unit. While effective land redistribution sometimes happens in poor countries, it is much rarer than this would suggest. Usually the laws are full of loopholes to let rich men keep their land; even where land is taken over, it often reverts to giant and inefficient forms of corporate farm organisation that vitiate both the above arguments for reform. In this case (as with free trade), marginalists explain the almost universal neglect of their counsels by saying, implausibly, that the politicians or bureaucrats do not understand their arguments; or by vague references to landlords' vested interests.

In fact the landlords, who usually receive compensation, often have little to lose from land redistribution; and in a centralised and urbanised state they have little power to resist it. The more they seek such power by aligning their interests with those of the urban elite, the less they benefit from using power to protect their rural, rather than their urban, concerns. But townsmen lose from land reform, because the small farmer or landless labourer, when he gets more land, initially tends to eat the product himself. He benefits from his efficiency by alleviating his hunger. This drives up the price of food to the townsman, forcing employees to seek, and probably employers to pay, higher money wages. Hence land re-distribution is usually unpopular with the urban elite.[53] (The co-operative farm, unless—improbably—it is an honest cooperative of equals, can more easily be used as a channel for compulsory extraction of a surplus, and is hence—for all its proven inefficiency—a less unpopular version of reform with the urban decision-takers.)

There are other instances where marginalists fail to recognise the class alignments underlying urban bias, and thus impeding or frustrating their advice: for example, the planning of farm output structures to meet growing demands (but whose?). But the analysis of land reform illustrates the problems of this would-be aseptic approach.

MARXISM AND THE RURAL-URBAN RELATIONSHIP

Marx, Marxism and domestic exploitation[54]

Marxists believe that capitalism, to develop, must first destroy traditional rural society. 'Natural economy', in which families or small groups provided their own needs, could supply industry with neither a 'home market' nor cheap labour. Nor would 'peasant economy', feudal or communitarian, deliver the necessary surpluses to capitalists. Hence capitalism had to pitchfork the rural population out of such 'commodity economy' into exchange relationships involving the 'cash nexus'.[55] This would have three effects: to transfer rural saving to capitalists; to 'differentiate the peasantry', making the poor 'wage-slaves' for capitalist enterprise, but transforming the rich into capitalist farmers or (after sale of land) into urban capitalists; and to enlarge cash demands for products of capitalist industry, as it displaced rural goods.

Marx showed how 'who gets what' depends on the power, unity and will of the contending groups. However, the Marxist *traditions* have confused our understanding of the early development process, in five ways.

First, Marx's trifurcation of classes—'rentier' landlords and lenders, 'bourgeois' businessmen and capitalist farmers, 'proletarian' employees in town or country—is (as he realised) unsuitable for poor agricultural countries. The Eurocentrism of Marx's class categories is concealed by the universality of his learning. In most poor societies it is more accurate to see city as exploiting village, than to argue that 'capital' and 'labour', as classes, even *exist* to fill the roles of exploiter and exploited. Marx's insights into class antagonisms are best applied in India or Nigeria today to analysing the nature, cohesion and conflict of the urban *class* and the rural *class*.

Second, insofar as rural differentiation proceeds with development, urban influence rather than 'capitalism' is responsible. Kautsky's application of Marxism to Austria of the 1890s—not too different from many LDCs today—shows how urbanism and capitalism interact.

Third, Marx, and more particularly Lenin, seem to overstress the need for urban capitalists to use state action to extract rural surpluses. Kautsky shows how the free market, despite stability-oriented *hindrances* from the 'bourgeois state', transfers resources from village to city.

Fourth, Marxists (except Maoists) see the peasant as objectively 'reactionary', to be polarised and destroyed by advancing capitalism, largely because they believe in the increasing technical inefficiency of small-scale farming. This belief leads them to advocate giant farms. Yet these bring just that alienation and unemployment of agricultural labourers and small farmers that Marxists rightly deplore in rural capitalism.

Fifth, there is in much Marxist analysis an unresolved tension between a residual 'golden-age' theory of pre-capitalist agriculture and an intellectual appreciation of the fallaciousness of that theory.

Classes, conflicts and sectors

For Marxists and anti-Marxists alike, 'the class a man belongs to. . . depends on whether or not he owns property and on the type of property he owns'.[56] The latter criterion, understressed in the literature, is vital in reality.

DOES 'RELATION TO THE MEANS OF PRODUCTION' BEST DELINEATE SOCIAL CLASSES? In LDCs, conflicts and inequalities are often more important *within* Marx's 'classes' than *between* them. This happens too often for classes, thus defined, to be generally useful analytic categories. In particular, consider the two main issues determining economic structure and income distribution in most LDCs: agriculture's share of investible resources, and the relative prices of farm and non-farm products. There are two sides here. On one side stand the peasantry (whether or not eroded by rural capitalism), the rural landlords, and (where identifiable) the new 'classes' of capitalist farmers — and the rural proletariat if, as is likely, these gain from high farm prices (chapter 13). On the other side stand the urban rentier, worker and businessman.

Over a time-span of fifty to a hundred years or more, the marks of a politically relevant social group are lasting common interest, actual or potential awareness of it, and actual or potential capacity for action to further it. Let us call such a group a 'class' when its members benefit from moving, in the same direction, the one or two key, disputed variables and the associated decisions most affecting economic structure and income distribution over that period. It is then more useful *in LDCs* to conduct our analysis of class interaction in terms of an 'urban' class and a 'rural' class dependent on agriculture than in terms of classes comprising capitalists, rentiers and proletarians. *The type of product affects group interests and actions more than does the relationship to the means of production.*

ARE RURAL CLASSES 'REACTIONARY'? 'The peasant has so far largely manifested himself as a factor of political power only by his apathy. . .[this is] the strongest pillar not only of the parliamentary corruption in Paris and Rome but also of Russian despotism. . .the bourgeoisie [easily] render the socialist workers suspicious and odious in the minds of the peasants as. . .lazy, greedy-city-dwellers who have an eye on the property of the peasants,' wrote Engels in 1894. He and Marx, in the *Communist Manifesto* (1848), had written of 'the peasant' as one of those whose fight against the capitalist is 'not revolutionary, but. . .reactionary, for they try to roll back the wheel of history'.[57]

Even when capitalism—by driving out their home-made crafts with mass-produced cheap town goods, their farm products with cheap imported food—has almost destroyed the peasants, they 'cling tightly to their property, even though in reality it does not belong to them but to the usurer. Nevertheless, *it will have to be brought home* to them that they can be freed from the usurer only when a government dependent on the people has [nationalised and reduced debts]. . .this can be brought about only by the working class.'[58] The peasants must 'find their natural ally *and leader* in the urban proletariat',[59] and then the small, non-exploiting ones can be useful to the socialist cause. The Marxist analysis has done much to create political movements corresponding to its own categories. But the rural class, in dividing allegiances between 'proletarians' and 'capitalists' in poor countries, does not overcome the real cause of its impoverishment. That cause is the power of the urban elite. A labour aristocracy such as the 'urban proletariat' cannot provide the paternal leadership that Marx and Engels envisaged. It is part of the problem, not part of the solution.

The inherent defect in the majority of political parties in [LDCs] has been to approach [mainly] the working classes in the towns, the skilled workers and the civil servants—that is to say a tiny part of the population, which hardly represents 1%. . . .The embryonic proletariat of the towns is in a comparatively privileged position. . . . [Most] parties show a deep distrust towards the population of the rural areas. . . .These people appear to them to be bogged down in a fruitless inertia. . . .The [post-colonial] ruling class does not hesitate to assert that [rural people] need the thick end of the stick if the country is to get out of the Middle Ages . . . the peasants, confronted with the national middle-class [fighting] these [city] workers who after all can eat their fill. . .shrug their shoulders. . . . All make use of the peasant masses as a blind, inert force—brute force, as it were.[60]

Fanon here indicts every 'leader in the urban proletariat' who seeks to 'make use of' rural people in a tactical struggle against the bourgeoisie. Asia and Africa today are not the Europe of Marx and Engels; but the morality and the juxtaposition of forces are the same.

Moreover, peasants are no more 'reactionary' than they are reluctant to adopt paying innovations; no more the pawns of communist political than of capitalist economic mythology. Many peasants in LDCs neither exploit nor are exploited. They share many an interest with landless labourers and with big farmers: in fair prices for fertilisers and cotton; in the diversion of public investment from urban showpieces to irrigation; in adequate rural access to scarce supplies of health, education and administrative energy. Most poor countries must ultimately industrialise to grow rich; but rural-class pressures for rural emphasis are not 're-actionary'. Such emphasis must in most LDCs precede effec-tive industrialisation.

Differentiation of the peasantry

Many Marxists are ambivalent towards romantic communitarian-ism. They are attracted to golden-age myths of the primitive rural economy,[61] yet see that development must break it, and appre-ciate its constricting effect on the maturation of rural man. But they generally overestimate its equality and freedom from 'exploitation'; correspondingly exaggerate the extent to which exploitation, found in rural economies developing out of pre-capitalist structure, is caused by the capitalist impact; and implicitly underplay the extent to which the rural sector as a whole, yes, as a class, is exploited by the urban elite. Such exploitation renders the constant snuffling after the odd capitalist farmer — however justified it was in the 1890s during Lenin's battle against *narodnik* mythology in Russia — a dangerous diversion. It is even self-defeating: low ceilings on rural landholding are much harder to render acceptable when nothing is done about (much greater) concentrations of intra-urban property or about rural-urban inequality. Big farmers win sympathy if, in opposing land reform, they can plausibly claim that it denies the countryman the chance to climb a short ladder to modest wealth and influence, while the long ladders remain open to the townsman. Equalisation, to win friends even among the fair-minded well-to-do, should itself be distributed equally.

As for pre-capitalist differentiation, Lenin's own data show that the Russian village communes enlarged the holdings of the rich much more than those of the poor. That is what modern research into analogous pre-capitalist systems would lead us to expect. Hill first destroyed 'the myth of the amorphous peasantry' in West Africa, then revealed the extremely unequal, gerontocratic struc-ture of landholding there. Thorner showed how India's traditional rural inequalities impose themselves on the allocation of resources intended for cooperative exploitation.[62]

Unless very dynamic *and* constrained by labour shortage, capitalists need not destroy — and may even strengthen — earlier rural social formations. Surplus value often accrues to chief or Brahman. And urban exploitation, whatever the degree of capital-ism or socialism, finds a natural ally in the big feudal farmer. Capitalism and feudalism are allies, not enemies, in the Indian village today: allies in the urban alliance.

As for Lenin's influential argument that 'capitalism' forces pro-letarian status on peasants, it gains little support from the Russian data he cites. His rural 'proletariat' seems to have a good deal of arable land, if not owned then allotted by the village com-mune.[63]

I have three worries about the Marxist theses regarding rural differentiation (and Lenin's account of Russia in the 1890s *still* seems to be the only exemplar available in English of these theses fully worked out for a poor and largely agricultural nation). First, it was considerable before capitalism began to impinge on the rural sector. Second, in Lenin's examples, it ends up surprisingly small after a good deal of capitalist impact.[64] Third, pressures towards rural differentiation are urban rather than capitalist: in the rural phenomena they create; in acting with 'pre-capitalist' pressures towards rural inequality; and in their demonstrable origin in urban extraction of rural surplus, largely irrespective of the penetration of capitalism into either sector.

Lenin, in dismissing this, advances some surprising arguments. Thus in Russia in the 1890s 'there is not a single economic pheno-menon among the peasantry that does not bear this contradictory form, one specifically peculiar to the capitalist, i.e. [sic!] that does not express a struggle and antagonism of interests, that does not imply advantage for some and disadvantage for others.' Earlier he has asked us 'to take the picture as a whole: the renting of land, the purchase of land, machines, outside employments, the growth of commercial agriculture, and wage-labour', and sarcastically enquires, 'Or maybe Mr Chernenkov considers these also are neither "new" nor "capitalist" phenomena?'[65]

Let us now consider, not only Russia in the 1890s, but India, Nigeria and Colombia in the 1970s. In all cases, (1) all the practices described are compatible with rural situations where most families earn most of their livelihood from their own farms; (2) pre-capitalist rural relations were and often are extremely antagonistic; (3) many capitalist irruptions *unify* formerly opposed rural interests, for example, against urban capitalist pressures on the state to make privately produced domestic fertiliser profitable by protective tariffs. Not 'capitalism', but the urban interest in cheap food supplies, leads the policy-makers of the urban state to 'polarise' villagers into surplus-delivering maxi-farmers, favoured with cheap inputs, and the squeezed poor (though these rural groups share many interests). Usury and land rent are rampant in closed rural societies; capitalism can live with them; urbanism turns them into channels by which the rural poor support the urban rich.

Scale in agriculture

Marxists, then, tend to interpret, as results of the internal dynamics of agrarian capitalism, what seem to me to be consequences of the forcing of external urban decisions upon agriculture as a whole. The role of scale in agriculture is an important illustration of this.

For Marx, a system of small landholdings 'by its very nature excludes the development of social productive forces of labour, social forms of labour, social concentration of capital, large-scale cattle-raising, and the progressive application of science'.[66] There are three charges of incapacity against the small farmer: to accumulate capital,[67] to innovate,[68] and to develop cooperative productive activities.

As for capital accumulation, on Lenin's data, the differential among farms in the value of implements per acre in pre-revolutionary Russia was surprisingly small: 1.98 to 1 between his groups of largest and smallest farms.[69] Admittedly, 'improved' implements were confined mainly to the large farm; this makes sense where traditional implements require plenty of labour, such as only the family farm can provide cheaply. But accumulation of costly 'improved', labour-saving and largely imported, farm machinery is not obviously desirable in a land-scarce, underemployed country short of foreign exchange. If—as is not clear (chapter 10)—small farms cannot save enough to accumulate even desirable capital, hire can often solve the problem. Moreover—even in Marx's time,[70] certainly in Lenin's, and much more today—'working capital', in such forms as fertilisers, was increasing in importance relative to fixed capital; that reduces any possible advantages of scale associated with financing or overseeing big items of *fixed* capital.

As for innovation, Marx rightly argues that—in agriculture too—joint work on total productive processes both suggests and tests inventions. But this does not imply that large farms do better at inducing inventions and applying innovations than small ones on account of a greater capacity to integrate the production process. For the division of labour in agriculture takes place among seasons and not among persons (chapter 4, note 22); the same worker, even in a one-man form, concentrates his energies on ploughing, then on sowing, and so forth. Hence inventions depending on the interaction of 'divided' activities can, in agriculture, be as effectively tested in production[71] from many small farmers as from a few big ones. If small farmers get fewer chances to innovate, it is because urban pressures for higher surplus dictate concentration on big farmers. Moreover, small farmers do cooperate where cooperation pays, and can thus accept innovations requiring scale if they are profitable. It is the urban interest — in food surplus from big farmers, in sales to them of state-subsidised labour-replacing machinery whether or not socially efficient — and not the internal dynamics of rural development that links profitable innovation to large scale.

As for cooperation, small farmers welcome it — if it pays them. Exchanges of labour and animals among families at ploughing time were common in pre-revolutionary China, and still are in Western India; economies of supervision and of mutual labour help (Marx's 'social forms of labour') are thus easily attained by small family farms. There have also been few obstacles to the introduction of cooperation around suitable *new* techniques, such as tubewells and pumpsets in Bangladesh.

There are two proper uses of the term 'economies of scale'. Statically, they exist if and only if in any year farms using — say — 10 per cent more of all inputs (land, labour, fertiliser, tractor-time, etc.) of a given quality produce *over* 10 per cent more physical product (for example, wheat). Dynamically, they mean that if the average farm gets smaller, its efficiency declines; if larger, that it increases. Lenin's major empirical efforts, for Russia and the USA, prove neither case.[72]

In any case, these simple concepts of 'economies of scale' are not the real issue. When farm size doubles, and outputs double too, inputs normally go up in different proportions. Typically, small farms use family labour power to do jobs for which big commercial farms use machines (or electricity or internal combustion engines) so as to avoid high and rising unit costs of supervising and coordinating labour. In LDCs where labour is plentiful, and capital and/or land scarce, this argues against tying up scarce factors in big farmholdings, and hence against agricultural concentration. Contradicting that argument, however, is the urban interest in raising the relative prices of urban products. This artificially favours producers using much capital and little labour (chapter 13) such as *big* farmers. Since these supply the urban classes with most of their food and raw materials, this interest politically dominates the considerations of efficiency mentioned above.

As marginalism sets aside the classical economists' concern for the theory of economic development and class formation, so Marxism sets aside their complementary interest in market price and cost theory. Marxists thus fail to ask whether their allegedly universal tendency to large scale in agriculture may be inefficient. Bukharin and Preobrazhensky saw a universal progression — communist farming best, capitalist farming second-best, peasant farming least efficient — as if optimum scale and organisation of farming were determined independently of a nation's resources of land and labour and capital, and of the combinations of these with which each type of farm unit will produce its output. Engels similarly had seen the French small peasantry as doomed; the task of the party, he argued, was to dispossess the large private farmer, to ease and humanise the small peasant's voluntary transition to cooperation, but to grasp that large-scale farming, whatever the prices and scarcities, was the wave of the future. For Lenin too, that trend was a technically given universal, an 'indisputable fact', hastened by the effect of usury on the small peasant: 'The superiority of big capitalist agriculture increases; there is a growing application of machines; the peasant economy falls into the noose of money capital, declines and collapses under the weight of a backward technique.'[73]

Even great and honest thinkers, owing to this *determinism of scale,* do not feel the weight of their own evidence. Marx observed that the use of waste products 'in small-scale agriculture [enhances] productivity [and derives] from the prodigal use of human labour-power'. Lenin saw that 'the well-to-do peasantry . . . employ a [different] *farming technique'*, using less labour and more capital per unit of product.[74] Again, Lenin showed that in the Perm region small farms used less manure than big ones — but overlooked that, the bigger the farms, the less was used *per acre,* so that acreages were better manured if dispersed into small farms than if concentrated in big ones.[75] In all three cases, if an LDC has plentiful labour, but scarce land and capital, small-scale farming makes sense. The thrust towards big farms, capitalist or collective, helps the urban state to extract food surpluses (and cheap workers) from capital-intensive farm units; but that thrust has little justification, on equity or efficiency grounds, in today's half-employed Third World.

Urban-rural circuits: Kautsky's breakthrough

To Karl Kautsky belongs the credit of grasping, while still an orthodox Marxist, how Marx's insights into class relationships could be transformed to explain urban-rural relations.[76] Because his contribution is little-known and fundamental, what follows relies extensively on direct quotation and paraphrase.

DECLINE OF TRADITIONAL RURAL LIFE-STYLES Kautsky saw that after 'mediaeval' times there were few self-sufficient farm families. Even then, 'the farmers did go to market, but only to sell superfluous output, and buy items that were dispensable (save for a minimum amount of iron products). The chances of the market could determine his comfort and luxury, but not his existence.' As urban large-scale industry replaces rural handicrafts, the peasant is driven to increase his cash earnings—and hence his market-ings—to buy things he used to make for himself. The drive to cash is increased because rural usurers and landlords—who have always existed—similarly come to insist on cash payments.[77]

MARKETS AND CASH, OR THE BOURGEOIS STATE? Hence the peasant is driven to increasing dependence on the market, 'which he finds even more moody and incalculable than the weather. . . . A good harvest, formerly a blessing, becomes a curse,' because of low grain prices. Also, as Marx pointed out, the price fluctuations made so important with the spread of 'the market' increase the farmer's difficulties in planning; this may outweigh his gains from the extra options that the market provides (for example, from being able to sell crops that the family cannot use directly). Furthermore, as spare land becomes occupied, and as more of the peasant's require-ments have to be bought in the market, the need for cash forces many families to earn it by splitting up, through migration—especially as urban industry destroys opportunities for village handicraft work. More intra-rural migration, in turn, eases the task of capitalist (or, one should add, state or collective!) farmers in finding employees;[78] and so the growth of the market feeds on itself.[79]

Such later Marxist statements as 'capital is faced with difficulties because vast parts of the globe's surface are in the possession of social organisations that have no desire for commodity exchange', and references to 'the growing pressure of the market on the village community', echo Kautsky but lack his precision. Lenin, however, complements him by showing that, even for peasants who normally just manage to feed their families from their own output, the market matters. It creates the option to produce other crops from those eaten at home, sell them, and use the earnings to buy food for the family—an option that, in some form, will generally be taken up.[80]

Kautsky's account and his supporting data create a problem for Marxists. If it is the operations of 'the market' (any market) that make the rural sector dependent on the city by increasing its demand for cash to transact with the city, what becomes of Marx's insistence on the role of the 'bourgeois state'? True, by tariffs and other measures that turn the terms of trade against the farmer (chapter 13), the state forces him to part with more cash for a given amount of purchases from the city, and to accept less for a given amount of sales to it; and that speeds up Kautsky's process of 'monetisation by markets'.

But such bridge-building between the two ways in which farmers are made dependent on cities—the effects of markets and the action of states—only underlines the fact that there is nothing specifically capitalist about the process. The state *is* acting as an executive committee, but for managing the common affairs not of capitalists but of townspeople: not a bourgeois state, but a burghers' state. Communist development, like capitalist development, draws the farm sector into the cash nexus in ways making it dependent on the city; communist states, like capitalist states, in the interests of primitive accumulation in early development, manipulate prices to increase the resource drain out of the villages (pp. 129-30). Kautsky, writing before the birth of the USSR, could not prove this; but he does, in effect, predict it.

FROM RURAL CIRCUITS TO URBAN CIRCUITS   Kautsky summarises this process in a chapter entitled, not 'Capitalism versus the Peasant', but more accurately, 'Exploitation of the Country by the Town'. He argues that, as villages become more and more dependent on cash, and as rural moneylenders acquire urban interests and compete with urban lenders, 'only a part [of lenders' income] stays on the land to be consumed or invested; a growing portion flows to the city'. As loans from urban banks replace (or compete with) traditional usury, borrowing gets cheaper. 'Useful as this is for the individual peasant, in the large it represents a growing tribute from country to town.'

This is mainly because money that used to circulate in the rural sector now circulates in the city instead. Rural moneylenders used rural interest receipts to have canals dug or temples built (employing rural labourers), to buy food (employing farmers), or to make new loans to villagers; the urban lenders who replace them (or whom they become) spend rural interest receipts in the city. Similarly, as the city-village gap widens and communications improve, the landlord goes to live in the city—Kautsky cites Sicily and Ireland as extreme cases—and leaves agents to supervise the farm, or else rents it out; once more, landlords 'spend their rents in the city', instead of in the village as before. This dramatically affects employment. The landlord's entourage of servants is dismissed; instead there is 'attraction of labour-power' to the cities. The process is reinforced as urban industry and commerce are strengthened by the new sources of funds from rural rents.[81]

Kautsky here observes a process in which spending that used to stay in the rural circuit, bidding up both demanded outputs and prices for rural people's products, moves into the urban circuit instead. Hence city-dwellers—better off to begin with—find that both the volume of their output that is demanded and the prices they can command for it improve, while the villagers' deteriorate. Kautsky's discussion anticipates in concept, though not in mathematical method, the 'matrix multiplier' that Goodwin developed out of Keynesian materials over fifty years afterwards.[82]

Moreover, Kautsky's perception that cheap loans from cities instead of dear loans from villagers are *both* 'useful for the individual peasant *and* 'in the large, represent a growing tribute from country to town' implies an integration of two major analytical frontiers of modern economics — the consequences of flows of funds among sectors (including 'matrix multipliers') and the divergence between private and social benefits and costs arising from financial transactions. Even in economics, where originality is so often the reward of ignorance, it would be hard to parallel Kautsky's case, where the debates of the 1970s had been prefigured, in directly policy-oriented fashion, by the thinking of seventy-five years ago.

While stressing the role of market mechanisms in furthering urban bias, Kautsky pinpointed the role of the state in transferring cash circuits from village to towns by the *pattern* of taxes and outlays. Agricultural production, he argues, is hard to tax because it is still largely consumed by the family farm; hence the growing burden of indirect taxation falls especially on non-farm output. Rural people, being poorer, spend a larger share of their income than urban people; providing their own food, they also devote a larger share of cash spending to non-farm products; for both reasons, the share of indirect tax burden is greater in rural cash income than in urban cash income.[83] Kautsky could have added that indirect taxes form a large part of government revenue in most LDCs, with their underdeveloped tax systems (chapter 12), so that the poorest people — mainly agriculturists — bear relatively heavy tax burdens. The need to meet tax demands in cash, Kautsky observes, forces further 'marketisation' on the peasantry, thus accentuating the processes of market 'exploitation' analysed earlier.

The government's impact on urban-rural circuits depends not only on taxation, but also — and in a particularly alienating manner — on government outlays.

Only a minimal part . . . is spent in the countryside. In the towns are the barracks, the cannons and the munition factories; in the towns the ministries and the courts of law, and there consequently are the lawyers, whom the farmer must pay if he has to litigate; in the towns are the publicly-supported middle and high schools, the museums, the theatres enjoying state subsidy, etc. Farmer and townsman alike must contribute to the cost of cultural institutions, but the farmer remains almost totally excluded from their benefits. No wonder that he does not grasp their meaning, that he feels enmity towards this 'culture' that is a pure burden to him — to the delight of the reactionary demagogues who, allegedly concerned for public economy, demand restriction of all cultural outlays!

For Kautsky, militarism is one way in which not merely cash but human talent is taken from rural circuits to feed into urban circuits. Army recruitment draws off the strongest, and often the brightest, young rural workers, often never to return. As for rural skill drain in general, 'not just the . . . strongest, but also the most intelligent and energetic, . . . are likeliest to flee the countryside, because they are likeliest to find the strength and courage, and to feel most quickly and keenly the contradictions between the growing urban culture and the growing rural barbarism. . . . The economic links of town and country are too close for it to be possible to keep the rural population from the "temptations" of the town.'[84]

Kautsky's Austria also anticipated subsequent processes of early development in matching pro-urban action with pro-rural talk, and in giving the latter an air of reality by farm subsidies. 'Today's governments are all great friends of agriculture and . . . support it . . . with . . . all sorts of subsidies. All these exercises only raise rent and benefit the urban-resident landlord and hence the towns.' Certainly the main benefit goes to the big farmer, who uses more of the subsidised inputs, and if they are scarce is better able to negotiate (and sometimes to grease) the bureaucratic obstacle course that separates them from the soil; and it is the big farmer, likely to sell his output to the towns and to invest his savings there, at whom subsidies are principally aimed.[85]

CAPITALISM OR URBANISM? Kautsky is ostensibly writing about capitalism in agricultural development: its transforming, yet destroying, role. Yet almost everything he says concerns urban-rural relations as a whole, and seems almost independent of the feudalism-capitalism-socialism transitions. For example, consider his insights into the impact on the production structure of what this book calls 'urban bias'. He shows how wheat output expanded, and the output of rye (a cheaper grain) fell, between 1789 and 1848 in France; and he points out that in 1822 meat consumption per person in Paris was 3.5 times rural levels, and in other towns 2.5 times. The more rapid growth of urban incomes had been inducing a shift in the pattern of output, and making the foodstuffs of the rural poor scarcer. This happened even in France, where urban-rural inequality (though growing) was much smaller at the start of the development process than in most LDCs today (table 5.4), and while the government of Louis Napoleon (1848-71) was based on a peasant-backed *coup* and presumably felt some pressures to deliver the goods. The cause of such shifts in production structure lies in the selectively urban nature of growth, not in 'capitalism'. Kautsky says that 'capitalist development' leads 'to a steadily growing exploitation of agriculture', but the sense of his argument requires the word 'urban' rather than 'capitalist'. His view of Marxism confined him to a particular use of class analysis, even when his evidence points to an urban-rural class split.[86]

This curious decision, to name clearly perceived urban-rural phenomena 'capital-labour relationships', runs through much Marxist literature. Marx himself wrote of nineteenth-century France: 'The smallholding is burdened by taxes. Taxes are the source of life for the bureaucracy, the army . . . the whole apparatus of the executive power . . . Smallholding property forms a suitable [target] for an all-powerful and innumerable bureaucracy. It creates a uniform level of relationships and persons over the whole surface of the land. Hence it also permits of uniform action from a supreme centre on all points of this uniform mass.' The strength of a concentrated, urban-based state — whether feudal, capitalist or communist — against a dispersed peasantry is brilliantly conveyed; yet Marx still feels constrained to blame these quite general problems of urban bias upon 'capitalism'. Lenin, too, when he claims to have discussed 'the progressive historical role of capitalism in Russian agriculture', and to have exposed the disparity (chapter 5) as a 'phenomenon characteristic of all *capitalist* countries', has in fact identified the effects of determined *urban* power.[87]

The attribution to 'capitalism' of the results of urban bias permeates more recent Marxist analyses of the development process. Luxemburg's 'Capitalism needs non-capitalist social strata . . . as a source of supply for its means of production and as a reservoir of labour-power for its wage system' translates into recent non-Marxist remarks about the need in industrial development for rural surpluses (pp. 63-4). Indeed, a few years later, both the 'socialist' sides in the Soviet industrialisation debate (pp. 121-30) allegedly 'came to understand the *fact* that the peasant must *inevitably* bear the cost of industrialisation'. Later Mao Tse-tung 'solved' the problem by begging the question: for him, though the urban-rural 'contradiction' remains after capitalism gives way to socialism, this process turns the contradiction from an 'antagonistic' into a 'non-antagonistic' one! The peasants who starved to death under Stalin

would have been comforted to hear it, but happily Mao's actions—
sending doctors to the villages, turning the terms of trade in favour
of the farmers—are more to the point than his words. Fanon saw
that the post-colonial regimes exploited the countryside as avidly
as their colonial forerunners, but he still believed that 'socialism'
would change matters. For Gunder Frank, the *world* capitalist
system polarises town and country, and 'liberation from . . . capitalist structure' would ensure that rural areas are no longer 'condemned
to underdevelopment'. In this chorus of Pollyannas, it is Kautsky's
virtue to have presented both the contemporary evidence of rural-
urban transfers, and an analytic framework for appraising their
impact under *any* economic system. His much-imitated obeisance
to their 'capitalist' nature is an unfortunate irrelevance.[88]

THE SOVIET INDUSTRIALISATION DEBATE
In 1928, 71 per cent of Soviet employment was in an agriculture
still backward and primitive.[89] Today, Russia is the world's second
greatest industrial power. These facts have mesmerised the elites
of most poor countries, which accordingly (however capitalist or
democratic) often use the language of socialist, mobilised transformation. What really happened in Russia? How relevant is the
example to poor countries today? In this light, what do the prag-
matic developments of Marxist ideology in the Soviet post-revolu-
tionary debates tell us about the scope and limits of the 'squeeze
on agriculture' as a method of development?

Tsarist Russia had attempted agricultural transformation in
three spheres: class structure, production, and the relationship with
industry. The Soviet leadership came to follow the Tsarist finance
ministers, Vyshnegradskii and Witte, in interpreting that relationship as the support of industrial development by food, raw materials
and savings squeezed out of the farm sector.[90] With this in view,
the Tsarist transformations of class structure, and hence of production, were diverted. As for class structure, serfdom had been
abolished in 1861. Capitalism (as Lenin showed) gained ground in
Russian farming in 1870-1900.[91] Immediately after the Revolution,
peasants all over Russia seized land, either for egalitarian capitalist or for communal joint farming. The Soviet state, concerned to
obtain farm units big enough for surplus food to be easily extracted
in support of socialist industry, at first dared not reverse these land
seizures,[92] so it sought to squeeze food and fuel out of the peasants;
and finally, under Stalin, enforced state-run farming (misnamed
'collectivisation') for the same purpose. The impact on production

was that from 1929 to 1936 'the cumulative loss of agricultural output was around 40% of 1928 GNP . . . a minimum estimate of the costs of collectivisation'; even in 1953, when Stalin died, food output per Russian was less than in 1913.[93] This latter figure compares with the results of the post-Independence squeeze on agriculture by non-Communist LDCs too closely for comfort: food output (and total farm output) per person, between 1934-8 and 1968-72, fell by about 10 per cent in South America and 3.5 per cent in Asia (excluding West Asia) and rose by only 3 per cent in Africa.[94]

The overwhelming difference is that the sacrifices of the Third World's peasantry in thirty-five years produced little industrialisation; those of Russia's produced enough to play a major role in the defeat of Hitler, and by the 1960s to be felt in nation-wide leaps forward in levels of consumption. There were four preconditions for such a sequence. First was the prior social and productive transformation of agriculture (1861-1900); the resulting income per person in revolutionary Russia, while not above that of many South American or West Asian countries, was far above that of most of Asia and Africa today, and so therefore was Russia's chance of extracting a big surplus, and hence of developing despite low-yielding, battering-ram approaches to initial industrialisation. Second, a totalitarian, centralist system was able to extract very large shares of income for saving and reinvestment. Third, Russia's peasantry was sacrificed to industrialisation on a much more massive scale than today's poor countries, however urban-biased, would contemplate: millions died of hunger, because of compulsion either to deliver food to the towns or to accept the meagre product of the state-run, pseudo-collective farms that could be squeezed for such deliveries. Fourth, only the sheer size and diversity of Russia made her industrialisation strategy conceivable: in today's Third World, only India, China, and possibly Indonesia and Brazil[95] could similarly isolate themselves from the relative valuations in international trade of inputs and outputs, so as to build a wide range of industries, ultimately self-sufficient as a whole (at whatever cost in short-run efficiency), by forcing out farm products at far below world prices for very long periods.

So the Soviet path is of limited applicability for today's LDCs; continued from a Tsarist agricultural transformation; involved enormous human cost; and did not lead to a successful agriculture, a failure that later limited Soviet options by compelling massive imports of US grain. For all that, the model and its underlying ideology have appealed enormously to subsequently independent LDCs; for it did industrialise peasant Russia.

The Soviet path

Almost nothing in Marxist theory prepared the Soviet economists of the 1920s for their task. Yet the debates of the 1920s explored all the central issues of industrialisation. By 1922, with recovery from the economic ravages of war and civil disaffection, a lively debate was beginning. At first, Lenin's 'new economic policy' (NEP) made concessions to peasants, to persuade them to sell food to the cities; Bukharin especially felt that that policy must continue. Yet, if only state industrial enterprise counted as 'socialist', how could it be built up? Only—or so Preobrazhensky argued, against Bukharin—by squeezing the peasants, and principally by making them sell cheap to, and buy dear from, the state-owned industrial sector. He distinguished this 'primitive socialist accumulation' from 'capitalist plunder', and believed that rapid agronomic advance (plus social services) would allow peasants to prosper even while being squeezed. Stalin eliminated both Bukharin and Preobrazhensky, enforced collectivisation, and compelled farmers to deliver grain at starvation prices. Was this a dogmatic botch? Or did Preobrazhensky's formula, if applied, produce terrible results that he would not face and Stalin did?

In the heat of debate, did the pro-peasant 'Right' (with Bukharin) and the anti-peasant 'Left' (with Preobrazhensky) ignore their convergence on policy until Stalin eliminated each in turn? Was the harshness of Stalin's version of Preobrazhensky's policies of *perekachka* ('pumping action' to force farm savings into socialist industry) avoidable if only milder *perekachka* had been applied earlier?[96] No; once the USSR opted for instant industrialisation through cheap *and* plentiful food deliveries from the peasantry, the starving rural millions of 1933 followed inevitably. That applies more forcibly to most LDCs today, because the rural sectors *start* closer to the margin of survival. It applies, too, whether the 'primitive accumulation' aimed at be socialist or capitalist. The paths of *perekachka* lead but to procurement.

Bukharin's logic and Preobrazhensky's dilemma

By 1923, the line-up was: Trotsky and Preobrazhensky seeking greater toughness against the peasants; Zinoviev, Kamenev, Stalin(!) and Bukharin arguing for softness. Bukharin 'demanded greater facilities for the *better-off* peasants, who were responsible for a large part of *marketed* output'. By 1923, with grain purchases from the peasants seriously deficient, Lenin agreed: 'It is impossible to improve the collection of grain and the delivery of fuel [presumably firewood] except by improving the condition of the peasantry.' Stalin then supported this view.[97]

High farm prices *were* needed, if peasants were voluntarily to deliver sufficient grain and fuel to the (largely socialised) non-farm sector. But Preobrazhensky was also right, in that the socialised industrial sector required cheap farm inputs, and cheap food for urban workers, to keep up its profitability and hence its capacity to finance growing investment. The peasants would supply sufficient inputs only at attractively high prices; they could permit a growing socialist industry only by charging low prices. *If socialism meant state industry,* therefore, there was no alternative to brutal compulsory procurement on the cheap.

But *should* a transfer of investible resources out of agriculture, through cheap food, have been a major policy aim? At least one 'Bukharinite', L. M. Shanin, saw the need not just for obtaining investible resources but for obtaining a good return on them: 'The main emphasis has therefore to be put on investment in agriculture, which requires an incomparably smaller outlay of capital per unit of output, [and] will throw the goods on the market much faster than industry.' Trotsky and Preobrazhensky understood this, and Bukharin's point that initial emphasis on rapid rural growth would mean more 'marketable produce [and hence] more resources for socialist accumulation';[98] but they objected that concentration on rural growth must strengthen rural 'capitalists', and seemed 'efficient' only because of relative world prices created by the capitalist 'law of value', which should take second place to the socialist 'law of accumulation'—that in building socialism capital had to be transferred to state industry, from an initially private agriculture.

It was also argued that only through industry could the USSR catch up with Western industrial capitalism and increase employment.[99] That argument ignored both the rapid technical progress in Western agriculture, and the low labour-intensity of efficient Western industry.

Preobrazhensky's case for squeezing the peasants

TWO UNUSED ARGUMENTS   Did Preobrazhensky hold the standard view (p. 64) that, because 'the small and weak socialist sector could not possibly bear the whole burden of investment', it followed that 'resources must be obtained . . . in the main, from the peasant, since these constituted about four-fifths of the population'?[100] I cannot find this bad argument in Preobrazhensky's work. In the quoted statement one could replace 'peasant' by 'poor' without affecting the argument.

Nor does Preobrazhensky crudely write off peasants as politically 'reactionary' *kulaks.* There were lots of small peasants left in

1917, many able to feed their families without either hiring labour or being hired as labourers. They enforced, and gained in, the land redistributions of 1917-18. They had mobilised much of the agitation of 1905-17,[101] and were not inherently 'reactionary'.[102]

Yet suspicion of peasant 'reaction' underlay much of the emotional support behind the movement to squeeze the rural sector. Lenin's deputy, Rykov, wrote in 1922: 'If the party were . . . no longer to direct the peasantry, proletarian dictatorship would cease . . . and capitalism would be re-established.'[103]

TWO SERIOUS ARGUMENTS   The USSR did not obtain a series of revolutionary allies in the industrial nations, but had to pursue 'socialism in one country'. To Preobrazhensky a USSR 'surrounded by enemies' needed rapid industrialisation, even at the cost of 'internal colonisation' of the peasantry.[104] This was presumably because of the need for military self-sufficiency, and the impossibility of prolonged reliance on foreign countries for loans or even heavy industrial imports. This argument is special to a country at serious risk of invasion or economic war, *and* large and diverse enough to consider responding by a drive towards self-sufficiency in almost everything. Even then, food shortage (and the need to please foreign suppliers of food) may well present the main risk to genuine national independence: a risk worsened by an industry-first strategy.

Preobrazhensky's second important argument for financing industrialisation by a squeeze on the rural sector has crucial modern parallels. He believed that agriculture was about to reap enormous windfall gains from improved techniques. The agronomists assured him that farm output could 'easily' be tripled with rational farm organisation, and he chose to believe that the latter was swiftly attainable. Hence he could argue that the peasants, though squeezed, would get 'still larger incomes . . . secured to the petty producer by the rationalisation of the whole economy, including petty production, on the basis of industrialis[ation] . . . and intensifying agriculture'.[105] This belief also seemed to justify the view that agriculture could achieve its targets without much investment, and could therefore divert its savings to finance industrial investment.

This was (and is) an illusion, because new technology is seldom that dramatic; is usually embodied in investment; and, if promising, justifies *increasing* the share of farm investment. But Preobrazhensky's model of Soviet development was made consistent internally (if not with reality) by this naive agronomism. Krushchev's 'virgin lands' campaign of the early 1960s and the pan-Asian reliance on the 'green revolution' since 1965 also exemplify naive agronomism. If it is justified, such comforting beliefs permit urban decision-takers to get from agriculture what they need; *and* to make its practitioners happier; *and* to avoid facing urban pressure groups with the unpleasant consequences of giving the farm sector better internal terms of trade, or a higher share of investment. If wishes were horses, planners could ride.

THE FUNDAMENTAL ARGUMENT   To build up the socialist sector, its share of national productive capital must be increased; could this best be done (given the non-availability of foreign loans) by transferring savings from the non-socialist sector? Does socialism require 'primitive socialist accumulation [or] accumulation in the hands of the State of material resources mainly or partly from sources lying outside the complex of the State economy'—peasants?[106]

This argument depends on four assumptions: that 'state' means 'socialist', and 'private' means 'non-socialist'; that 'industry' means 'state and potentially socialist', and 'peasantry' means 'private-cum-bourgeois'; that it is slower to enlarge the industrial sector by reinvestment of its own surpluses than by transfers out of agriculture; and that it is impracticable to sell farm exports, to import the capital goods needed for socialist-cum-industrial expansion, to borrow from (or tax) equitably the peasant and non-peasant sectors, and to use the proceeds largely for non-farm investment only after the flow of farm goods is adequate. The last is the 'socialism in one country' assumption—arguable in inter-war Russia, irrelevant for today's LDCs. What of the other three assumptions?

In the USSR it is at least arguable that state control has brought socialism nearer. But can *only* the state be socialist? The conditions for a sector to be socialist in the framework of a socialist economy are, I suppose, that it be non-exploitative (no 'wage-slavery'), plannable, and — except inasmuch as the transitional period of 'building socialism' requires 'material incentives' — egalitarian. All three conditions can be secured outside the state economy. For instance, biggish units can be 'self-managed' by the workers on the (alleged) Yugoslav pattern. Alternatively, smallish units can comprise families owning their means of production, hiring in no more labour than they hire out (and on similar terms), and not enjoying a scarcity premium or 'monopoly rent'. In either case, the state can vary output or input prices, and thus, through predictable reactions by sellers and buyers, can secure a wide range of planned responses.[107] In agriculture these forms of organisation correspond, respectively, to a cooperative farm and a family farm roughly big enough to provide its members with the national average income per person. Units like the latter existed in the USSR before 1917; more were created by the land redistribution of 1917-18; more still could have been created (as could cooperative farms) if, instead of turning against peasant radicalism after 1924, the Soviet state had supported it in redistributing large landholdings. To increase the share of capital investment in such a reconstituted agriculture would have been no less to increase the socialist share of the economy (and no more 'petty-bourgeois') than Preobrazhensky's preference, a squeeze on agriculture to support state industry!

Second, even if in the USSR of the 1920s the state sector *was* the only potentially socialist sector—an identity even harder to accept in most LDCs today—the fact that industry was state-owned and agriculture privately-owned was accidental and alterable. The transfer of resources from agriculture to industry is not a random or insignificant consequence of a decision to enlarge the state sector at the expense of the private sector. Would-be 'socialist' LDCs with much state ownership in industry are trapped today into ruinous underspending on small-scale agriculture by such a consequence. Other LDCs, with few pretensions to socialism, use that blessed word to sanctify enlargements of the state sector in fact motivated by the natural wish of bureaucrats and politicians to increase the number of jobs in their gift. If the state and non-agriculture do substantially overlap, gains from a larger state sector must be set against losses from a smaller agricultural sector. If the conflicts are intolerable, a larger sphere of state activity in agriculture may be a way out.

Third, supposing that 'state = socialist = non-agricultural', is a rise in the investible resources of this portmanteau-sector, by enforcing their transfer from the rest of the economy, the most efficient way to increase its share of total national capital? Preobrazhensky saw that it could not go on for ever: '[primitive socialist] accumulation must . . . hasten to a very great extent the moment when . . . the state becomes able to support its own accumulation.' But why should an increasingly rich and powerful urban state ever stop squeezing the peasants—or the collective farms? Stalin soon argued that such 'supertax' will be needed for 'several years'.[108] There are three reasons to doubt the dynamic efficiency of such a squeeze (in practice, unlikely to end soon). First, the maximisation of the socialist *share* of national capital cannot be the only goal. The volume of socialist capital must matter too, not least for bargaining with non-socialist nations or seeking to impress neutral ones. An inefficient policy, sacrificing growth to a high socialist *share* of capital, could well retard the *volume* of socialist capital.

Second, the provision, for the state sector, of a price policy to ensure a large infusion of funds from agriculture will reduce the pressures on socialist managers to generate a surplus, since they will know they can increase their power even if they are not efficient. Hence 'primitive socialist accumulation' might actually reduce the socialist *share* of capital, as compared with compelling socialist management to rely on — and improve — its own dynamism for reinvestment. At best, it will saddle the state sector with activities making relatively small profits. This will raise the private sector's share of *income* even if its share of capital falls, especially since the squeeze on the private sector's investible funds will push what is left into extremely high-yielding activities. The infusion from agriculture thus provokes unfavourable comparisons between private and public sectors, a growing need for artificial methods to get either savings or good managers into the latter, and general *malaise* of the socialist sector.

Third, excessive blood donation so weakens agriculture as to endanger its capacity to sustain industry. (This had happened in the USSR by 1933.) It happens sooner if the method of transfusion is a price squeeze, creating a contradiction: either the rural sector is sufficiently stimulated by price, and assisted by investment, to feed the state sector's workers; or it is squeezed sufficiently to provide forced savings to meet the state's investment bill.

The methods of the squeeze

NON-PRICE METHODS   Some of Preobrazhensky's proposals, for instance that railways be run at a reasonable surplus, were less for squeezing the peasant than for restoring order to the state sector. He also opposed loans to the private sector — even at high interest rates — and advocated borrowing from it instead, to raise money for the state: an arguable case, though a credit famine in agriculture is not a recipe for adequate marketings to the towns. But he suspected rural taxation, because of its high collection costs; instead, state industrial monopolies required 'a price policy so calculated as to alienate a certain part of the surplus of the private economy in all its forms'. In Lewin's words, 'the most important source [of *perekachka*] was to be . . . "non-equivalent exchanges"' which would result from 'manipulation of the prices for industrial goods'.[109]

Not only was maximum growth in the share of the socialist *sector* preferred to a socialist *price policy* (rewarding farm and non-farm labour roughly equally, allowing for the need for 'material incentives'); prices even harsher on farm output, and hence farming labour, than capitalist prices were advocated without any consideration of 'socialist' alternatives, notably the alternative that agriculture, perhaps already in part non-exploitative, could be made more so by policy. Naive agronomism played a major role: 'the task of the socialist state here consists not in taking from the petty-bourgeois producers [sic: that is, the peasants] less than capitalism took, but in taking more [that is a larger proportion] from the *still larger* incomes which will be secured to [them].'[110]

HOW IS A PRICE SQUEEZE ACHIEVED?   The state was thus advised to use — and, under Stalin, did use — its industrial near-monopoly to make farmers pay high prices for their purchases. This would work only if peasants did not respond to higher industrial prices by doing without the products; that implied concentrating the rises in industrial-goods prices upon necessities with few substitutes. Such higher prices mean that cash, which the peasants once had at their disposal for saving (after buying what they needed from industry), is transferred to the state monopolies instead. The state's savings are swollen at the expense of the peasants'.

Peasants might react by purchasing imports instead of state monopoly products. Hence effective price *perekachka* implies selective protection of such products. Preobrazhensky therefore argued that the state monopoly of foreign trade was a key weapon of socialist accumulation, enabling the state to keep prices received by and paid to peasants different from world prices. Deliberate currency overvaluation, and the printing of paper money to swell the share of industrial investment, were other pieces of anti-peasantry associated with his position.[111] Similar techniques, with similar inefficiencies, permeate LDCs today (chapter 13).

Preobrazhensky's priorities, peasant response,
and the inevitability of Stalinism

Trotsky's approach — that the Preobrazhensky policy would have worked but for Stalin's blunders and crimes[112] — seems implausible. Of course, they existed, in part as Trotsky analysed them: 'Bacchanalian planning' with unreal targets and disregard of efficiency; elevation of bureaucrats above workers (and also above experts and managers); disregard of opponents, victims, even facts. Yet, even without all this, the responses of peasants to price disincentives compel any government, determined to apply them *and* to extract food, to use force. Stalin's methods could not have been avoided, given Preobrazhensky's — and Stalin's — priorities.

This can be doubted only if one believes that, if prices are turned against peasants, they will not substantially reduce their production of key crops, their total output, or their marketing. This is refuted by the Soviet evidence—reduced sowing after the forcible acquisition of surplus grain (a form of price-cutting) in 1918-19, the reduced marketings following grain price control in late 1924— and by abundant recent work in LDCs.[113]

What, then, could be expected as after 1928 Stalin began to work Preobrazhensky's pump—with peasants increasingly 'paying too much for manufactured goods, whose prices were relatively high. . . a form of supertax. . . to increase the present tempo of industrial development'[114] —with increasing vigour? Peasants could respond in three ways. They could reduce total crop production; they could consume a larger proportion of it in the farm household; or they could shift production towards crops so consumable. All three responses would reduce surpluses of food for the cities; only the 'eat-it-myself' response (open principally to poor households) could be met by compulsory procurement, and that expensively. The other two responses could be met only by labelling all peasants as kulaks, crushing their resistance, and forcing them into directed farming (bogus collectives). There, the mixture of crops to be grown, the prices to be paid for them and the proportion to be retained on the farm were all in effect determined by the state.

It comes back to the dilemma described on p. 124: in Stalin's Russia, as in most LDCs today (if, to date, with less grisly outcomes), the two components of the Doctrine of Surpluses are inconsistent. The peasants are supposed to support industry both by supplying more food (and raw materials) and by giving it cash for its saving through buying its output dear and selling farm output cheap. But the second form of support destroys the first. Farmers respond to low prices by non-delivery of the goods. The dilemma was 'resolved' by Stalin in the only feasible way, if one accepts the priorities of instant, statist industrialisation, and the equation of 'peasant' and 'non-socialist': by seizure of grain, at the point of a tractor allocated or refused, from the compulsorily pseudo-collectivised.

A NOTE ON PASTORAL AND POPULISM

The literary influence

People with dispositional urban bias want to transfer rural resources to support urban expansion. Their opponents, however, are divided. Many want rural life, not supported or made prosperous, but just left alone. Why?

Shelley called poets 'unacknowledged legislators'. Powerful literary representation is itself a social fact. English poets influenced, and sometimes were, English social, moral and political thinkers.

Together, these shaped the sensibilities of British colonial administrators and politicians, and of the new indigenous elites of Britain's
colonies. (Similar processes applied to French and German[115]
colonial possessions.) And most English poetry, from Shakespeare
to Arnold, presented an idealised picture of rural life. Marx and
(more particularly) Engels were powerfully affected (note 61),
producing an ambivalence towards rural life that pervades Marxist
writing and policy on development. Gandhi's social thought was
formed by Ruskin and other heirs of a literary-social tradition
linking natural beauty and rural simplicity and self-sufficiency,
and stressing the morally polluting impact on the village of urban
contact and urban outlay.

In many LDCs today, pastoral and populism interact. Inspiration is drawn from European models of self-sufficient rural life;
from parallel indigenous traditions (as with the *ujamaa* village in
Tanzania); and from such new versions as 'intermediate technology'
and the doctrine of 'small is beautiful'.[116] These things sound pro-
rural, and might be so, if the models and technologies were properly
researched and applied. In practice, however, rural self-government
is often a convenient excuse not to put good administrators into
rural areas; and traditional rural technology, for not putting resources into more efficient ones. Usually, for all its good motives,
pastoral-cum-populism damages the rural poor. It is usually not
sufficiently accurate and thought through, not free enough from
aesthetic myth-making, too saturated with idealisation of the past,
to rally the rural poor in the harsh competition against urban power
for scarce resources.

How did pastoral and the cult of rural spirituality acquire their
present political force? They are useful to the urban classes, because
they reduce both rural demands and urban guilt. Shakespeare's
Amiens summons to the rural banner everyone 'who doth ambition
shun, and loves to lie in the sun';[117] apparently countryfolk enjoy
simple, communitarian, spiritual satisfactions denied to townsmen;
they then either benefit from, or principally require, spiritual regeneration, which is inexpensive to the urban interest. Since the
idyll omits all mention of exploitation of the rural poor, no remedial
action is required.

'We must . . . use some illusion to render a pastoral scene delight-
ful; and this consists in exposing the best side only of a shepherd's
life, and in concealing its miseries.'[118] In the eighteenth century,
such poets as Gray, Goldsmith and Thomson followed Pope's pre-
cept. Even poets aware of rural realities idealise rural life in general;
Gay, for instance, not less so because his peasants clear out pigsties
and quarrel.

Wordsworthian 'nature poetry', as Wordsworth and his successors attempted it, conveys — as convincingly as the pastoral idyll and more subtly — that rural life is sweet and simple, and that progress and material well-being will only destroy it. Wordsworth chose 'humble and rustic life' as the scene for most of his *Lyrical Ballads* 'because in that condition, the essential passions of the heart . . . speak a plainer and more emphatic language . . . [because] the manners of rural life germinate from those elementary feelings; and from the necessary character of rural occupations are more easily comprehended; and are more durable; [and because] the passions of men are incorporated with, the beautiful and permanent forms of nature'.[119] Man is not alienated from his work ('necessary character') and thus human action is close to the sources of natural inspiration. The intrusion of urban learning, sophistication, levels and expectations of material welfare would destroy this 'natural piety'. The fusion of personal morality and rural aesthetics, in those two words and in the brief poem that incorporates them,[120] embody not only much of Wordsworth's view of life, but also much of Ruskin's, Gandhi's and perhaps Nyerere's.

Only one major English poet has tried to grasp and convey the whole turth about rural life. Crabbe's *The Village* refutes not only the golden-age myth-making of Goldsmith's *The Deserted Village*, but also Wordsworth's apolitical identification of nearness to nature with moral order:

> But when amid such pleasing scenes I trace
> The poor laborious natives of the place,
> And see the midday sun, with fervid ray,
> On their bare heads and dewy temples play. . .
> Then shall I dare these real ills to hide
> With tinsel trappings of poetic pride? . . .
> Can Poets soothe you, when you pine for bread,
> By winding myrtles round your ruin'd shed?[121]

Then he turns from the village poor to the visiting urban pastoraliser:

> Go then! and see them rising with the sun,
> Through a long course of daily tasks to run, . . .
> See them alternate sun and showers engage,
> And hoard up aches and agues for their age. . .
> Then own that labour may as fatal be
> To these thy slaves, as thine excess to thee. . .

> Or will you praise that homely, healthy fare
> Plenteous and plain, that happy peasants share?
> Oh! trifle not with wants thou cans't not feel,
> Nor mock the misery of a stinted meal!

Nor does Crabbe romanticise the victims; a 'bold, artful, surly, savage race' who 'scowl at strangers with suspicious eye', results naturally from the realities of rural life.

That the literary sensibility did not go in this direction owes much to the half-serious belief that, long ago, all was well in the village. Much poetry of rural idyll is the poetry of nostalgia: Clare lamenting that, owing to enclosure, 'Helpstone' is not the same village he knew as a child; Goldsmith, that he cannot retire to 'Auburn', because the memories have been driven out, with the villagers, to make room for a great house.

Some Third World politicians, like Goldsmith and Clare before them, bemoan the loss of the rural idyll of their youth.[122] For their non-hierarchic, cooperative idyll there is no evidence. Its literally reactionary implication is, however, powerful and clear. So, often, is the responsibility of the literary tradition: of Goldsmith's fiction,

> A time there was, ere England's griefs began,
> When every rood of ground maintained its man.

Later Wordsworth invented equal, self-sufficient Lakeland peasants. Access to land (whether based on individual ownership or on the primitive communism Maine alleges to have preceded British rule in Inida) was not equal, in this golden-age fashion, before 'development' came along to distort it.[123]

It is hard to be reactionary and conservative at once, but the literary *tone* of pastoral has passed on both attitudes to much modern 'peasantist' thought. Such literature lauds the past 'glories' of the peasant community, yet so discourages efforts to improve on its avowedly degenerate successor. The causes of decline—land seizure, to build the 'great house' in Auburn, to enclose for large-scale farming in Helpstone—are mourned as achieved tragedies, not attacked to propose a basis for positive change. Abuses in rural society are so described as to make the reader accept them. Empson comments on Gray's

> Full many a gem of purest ray serene
> The dark unfathom'd caves of ocean bear;
> Full many a flower is born to blush unseen,
> And waste its sweetness on the desert air:

'What this means. . .is that eighteenth-century Britain had no scholarship system. . . . This is stated as pathetic, but the reader is put into a mood in which one would not try to alter it. . . . A gem does not mind being in a cave and a flower prefers not to be picked; we feel that the man is like the flower, as short-lived, natural and valuable, and this tricks us into feeling that he is better off without opportunities.'[124]

Idealisation of the village leads to opposition to 'progress' in two senses. Rural 'progress' disrupts the idealised community; and the fruits of urban 'progress' are not to be preferred to it. The two views combine when Goldsmith mourns that

> . . . times are altered; trade's unfeeling train
> Usurp the land, and dispossess the swain.

Pastoral and its successors also convey a reluctance to seek rural development by suggesting that urban 'progress' creates a city life far from enviable. The classic statement of the poet's case against the city is in the preface to Wordsworth's *Lyrical Ballads* (1801):

. . .a multitude of forces, unknown to former times, are now acting as a combined force to blunt the discriminating powers of the mind, and, unfitting it for all voluntary exertion, to reduce it to a state of almost savage torpor. The most effective of these causes are the great national events which are daily taking place, and the increasing accumulation of men in cities, where the uniformity of their occupations provides a craving for extraordinary incident, which the rapid communication of intelligence hourly gratifies. [All this produces a] degrading thirst after outrageous stimulation.

If the city is so terrible, if its 'time is running out' in Rilke's industrial Europe as in Ruskin's Manchester,[125] then the urban-biased policy-maker can salve his conscience; for what is the service done to the villager by offering him — in the city or in the country — the fruits of urban 'progress'? But feeling for the moral and aesthetic squalor of the industrialising city, however valuable as a source of poetry, cannot on its own form a defensible social sensibility. It is not surprising, though, that the audience for literature and the visual arts — an audience largely urban, well-off and in search of moral justification — responds warmly to the idealisation of rural life and landscape; and to being informed that it is really not privileged, that rural people are 'better off' spiritually, and that to enrich them materially would damage their spiritual advantages.

In 'modernising' England, urban bias and exploitation of the village were small (table 5.4) and the already-urbanised part of the population large, compared with today's Third World. How much greater are the temptations of *its* urban elites to justify their relative wealth, and the exploitation of their villagers, by reference to rural idylls and urban horrors: especially since the horrors are more than ever horrible and plausible; and since home-grown 'idyllisation' remains common, and the inspired common sense of a Crabbe (or a Premchand) rare.

The example of medical care

Consider the praise heaped on primitive medicine. Some of the techniques of acupuncture, and a very few of the herbs used by indigenous practitioners in poor countries, sometimes work for some conditions. However, villagers almost always choose modern drugs or surgery, rather than, say, Indian 'ayurvedic' homeopathy, if they can afford and obtain either. A tested, comprehensive theory of disease underlies modern drugs and surgery, unlike any traditional medicine, including that of eighteenth-century Europe. The sophisticated urban advocate of traditional methods seldom uses them himself.

Medical indigenism provides ideological 'support' for spending on traditional, largely rural medicine. Given the realities of ministerial budgeting, that means less for effective rural medicine — including rural health centres, 'barefoot doctors' and drinking-water purification. Yet I have seen well-meaning foreign experts advising Sri Lanka to play down its advanced, scientific rural medical provision in favour of ayurvedic schemes.

Medical indigenism also underpins spending on big urban hospitals and on the private sector. Urban bias, plus Western-oriented medical training, render poor countries prone to this anyway. If sages tell governments of poor countries that traditional rural medicine is fine — and even that residual rural ill-health (manifested mainly in high infant mortality) represents a kind of natural equilibrium[126] — why not give the urban elite the costly benefits of real medicine, and even so structure them as to produce kidney machines? These may cost a thousand times as much, per prevented death, as the simple rural improvements they drive out; but they leave the villagers to their idyll, their Auburn and Helpstone, their malaria and witches and dying children.

Neo-pastoral, populism and sanctity: the case of Mahatma Gandhi

Both Preobrazhensky and Gandhi well-meaningly advocated policies permanently damaging to the rural interest and hence, indirectly, to the (very different) developments they sought. Each concealed the damage: Preobrazhensky, by faith in instant rural transformation (through agronomy and socialism) permitting villagers to prosper though subject to 'pumping action'; Gandhi, by faith in the natural fineness of the human personality in the self-sufficient village. Preobrazhensky's futuristic vision of progress is a dynamic counterpart of Gandhi's vision of the 'golden age' of his youth. Walter Mitty's imagined incarnations are mutually inconsistent, but stem from the same confusion of reality and dream.

Gandhi lacked three usual vices of pastoral-populists. First, there was nothing vicarious about his simple-lifery: he acted out his vision of rural transformation through egalitarian and self-sufficient community life (though, as the sad condition of the village he once transformed, Sevagram, today suggests [Introduction, note 15], he understimated the extent to which his local successes were due to his own charismatic presence). Second, he did not leave urban exploitation out of his account of rural degeneration. Third, his recipe for rural *re*generation had policy consequences extending far beyond the unpromising formula 'leave them alone'. Indeed Gandhi, despite his many years of argument with Nehru about industrialisation, inspired policies of 'community development' and rural self-government (*panchayati raj*) which — by diverting attention from the villages' need for developmental resources and the high returns to scientific rural modernisation — chimed in perfectly with the priorities of the industrialisers.

Gandhi read Ruskin's *Unto This Last* on a train in South Africa in 1909, transformed his newspaper into a farming commune, and, as he said, 'decided to change [his] life in accordance with the philosophy of this book'.[127] For the rest of his life he strenuously advocated, and frequently practised for long periods, what he took to be Ruskin's philosophy of the need for all to do physical labour, preferably rural, for roughly equal reward. Yet the egalitarian maxim 'that a lawyer's work has the same value as the barber's', added by Gandhi to the pastoral populism of *Unto This Last*, is just not there. It stems from Gandhi's need, political and psychological as well as spiritual, for a master source of a vision he had already half-formed: a vision of the self-sufficient, cooperative and rural community, 'an amalgam of Tolstoy, Edward Carpenter's Simple Life doctrine, the memory of Marian Hall [two of his London friends], the theory of the *ashram* [spiritual retreat] in Hindu religion, and the theory of corporate property in Hindu law (which had lodged in Gandhi's mind when [as a law student] he read Maine)'.[128]

Gandhi admits, as Maine does not, that he has 'no historical proof', but believes 'that there was a time when village economies were organised on the basis of . . . non-violent occupations, not on the basis of the rights of man but of the duties of man. . . . Labour contributed to the good of the community.' But if his memories of Kathiawad seem bathed in a Mainean glow, he is too realistic to rest his deeply felt case for village regeneration entirely on Maine's myth of common property. Thus Gandhi implies individual family farming when he speaks of the farmer 'content to own only so much as he can till with his own labour',[129] and he asks the rich to accept 'trusteeship for', not equality with, the poor. Nevertheless, he sees the village as naturally non-exploitative, unless perverted by urban contact. In this sense Gandhi's plea for a self-sufficient village, independent of the town and combining agriculture and cottage industry, echoes Maine's view that common property is 'natural'. Both — like the Russian populists[130] — envisage a return to a golden age of village isolation, self-sufficiency, and relative non-exploitation. This golden age can feature the 'common mark', in Maine's theory of property; 'unconscious *ahimsa*', as in Gandhi's account of absence of exploitation as non-violence; or the equal status of the populist vision of the Russian *mir*. All are redolent of Auburn and Helpstone; all encourage the townsman to believe that he helps the village, not by integrating it, but by isolating it.

Yet a village producing exactly what it requires, apart from being wasteful in a way that a poor country cannot afford, would either have to be quite implausibly isolated from knowledge of market opportunities, or would soon respond to them. Isolation would impoverish the village; response exposes it to urban market-power. In neither case does 'village swaraj' in Gandhi's sense secure freedom from exploitation from without; and to expect it to secure equality within is wishful golden-agery.

The view that rural isolation can end exploitation leads Gandhian populists to fight exploitation by trying to roll back genuine (not just socially inefficient) technical progress. This seldom succeeds. But it tars the anti-exploiters with the Luddite — or anti-green-revolutionary! — brush, and diverts their attention from the activities of powerful urban classes, which unless their wings are clipped will get their way irrespective of the nation's choice of techniques, products, or degree of rural-urban integration.[131]

Nor can urban exploitation be exorcised by damning urban life, as Gandhi does. '[The attempt to] gain America's wealth but avoid its methods is foredoomed. . . . It is not possible to conceive of gods inhabiting a land which is made hideous by the smoke and din of mill chimneys and factories and whose roadways are traversed by rushing engines, dragging . . . men who know not . . .

what they are after . . . in the midst of utter strangers who would oust them if they could and whom they would oust similarly.'[132] The echoes are of Arnold and Carlyle, Wordsworth and Ruskin, even Rilke and Eliot. Politicians echo poets in the language of romantic rhetoric, even if Gandhi's is the rhetoric of a *mahatma* — a great soul. The US is typically far less polluted than a Harijan well in a typical Indian village. Poverty, by making cleanliness too expensive, is the world's main source of air and water pollution. Resources, and hence growth, are needed to produce goods cleanly, and small-scale production need not help at all. Nor is the villager, because poor and ignorant, clear about his aims, or lacking in competitive aggression.

The main neo-populist manifestations in India of the Gandhian spirit — community development, village self-government, cottage industry, land-gift — have been disappointing. Intra-rural and urban-rural exploitation are too deep-seated (and interconnected) to be effectively challenged that way. Hence many Indians came to regard rural development as unpromising because routed along pastoral and reactionary paths. Its ideology seemed to rest upon hopeless efforts to regenerate a probably mythical rural golden age, rather than on scientific agriculture; on opposing industrial development, not on providing a necessary preliminary to it; and on appeals to goodwill, rather than on recognition of the facts of power.

Nehru's alternative was a rural sector acting as handmaiden to industrialisation.[133] Thus, in India as elsewhere, between pastoral-populist and instant-industrialising dreams, the possibility of a prosperous, scientific, labour-intensive and egalitarian agriculture was crowded out. Yet that possibility was, and is real. Its cost, in terms of foregone *immediate* urban investment, would be high; but its yield, unlike that of such investment, would be high too.

Populism transcended: Fanon

Fanon moved from fascination with black pastoral — '*négritude*' — to, and beyond, the awareness that rural-urban exploitation was not (or not simply) a colonial intrusion on African rural communities, but an internal phenomenon. Initially, he was attracted to the view of Leopold Senghor, an African poet (in French) and later president of independent Senegal to 'the view of the Negro as an essentially emotional man whose roots are deep in the earth, a man who joins himself cosmically to the world, whereas the European divorces himself from nature in order to master and subdue it' — Wordsworth's peasant. 'Then abruptly Fanon's rationality reasserts itself; the dream is over. "Nevertheless", he writes, "one had to distrust rhythm, earth-mother love, the mystic, carnal urge of the group and the cosmos."' Fanon came to realise that although 'the aboriginal cult is paid tribute by Western ethnologists. . . with sentimental affection', acceptance of that portrayal by Africans would mean that 'the dynamics of social change are blocked'. There is indeed an echo of Illich and the ayurveds in the advocates of '*négritude*', who 'tend back to the countryside, to the peasants, and cultivate a spirit of reverence towards the most primitive aspects of local culture and folklore, including Voodoo'.[134]

As Nehru rejected Gandhi's pastoral, Fanon might simply have rejected Senghor's. Like Nehru, Fanon might have built on his experiences — of the colonists' cultural 'swallowing', rural romanticising and restriction of indigenous industry — to argue that independent countries of Africa, or the Caribbean, should gain cultural and political strength by rapid, autarkic industrialisation. Yet — perhaps just because Fanon, as a doctor and a *littérateur,* lacked social-scientific blinkers — he did not just react against populism into an equally naive urban-elitist advocacy of instant industrialisation. He transcended it.

Fanon's insights into urban-rural relations in poor countries centre upon the pro-urban impetus of the colonial power; the demonstration (by the often greater urban bias of the nationalist movements and later of the independent government) that such impetus is not the main cause of rural-urban injustice; and the need for a change of heart towards rural *development,* not populist revivalism or urbanist exploitation, if political consent and independent nationhood are to be compatible. 'In the colonial territories the [urban] proletariat is the nucleus of the colonised population which has been most pampered by the colonial regime,' because it is 'that fraction of the colonised nation which is irreplaceable if the colonial machine is to run smoothly'. Nationalist movements mistakenly recruit in the politically obvious places — from among urban 'skilled workers and civil servants, . . . a tiny proportion of the population', which because 'pampered' is hard to mobilise against the colonial power.

The colonial attitude towards villagers infects the nationalist parties with 'deep distrust towards the population of the rural areas [as] bogged down in fruitless inertia. [They], town workers and intellectuals, pass the same unfavourable judgement on country districts as the settlers', overlooking that the despised 'medieval structure of [rural] society [often was] maintained by the settlers'.[135] The style of politics of the colonising power, and the urban structure of its class conflicts, infect the leaders of the independence movements, who accordingly do little for the rural masses: 'The trade union officials who have won their colours in the field of the union organisations of the mother country have no idea how to organize the mass of rural people. They have lost all contact with the countryside, and their primary preoccupation is to enlist dockers, metallurgists and State-employed gas and electricity workers in their ranks.'[136]

Fanon saw that the vicious circle — colonists who 'pampered' the urban elite, countryfolk who mistrusted it, and its tendency to recruit townspeople rather than villagers into political movements — persisted after independence. To villagers, 'townspeople are "traitors and knaves" who do their best to get on within the framework of the colonial system. [This is not] the old antagonism between town and country [but] between the native who is excluded from the advantages of colonialism and his counterpart who manages to turn colonial exploitation to his own account.' Even if the townsman represents an independence movement, he 'dresses like a European; he speaks the European's language,[137] works with him, sometimes even lives in the same district'. Partly because of this background, even after independence 'the men at the head of things distrust the people of the countryside [and sometimes] consider the interior . . . as a nonpacified area . . . the young ruling class does not hesitate to assert that "they need the thick end of the stick if this country is to get out of the Middle Ages".' After independence, indeed, the gulf widens between the urban alliance — including, according to Fanon, 'landed bourgeoisie . . . working class of the towns . . . unemployed, small artisans and craftsmen' — and the rural masses. 'The masses begin to sulk; they turn away from this nation in which they have been given no place and begin to lose interest in it.'[138]

Despite the short experience of African independence — and Fanon's *marxisant* rhetoric — his call for a change of heart is blunt, specific and practical. Urban politicking, 'a limited settling of accounts . . . between the national middle-class and the union workers', will leave the hungry peasants 'shrugging their shoulders' so long as all the urban interests 'make use of the peasant masses as a blind, inert tactical force: brute force, as it were'. The flags and processions of the independence movements will not fool the peasants into integrating willingly into this manipulative, urban-centred system. The only solution is for 'citizens of the under-developed countries . . . to seek every occasion for contact with the rural masses. . . . The indigenous civil servants and technicians ought not to bristle up every time there is question of a move to be made to the "interior". We should no longer see the young women of the country threaten their husbands with divorce if they do not manage to avoid being appointed to a rural post.' The choice confronting planners should be explained to the rural masses in 'the language of every day'.[139]

This is neither an explanation of the logic of urban-rural exploitation, nor a list of priorities for rural development. But it reveals almost unique awareness of urban bias, as an enemy of national integration, springing from townsmen's perception of their advantages and their power rather than (though not independently of) either colonialism or the nationalist reaction against it. Fanon saw that the rural poor of 'the interior', the 'back-country', would remain 'the wretched of the earth' after colonialism — and even after 'neo-colonialism' — until they mobilised against urban power, or else until urban power realised that rural development was necessary for its own security. 'Exploitation can have a black or brown face as easily as a white face'; its modality is chiefly urban-to-rural; and Fanon, having seen through '*négritude*', knew there was no escape in rural retreat to an imaginary Auburn or Kathiawad.

Part III
Urban Bias: Some Evidence

5 The disparity in welfare and earnings

Two related inequalities underlie the differences between city and country, between farming and other activities, in poor countries. The first gap separates urban and rural income and output per person. The second gap separates agriculture from non-agriculture in the endowment and efficiency of 'capital'.[1] These gaps are dealt with in chapters 5 and 6, and 7 and 8, respectively.

The gaps are related in three ways. First, each helps widen the other: for instance, agriculture's underendowment with capital is (1) a major cause *of* the low productivity of farm labour, and hence of low rural income, (2) partly caused *by* rural poverty, and consequently impaired capacity to save. Second, each gap is widened by urban bias: for instance, both rural income and farm investment are kept down partly by government action to depress food prices, which renders agricultural effort less rewarding. Third, as this example shows, neither gap can be accurately measured, unless one adjusts prices to allow for the impact of urban bias.

Chapters 5 to 8 examine the causes—on the side of both labour and capital—of the fact that between agriculturists and others the first gap, in income per person and output per worker, is large and probably widening.[2] It reflects not only the capital gap, but also other rural-urban differences in endowments: of current producer inputs such as oil, of educated persons, and of administrative attention. On balance, rural-urban welfare gaps are underestimated by the information available (pp. 146-8 of this chapter), especially information from rural and urban surveys and from estimates of earnings, useful as this is. The most significant single indicator of the gap is here termed the *disparity:* the ratio between productivity—output per worker—outside agriculture and productivity inside agriculture. The differences between less developed countries (LDCs) now, and now-rich countries (NRCs) in comparably early development, in this key indicator of rural-urban imbalance are huge (table 5.4). Six of the nine NRCs with usable data showed a smaller disparity, in early development, than sixty-three of the sixty-four LDCs showed around 1970; and forty-seven of the LDCs showed a disparity greater than any of the nine NRCs (table 5.4). Chapter 6 examines when disparities themselves are inefficient—especially when price distortions are allowed for. Chapters 7 and 8 relate the disparity to the *quotient* — the ratio of yield (output per unit of capital) in agriculture to yield elsewhere in the economy.

As chapters 7 to 13 show, most LDC governments have allocated public resources, and provided incentives to private persons, in ways tending to widen the gaps: to increase both the disparity and the quotient. This has plainly increased inequality; chapters 5 to 8 argue that narrowing both gaps would also reduce the inefficiency with which labour and capital are applied. Several other inefficiencies, touched on briefly here, are examined more fully in later chapters.

This shared error of most LDC governments is due neither to stupidity nor to wickedness. It is due to pressures on and within them from those who reap private benefit from the public loss. This perfectly normal self-interest, however, does not mean that it is useless to demonstrate the existence of that loss. To expose urban bias may convince few of its beneficiaries that it should be reduced; but it will alert many people with other, or mixed, interests. Governments indeed contain agents of the forces that benefit from urban bias; but governments are neither monolithic nor deaf.

URBAN-RURAL GAPS IN INCOME AND OUTPUT:[3] INFORMATION AND DEFICIENCIES

Three sources of information are available on rural and urban output and income: surveys of income and consumption; estimates of wages and earnings in different occupations; and output per person and output per worker figures for agriculture and industry. Taken together, these three sources reveal that rural rewards lag far behind urban rewards. All three leave out some components of the welfare gap and overstate others. Yet, while much is made of the concealed benefits (B) of rural life, little is made of its concealed drawbacks (D). Planners, scholars and governments are thus led to underestimate urban-rural welfare gaps.

(B1) The cost of living is generally a little higher in urban areas. In India in the late 1960s urban prices exceeded rural prices by about 15 per cent, and in Ghana in 1961-2 by about 8 per cent (though by 1967 there was no difference). These differences in the cost of living[4] reduce the townsman's welfare advantage somewhat below the level suggested by income per person, earnings or (value of) output per person.[5]

(B2) The rural-urban 'welfare gap' is also narrowed by the existence of unavoidable and concealed costs of living in urban areas, largely absent in villages. These include commuting, and higher costs of housing and sanitation. Quite unacceptable overestimates of such costs are prevalent, but two independent and careful estimates for India suggest that the combined impact of (B1) and (B2) would be unlikely to raise the minimum subsistence cost in urban areas by as much as 40 per cent above rural levels.[6] Typically 20 per cent is a likely average. These (B2) costs are not pure costs,[7] since they sometimes correspond to extra benefits available, notably better transport and drinking water.

(B3) One could hardly class it as a hidden rural 'benefit' that generally rural families receive poorer water supply, sanitation and medical care than urban families; or that their diet is more prone to seasonal and year-to-year fluctuation. Yet the resulting, tragically high, infant and child mortality rates do have two side-effects that enable a given income per head to go further in rural areas than it otherwise would. First, to ensure a surviving child despite the great risk of early death, rural parents seek frequent births and hence (while all the children remain alive) have big families; the average household in villages thus usually contains rather more people than in cities,[8] and big households can spend less per person on several items—cooking, heating, roofing—than small ones. Second, for the same reason, rural households include a higher proportion of infants and small children, which cuts down the 'average' household member's consumption requirement. Partly offsetting this, the rural sector has a slightly larger proportion of adolescents than the urban sector; and adolescents cost more for food, training and changes in clothing sizes than do adults. Also, if our three measures of urban-rural gaps ignore benefits from large, young rural households, they also ignore the corresponding emotional costs—and physical risks—of frequent pregnancies, and of dying and sick children.

(B4) Some rural benefits are concealed by only one or other *type* of information. These will be considered when each type is analysed.

(D1) The first drawback of rural life, not shown by the measuring rods in this chapter, is that many items not normally included in cost-of-living indices are either absent or much dearer in many rural areas. These range from health and secondary education, through journeys to markets or doctors or cinemas, to trade and other forms of credit.[9]

(D2) Corresponding to (B2) are concealed costs specific to *rural* life in poor countries. Piped water and processed food are seldom available in the countryside, and rural women commonly spend much of the day grinding grain or fetching water. Small farmers and agricultural labourers must use energy in long, muddy walks between fragmented plots; the urban worker can travel by bus (however horrible) or, if too poor, can walk on a firm pavement. The seasonality of farm output imposes further concealed direct and indirect rural costs that the household can avoid in most cities: storage; frequent trips, often to distant markets; above all, borrowing in seasons when no farm work is available.[10] Interest payments eat up much more of rural than of urban income, partly because rural credit is less competitive, but mainly because far larger proportions of rural people need producer credit (being small farmers who must buy inputs before the crop is ready to be sold) or consumer credit (being poorer). None of these costs normally shows up in comparisons of income, earnings, or output per head.

(D3) The demographic structure of the countryside also imposes hidden costs upon it. More time than in the cities is taken up in preparing infant food, in feeding and looking after children, and in earning income to pay for an education that increasingly benefits a sector in which the parents do not reside (chapter 11). Higher infant mortality rates compel rural women, aiming at a given family size, to go through more pregnancies than in the city. Also migrant relatives impose major costs upon rural families[11] by returning to them for care in illness and pregnancy; few rural surveys allow for the cash costs, whereas the costs of time, effort and worry are completely neglected.

(D4) Relative urban benefits concealed only by some *types* of information are, once more, discussed when those types are reviewed.

In the present state of knowledge, a final assessment must be subjective. My own experience suggests that type (D2) alone outweighs rural benefits (B1) to (B4). If so, the evidence in the following sections understates the rural-urban welfare gap.

RURAL AND URBAN SURVEYS

Even this most direct source of evidence conceals many factors affecting the level of living. The gap stated between rural and urban consumption[12] in these surveys is indeed surprisingly small. Although output per worker in LDCs is normally three to six times as high outside agriculture as inside (table 5.4), survey estimates of spending per head of population, as in table 5.1, are typically only 1.5 to 2.5 times as high in urban as in rural populations. Why the big difference?

Part of the explanation is that the rural-urban gap is less than the gap between agriculture and non-agriculture, because urban agri-culturalists are below the urban average in their living standards, and rural non-agriculturalists a little above the rural average. Another part of the explanation is that the ratio of workers to popu-lation is slightly higher in agriculture than elsewhere, because women and children are likelier to be workers; this means that, on top of being able to spend only about half as much as the urban family, the rural family must put in more income-earning work, often by pregnant women and school-age children, despite the high work-costs of rural life itself.

However, it is income, not outlay, that measures what people receive in a sector. And the rural-urban gap in outlay is less than the gap in income. The greater poverty of countryfolk compels them to spend higher proportions of income than townspeople.[13] Even this disparity in *disposable* income is in turn less than that in *earned* income,[14] because rural persons must rely on borrowing (as opposed to earning) far higher proportions of disposable income (see p. 148 above). And the disparity in *earned and usable income* (very seldom available in the surveys) is biggest of all, because the commitment to repay debt interest and capital represents a larger share of rural than of urban income. It is the capacity to save, against a bad harvest or old age[15] — after meeting basic con-sumption needs and repaying a debt — that is eroded by rural poverty. Net urban-rural remittances hardly affect this poverty (see p. 236); yet migrants often return to the village in sickness, pregnancy or old age, eroding rural savings even further.[16]

Yet even the urban-rural income gaps in table 5.1 remain less than we should expect from the disparities of output per person between agriculture and other sectors (table 5.4). Since agricul-tural income largely 'makes' rural well-being, this is a puzzle. Is the solution that some of the higher income-earners, resident and surveyed in rural areas, may be crypto-townsmen; while many of those receiving no, or little, income, while resident and surveyed in urban areas, are crypto-countryfolk? Some of the higher surveyed rural incomes are probably pulled up by incomes earned from, and spent in, urban activities: incomes derived by moneylenders, traders and landlords (still residing, and hence surveyed, in rural areas) from their real-estate, business and political activities in urban areas. Similarly, some of the higher surveyed rural outlays are spent on urban high living.[17] This inflation of surveyed, measured rural income and consumption by a few rich crypto-urbanites, however, is a relatively small part of total rural income. Conversely, however, survey estimates of urban outlay and income per person are (I suspect) substantially pulled down below the true level by the very low incomes of two crypto-rural groups: 'fringe villagers' (village-born students with poor prospects, or unemployed migrants) living on rural savings or remittances and likely to return to the village after a few years; and 'engulfed villagers' who, without great changes in their agriculture-based environment and life-style, have been gradually surrounded by the sprawling city.

If surveys estimated 'true' urban and rural incomes, the low incomes of fringe and engulfed villagers would bring down the rural average instead of the urban average; and the relatively high incomes of those rural residents with largely urban economic activities would swell the urban instead of the rural average.[18] Thus the income gap between 'real' urban and 'real' rural persons certainly exceeds the gap measured by surveys based on formal residence. To make sense of the figures in table 5.4 it has to be nearer 3:1 or even 6:1 than to the 2:1 implied in table 5.1.

Nevertheless, useful — if underestimated — measures of the true gap are presented in table 5.1. The most comprehensive information is for India, where the value of monthly rural consumption per person, in nine rounds of the National Sample Survey over the 1950s, averaged 18.4 rupees, as against 26.3 rupees (1.43 times the rural level) in urban areas. That is not a very large gap, especially as living costs are about 15 per cent higher in urban areas (chapter 5, note 4). In the 1960s, however, the consumption gap widened. Moreover, as explained, urban-rural disparities in income exceed disparities in consumption. Personal disposable income in Indian urban areas in 1959-60 averaged 1.67 times the rural level; the gap had grown through the 1960s, and by 1975 had almost certainly reached 1.8 : 1. Earned-income surveys, as expected, show larger disparities — at least 2 to 1 between urban and rural income per person, also increasing somewhat over time. Data net of repayments of debt interest and capital, if available, would show bigger gaps still. Moreover, the poorest third of India's 400 million or so villagers — those who rely mainly or wholly on income earned by work on others' land — may well, in most areas, have become poorer — not only in the 1950s and early 1960s but right through the much-vaunted 'green revolution', and despite sluggish but undoubted growth in Indian average incomes.[19] The best available estimate is that the proportion of rural people below a (very basic) poverty minimum rose from 39 per cent in 1960-1 to 54 per cent in 1968-9.[20]

The gaps between country and city in India — and government actions tending to widen them — are less marked than in most poor countries. In neighbouring Bangladesh, while it was part of

Pakistan, rural income per person fell from 44 per cent of urban income per person in 1949-50 to 37 per cent in 1963-4. Furthermore, the real income of agricultural labourers fell, while average and even labourers' urban living levels at least crawled upwards.[21] Urban income per person over 2.7 times rural levels is especially striking in Bangladesh, a country with few big landlords and with a very small industrial sector. In Bangladesh, rural-urban inequality must be overwhelmingly the main component of overall inequality.

It is noteworthy that rural-urban inequality was smaller in West Pakistan than in East Pakistan in the 1960s.[22] The big farmers of West Pakistan, and even to some extent their labourers, gained because the city needed their wheat, and because they were organised into large units providing a surplus for the cities, albeit at huge cost in (subsidised) imports of tractors, pumpsets and fertilisers. The smaller, more equal farm units of the Eastern wing ate most of the rice they grew, and hence were of little use to — and were neglected by — the urban alliance. Within agriculture also (chapter 3), urban bias introduces inequities and inefficiencies of policy, and these surveys help reveal them.

For Brazil, where 1970 shows no 'greater welfare in rural areas' than 1960 despite extremely rapid growth in real national product per person,[23] the gap revealed in table 5.1 is large and (like those in table 5.3) growing. As so often, however, one is struck by the lack of usable data on the Latin American rural sector. Perhaps arguments about 'dependency', characteristically conducted among the urban rich, provide at once a foreign scapegoat for the conditions of the rural poor, and an intellectually respectable alternative to analysing them? Anyway, the similarities between Asia and Latin America, both in their disparity between non-agricultural and agricultural output per person (table 5.4) and in their use of price policy against the farm sector (chapter 13), suggest that urban-rural gaps in income per person might be in the Asian range.

Disparities between non-farm and farm labour productivity are a good deal higher in most African countries than in most other LDCs (table 5.4), and this is reflected in somewhat higher rural-urban gaps in consumption. In Ghana, monthly urban consumption per person was about 1.5 times rural levels in the early 1960s, and by 1967 the cost-of-living differential, always small, had shrunk to zero; that would suggest real earned-income disparity by then considerably over 2 to 1. In Zambia, rural income per household rose from 60 to 76 Kwachas per year between 1954 and 1968; meanwhile the copper boom raised average earnings per African urban *employee* from 156 to 713 Kwachas per year, producing a staggering disparity of 9.4 to 1. In Uganda, surveys of peasants in 1957 and 1964 showed income per active worker rising only from 35 to 36 Ugandan pounds per year, while income from wage employment per urban employee rose from 55.6 to 116.8 Ugandan pounds, producing a disparity of 3.2 to 1.[24]

Finally, the gap between rural and urban areas in wealth — which reflects not only differential reserves with which to resist misfortune, but differential access to income without work — is even greater than in income. India, one of the less unequal LDCs in this regard, is one of the very few with available data. Indian urban wealth per person rose from 2.5 times rural levels in 1950-1 to 2.7 times in 1961-2.[25]

EARNINGS GAPS

Agricultural and non-agricultural earnings and wages data are available for more countries than are comprehensive surveys of rural and urban income or outlay. Though they miss out non-farm rural income and farm urban income, they avoid the problem of fringe villagers in cities and crypto-townsmen in the countryside (p. 150). Earnings figures exclude remittances, but rural support of countryfolk undergoing unemployment or education seems roughly to balance the much more familiar flow of remittances in the opposite direction (except in a few mining economies of Africa with intensely seasonal, eroded and 'feminine' agricultures).[26] Earnings figures might therefore give quite a useful picture of urban-rural disparities, but for four drawbacks. First, they are scrappy, concentrating heavily on permanent employees and organised taxpaying units — plantations and government departments — with the effect of overstating average rewards in both sectors. Second, they play down the share of capital (much larger in non-agriculture) and land (much larger in agriculture) in total income. Third, they are collected in many different ways (table 5.2). Fourth, they do not directly show the rewards of those who farm on their own account, who form the great mass of rural workers in many LDCs, and a substantial portion in almost all. Earnings data are probably more useful indicators of trends in the welfare gap than of its level, though they do tell us something about that.

Table 5.2 compares the earnings data reported to the International Labour Organization. Before I did any calculations on these data (lest the result bias my selection), I excluded one or two sets of statistics known to be worthless (for example, for Burma); data of minimum rather than actual payments; and estimates not comparable between agriculture and other sectors. The remaining figures are of mixed quality, but have no apparent systematic bias. They reveal larger rural-urban gaps than the surveys.

Both on survey data and on earnings data, the disparities were increasing in the 1960s in most LDCs (table 5.3). For whatever reasons, the impact on non-agriculture of pricing and investment policies has in most LDCs been felt in a large and growing wage gap. *Either* there is no flood of migrant workers out of agriculture in search of high urban wages (and no flood of capital into the rural areas in search of 'cheap' rural labour) *or* such movements are not closing the gaps. A widening gap during the decade of the 'green revolution', and while urban population shares grew slightly with no obvious matching growth in urban job prospects, is a powerful testimony to the impact of urban bias. Moreover, the gaps may be outpacing the estimates in table 5.3; most estimates exclude wages in kind (table 5.2) and these are generally paid in the less progressive parts of agriculture, so that the estimates tend to overstate the growth in average farm wages. Rural situations in the early 1970s worsened relative to the towns with the slowing-down of the 'green revolution'. The temporary improvement in 1973-5, resulting from high prices for farm products, caused by world food scarcity due to simultaneous bad harvests in several developed countries, signifies neither a change in developing countries' conditions nor a reversal of the trend against relative farm incomes.

THE OUTPUT DISPARITY: METHOD

Verdicts and advantages
Surveys of consumption understate gaps in rural-urban welfare, largely because the savings capacity is more unequal than consumption. So do earnings comparisons, largely because they omit income from capital (much more important in the towns) but implicitly include much income due to land (because the commercial farmer can seldom attract workers without paying as much as they could earn, from effort and land, on the family farm). Our main emphasis is therefore on the ratio of output per worker in the rest of the economy to output per worker in agriculture, valuing output at prevailing prices.

This ratio, hereafter called *the disparity*, ranged from 1.1 to 3 in most NRCs while they accelerated their growth in the agricultural, and later industrial, spurts of the late nineteenth century – and was tending to fall. But in most LDCs today the disparity ranges from 3 to 7 — and is tending to rise. Inasmuch as some analogy may exist between the development process in NRCs then and LDCs now, it suggests that the disparity, unless it falls early, stays high for a long time: in NRCs the disparity, after its initial fall, stayed fairly constant until the mid-1930s, and it was only after 1945 that the rural-urban income gap began to close.[27] Moreover, the constellation of forces in most LDCs is much more unfavourable to the rural poor than it was in the NRCs during their early development (chapter 1).

Can I use the disparity — the ratio, at current prices, between the *output*, on *average*, of *workers* in *agriculture and non-agriculture* — to assess the gap between the *well-being* of *typical* resident *individuals*, in *rural and urban areas*? The procedure, if admissible, has obvious advantages. First, information about the disparity is more readily available than information about earnings or living standards, both for LDCs today and for NRCs during early development. Second, the disparity typifies the position in entire sectors, as earnings data (in countries where most farmers and many craftsmen are not employees) cannot do. Third, output per worker in a sector is also its productivity of labour, and tells us not only about 'welfare' but about labour's endowment with supporting factors — skills, physical inputs, even nutrition. Fourth, the sustainable well-being of rural people depends on agricultural output per person: on the amount of it consumed in rural areas, and on the purchasing power of the amount of it sold to urban areas, and on the rural jobs it causes bigger farmers to pay for (either in cash, received from food sales, or in kind, with rurally retained food). But is the procedure admissible? What of those italicised dichotomies: between output and well-being, the average and the typical, workers and individuals, agriculture-nonagriculture and rural-urban?

Output and well-being

What an average worker produces, times the price it will fetch, equals the current value of goods that can be bought with his product. Hence the disparity properly measures the ratio of purchasing power per head outside agriculture, to purchasing power per head inside agriculture (leaving aside intersectoral differences in income taxes, income subsidies, and price levels). Of course the worker does not get the full product of his labour in either sector — some goes to owners of capital and land, who may or may not be the same people as the workers. But the disparity correctly measures the ratio between *potential* welfare created by outputs outside and inside agriculture, and as such is comparable over time and between nations. By using prevailing prices to measure the disparity in each case, we ensure that a disparity of 3.1, for instance, means that an average income outside agriculture will buy 3.1 times as much of any bundle of products that can be bought with an average agricultural income at that particular place and time.[28]

The output disparity may well overstate the ratio of urban to rural welfare slightly. Welfare is not increased only by income, but also by leisure. Leisure per person is probably on balance less inside than outside agriculture in most LDCs (due to the greater time involved in preparing water and fetching food, and to the greater incidence of infant and thus of child care); but the gap is small and certainly far below the ratios indicated by the disparity. The ratio of urban to rural leisure time may be 1.1 or 1.2 to 1; the output per person disparity between 'non-agriculture' and agriculture (table 5.4) is typically 3 or 4 to 1. Hence the disparity probably overstates the *ratio* of 'potential welfare' between sectors,[29] since leisure per person is less unequal between sectors than potential purchasing power per person. However, intersectoral inequality in this latter (and in 'underemployed' LDCs much more important) component of the potential welfare gap is correctly measured by the output disparity.

Average and typical

Unless income is equally distributed in a sector, the typical or 'median' person (or worker) in that sector—the man in the middle, with as many people better off as worse off—will receive less than the average income per person (or per worker).[30] The more serious is inequality within a sector, the greater is this shortfall. Now intra-urban inequality usually exceeds intra-rural inequality (p. 167). Therefore income per worker overstates the typical worker's income more outside agriculture than inside. Hence the disparity somewhat overstates the non-farm sector's advantage in actual well-being, though not of course in *potential* well-being from equal distribution of each sector's output. The other side of the coin is that, by distributing its benefits more evenly, agriculture produces more actual welfare from a given value of output than non-agriculture.

Workers[31] and individuals

The measurement here of the disparity between sectors per worker, instead of per person, is to permit its use later as an indicator of the comparative efficiency of labour in the two sectors. But it would invalidate the disparity as an indicator of comparative welfare if the ratio of workers to persons were very different in the two sectors. Fortunately that is not so. The rural sector, with its higher child mortality rates and the selective emigration of persons aged fifteen to thirty-five, does have a larger proportion of small children; on the other hand, young persons enter the labour force sooner in rural areas, both because education is scarcer there (chapter 11) and because part-time work is commoner — helping with the harvest in school vacations, for instance. Rural women are more often pregnant, but on the other hand are more likely when in good health to work, especially on the family farm. On balance the proportion of workers in agriculture is in most LDCs *very* slightly above the proportion of population dependent on agriculture.[32] Hence the disparity gives a fairly good indicator of the welfare advantage of non-agriculturists over agriculturists.

Agriculture-nonagriculture and rural-urban

The sustainable well-being of the rural sector in LDCs depends largely on the value of farm output (p. 154). However, some rural people do not farm and some urban people do — in both cases, typically 8 to 15 per cent in most LDCs. Urban agriculturists are somewhat poorer than most urban persons; indeed many, perhaps most, are engulfed villagers, around whom the town has expanded without much changing their rural life-styles (perhaps this is one reason for taking the non-agriculture-agriculture disparity as the best indicator of the *real* urban-rural gap). Conversely, rural non-agriculturists are somewhat richer than most rural persons (similarly being often urban in all but residence — sometimes even commuters). Hence the disparity in most poor countries probably overstates the urban-rural welfare gap, in this respect also, in letter but not in spirit.

Output measures

All in all, the disparity emerges pretty well as a welfare-gap indicator, albeit — as we should expect from its large excess over the earnings, expenditure and income gaps — something of an overstatement. The overstatements, however, are not systematically greater for particular continents or epochs. Certainly they do not explain away the dramatic evidence of tables 5.4 and 5.5: the far greater disparity in LDCs 'now' than in NRCs 'then', the outstanding position of Africa even among today's high disparities, and the clear tendency for the latter to increase in both Asia and South and Central America. However, output disparities are no more accurate than the output data underlying them. Agricultural output estimation has been improving with the introduction of crop-cutting sample surveys; since the traditional method of accepting village headmen's reports led to about 10 per cent underestimation of output, the gradual transition to the new method of estimation in several LDCs tends to overstate growth of agricultural output per person and hence to understate growth (or overstate shrinkage) in the disparity. Thus the use of the disparity is most unlikely to artificially strengthen our case — that current LDC disparities are historically unprecedented, growing, and inefficiently and inequitably large. If agricultural output is somewhat understated where official estimates fail to 'catch' all subsistence production, the same applies even more forcibly to output of traditional craft services, a big sector in many LDCs — and it applied, also, in the historical cases with which we want to compare current disparities. And the estimates of *changes* in disparities are, by the same token, if anything nowadays biased *against* recording increases even where they exist.

There are two more issues of output measurement. First, most output information is for domestic product, not national product.[33] That is, it includes all output produced 'domestically' within a country (even if it accrues not to 'nationals' but to foreign suppliers of capital, skills, enterprise and labour). This is useful in comparing the productivity of labour or capital as between agriculture and the rest of the economy, but misleading in assessing the intersectoral welfare gap — unless (1) the foreign share in domestic product is small, or (2) foreigners receive similar shares of the value of output in agriculture and non-agriculture. Where foreign involvement is more pronounced in agriculture than in industry — as in economies where plantations are very significant, such as Sri Lanka (Ceylon) and Barbados — the intersectoral disparity understates the true welfare gap, because a larger share in the value of the agricultural output than in that of other output leaks abroad. In economies with a major foreign presence concentrated outside agriculture, notably such mineral economies as Saudi Arabia and Zambia, the disparity overstates the welfare gap, because much more of the income generated by output flows abroad — as profits — from Arabian oil or Zambian copper, than from either country's farm output. Fortunately such distortions are surprisingly small (even for Venezuela, 'only' 7 to 8 per cent of domestic output in the 1960s flowed abroad as returns to foreign capital) and for many LDCs are negligible.[34]

The second issue arises out of price distortions. The disparity, in measuring outputs at market prices, correctly measures the ratio between sectoral workers' potential welfare. But it is tempting to use it as an *efficiency* measure — to say that, if output per worker is three times higher outside agriculture than inside, agriculture uses labour three times less efficiently. We shall indeed want to say things like that, and to make the opposite comparisons for output per unit of capital, where agriculture is more 'efficient'. However, in comparing the social efficiency with which sectors transform any input into output, we should measure both, not at market prices, but at prices reflecting the true value of each type of output to the economy. The value of farm output is artificially lowered relative to the value of non-farm output by various forms of private or public power to manipulate prices or markets (chapter 13). Therefore (1) the welfare gap (the disparity) owes some of its size to the exercise of such power; (2) the relative efficiency of the non-farm sector in labour use — in producing higher values of output than the farm sector per person and per worker — is smaller than the disparity, because 'real' output in the non-farm sector is worth less (and in the farm sector more) than market prices indicate; (3) for the same reason, the relative efficiency of the farm sector in capital use — in producing higher values of output per unit of capital than the non-farm sector — is more than would be indicated by comparing such outputs at market prices. To this crucial issue we revert on pp. 177-9 and 187-8.

THE OUTPUT DISPARITY: RESULTS

Table 5.4 shows domestic output per person outside agriculture, as a multiple of that in agriculture, around 1970 in sixty-three LDCs: twenty in Asia, twenty-four in Africa and nineteen in Latin America and the Caribbean. It also shows the disparity for the nine NRCs for which calculations can be made for a comparable stage in their development.

The contrast between the historical and the recent situation is stark. Six of the nine NRCs showed smaller disparities than sixty-two of the sixty-three LDCs, and *less than half* the disparities prevailing in forty-seven of the sixty-three LDCs (including all but two of the African ones). All these forty-seven LDCs showed a greater disparity than any recorded in any NRC at a comparable stage.

What of the trends in the disparity? Of the nine NRCs, only three showed disparities higher than 2.6, and all brought them down quite sharply in early development (Norway from 3.43 around 1865 to 2.06 around 1910, Japan from 2.73 around 1880 to 2.57 around 1904, and Sweden from 2.66 in 1863 to 1.98 around 1903).[35] The other six NRCs, all starting with disparities below 1.75, raised them in early development, usually gently (only

Germany (2.57) and the Netherlands (2.17) surpassing 2 in the first forty years after the acceleration of growth).

At the extremes, a similar convergence can be seen for LDCs during the 1960s. Of the sixty-four for which comparisons are possible (table 5.5), thirty-four showed a rising disparity and thirty a falling disparity, but of those with low rural-urban inequality (disparity below 2.5) the trend was up for seven and down for two, whereas the LDCs with enormous disparities (above 7.5) showed uptrends in four and downtrends in eleven.[36] Hence the countries that accelerated their growth in the nineteenth century converged upon a disparity of 1.5 to 2.5; among the much larger group of countries accelerating their development since 1945, a similar convergence seems clear for those with exceptionally large or small disparities, but towards an alarmingly higher level of 2.5 to 7.5. The implications of analogy should not be taken too literally, but alarm must nevertheless be sharpened by Kuznets's finding for NRCs that, between the period of acceleration and 'the recent decade or two . . . the [disparity] did not decline . . . and in many countries [it] tended to [increase]'.[37] Poor countries may be stuck for a long time with the high disparities of 2.5 to 7.5 upon which they are now converging, unless dramatic changes occur in the power balances that underlie urban bias.

For the majority of LDCs with disparities already in the range 2.5 to 7.5, the disparity shows no particular trend towards a middle point. Indeed, of the seven LDCs between 5.8 and 7.5 in 1970 (immediately below the group with enormous but, on balance, shrinking disparities, above 7.5), five showed disparities increasing since 1960; and all five LDCs with 1970 disparities between 2.5 and 3.0 showed declining figures over the 1960s. It is safe to conclude only that the disparity in LDCs is tending towards 2.5 to 7.5, with no clear tendency once it reaches this range. This is two to three times the 1.5 to 2.5 range towards which NRCs tended during early development. Hence the figures underscore the conclusion reached during the brief comparison of class and institutional structures in chapter 1: the pressures of rural-urban inequality are much stronger and more durable in today's 'developing' countries than in yesterday's.[38]

6 The disparity: explanations, evaluations, significance

WHY DISPARITIES DIFFER

Why is the disparity in LDCs today so much greater than in NRCs yesterday? Chapter 3 rejected some sorts of general explanation of persistent inequality in growing LDCs; capitalism or socialism, openness or closedness to foreign influence, and population pressure. Do tables 5.4 and 5.5 suggest that, far from replacing these with another general explanation ('urban bias'), one should reject general explanations altogether, in favour of explaining different levels of the discrepancy by the distinct characteristics of particular small sub-groups of countries? In other words, are variations among LDCs in the disparity more significant than variations between LDCs as a whole and the past of NRCs as a whole?

Special explanations: products

At extremes, this is possible. The four LDCs in table 5.4 with monster disparities above 23 in 1970 (no other LDC exceeded 14.3) all featured small, largely foreign-owned enclaves producing oil or copper; several other LDCs high in their continental rankings (Iraq; Chile; Bolivia, with tin; and Liberia, with rubber) were to a lesser extent in this category also. Such economies feature very high capital per man, and hence output per man, in a small modern mineral sector with little prospect of higher levels of employment and little concern for them by businessmen or organised workers within that sector. A second, somewhat factitious, category comprises LDCs where statistical issues have affected the disparity: the much higher disparities revealed by table 4 for Africa owe something to its more recent statistical machinery, and hence to its greater tendency to omit some subsistence farm output. Again (p. 157), several of the very low disparities are understated by *domestic*-product figures, owing to the presence of foreign-owned plantations.[1]

Special explanations: places

Such special explanations, however, cover only a few of the countries in table 5.4 and create as many mysteries as they solve. For example, why has Iran, still to some extent an enclave mineral economy, a low disparity; or Kenya, where foreign-run plantations remain important, a high one? No more illuminating are sub-continental explanations. Africa's specially high disparities (twelve of the thirteen LDCs over 8.0 are African) are outstanding, as is the great similarity between the Asian and Caribbean-plus-Latin-American data. However, it is hard to know what to make of this, since Africa's levels of living are between Asia's and South America's.

Greater poverty?

That in turn suggests that, when we do seek a general explanation for the excess of today's disparities in LDCs over yesterday's in NRCs, we should remember that the former are almost certainly poorer.[2] Perhaps poverty itself widens the disparity? Statically there is much truth in this: the poverty of a society, in several ways, prevents people from moving away from its areas of extreme poverty, rural or other (chapter 9). But one could not predict an LDC's disparity just from its income per head, as Kuznets has shown. Although in 1958 his 'richer' countries showed smaller disparities, his historical series show that until the Second World War 'in the majority of developed countries the long-term trend in the [disparity] was upward',[3] and table 5.5 suggests that this is on balance true for LDCs also. A snapshot of the world, at a particular date, shows a bigger disparity in poorer countries; but a film of each particular country does not show that they reduced the disparity as they got richer.

The existence of NRCs?

Can we explain the disparity not by levels of income, but by the histories of income growth? One might enquire whether today's greater disparities were forced upon LDCs by the need to attain 'development in a divided world'. The existence of developed countries, absorbing the lion's share of world income and power, indeed renders the policy options open to today's LDCs structurally different from those that faced NRCs in the nineteenth century.[4] It is not clear, however, why this should lead today's LDCs to seek instant industrialisation, especially by methods as inefficient as the widening of the disparity will be shown to be. Rather the industrial 'head start' of the NRCs might lead LDCs to seek *initial* enrichment by the less difficult path of developing a prosperous agriculture.

NRCs and non-farm growth

Perhaps the earlier development of the NRCs has widened the LDCs' disparities, not by restricting choice, but by creating new *non-farm* opportunities and inducing imitation in LDCs? Professor Dore has suggested[5] the following ingenious stylised explanation. Non-agriculture comprises mainly manufacturing and services.

The sources of recent growth in manufacturing, available to LDCs, have involved major increases in capital per worker; in agriculture, new paths to growth (water-control, fertilisers) have instead increased labour requirements; hence agriculture has tended to raise output per capital unit, while manufacturing has tended to raise output per worker, thus increasing the disparity. As for services—the proposed explanation continues—they too have contributed to the disparity, though artificially: service 'output' is often measured by wage levels, which have been pushed up by colonial practice, by labour mobility to rich countries, and by global practices and expectations of labour organisations.

There is much truth in this. Yet in effect, it pushes the search for an explanation of the LDC-NRC gaps in table 5.4 one stage back. If manufacturing offered new techniques so badly suited to the initial circumstances of poor countries—ample idle labour, scarce savings and capital—why has it been chosen for the initial thrust of development? Why not transfer agricultural techniques, suitably adapted, first—especially since in 'the West' they have increased in their efficiency even faster than those in manufacturing or services? What, in the LDCs' situation of labour glut, enables (some) urban service workers to pull up their relative rewards in this way? Why do not private and public employers, in both services and manufacturing, seek out techniques that employ many inexpensive workers and little costly capital, rather than few overpriced workers with much costly capital? The techniques of 1800 and 1900 and 1930 still exist: nobody forces automatic luggage-loaders upon any poor country; they are part of the disparity syndrome, not an external cause of it.

Catching up

But let us assume that today's LDCs see development as accelerated industrialisation. Their leaders might then justify high disparities with Gerschenkron's argument that 'late developers' (such as Germany, Italy and Russia in 1860-1910) are bound to lay special stress on three policies likely to increase the disparity by depriving agriculture of the consumer goods that its practitioners require. The three emphases are on output of producers' goods, downward pressure on consumption, and a coercive supply of capital to nascent industries; these are all seen by Gerschenkron as necessary, if late developers are to achieve the 'great spurt' needed to catch up with early developers.

It is not clear that this strategy was consistently adopted by nineteenth-century 'late developers', that when adopted it worked, or that it could work now. First, Gerschenkron's own superlative analysis of early Russian development shows that the agricultural reforms of 1861 were conceived by their authors as creating a stable and conservative agriculture and not at all as a 'prerequisite of industrialisation'; and that the tremendous industrial spurt of the 1890s aborted after 1900 because of 'the exhaustion of the taxpaying capacity of the peasantry'. Second, neither Germany nor Italy showed the huge disparities that one would expect if agriculture's role as milch cow were so crucial for latecomers to development; Norway and Sweden came closer, but contracted their disparities fairly soon in their development processes. Third, even if we reject these two indications that 'squeezing the peasant' by diverting resources towards import-substituting industrialisation (ISI) was either a minor or an abortive component of 'late development', Hirschman has argued powerfully that ISI is a much more artificial, less sturdy, and slower-growing plant in the 'late late' industrialisers of 1945-85 than in the merely 'late' industrialisers considered by Gerschenkron.[6] Fourth, 'catching up' is not obviously a sensible goal (improving welfare is), nor obviously attainable by a 'great spurt', nor obviously advanced by seeking such a 'spurt' in a sector that uses much of a nation's scarce capital and little of its half-employed labour.

Man/land ratios?
Lord Balogh, in discussion, attributed the historical divergences in table 5.4 largely to the fact that the man/land ratio, because it is much higher in LDCs than it was in NRCs, pushes farm incomes down and the disparity up. However, a rising man/land ratio of itself, compels each farm family (since it has less land per person) to retain a growing share of food output. That leaves less foot output to sell to the growing urban population. Why should farm incomes not be restored as the consequent shortages of farm products drive up their price?[7] And why should not income-generating resources of capital be attracted into agriculture by this process? Urban biases in private and public power, and hence in pricing and resource allocation, are needed to explain high disparities, even by means of high man/land ratios. Moreover, Africa, the Third World continent with the lowest man/land ratios, has the highest disparities of all (table 5.4).

WHY RURAL-URBAN DISPARITIES ARE SIGNIFICANTLY INEQUITABLE
Neither historical compulsions, then, nor the specific features of groups of LDCs, can account for today's huge and on balance

growing disparities. Before attributing them to the socio-political and ideological features of urban bias in LDCs, however, we need to establish a *prima facie* case that something is wrong with them.

A welfare gap between two groups in a society is inequitable — that is, contrary to justice — if it causes a society to impose burdens (or to distribute benefits) in a way that most or all reasoning members of that society, if they could free themselves from self-interest,[8] would consider both unfair and unfruitful. Some inequitable welfare gaps do not matter much, for one of four reasons. First, they may be swiftly corrected; for example, the victims of discrimination may be able at low cost to migrate until the discrimination stops. Second, they may arouse such anger among a sufficiently powerful group that, although another powerful group seeks to maintain them in its own interest, the resulting confrontation removes them and produces a net benefit to society in the process. Third, they may simply not arouse much anger, even in the presence of full information; it is not *significantly* inequitable to segregate lepers if (despite widespread knowledge of available methods of treatment and prognosis) general agreement on that policy has been freely arrived at, even among actual and potential lepers. Fourth, welfare gaps generated by inequalities may be unimportant, or incorrigible, or (as in the case of the unequal distribution of such welfare as is generated by the ability to waggle one's ears) both.

The first and the fourth possibilities can be ruled out in the case of inequitable welfare gaps generated by the disparity. It is not swiftly corrected by movements towards 'equilibrium' (table 5.5); and it is clearly important, whether or not urban bias is (as argued here) the main cause of inefficiency and inequity in LDCs. But what of the other two attempts to play down the welfare gap created by rural-urban disparities: the 'conservative' claim that the resulting inequity causes *little* anger, and the 'radical' claim that it causes *effective* anger that substantially reduces it? Unfortunately, experience suggests a much more usual third possibility: *frustrated* anger, undermining the rural will to 'develop', individually or collectively, by the knowledge that the village will bear most of the costs of development whereas the town will enjoy most of the benefits.

What determines whether a major inequity arouses much or little anger? Some random advantages, from betting wins to Nobel prizes, are widely accepted, either as 'matters of luck' where potential beneficiaries regard the prospect of success as fairly distributed even though not everyone can realise that prospect, or as 'fair reward' for application or skill. Other random advantages arouse little anger because the gainers brainwash or terrify the losers into accepting them; but an urban 'big stick' (or big loud-speaker) could hardly *justify* urban bias, and anyway could seldom cover its many severe manifestations, in many dispersed rural communities, sufficiently to defuse rural anger: we are, after all, talking of income gaps of at least 3 to 1, and of price distortions effectively seizing about one-quarter of total farm output (chapter 13, notes 54 and 100) imposed purely by accident of rural birth. To allocate wealth, status or power (or in general claims on resources) by accident of birth, moreover, has been increasingly rejected at the level of expressed belief since the late eighteenth century, providing potential opponents with a choice of ideologies: the Left has espoused equality, and the Right has increasingly responded by advocating 'equality of opportunity' rather than by defending inherited advantage; such advantage has been seen by Marxists and marginalists alike as an immobilising force, impeding desirable change and wastefully perpetuating functionless mono-poly power. Therefore, one would expect systems allocating power, wealth and status — and the resources generating them — mainly to a lucky, town-born minority to generate much rural anger.

Absent or muffled protest at major, inherited inequality should not, however, be interpreted automatically as absence of anger. Many people whose life-chances are substantially restricted by the accident of birth — French manual workers born in Algeria, Soviet dissidents, low-caste Indians, even South African blacks — often seem surprisingly reluctant to use even legal, let alone revolutionary, means to challenge the discriminations against them. There are several reasons for this *other than* lack of anger. First, relative deprivation makes people extremely averse to risk: if one stands low on the ladder of life, and in anger grasps for a much higher rung, falling may mean falling off. Second, the *professed* egalitarianism of the elite — the eighteenth-century tradition that makes leaders claim that there is a *carrière ouverte aux talents* in France, that there is no 'new class' of party functionaries in Eastern Europe, that untouchability is banned in India, even that in South Africa (in the repeated words of its Prime Minister) blacks are to be regarded as equal to whites — can create a mixture of deference and conditioning among the led; once they accept that life-chances are really equal as the elite claims, they would, by overt protest against their rank, merely be advertising their own inferiority or laziness. (There is little doubt that the rhetoric of 'top priority for agriculture' in poor countries plays a similar role of social ordering, of silencing anger: but to silence is not to dissolve.) Third, discrimination against a group or sector can itself lessen its ability to protest: the undereducated ignorance, mutual isolation and bargaining weakness of the rural poor[9] are partly caused by urban bias, and help to sustain it.

Induced to feign acceptance by fear or by deference, the French worker of Algerian origin or the Soviet dissident, the South African black or the Indian sweeper-casteman, is regularly outraged by the discrimination against him: and so are the rural people almost everywhere in the Third World. Systems that hold many people at high levels of suppressed anger, yet deter rebellion by increasing its psychological barriers or high risks or costs, may be stable but cannot be healthy. They cause ulcers, both private and social.

Hence the huge disparity, and the associated urban bias that it epitomises, cause important, inequitable loss of welfare. It might nevertheless so improve the allocation or amount of resources that tomorrow's poor gain more than today's poor lose. That hope has four sources. The first is the naive feeling that the losses of today's poor from disparities are balanced by the joys of rural life (pp. 130-2). The second is the view that high non-rural resource allocations are efficient even if unfair — a view considered in chapter 8. The third is the expectation that non-rural allocations, even if neither efficient nor fair, generate the capacity to save, to develop, and hence to benefit poor and rich later: this important and respectable strand of urban bias is discussed in chapter 10. The fourth, and the most directly relevant to the attempt to justify a high disparity despite its important current inequity, is the belief that the rural sector, because it is rigidly traditionalist or hierarchical or immobile, is likelier than the town to allocate such benefits as it does receive to the rich, and moreover to the uncreative and undeserving rich who will not use their gains in ways that benefit the poor. In other words, apparently inequitable urban-biased allocations, and high and rising disparities, are justified on the grounds that they do good to the poor, owing to the likely distribution *within* each sector of gains from any allocation *to* it.[10]

This 'argument from concealed equity' has three flaws. First, in most LDCs rural sectors are less internally unequal than urban sectors, and probably therefore distribute new benefits less unequally. Second, agriculture is especially likely, and urban industry and construction are especially unlikely, to use extra productive resources in ways employing many people per £1,000 of extra resources. Third, rural people tend to use extra incomes to buy, and hence to cause to be produced, goods using much effort and hence employing much labour; townspeople's extra income is likelier to be saved, or spent on imports or on goods produced mainly with machinery. For all three reasons, in most LDCs the indirect and secondary impact of expenditure upon poor people is better if that expenditure is rural.[11]

There are several reasons to expect the rural sector in LDCs to be more internally equal than the urban sector. First, in many LDCs, the disparity renders average rural income so low that the mere subsistence of the labour-force leaves little 'fat'; this reduces the surplus that can be extracted by the rich and powerful without weakening or even starving their workers, and eventually thereby impoverishing themselves. Second, the labour-intensive nature of most rural output tends to produce a less unequal distribution of income than the more capital-intensive production processes of the cities. Third, except perhaps in Latin America, capital and land are distributed much less unequally in the village than in the town.[12]

The evidence confirms this rather airy theorising. For the ten poor countries with available data, in seven the best-off 20 per cent of *rural* households get a smaller share in rural income than the best-off 20 per cent of *urban* households get in urban income; in two the share is the same; only in one are the rich 'more un-equal' in rural than in urban areas.[13] Hence a given amount of income looks likely to be more equally shared — and thus, especial-ly under conditions of great poverty and inequality, to bring more total benefit — in rural than in urban areas. If we add this to the facts that the rural areas are poorer, and that (chapter 8) each unit of investment generates not 'a given amount' but a greater amount of extra income inside agriculture than outside, the initial equity argument, against resource allocations producing and maintain-ing (let alone increasing) the disparity, seems formidable. But does the more equal distribution of *existing* rural income suggest that *extra* incomes, from extra resources, will also be distributed more equally in rural than in urban areas?

The power to command flows of extra income, within any sector, must be strongly influenced by the distribution of *initial* income. for several reasons. First, there is a tendency[14] for the social sys-tem of a village or a metropolis to generate institutions preserving its hierarchies and thus, to some extent, its income differentials. Second, past income confers present wealth and status and hence the power to affect future income. Third, past rewards roughly mirror the demand and scarcity of services provided by those receiving them, and these economic considerations are likely to operate on future rewards also. Hence the relatively 'egalitarian' rural sector will probably also distribute *extra* incomes less unequally among its members than the relatively 'inegalitarian' urban sector.

Even so, however, secondary benefits to the poor, from production or expenditure, might be greater if extra resources were initially concentrated in the city. This is, however, extremely unlikely. On the side of production, the activity of housebuilding is typical: plainly the building of rural mud-houses generates incomes mainly for poor labourers,[15] while urban housebuilding is far likelier to reward owners of brick-kilns, cement plants and tower cranes; more generally, a much bigger share of income paid for extra output goes to hired workers, or as 'imputed income' to members of the working family farm, in the country than in the city. On the side of consumption, the greater poverty of rural people induces them to spend; hence their spending generates a larger share of extra 'secondary' income on food, creating more incomes for rural people (and a bigger share of labour-income) than does the extra spending of townspeople, which is normally directed more towards imported and domestically produced durable consumer goods.

So the disparity between farm and non-farm incomes produces important, inequitable gaps between rural and urban welfare; there is little basis for either short-run or long-run efficiency arguments purporting to justify such inequities and the resource allocations generating them and socio-economic structures, uses of income, and forms of output are such that the *indirect* effects of allocating resources to the towns rather than the countryside are also inegalitarian. Since extra resources matter more to poor people than to rich ones—especially given the great poverty and inequality[16] of LDCs — all this means that any 'output inefficiency', associated with an excess urban share of investment or doctors or Cabinet time, is translated into a greater 'welfare inefficiency'. Not only are £100 of extra incomes generated with more resources than necessary, because they are created capital-intensively in the cities; that £100 would have generated more extra welfare in the poorer, and usually less unequal, rural areas.

A last-ditch defence of the disparity (typical of the 'we always knew this and it doesn't matter' response to unwelcome findings) is to argue that, while all the above arguments are valid, the disparity is not an important source of inequality in LDCs. The very fact that the disparity is much larger in LDCs now than it was in NRCs (table 5.4) casts doubts on this defence. Moreover, the disparity is demonstrably an arithmetically important component of overall inequality in most LDCs, and arguably a strategic obstacle to equalising policies in almost all.

It is not easy to see how the contribution of *rural-urban* inequality to *total* inequality in a country ought to be measured and separated from the contributions of *intra-rural* and *intra-urban* inequality. The attempts so far made seek a single statistic to summarise or encapsulate each of these four inequalities, and an algebraic relationship to 'decompose' total inequality into the three others, which are estimated as proportions of it. Thus Anand estimates that inequality between metropolitan towns and towns, and between both and rural areas, accounts for 13.7 per cent of the 'Theil index' of total inequality in Malaysia in 1970, while occupational differences in income—almost all due to the disparity between agricultural and non-agricultural incomes— account for as much as 32 per cent. Mangahas, working with a different inequality measure, the 'Gini coefficient', reaches lower contributions, about 10 per cent and about 14 per cent respectively, for the Philippines in 1965—the 14 per cent, again, mainly due to the disparity.[17]

These interesting pieces of applied statistics, however, while hinting that the disparity is fairly 'important' even if intrasectoral gaps are assumed to be independent of it, tell us little. First, inequality among millions of people cannot be reduced to a single measure without misleading and ambiguous simplifications. Second, rival measures give quite different results (yet another, the 'log-variance measure', makes Malaysian occupational differences account for only 22 per cent of overall inequality on Anand's data), and there are no grounds for preferring one measure to others. Above all, the measures fail to illuminate the key policy question: if assaults were made on inequality, comparable and plausible in respect of the political obstacles and risks involved, by redistributing income (1) within urban areas and/or among non-farm occupations, (2) within rural areas and/or among farm occupations, (3) between urban and rural areas and/or between non-farm and farm occupations, which would have most effect in reducing poverty? One way to define 'comparable and plausible assaults on inequality' is as follows. Let policy (1) be to reduce the incomes of the top 20 per cent of urban persons to the level of the next best-off 10 per cent, and so to redistribute the yield in the cities to maximise urban poverty reduction. Then a comparable policy (2) would be to reduce the income of the *same number* of rural persons as the urban persons who would suffer in (1)—the best-off rural slice (but less than 20 per cent of rural populations in most LDCs, because far more people live in rural areas than in towns, and 'the same number of people' is thus a smaller percentage of rural than of urban populations)—and so redistribute the yield as to maximise rural poverty reduction. A comparable policy (3) would be to mulct the top urban 20 per cent as in (1), but benefit the rural poor as in (2).

There are obvious *a priori* reasons why an attack on inequality such as (3) would do more to reduce poverty than politically comparable attacks on (1) or (2), or both. First, average income is higher in urban areas than in rural areas, so that—if intra-area distribution is similar—more is to be gained, for redistribution later, by reducing otherwise comparable income strata to the level of the 'next stratum down'; this favours (1) and (3) over (2). Second, there are more poor people to be helped in rural than in urban areas; this favours (2) and (3) over (1). Third, the very rich are further above the next-richest in urban areas than in rural areas; this again favours (1) and (3) over (2).

A crude comparison was tried for India in 1961-2, which provides the only sets of sufficiently detailed figures. To bring down the richest 20 per cent of urban *households,* containing some 16.3 million *people* or 27 per cent of the urban population, to the same level of income per head as the next richest 10 per cent of urban households would have raised at least Rs. 7,460 million for redistribution. About the same number of people (16.6 million) lived in the top 3 per cent of rural households; to bring them down to the same level of income as the next richest 10 per cent of rural households would have raised about Rs. 5,200 million. So there was clearly much more available, by measures preserving the ranking of social groups and causing hostility from similar numbers of persons, from the urban rich than from the rural rich.

Conversely, much more was required to remove rural poverty, even on a very modest definition of Rs. 200 per person per year as the 'poverty line', than to remove urban poverty. Some 40 per cent of urban households, containing 31.2 per cent of urban people, were below this level, and the average shortfall was Rs. 51 per year. At least 50 per cent of rural households, containing 44.5 per cent of rural people, were below the 'poverty line', though the average shortfall was smaller at Rs. 32 per year. Since the urban population (at 60.5 million) was barely one-sixth of the rural population, the elimination of urban poverty would not use up even the rather small sum that could be raised from the modest attack on *rural* concentrations of wealth considered here.[18]

Hence there is much greater urban average income, urban income-concentration, and relative rural need; and *from a policy viewpoint,* if intra-rural, intra-urban and rural-urban inequality are independent, the last component is plainly very big in an arithmetical sense (for in all these respects most LDCs are more extreme than India). However, a big component need not be a strategic component. Political will and power to reduce inequality, in face of powerful interests favouring it, must be scarce. Those with will and power must seek to use them in an efficient way — if possible — so as to make equalisation cumulative and self-sustaining. They will be concerned with the impact of a reduction in any one component of inequality on others. Thus, to argue on grounds of equity for concentrating the fight against inequality upon the disparity, we must do more than show that it is arithmetically important; for either the intra-urban or intra-rural gap might still be more strategic, more central in weakening the *other* components of inequality.

To start off with a reduction in intra-urban inequality — by redistributing income to people who use a bigger share of it to buy food — would probably raise food prices and thus improve the rural-urban terms of trade. That would somewhat reduce rural-urban inequality, but — by giving the greatest benefits, within the rural sector, to farmers with surpluses of food — would also raise intra-rural inequality. As for starting off with reductions in intra-rural inequality (especially by land reform), that would raise rural food consumption, lower rural dependence on the city, and thus probably improve the villager's terms of trade and cut back rural-urban inequality. Once again, however, the effect within the sector *not* initially 'equalised' may be unequalising, because the urban poor spend a larger part of their income on food than the urban rich, and hence lose more if food prices rise. Government measures against inequality within either sector seem likely to increase inequality in the other sector, although they may well reduce inequality between the sectors (and this proviso may be one reason why they so seldom happen).

Much more could be said about equalising methods within sectors,[19] but clearly they are double-edged in their impact on overall equality. On the other hand, there are at least five reasons why an initial assault on rural-urban inequality, aiming to reduce the disparities of table 4, is likely to be strategic in a campaign to shift the benefits of growth towards the poor as a whole.

First, the case for equalisation within the rural sector — and especially for land reform, the most-discussed and (despite frequent evasion) most serious of intra-rural equalising measures in many LDCs — is weakened by the size of the urban-rural gap. It is weakened in rhetoric, in that (for instance) the big farmers of the Punjab argue plausibly that emphasis on land redistribution is 'unfair' while the higher urban incomes remain so far above the higher rural incomes. It is weakened in reality, in that rural entrepreneurs, if damaged by purely intra-rural equalising measures, will forsake the villages for the towns if the latter remain much more prosperous; politically plausible intra-urban equalisation could reduce this exodus, but not much, given the high initial levels of the urban-rural gap and of intra-urban inequality.

Second, income redistribution from the city would necessarily be at the expense mainly of the urban rich. The urban poor simply have too little to be squeezed much. They would probably lose something at first, because redistribution from the urban rich to the rural poor would raise the demand for food, and hence its price; but this damage to the urban poor could be offset by the close rural ties of those among them who are recent migrants (chapter 9), and should anyway be temporary, because a pro-rural policy both enables and encourages villagers to raise food output, thus bringing food prices down again.

Third—a related issue—insofar as the poorest 'townsmen' are really fringe villagers, better rural prospects (or dearer food) will pull them back to the village.[20] This reduces inequality in the towns, as its victims leave for new rural opportunities.

Fourth, rural-urban inequality is in several ways the *fons et origo* of inequality within each sector. The 'urban alliance' — uniting big farmers subsidised to supply cheap food, the urban labour aristocracy, and urban employers — tends to stabilise inequality within each sector. The great poverty of the countryside offers a grim alternative to the urban 'reserve-army' of half-employed, and thus lowers its earnings and bargaining power; all this helps to maintain urban inequality. The growing tendency of rural landlords and moneylenders to transfer to *urban* investments their savings from *rural* exploitation — because it stops the recirculation of such property income to the rural poor (chapter 4, note 81) — must worsen rural inequality.

Fifth and foremost, why are we worried about inequality, and why do we see excess of it as contrary to equity — as iniquitous? To a small extent, because it hardens the hearts of the rich, splits society, increases envy; but overwhelmingly, especially in very poor and very unequal societies, because it adds socially remediable scarcities to the already desperate hardships of the poorest: in particular, because it makes the poorest people hungry, so hungry that they die from otherwise trivial illnesses, lack energy to develop their capacities, possibly see their children suffer irreversible mental retardation from early protein-calorie malnutrition, and above all feel *chronically miserable*. Reducing the disparity means putting a higher proportion of public resources into agriculture, and correcting price incentives so that a higher proportion of private resources goes there too. This means more food, at first at slightly higher prices; eventually, cheaper food (achieved not by artificially depressed prices but by much higher supply); and, both now and later, less hunger. Since hunger is the main difference between the rich and the poor in LDCs, and is likely to be reduced by the output consequences of measures to cut the disparity, such measures attack the worst aspect of overall inequality, and reduce inequality within as well as between sectors.[21]

THE INEFFICIENCY OF INEQUITY

Large disparities are probably inequitable, and (chapter 8) correspond to inefficient resource allocations. But there is an intermediate point: are large and growing disparities of themselves inefficient? There are at least four senses in which they are: psychological, allocative, selective and arithmetical.[22]

Psychologically, a new nation-state in particular will probably find it hard to mobilise mass support for the sacrifices of current consumption needed for development, if its 50 to 90 per cent of countryfolk feel that, though much poorer initially, they are sharing more fully in the costs of growth than in its benefits. We lack scientific knowledge of rural mass psychology, and, though this effect may become increasingly important as rural literacy and communications improve, no more will be said of it here. The allocative aspect is dealt with in chapter 11. Selective inefficiency is revealed whenever a bright rural child is compelled, by the relative poverty of his or her family, to forego an educational opportunity that is snapped up by the less bright child of a less poor urban family.

This section points to a surprising consequence of kindergarten arithmetic. If poor (rural) people have been receiving much less of the benefits of growth than have rich (urban) people, it is possible for quite a long time — if the overall rate of growth remains the same — to redistribute its benefits so that (1) the rich townsmen suffer a barely perceptible fall in the rate of increase of income to which they have become accustomed, yet (2) the poor countryfolk enjoy a clearly perceptible, indeed dramatic, rise in the rate of increase of their income.

Table 6.1 is for an imaginary, but realistic,[23] LDC with ten million people each in urban and rural areas in 1974, both increasing at 3 per cent yearly. Urban income per person in 1974 is $300, rural income per person $100, and national income per person therefore $200. For several years, urban income per person has been growing at 2½ per cent yearly and rural income per person at ½ per cent, currently giving an increase in national income per person of 2 per cent.[24] Now, provided total income grows fast enough each year to support 3 per cent more people and 2 per cent extra income per head (that is, can sustain the recent rate of (103 x 102) − 100, or 5.06 per cent, per year), that extra 2 per cent per person could in principle be henceforth distributed equally between the urban, richer half and the rural, poorer half. But then the richer half would suffer a barely perceptible decline in the growth of income per person, from 2½ per cent to 2 per cent yearly; while the poorer half would enjoy a rise from ½ per cent to 2 per cent — much more clearly perceptible (certainly after five years).

Table 6.1 illustrates the effect. To divide a given amount of extra output and real income as indicated in option A — continuing the trend — is to deny the rural poor a clearly perceptible gain, in order to protect the urban rich from a barely perceptible loss. It seems fair to label this 'the welfare-inefficiency of increasing inequity' — even if output is unaffected, the poor are deprived of much welfare while the rich gain little.

There are further quasi-arithmetical reasons why urban bias wastes potential welfare associated with a given output level (quite apart from the output inefficiencies). First, the greater costs of servicing urban outlays — especially owing to congestion, city transport and food movement — erode even the small urban benefit associated with option A. Second, this effect will be sharpened insofar as townward migration is greater under option A than under option B. Third (and quite distinct from the greater perceptibility of 1.5 per cent more than of 0.5 per cent less) the usefulness of an extra absolute sum of $1.5 per person per year is greater for the poor man with $100 than for the richer man with $300, since the latter has already been able to go further down the spectrum of diminishing urgency in satisfying his needs.[25]

DO THESE LARGE DISPARITIES EXIST AT THE MARGIN AND REDUCE TOTAL PRODUCTION?

For labour resources to be used efficiently, any change in the way they are used must entail loss of output. Hence the difference made to output by transferring one worker away from any job — the marginal product of labour (MPL) — should be roughly the same in all jobs, and in particular in agricultural and non-agricultural uses. Table 5.4 demonstrates very large disparities only between *average* products of labour — output per person (and per worker). Do these suggest major inefficiencies — losses of total output — in the sense of big intersectoral gaps between MPLs? Are there too many workers in agriculture (or too few productive agents in their support) so that their marginal product falls below that of workers elsewhere in the economy?

We need to distinguish two concepts. 'Marginal product of labour' (MPL) — the change in output when labour increases by one unit and nothing else happens — is hard to measure for big sectors like 'agriculture' or 'non-agriculture', and hence hard to compare between these sectors. 'Extra product associated, on average, with extra labour' (PAEL) — the extra output in a sector, per extra worker joining it, between two points of time — is not quite what we want; but at least relevant measures can be constructed for some LDCs (table 6.2). This construction is of limited value: it can be carried out only for LDCs with reliable and comparable estimates, at least six or seven years apart, of agricultural and total workforce and output; it makes sense only if both output and workforce have risen, both inside and outside agriculture; and comparisons of extra 'real' output per extra worker depend heavily on the relative prices of the base year, in 'constant' prices of which real output must be measured. Nevertheless, for what it is worth, in the LDCs for which comparison is possible 'non-agriculture' has usually achieved a higher PAEL than has agriculture. The historically huge disparities of table 5.4 support this suggestion, for there seems little reason to expect the PAEL in agriculture to fall much further below the average product of labour than in other sectors. Moreover, the disparities have not in general declined (table 5.5) as they would if the intersectoral ratio between PAELs were much smaller than the disparity and were thus pulling it down. And the high and rising earnings ratios (tables 5.2 and 5.3) suggest that the ratio between PAELs in agriculture and non-agriculture was also large.[26]

If the ratios between MPLs were as high as the ratios between PAELs in table 6.2, we could infer that most LDCs should substantially reduce the proportions of their workers in agriculture, and/or increase the proportions of capital, skills and research supporting agriculture. In fact the MPL ratios are not as high as the PAEL ratios. A PAEL ratio of 2.6 to 1 — the unweighted average of the ten countries in table 6.2 — between non-agriculture and agriculture might reflect, say, an MPL ratio of 2 to 1; if such figures are about right, the shortfall of MPL ratios behind PAEL ratios will not invalidate the inference that agriculture has too much labour and/or too little of all other resources.

Any sector's PAEL, especially during growth, tends to exceed its MPL. The PAEL is boosted over time by all sorts of dynamic factors — extra equipment, skills, and hence techniques — that need not increase the MPL. Probably, since 1945, these effects in LDCs have operated more strongly outside agriculture than inside. So the high PAEL ratios in most countries in table 6.2 overstate the ratios between MPLs, and hence the case for labour transfers off the land. Because more capital, skills and research have backed the typical new worker outside agriculture, a smaller part of the extra product associated with him has been, properly speaking, caused by him than in the case of a typical new worker inside agriculture.

However, this effect is probably smaller than it seems, for three reasons. First, much of the extra capital that supports workers on the land has cost the economy less than its valuations suggest, notably because it comprises drainage and irrigation works built or maintained by family farmers in the slack season when there is little else for them to do; thus the real worth of a unit of capital, and hence its impact in boosting the PAEL above the MPL, while more outside agriculture than inside, is not as much more as a comparison of *outlays* on capital might suggest. Second, the recent agricultural 'innovation explosion' culminating in the 'green revolution' has dramatically increased agriculture's capacity to link major technical change with small inputs of durable equipment; this has again raised its MPL relative to its PAEL. Third, even outside agriculture, long-run profitability steers the innovator, in a capital-poor country, towards techniques requiring extra labour rather than extra capital;[27] innovators may well tend to select new techniques such that most of the extra product, associated with an expanding workforce, requires little else than those extra workers, so that the MPL is almost as great as the PAEL. These three effects mean, probably, a rather small shortfall of the ratio between non-agricultural and agricultural MPLs behind the PAEL ratios of table 6.2; some shortfall probably remains,[28] but probably too small — given the typically high PAEL ratios — to bring down the MPL ratios anywhere near to unity.

One further factor — more easy to measure this time — has made the *apparent* PAEL and MPL ratios diverge from the *true* ratios in most LDCs. This is the existence of government actions to influence relative prices of farm and non-farm products. Such actions obviously affect the average-product disparities of table 5.4 as well. They also mean that intersectoral gaps between the returns to capital — considered in later chapters — need adjusting, to allow for the 'true' value of those returns in each sector. Hence, before passing to the issue of capital use, we must see what happens when prices are adjusted.

Government price manipulation in most LDCs brings farm prices down and non-farm prices up. Thus farm output is worth more than it seems to be at manipulated prices, and non-farm output less. As *productivity* measures, the data in table 5.4 and the PAEL ratios of table 6.2 need scaling down; and the inefficiencies of labour allocation, implied by MPL gaps, reduce total product *less* than measurement at market prices would suggest. Conversely, though, average and marginal products of capital are much higher inside agriculture than outside it (chapters 7 and 8) and correcting for price manipulation will scale these gaps *up*. Because farm output is worth more and non-farm output less than the manipulated prices suggest, the allocation to non-farm production of excessive capital means *more* lost output than measurement at such prices suggests. Since it is capital, skills and training that are scarce in LDCs, it matters greatly that their contribution to output is cut back, even more than market-pricing would suggest, by their over-urbanisation.

Since unskilled labourers are relatively plentiful, it matters less that (especially at 'correct' price of output) their average output is cut by their under-urbanisation. On balance, therefore, correcting for mispricing (as in the following section) increases the estimate of damage due to urban-biased resource allocation.

This conclusion is strengthened by two facts. First, farm output is undervalued not only because of selective intervention in favour of (and greater monopoly power within) the non-farm sector, but also by the great inequality of most LDCs. Since it is poor people who spend most of their incomes on food, this inequality reduces demand for farm products (relative to others) and hence cuts their prices compared to the valuation placed on them in a less unequal society. Second, not only are the outputs of the non-farm sector worth less than market prices indicate; its capital inputs are worth more than market prices indicate (pp. 303-4). Hence its average and marginal output per unit of capital, with both output and capital properly valued, is doubly reduced, both absolutely and relative to the output per unit of capital (average and marginal) in the farm sector.

EFFECTS OF MEASUREMENT AT 'CORRECT' RELATIVE PRICES

Though uncorrected (market-price) comparisons of the disparity indicate the relative command over economic *welfare* enjoyed by average members of sectors of the economy (pp. 154-6), comparisons in prices 'correctly' valuing outputs are needed to assess the relative *efficiency* of the sectors in producing outputs from any input, such as labourers or acres. Endless arguments are possible about what 'correct' prices may be. For tradeable goods, however, it seems reasonable to assess true value as what the producing country would pay if importing them, or receive if exporting them. This creates problems if the country looms so large (in a commodity market) that it would alter the price if it substantially changed the volume it traded, as with India's tea exports or wheat imports; or if prices fluctuate so severely that reasonable expectations of import or export prices are hard to establish. Nevertheless, such problems can be minimised by sensible assumptions about the impact of alternative decisions on prices, and by selection of reasonably typical years to establish 'normal' relative output prices. Two recent attempts at output revaluation do this, and both deal with the non-tradeables — services, including transport and communication, public administration and defence — by accepting the valuation given by relative market prices (though a superior, albeit more difficult, approach has been suggested). Table 6.3 shows their results, and the implications for ours.[29]

The corrections are fairly small, except for Brazil and Pakistan. These are big, diverse LDCs, and as such particularly tempted to autarkic measures, involving special protection for non-farm products. Hence non-farm output in these countries is boosted in price especially far above world levels; and the relative *efficiency* of non-farm activities in getting output from each extra worker is much less than it appears. Of course, from the standpoint of equity, the disparities are not reduced from column 3 to column 4 levels by the procedures of table 6.3; indeed one can argue that the social iniquity of the disparities is increased, insofar as they do not even correspond to the relative worth of sectoral outputs. The adjustments of table 6.3, even for big LDCs, do not therefore weaken the conclusions from table 5.4.

Moreover, any advantage that agriculture may reveal, in the efficiency with which capital is used, is increased by allowing for the underpricing of farm goods. Even at market prices, extra capital produces more in agriculture (table 8.2 and discussion); when agricultural output is appropriately upvalued, the advantage of agricultural investment, especially in big LDCs, becomes even more marked. This effect is sharpened if we allow for the fact that agricultural capital, with its substantial component of on-farm irrigation works, contains a lower proportion of imports than other capital. Hence not only does the special protection of non-agriculture make agricultural output worth *more* than it seems; the undervaluation of foreign currency by the official exchange rates of most LDCs also makes the share of agriculture in properly valued investment *less* than it seems. Both private market power outside agriculture, and public policy in support of that power, have ensured that in most LDCs agriculture gets proportions of capital astonishingly low by contrast to the NRCs in early development; this is inefficient; and it substantially accounts for the inequalities mapped in table 5.4.

7 Unbalanced shares in capital

THE ALLOCATION OF EXISTING CAPITAL STOCK: WHAT THE LABOUR-PRODUCTIVITY INEQUALITIES IMPLY

For most of the year, in most parts of most poor countries, labour is plentiful. Population growth is making extra labour even more plentiful. Hence the disparities in table 5.4, even if they do imply major gaps in MPL (marginal product of labour) (p. 175), might seem to do little damage to efficiency. Since there are plenty of workers half-idle, what does it matter if some of the time spent at work produces less than it might? Morality apart, such a view would be superficial; for the disparities imply large gaps, between agriculture and the rest of the economy, in the returns to factors supporting human effort; and these factors are indeed scarce. If these large gaps indicate inefficiencies, it is serious.

Suppose output is produced by human effort plus a composite input, 'everything else'. If part of the economy, say farming, produces a lower value of output per hour of human effort, that sector must enjoy smaller endowments of 'everything else' per pound's worth of output — that is, it must produce more output per 'unit' of 'everything else'. For if it needed more of labour *and* 'everything else', to produce one rupee's worth of farm output than to produce one rupee's worth of non-farm output, people will tend to reduce their farm activities in favour of production elsewhere in the economy.[1] Large disparities in labour productivity, with agriculture doing 'badly', correspond to large differences in the productivity of 'everything else', with agriculture doing 'well'. We have seen that the big disparities suggest that labour is not allocated efficiently, and that there is some direct evidence of this. Corresponding inefficiencies are likely to be indicated by big gaps between sectoral outputs per unit of inputs in support of labour.

Another side of the same coin is this. Labour produces little (per unit) in underdeveloped agriculture, because it is combined with little of 'everything else'. In the non-agricultural part of poor economies, a unit of labour produces more, because it is combined with more 'everything else'. This is true of extra labour as well as of average labour (tables 5.4 and 6.2). But it is 'everything else', not labour, that is scarce in almost all LDCs, which find it hard to save at home or to borrow on reasonable terms abroad, and hence to finance such non-consumption activities as dam-building, land reclamation, or the training of engineers.[2] Hence it is important to saturate 'everything else' with as much labour as possible. If output per worker is much higher in 'non-agriculture', the latter is getting more 'everything else' per worker. Hence 'everything else' is being less saturated with labour than in agriculture. This implies that a shift of 'everything else' resources into agriculture is desirable if (1) it is an *allocable* part of 'everything else' that is undersaturated, so that matters can in principle be changed; (2) there is some direct evidence that this allocable part is adding more to the general welfare (or to some indicator of it) inside agriculture than outside; (3) both (1) and (2) hold of extra and future units of that allocable part, not only of average units previously allocated.

ALLOCABLE AND NON-ALLOCABLE SUPPORT FOR EFFORT

Unimproved land is a very small part of the sources of non-farm production in most poor countries. Except at the margin of urban expansion, there is little scope, for the individual or for policy, to allocate land between agriculture and other uses.[3] Moreover, since agriculture uses overwhelmingly *more* land than other activities — both per worker and per unit of output — land endowment cannot account for the fact that agriculture produces so much *less* output per worker.[4] Similar arguments apply to unimproved natural resources used with land — river-water, sunlight, etc.

If land (and its associated natural resources) neither explain agriculture's lower labour productivity, nor can be substantially reallocated to or from agriculture to increase overall efficiency, that leaves only 'capital'. This source of output gives rise to great definitional arguments; and three senses in which 'capital' might explain the disparities of tables 5.4 and 6.2 — or be so reallocated as to reduce them — had better be ruled out at once.

By 'capital' (or 'investment', which means 'extra capital') we do not mean finance, but fixed equipment. Agriculture certainly suffers from natural and artificial derogations from its capacity to attract finance with which to buy such resources, but they are not our concern here. We are concerned with agriculture's capacity to turn real resources — effort, water, soil, horsepower — into output; and with the reasons why these capacities differ from non-agriculture's.

We shall try to exclude 'working capital': current inputs to production such as electricity and fertiliser, and stocks of inputs and of end-product. Plainly one cannot treat a producer's stocks of his own product, or of inputs, as if they were sources of production like workers or machines.[5] It is, however, often plausibly argued that human effort has lower productivity in agriculture than elsewhere because of agriculture's lower intake of current inputs of raw materials, which are properly a form of producer's capital; but this reasoning is dubious (although it would strengthen my argument if correct, since agriculture normally uses less working capital per unit of output than non-agricultural sectors, and since agriculture's shortage of inputs is due largely to deep biases in the allocation of knowledge, research and transport). First, 'labour-productivity' is net output per worker; 'net output' means gross output *minus the value of raw-material inputs*; and agriculture's low ratio of such inputs to gross output need not push *net* output per worker down. Certainly producers will not buy, say, electricity unless they expect it to raise net output—but not necessarily net output per worker, for many more workers may be needed to work with the electricity. Second—a linked point—agriculture has higher net output per unit of fixed capital than other sectors (table 7.1); if we blame low levels of current inputs for agriculture's low labour productivity, ought we to praise them for its high productivity of fixed capital? Third, it is agriculture's under-endowment with fixed capital that largely causes its shortage of current inputs—no irrigation facilities mean little controllable water and this in turn discourages the use of fertilisers.[6] Hence we concentrate on the allocation of fixed capital, yielding flows of services to producers.

It would be excellent to include, in the 'capital' available to any sector of the economy, 'human' as well as physical capital: to measure the costs to society of training the workers and organisers in each sector. Urban workers produce and earn more than others in LDCs partly because they are on average endowed with more, higher, and more relevant education.[7] However, to avoid statistical and conceptual complexities, 'capital' in chapters 7 and 8 excludes 'human capital'. This exclusion means that I understate the principal result of the chapters: that agriculture receives inequitably and inefficiently low endowments of allocable capital, both historically and at the margin. Since in most LDCs agriculture falls short of other parts of the economy in its endowment of trained persons by an even larger proportion than in its endowment of physical capital,[8] the gap between the sectors in capital endowment would have appeared even higher had I been able to include 'human capital'.

So far, we have explained why certain bits of 'everything else' —some non-labour inputs into production, whose sectoral allocations might account for the huge disadvantages of labour in agriculture — are omitted from the analysis of this chapter. We are left with 'physical capital' — machines, means of transport and traction, docks and roads, and structures ranging from dams and factories, through roads and schools, to dwellings. We shall show that net output, per unit of such capital, is in most LDCs much higher in agriculture than outside; that this is true also of extra net output per unit of extra capital; and that the objections to such measurements and comparisons, when analysed, strengthen the implied conclusion that in most LDCs both efficiency and equality would benefit if, instead of getting about 20 per cent of physical capital (and of investment in additions to it),[9] the 70 per cent or so of people engaged in agriculture were to enjoy 30 to 35 per cent of it at least.

First, it is necessary to examine two items normally included in 'capital': livestock and dwellings. Typically in LDCs, one-quarter to one-half of agricultural capital (but hardly any other capital) comprises livestock. Plainly, if output per unit of measured capital (or extra output per unit of investment) is larger in agriculture than elsewhere anyway, the excess if livestock are excluded from measured capital (or investment) is greater still. The case for such exclusion is that we are enquiring whether LDCs would do better to allocate to agriculture a larger share of capital-forming resources — savings and foreign borrowing. The volume and value of the livestock herd (unlike, say, the volume and value of roads) is not solely, and often not substantially, affected by such allocation-decisions. Livestock reproduce themselves; moreover, in most poor countries, they get the calories to do so largely from stubble, stalks of cereal crops, and grasses from non-arable land, all of which have few alternative uses.[10] Such livestock feeding has been encouraged as population pressure compels the diversion to crop production of more formal pastures. Certainly any outlays on veterinary training and buildings, on import of improved bullocks or semen[11] — and above all on pasturing and otherwise feeding heifers and pregnant cows — are properly counted as allocating resources to 'investment in livestock'. But most livestock 'investment' (and indeed most of the stock of livestock *capital*) has little to do with such allocative decisions. It stems much more from the sexual instincts of cattle than from the savings decisions of people. Much livestock belongs, not to agriculture's capital stock, but to its natural resources. Such beasts help raise farm output per worker and per unit of allocable capital; they do not constitute a significant burden on the nation's capacity to save and invest, and ought really to be excluded from any measurement of the extent to which that capacity is being direct-ed towards agriculture.[12] However, separate measurements of the share of measured capital or investment 'on the hoof' are not always available; moreover, the above argument is controversial. Hence, in table 7.1 and thereafter, estimates are presented, to the extent possible, of sectoral allocations and returns to 'capital' both with livestock and without.

Dwellings comprise another part of 'capital' with a somewhat problematic relation to output. I shall split output and physical capital (and extra output and 'investment') into agricultural and other, and contrast the average (and incremental) capital require-ments per unit of output in the two sectors. Is this fair, given that all dwellings (including those in which agriculturists live) are assigned to the non-farm sector, and that this 'non-productive' form of capital and investment artificially pushes up that sector's capital costs per unit of output? It is, in fact, quite fair. Dwellings are not 'non-productive' but yield an output of services, which are counted in national income figures, either as house rents or (in the case of owner-occupied premises) as imputed house rents. Such output is all assigned to the non-agricultural sector, so it is perfectly proper to assign thither the capital that yields these returns.[13] If a rural-urban (instead of an agriculture-'other') contrast of capital/output ratios were possible, dwellings would be assigned to geographical instead of economic sectors; this would boost the gaps between ratios above the figures in tables 7.1 and 8.2, since construction costs much less, per person housed, in rural than in urban areas.

SECTORAL DISTRIBUTION AND YIELDS OF CAPITAL

Four criticisms must be anticipated (some others are treated in detail later) before the data are presented. First, I compare 'agri-culture' and 'non-agriculture', despite the strictures on pp. 60-3. This is because it is not so much 'industry' as infrastructural costs in transport and building that are the chronic capital-wasters in most LDCs. An 'urban-rural', comparison (which would probably suggest even greater gaps in the endowment and efficiency of capital) is possible for very few countries, and abstracts from the fact that agriculture largely determines sustainable and circulat-ing rural incomes (p. 154). Planners, of course, must compare the performance of many sorts of 'capital' in many sectors—for example, in growing different rice varieties in different regions. However, for the purposes of this discussion, it is the crude, broad, rough contrast of agriculture and 'non-agriculture' that is most relevant.

Second, I look at sectoral requirements, per unit of output, of capital *installed*, whether or not it is 'used in production'. To do otherwise is to pretend that a sector, by wasting capital in idleness, commits either no crime, or at worst a temporary and self-correcting one, against efficiency.

Third, in assessing a sector's use of *extra* capital in a year, I include the investment used to make good depreciation. To do otherwise is to pretend that the burdens, placed by production in a sector upon the economy by wearing out capital, do not count in assessing efficiency of capital use.

Finally, capital and investment in agriculture mean capital placed there, even if its impact on output is in part elsewhere (pp. 204-5). A fertiliser plant yields output that raises farm production, but it is still non-farm capital. Cotton irrigation yields output that raises mill production, but it is still farm capital. The choice (let alone the compulsion) to buy fertilisers or cotton made at home, instead of competitive imports, represents at best a tiny benefit to a sector, and does not justify complicated statistical manipulations.

I concentrate on output per unit of capital that is physical, directly reproducible by human action, and allocable among sectors. *Existing* capital may seem not to fall into this category at all. A blast-furnace is of no use to a farm, nor an irrigation channel to a steel-mill. Yet these items embody *past* decisions, private and public, about how much saving (or import surplus, that is, foreign borrowing) was justified to increase capital stock, and about how the capital stock resulting from such a decision was to be allocated among sectors and projects.[14]

Table 7.1 shows the distribution and yield of directly reproducible, allocable capital (DRAC), inside and outside agriculture. For convenience, data for other concepts of capital (including livestock, and including both livestock and inventories) are also given.

Table 7.1 refutes a number of strange attempts to show that agriculture gets 'too much' DRAC, uses it 'inefficiently', etc. Thus in 1957 Ganz claimed that 'manufacturing [capital has] higher productivity [than agricultural] deriving from its advance in technology and longer life-span'.[15] First, technical progress (especially the sort that saves capital rather than labour and is hence best suited to LDCs) is not obviously faster outside agriculture, and farm capital is not obviously short-lived. Second, even if such characteristics were general, they would not necessarily raise the economic yield of non-farm capital at all—let alone push it above that of farm capital; more efficient capital usually costs more, as well as producing more. Third (and this is hinted at by tables 7.1 and 8.2), the performance of most non-farm capital (and investment) in poor countries has been bad since 1950; the performance of manufacturing investment in Latin America, since Ganz wrote, has been especially bad, despite massive and selective protection.[16] The fourth and central criticism of Ganz's judgement, however, is not based on wisdom after the event but on simple logic. Agriculture simply *must* show higher output per unit of DRAC; for if it needed more DRAC per unit of output (given that it also requires more land and more labour) no family would stay long in farming.

Might this argument fail? Might small farmers find the formation even of apparently low-yielding DRAC (for example, by putting up a simple toolshed to protect farm implements—not very efficiently—from weather damage) very cheap, since they could do it with otherwise idle family labour in the slack season? Admittedly, in such conditions, the real scarcity value of such farm DRAC, and hence the ratio of total farm DRAC to output, would be overstated by normal estimation procedures. The small farm does enjoy, in effect, cheap family labour for DRAC formation; and this indeed gives it a developmental advantage. Why, though, should such labour be allied with the formation of *farm* capital, unless the alliance is productively efficient? If farm DRAC can be cheaply formed by off-season family labour, so can DRAC in non-farm activities, including many crafts already often undertaken by small farmers part-time.[17] Hence the capacity of small farmers to form DRAC cheaply would not lead them to form it on the farms, if its yield per unit—as well as that of labour—were higher in manufacturing or other activities suitable for home production.[18]

Most of our picture of the performance of farm and non-farm capital must come from estimates of *extra* capital (investment), in relation to labour and output, as in table 8.2. Indeed, so few are the estimates of the *total* amount of DRAC, and in general of capital, by sectors in LDCs that we have included in table 7.1 some countries that are dubiously 'underdeveloped' in order to present a not-too-restricted range of findings.

As with labour (chapter 6) so with DRAC: all the sets of average ratios in table 7.1 point in the expected direction, not only for DRAC but even when livestock inventories are included (except in one case[19]). Workers in agriculture in LDCs have been supported, typically, by only 10 to 35 per cent as much DRAC in agriculture as elsewhere. This is in striking contrast to Japan's situation in 1881, at a comparable stage of early modern development to that of many LDCs in the 1950s; there, 'gross fixed capital stock, residential buildings excluded, was . . . 72.4 per cent [in the] primary sector', so that 'gross capital stock per gainful worker in the primary sector was . . . 62 per cent of that of the non-primary sector'.[20] Agriculture's capital starvation in LDCs means that its workers have produced less output-per-man than those in other sectors; but 'their' DRAC has been typically 1.6 to 6.8 times more productive. One cannot, of course, therefore be sure that *extra* capital has been, and is, supported by more extra labour and thus linked with more extra output in agriculture than elsewhere. Yet the average data do carry three hints about marginal performances.

First, the 'productivity ratios' in rows 18 to 20 of table 7.1 are large. Average DRAC seems to be linked with 1.6 to 6.8 times more output in agriculture than elsewhere. For this gap to be eliminated with respect to extra DRAC, the returns to it would have to fall much more rapidly, as its volume increased, in agriculture than in other activities. That returns should fall somewhat more rapidly is credible; but not so much more rapidly as to turn, say, a 'productivity ratio' of 3.4 to 1 (India 1950) for existing DRAC into a ratio of 1 to 1 for extra DRAC, as would be required for efficiency.

Second, where average data are available for more than one point of time, agricultural DRAC's 'productivity advantage' seems at least as pronounced for the later as for the earlier observation.[21] This could not be the case if DRAC, installed between the two observations, had shown a 'productivity advantage' in agriculture significantly smaller than the DRAC already installed at the time of the earlier observation. So extra DRAC, for the few countries with two sets of average data, appears to be associated with more output inside agriculture than outside, almost to the same extent as initial DRAC.

Third, both the above observations are strengthened by the fact that, in most of the 'table 7.1 countries', the impact of private monopoly and public power has substantially and increasingly made agricultural output cheaper relative to other output (and agricultural capital correspondingly dearer) than it would have been without those influences. For example, the 'DRAC productivity ratio' (row 8) for Argentina in 1955 was 1.94. If agricultural and non-agricultural output are revalued at world prices, agriculture's share in GNP rises from 17.1 per cent (row 6) to at least 25.4 per cent.[22] The higher 'true' value of farm output raises the 'true' row 8 entry — measuring agriculture's 'true' output per unit of DRAC as a multiple of that in other sectors — from 1.94 to

3.21. It would rise further if corresponding adjustment for the relative overpricing of farm capital were possible. Similar corrections would apply to other 'table 7.1' countries if data were available. If *average* 'productivity ratios' are even bigger at corrected prices than in row 8, they can scarcely be as low as 1 to 1 for *extra* capital, as efficiency would require. Moreover, if (as seems likely) agricultural capital was more severely overpriced, and agricultural output more severely underpriced, at market prices at the second period of observation than at the first period in Argentina and India, and if (as table 7.1 suggests) agriculture's advantage in output per unit of DRAC hardly contracted even at market prices, then its advantage at 'true' prices must have expanded. There is no evidence that extra DRAC suffered so much more seriously from 'diminishing returns' in agriculture than elsewhere as to wipe out the productivity advantages of *average* agricultural DRAC.

However, these findings are tentative, indirect, and based on dubious capital-stock data. To estimate whether LDCs have associated more output with farm investment than with non-farm investment, we must turn to direct estimates. Even these require great caution, and cannot on their own prove that agriculture was getting too little investment, but they can provide strong indications, especially because most of the investment data do not separate investment in DRAC from investment in assets that are, more or less, non-allocable between sectors (livestock, inventories). If agriculture shows substantially higher ratios of extra output to extra 'capital', despite the fact that the latter includes major components not allocable away from agriculture, then the inference is almost irresistible that agriculture's ratios of extra output to extra *DRAC* are so high as to be certainly, at least in part, signs of a causal sequence running from an inadequate share of agriculture in DRAC, via low yields on total DRAC, to wastefully low growth in total output. It is to the direct evidence relating extra capital to extra output that I now turn.

8 Capital efficiency

THE ALLOCATION OF EXTRA CAPITAL (INVESTMENT): THE QUOTIENT AND THE K-CRITERION

Table 8.1 shows that agriculture's share in investment has usually fallen far short of its share in output, let alone employment, in most less-developed countries with available data. This has been a matter partly of price policy and other influences on private investment, partly of public investment allocation – and partly of implementation, for the achieved shares of agriculture in investment have normally fallen short even of the planned shares.[1] Moreover, as shown below, the shortfalls would be greater measured at 'correct' prices. Since agriculture is poorer to begin with, starts with less capital per person, and can attribute much of its poverty to undercapitalisation, such allocations are not very just. But they may be efficient. Are poor rural workers sacrificing extra capital support in order that tomorrow's rural and urban residents may have more output to share?

Table 8.2 gathers the crude evidence regarding the efficiency of these apparently low allocations of capital to agriculture. In LDCs as a whole, an extra pound's worth of extra capital seems to be associated with about twice as much extra output in the agricultural sector as elsewhere in the economy. I hereafter call a sector's ratio of extra capital to extra output its k (short for incremental capital/output ratio); I call non-agriculture's k, divided by agriculture's k, the *quotient*; and I call the suggested efficiency-criterion, that sectoral k's should be about the same (so that the quotient should be close to 1), the *k-criterion*.

Table 8.2 understates the quotient, because it measures both capital installation costs and output – and hence the k's and the quotients – in constant prices of a base-year, which (while allowing for general inflation) accepts the relative valuations of products given by each country's prices in its base-year. However, such valuations understate the payments that would have to be made (or foregone) if farm output were reduced and had to be imported (or not exported); conversely, the valuations overstate the true value to the LDC of non-farm output. For example, in the Philippines, an extra peso's worth of output in 1960-5 appeared to require 3.6 times more investment outside agriculture as inside it (table 8.2). But table 6.3 showed that, for the Philippines, agricultural output was worth 1.12 times its market value on Balassa's

189

estimate for 1967 ($\frac{34 \cdot 9}{31 \cdot 0}$), or 1.11 times on Little's 1965 estimate ($\frac{35 \cdot 4}{31 \cdot 9}$). Conversely, non-farm output was worth 0.94 to 0.95 times its market value. Hence a unit of 'real extra output in the Philippines was associated with about $3.6 \times (\frac{1.11}{0.95})$, or 4.2, times as much extra capital outside agriculture as inside.[2]

Even these corrections understate the true quotient. They allow for the mispricing of output, but not of capital. A much larger proportion of non-farm than of farm capital is imported,[3] and imports are worth more than is indicated by the official exchange rate. The extent of such overvaluation in the Philippines was modest by LDC standards—in 1965 about 14.5 per cent—but, on the conservative assumption that the proportion of imports in agricultural capital was as high as 25 per cent, and in non-agricultural capital as low as 60 per cent, this further raises the ratio of the true value of capital associated with an extra unit of output outside agriculture, to that value in inside agriculture, from 4.2 to 4.4.[4]

Hence, in the Philippines around 1965, at market prices a unit of extra farm capital was linked to 3.6 times as much extra output as was extra non-farm capital. Correcting for undervaluation of farm output raises this ratio to just under 4.2, or by 16 per cent. Correcting for undervaluation of (imported) non-farm capital raises the ratio further, to 4.4, or by another 6 per cent of the original level of 3.6. Yet our correction was conservative: we used the lower of the two estimates of *product* mispricing cited in table 6.3, and deliberately underestimated intersectoral divergence in the use of imported *capital*. Moreover, the Philippines is a mild case, both of currency overvaluation and of farm-output undervaluation.[5]

The quotients in table 8.2 probably need to be raised, on average, by 20 to 30 per cent, to reflect true divergences in the extra output associated with extra capital as between non-farm and farm sectors in typical LDCs.[6] For the seventeen countries Szczepanik analyses for 1960-5, k was about 3.9 in non-agriculture and about 1.73 in agriculture, a quotient at market prices of 2.25. Raising this by 25 per cent to correct for mispricing, we come to 2.82.

Could LDCs have got 2.82 times as much real output from their non-farm investment, had it all gone to agriculture? Of course not; although most defences of inefficient investments as 'complementary' with efficient ones are weak (pp. 204-5), they contain an element of truth. The yield of agricultural investment would decline if *nothing* were done to add to, or even keep up, the nation's stock of fertiliser factories, power plants, rice mills or cotton looms. Statistical analysis, however, shows that—except for LDCs with enormous quotients, requiring special explanations — there was in 1960-5 some association between (1) the extent to which the sectoral pattern of investment followed that of output, and (2) the success of the LDC in getting the *extra* output per unit of non-farm and of farm investment close together, that is, a quotient close to 1. That seems to be achieved when agriculture gets a share in investment somewhat higher than (actually about 1.1 times as high as) it share in output, as against the 20 to 45 per cent actually achieved.[7] (For instance, in an LDC with 45 per cent of its output in agriculture, the typical share of investment in agriculture would have been half that—22 per cent or so; but the share required to equate sectoral k's would have been around 50 per cent.) If, however, farm output is generally worth more than it seems (and farm capital less), then to allow for that mispricing we need to aim at a market price quotient well below 1. A 'real' quotient of 1 (equating the 'properly valued' extra output associated with extra capital outside and inside agriculture) could well correspond to a quotient at market prices around 0.80. To achieve the latter in a typical LDC would have required an even higher share of investment in agriculture—a share, according to the statistical analysis based on tables 8.1 and 8.2, as high as 55 to 60 per cent if agriculture produced 45 per cent of output, both measured at market prices. Moreover, we must recall that tables 8.1, 8.2 and this analysis refer to *total* extra capital, including extra livestock and changes in inventories. The 'advantage' of agriculture, with respect to the sort of capital whose allocation between agriculture and 'non-agriculture' is at issue, would be larger if we could measure the quotients for extra directly reproducible, allocable capital (DRAC) alone.

But is a quotient of 1 a sensible criterion for allocating investible resources—savings plus imports-less-exports—between agriculture and other sectors? What needs to be equated among uses, for efficiency, is the true social return, to the last unit of each *sort* of capital employed, in each particular activity (pp. 100-1). From this almost unexceptionable 'marginal-social-product-of-capital criterion' to the k-criterion here proposed (a quotient of 1) seems a long way. However, if agriculture has received too little investment on the k-criterion, then it has almost certainly received too little on the 'marginal-social-product' criterion. The substantial divergences between agriculture and non-agriculture, in most LDCs, in their true k's — remember that the readings for the quotient in table 8.2 really need scaling up by 25 per cent or so — mean great divergences, too, in their true marginal social products of capital.

THE *K*-CRITERION UNDER FIRE
The *k*-criterion asserts that, for efficient growth, the incremental capital/output ratios in major sectors (such as agriculture and 'non-agriculture') should be similar. A critic may reject the *k*-criterion because it embodies (1) the aim of a fast rate of growth, (2) the approach to that aim via increasing the efficiency, rather than the amount, of investible resources, (3) emphasis on the efficiency of capital, rather than of other resources, (4) the application of allocation criteria to something as broad as 'capital', and between such huge sectors as agriculture and (worse still) 'non-agriculture', instead of among many small sectors, or projects, or geographical areas, or types of beneficiary; or (5) the specific use of the *k*-criterion to allocate capital between agriculture and other sectors—to decide how much savings should go to support farm investment—despite such objections as the dependence of the yield from much investment on installations in other sectors, the delays between installation of capital and full production, the existence of idle capital, the high risks of agricultural activities, and the need to build sensibly upon past, possibly urban-biased, investment decisions. These objections are connected and may logically be advanced jointly.

I reject the values underlying criticism (1), and the logic of (2). However, (3), (4) and (5) are perfectly valid. All these objections accept that social marginal value-products should be equated, but deny that this boils down to the *k*-criterion. Carefully considered, these objections strengthen the conclusion from the crude *k*-criterion that the share of investible resources flowing to agriculture, and in general to the rural sector, has been much too low in most LDCs even on grounds of efficient production alone.

Application of the *k*-criterion has the advantage of requiring only simple manipulations of available data. The conclusions suggested by table 8.2 would be reinforced if objections (3), (4) and (5) were allowed for, but this would require dubious new estimates. Hence these objections, while valid, can be ignored in presenting the conclusions.

A criterion for growth?
Little will be said here to justify the aim of economic growth in LDCs. The rich can say they have had enough of growth; but they have neither the right nor the power to enforce abstinence on the poor. Anyway, extra output, especially agricultural output, has much less power to damage the environment or to exhaust natural resources in poor countries than in rich countries. Indeed, most of the productive pollutants (from oil to fertilisers) possess 'in-

creasing external costs' and 'diminishing returns'. These mean, respectively, that they do more damage per unit, and yield less output per unit, if concentrated than if spread out. Thus an environmentalist ought to be specially concerned to see that growth is shifted from rich countries to LDCs, which currently use productive pollutants far less than do rich countries.

Moreover, while growth does not always bring improvements in the welfare of the really poor (see chapter 1), it is almost certainly a necessary condition for them. In LDCs the entrenched power of the rich is fortified by great initial inequalities (chapter 1, note 36) and by the dispersion, and hence disorganisation and immobility, of the poor. Without growth, the rich usually insist, if necessary by force (as in Chile in autumn 1973), that they will not appease the poor at the cost of absolute cuts in their own wealth. The weakness of the poor, moreover, is progressively remediable only as growth compels employers to train, concentrate and organise workers, in intention in the employers' interest, but in effect and ultimately in the workers'.

Efficiency criteria versus quantity criteria?
Both the k-criterion and the refinements required to handle objections (3) to (5) (pp. 195-209) purport to show how growth can be speeded by improving the efficiency in use of resources required for it. In a celebrated paper, Galenson and Leibenstein suggested that such improvements might retard the build-up of *more* resources for future growth, and in particular that going for a high social marginal product of capital — whether by adopting the k-criterion or by more subtle methods — would divert resources into activities with many workers, little capital, and hence not much profits to fuel future savings and hence to increase the future availability of capital.[8] This particular view is fallacious (chapter 10), but is there anything in the general point, that going for high yields on capital means accepting a slower build-up of capital?

It does not seem very plausible. Private persons or public authorities can normally increase the availability of a resource for *future* growth — savings for investment, or teachers, or administrators — only by reducing its availability to generate *current* benefits. Willingness to sacrifice jam today depends mainly on whether the sacrifice yields enough jam tomorrow. That is likely to depend on the output associated with extra units of capital input — whether for the private businessman through a better chance of profit, or for the politician through supplying more output to please tomorrow's public opinion. The future rewardingness and efficiency of any use of resources are likely to be judged on its performance in the recent past. Hence the best way to persuade firms (or governments) to undertake, and workers and owners of capital (or electorates) to sanction, sacrifices of current resources for future growth is to demonstrate the efficiency of such policies by raising the returns to similar resources sacrificed previously. It is not hard to construct economic puppet-shows in which current inefficiency assists subsequent growth, but the hand pulling the strings is usually highly visible. In real life, tomorrow's growth is usually a wishful excuse, rather than a real reason, for today's bottlenecks,[9] wastes and misallocations.

Capital is not everything

Policies to shift capital into sectors that have in the past shown low k may fail for three connected reasons. Such sectors (for example, agriculture) may use capital efficiently but waste some other scarce resource. Or they may require, for further rises in output, mainly increases in something other than physical fixed capital — for example, improved administration or management. Third, there may be so few improved techniques available, or round the corner, in (say) agriculture that — even though its recent yields on extra capital appear promising — more is to be gained by learning or by just waiting, while concentrating investment elsewhere in the economy. These possibilities, in practice, strengthen agriculture's claims for resources, as compared with those suggested by the k-criterion.

OTHER SCARCE RESOURCES WASTED? There are indeed resources other than capital (how else explain agriculture's lower k?) but those that agriculture uses intensively, in order to achieve its high return on capital, are generally not scarce in LDCs — less scarce than the price system suggests. They are above all 'unskilled' labour, which can sow and reap, weed and maintain irrigation channels, as it cannot perform most industrial activities. (It would be more accurate to call farm labour 'skilled', but trained free of cost by the experience and knowledge around it, as against the costly and highly job-specific training needed for most industrial skills.)

Agriculture also, of course, makes more direct use of a scarce factor — cultivable land — than other sectors. However, this has little to do with its low *incremental* capital/output ratio and hence with explaining its success on the k-criterion. *Extra* land brought into cultivation has been dwindling (in quantity and quality) since 1950; in most LDCs the quotient has not. Moreover, if such extra land costs little to render cultivable, its ready availability is a valid reason for preferring agricultural investment, because the yield of such investment is cheaply enhanced by the spare land. And if (as is increasingly the case) the new land carries substantial costs of 'bringing under the plough', such costs are included in agricultural investment, and if that investment achieves a low k, it is after such costs have been fully (and quite properly) taken into account.

Nor is extra agricultural investment (or the output it yields) especially costly of expensively trained skills. Initial *and additional* agricultural output are particularly underendowed with skilled persons, more so indeed than their efficient use would require (chapter 11).

The better performance of capital inside agriculture in most LDCs is due to its saturation with 'unskilled' labour, socially inexpensive because otherwise largely idle. Indeed the employment effect is itself a concealed social benefit. The high quotients of most LDCs can seldom be explained by a relatively high endowment of agriculture with other *scarce* factors than capital. But are some such factors, needed in agriculture, absent in a way that would frustrate mere capital inputs?

OTHER SCARCE FACTORS LACKING?　First, let us consider administration. Administrators might, naturally, attribute the higher past yields of agricultural capital to a great endowment with administration. If true — since administrative skills are scarce — that would moderate the force of the k-criterion's conclusion that agriculture should get a larger share of investment. In reality, however, it is usually non-farm investment that uses up most scarce administrators. Industrial expansion, because of its high foreign-exchange cost, in most LDCs features complex licensing procedures, with attendant officials, senior and well-paid to reduce the risk of corruption. Infrastructural expansion — which involves organising people and offices, or supplying goods and services, to many places less accessible than the 'easy' ones served at the early stages of the growth of a network — uses up many scarce officials in such fields as power and railways.

However, the organisation and status of agricultural services — unfortunately — are such that extra farm output expansion makes low-priority and hence low-cost claims on field services. In most ex-colonies of Britain, a rural region that is directed by a civil servant of the administrative grade has a population of about a million. The chief agricultural officer even for such a region (for example, an Indian district) and the overall civil service controller for the next rural area down (for example, an Indian block of

60-120,000 people) will normally be of executive grade and at the peak of his career structure (albeit often in his thirties) and hence with little career incentive to perform well. Moving down, we find officers, responsible for agricultural extension to 100-500 small farms averaging a couple of acres each, paid substantially less than clerks, drivers or sometimes even errand-boys in the ministries of the capital city. So there is not much to the argument that investment in agriculture produces high output only because each unit of extra output carries heavy administrative overheads.

Next, let us consider managerial skill. What if agriculture's success in achieving low k's in the past is due entirely to saturation of small amounts of extra capital with masses of extra effort so unskilled as to involve no acquisition of managerial skill: almost with unthinking, animal force? If true, this would bode ill for returns to future capital; but it is false. Abundant recent evidence proves that poor farmers are not only responsive to incentive, but eager to adopt low-risk innovations; there is no evidence that such innovations are diffused more slowly in agriculture *in general* than, say, in mining or construction. Agricultural innovation is often said to be slowed down by the need for precise local adaptation, but this is often false (note the very rapid spread of dwarf-wheat-plus-fertiliser technology across Northern India); even where topography and soils do vary critically, farmers are neither more different nor slower than their industrial counterparts, and are probably less handicapped in adaptation by the imposition of a common but inappropriate framework of 'Western' technology.

Farmers do not simply maximise profit. Status, power, leisure and security matter also; and every trade has its keen and its lazy, its enterprising and its conservative members. Yet I am led, by many instances of Third World success and failure, to conclude that small family farms — developing and modernising their traditional skills, in control of all the factors of production, and benefiting as units from them all — have managerial advantages of overview, incentive and gradual learning, which the steel mill, the large building site or (it must be conceded) the big farm or dam lack. Hence the capacity to apply three components of managerial ability — drive, innovativeness and techno-economic skill — seem likely to be at least as prevalent in agricultural entrepreneurs as in others in LDCs. Moreover, more farm capital means a wider range of rural possibilities, and hence better rewards to persuade those who are now farmers to develop their managerial talents, and the ablest of those elsewhere to return to the land.

AGRICULTURE: NEW TECHNIQUES, NOT MORE FACTORS? The third argument of this type is that extra agricultural output needs, not mainly extra capital (or extra anything), but a technical breakthrough. Even before the 'green revolution', and even today in those areas where it has little chance, there cannot be much force in such an argument. If there were, agriculture's low k's in the pre-1965 period of alleged technical stagnation would be inexplicable, as would the excellent agricultural and rural performances of the few LDCs prepared, like Taiwan, to allocate substantial shares of investment to agriculture.

This 'techniques not capital' argument fails, because it is impaled on a dilemma relevant to many analogous arguments against rural investment. If the techniques exist already, they must almost certainly be wholly or partly embodied in new capital equipment, so that farmers cannot exploit them without public willingness either to provide it or to make its purchase privately profitable.[10] If the techniques do not exist in a particular LDC environment—despite the advanced state of global knowledge— it has to be because hydrological or (less often) chemical or biological knowledge there lags behind world levels for similar ecologies; in such cases the return on investment in agricultural research is probably large.[11] Thus the 'no technique' argument, against a higher share of investment in agriculture, is almost always refuted by observing either that (as in Europe's medieval 'agricultural revolution') techniques wait only upon the capital to permit their adoption,[12] or that their discovery requires only (and almost *ipso facto* high-yielding) investment in local research into the transference of analogous discoveries from elsewhere.

All these three arguments, that agriculture needs little investment because its complementary requirements reduce its 'absorptive capacity' for investment, recall the 'explanation' by eighteenth-century physicians of the power of morphine to induce sleep: it had *virtus dormitiva*, soporific virtue. Just so are investments in agriculture supposed to fail because it lacks *virtus absorptiva*. However, the case is worse; at least morphine does induce sleep. Given the persistently lower k in agriculture in most LDCs, to argue that agriculture cannot use capital for want of absorptive capacity is like arguing that *coffee* induces sleep on account of its *virtus dormitiva*.

Such arguments are not dead. Today oil is the popular 'scarce factor' needed in agriculture to make investment there pay. Thus high oil prices are often alleged to erode the capital-saving advantage over industry of, at least, fertiliser-intensive 'green-revolutionary' farming. In fact, even this uses *less* mineral energy and petrochemicals per unit of output than does most construction or industry—just as it uses less extra administration. In general, because of agriculture's economical use of scarce factors other than capital, its true relative efficiency in capital use and hence its case for more investment are strengthened.

'Capital' to 'agriculture'?

THE OBJECTIONS Agricultural capital comprises sheds and barns, dams and livestock, tractors and the 'improvement value' of land, and more. Non-agricultural capital is even more diverse. Pricing the various items of capital can be done only by asking what each costs to install, or, better, to replace in its present condition. These prices reflect mainly the relative valuations of the capital items in the market. These in turn depend on the demand for the products of each item, and hence on income distribution. In a country where income is divided fairly equally, capital to make bread—and especially the agricultural capital to provide the raw materials for it—will be worth relatively more, and capital to make durable consumer goods less, than in a more unequal country.[13]

Worse still for attempts to value capital, the total valuation as well as that of individual items is highly suspect. As Joan Robinson has observed, what capital is worth (and hence what firms will pay to replace it) depends on the profit it is expected to earn; thus a high value in the marketplace for (say) the expected product of extra farm capital raises the demand and hence the price of such capital. So if non-agriculture does badly on the k-criterion, it need not be because of agriculture's greater efficiency in capital use. It may be because (correct) expectations regarding the demand for the output of non-farm capital have raised its expected profitability, and hence its market price, thus lowering the value of non-farm output relative to non-farm capital valued at that market price.

This problem of 'capital' divides for our purposes into two parts. First, what if any defence can be put up for valuing a sector's average and marginal capital/output ratios overall? Second, if the defence is not adequate, can we still advocate the 'pro-agricultural' policy changes, suggested by table 2 and the associated discussion, if we disaggregate? In particular (1) is agriculture using particularly scarce 'bits' of extra 'capital', and (2) is the range of efficiency with which various 'bits' are used so great that more could be gained by improving composition within farm, or within non-farm, investment than by shifting investment to the farm sector?

THE DEFENCES   The major defences of the crude distinction in the efficiency of capital use between big sectors — rather than among the uses by firms or projects of particular sorts of capital — in investment analysis are three. First, people dependent on sector have common features relevant to the case for supporting them with capital, notably greater or lesser poverty and the capacity to work capital more or less fully. Second, decision-taking is often structured around the sectoral allocations of total investment, both in planning agencies and ministerially. Third, and less negatively, even if total capital cannot be objectively measured, an LDC's total savings effort (and its supplementation from abroad) can be — and is — allocated among sectors for the purchase of investment goods (see chapter 7, note 14).

These arguments are quite convincing in the real world, where it is agriculture and transport that have ministries and pressure groups, rather than barns and dams and buses and roads taken separately. They are, however, not very satisfying theoretically. Just because we are stuck with an intersectoral decision procedure, an overall measure, and a way of categorising workers by major sectors of activity, we are not entitled to override the points made on p. 198. What really matters is whether these points make the crude k-criterion likely to overstate or — as is argued here — to understate the case for putting more investment into agriculture.

INCOME DISTRIBUTION AND THE K'S   First, income distribution in most LDCs is relatively unequal (chapter 1, note 36). This means that the needs of the poor find relatively little expression in market demand, as compared with the wishes of the rich. To believe that such a distribution is unjust is to believe that, at the existing income distribution, the large part of farm output which in LDCs comprises non-exported food is undervalued[14] in a sense more fundamental than, and additional to, that discussed on pp. 188-90.

At first glance this undervaluation means that the dependence of absolute and relative capital values on income distribution will, if allowed for, raise the quotient and strengthen the conclusions from the k-criterion; for the 'just' value of farm output is relatively more, and of non-farm output relatively less, than it seems to be, so that farm capital is even more efficient (compared to non-farm capital) in terms of 'just' values than in terms of market values, even after the latter are adjusted to correct for foreign-exchange distortions. However, if the value-per-unit of farm output rises (for example, because income equalisation raises demand for it), so will the value of the capital to make it (because expected profits, per 'physical unit' of such capital, grow). Does that mean that, in the marginal capital/output ratio in agriculture the numerator rises as well as the denominator when we value outputs as they might be priced after 'just' redistribution; that both correspondingly fall outside agriculture; and hence that the impact on the quotient (and on the case for more investment in agriculture via the k-criterion) is obscure?

No; the first glance is right after all, and the above query is a misapplication of Robinson's argument against valuing capital. What is being allocated is domestic savings and the import surplus (that is, foreign savings) *at the time of allocation*, and the cost of the investment goods these savings can purchase is reflected in their market prices at that time. It is valid to correct a sector's share of investment to the extent that such prices fail to reflect scarcities (p. 190), for example because they undervalue imported capital. It is also not just valid but vital to emphasise that market prices of *outputs*, even after this amendment, arise from a particular income distribution. We can then validly reprice outputs to reflect the preferences of buyers at a 'preferred' income distribution. But it is quite invalid to reprice the investment goods to correspond to the valuations of another time, place or income distribution, because the scarcities corresponding to such prices do not exist when the allocative choices are made. There is not (as there is with outputs from extra capital) any sense in which capital goods can be priced to reflect more or less 'just' valuations. Unequal income distribution may well force up yacht prices, relative to bread prices, far above a level reflecting proper social valuations; but proper valuations of sail-making equipment and flour mills are their real costs to the economy and nothing else.[15]

Hence, if we could work out a sector's 'just' k, we should reprice its investment only to allow for the failure of prices to reflect present relative scarcities, and by that sum divide the 'just' value of its extra output, that is, the value prevailing at an 'approved' income distribution. The 'just' estimate of each sector's k would be its extra output (priced to reflect 'approved' income distribution) divided by its extra investment (priced to reflect *existing* real costs). This 'just' estimate would raise the quotient and strengthen the conclusion from the k-criterion.

OTHER VALUATION ADJUSTMENTS   There are other senses, leaving aside problems of income distribution, in which agricultural investment costs the economy less than it seems, relative to other forms of capital. First, a smaller share of agricultural investment comprises DRAC. Much more of it is livestock, which imposes relatively little strain on *allocable* savings.

Second, the depreciation (replacement and maintenance) costs imposed by extra agricultural capital are a smaller proportion of its output than in the case of other forms of capital. A larger proportion of farm capital comprises slowly depreciating structures and simple hand implements, as against machinery that quickly wears out. Also, the real cost of maintaining (for example) irrigation works in the slack season with otherwise idle unskilled labour is much less than that of importing spare parts for industrial machinery. Moreover, if capital is small relative to output, so also will be the cost of maintaining it.[16]

Third, and probably most important, in LDC agricultures a large part even of net investment (though not as large as of replacement and maintenance) comprises drainage and irrigation structures built manually by farmers and their families in the slack season. This is not costless to the community — he who works more must eat more — but its cost is substantially less than that of even 100 per cent non-imported investment whose manufacture requires fuel, machines and skilled employees, all with alternative uses.[17]

Thus, if it were possible to allow for valuation errors in 'output associated with extra capital', the quotient would be higher still. A linked objection to the k-criterion, however, remains: that the line between agriculture and 'non-agriculture' does not sufficiently mark off the parts of the economy where extra capital is associated with large increases in output, from those where it is associated with smaller increases. This objection is in two senses well taken. First, finer subdivisions of sectors — indeed prior evaluations of *projects* — are desirable.[18] Second, if a dichotomy is sought, the rural-urban distinction might well be preferable. But again both these points strengthen the conclusions of the k-criterion.

INTRASECTORAL VARIETY IN K'S   There is an enormous range of success and failure with extra capital inside as well as outside agriculture. There are three sorts of cure: to improve the intersectoral allocation of investment, its intrasectoral allocation, or its efficiency in any particular use. But these are not simple rivals for more political and administrative energies. Improving the sectoral balance, by cutting out 'fat' in relatively overendowed sectors and providing necessary clothing to underendowed rural Cinderellas, helps intrasectoral allocation and project efficiency all round.

What of the range among k's within each sector? In one or two LDCs, statistics permit a fine enough breakdown to confirm that the heavy infrastructural sectors, notably power and transport, have much higher k's than industry, especially light industry. However, since the huge k's in infrastructure are due substantially to the low output prices pressed upon public utilities by the industrial interest (and to the intermittent demand provided in return), this cannot absolve industrialisation. And if there is a great range of k's among non-agricultural projects, the same is true of agriculture, where the projects showing the highest k's are heavily hardware-oriented schemes—giant dams,[19] surfaced rural roads[20] — suggesting that urban bias not only cuts rural resources but also lowers intra-rural returns; for such high-k schemes, like tractors, usually help the large farmer to produce and market urbanised surplus, rather than helping farmers as a whole to raise total farm output.

Hence (1) reducing urban bias in project selection within each sector, without changing the given volume of investible funds in either sector, would help to lower k within each sector, (2) this desirable process would not, of itself, necessarily change the quotient. More obviously, (3) the ready availability of funds to non-agriculture has been a major factor encouraging its spread into high-k projects, so that a concealed benefit of reallocation towards agriculture would be the reduction of future spending on such projects, and (4) the intrasectoral future (in default of strategic decisions about intersectoral priorities) will be similar to the past. Non-agriculture has shown little capacity to reduce its share of albatrosses, since an outmoded steel mill can be used only for outmoded steel production; but even ill-conceived irrigation and barrage projects, being usable for many different crops and farming systems, have often been put at least half-right after the event by advancing agricultural technology;[21] hence most LDCs' quotients have probably edged upwards (table 8.2), suggesting that it is starry-eyed to expect relative improvement in the non-agricultural sector to reduce them in future unless relative pressure on funds is intensified.

Indeed, the case for comparing k's in agriculture and 'non-agriculture', despite the huge diversity of both, is that this comparison is *not* starry-eyed. The bundle of recent extra non-farm investments, as it actually was composed, is compared — in cost and in product -- with the similarly real-life bundle of farm investments. In a theoretically ideal plan, we should compare the marginal product of capital in *optimally selected* products within each sector; but in practice it is wise to consider the actual pressures on project selection, and to ask how sectoral yields compare, given such pressures.

AN URBAN-RURAL QUOTIENT? The central bias of policy in most LDCs is urban, rather than 'non-agricultural' (chapter 2) — although rural welfare usually depends on agricultural prosperity, so that growth in the former is likely to be self-sustaining only if based on growth in the latter. It is unfortunate but not fatal, therefore, that statistical limitations have compelled the use of a quotient relating non-agricultural and agricultural, not urban and rural, k's. Some straws in the wind suggest, anyway, that urban/rural quotients would be at least as high.

First comes the generally low yield of residential building: 'In capital-poor Latin America a fixed investment of $100 produces an average annual product of $40-50, but only $10-12 if put into residential building.'[22] Fire and infection risks compel construction at far higher unit cost in cities than in villages; moreover, urban construction is much less likely to have its real costs cut through the slack-season contributions of otherwise idle labourers.[23] Second, the temptation to integrated showpiece development, good for the morale of the tiny minority who benefit but yielding next to nothing, is peculiarly urban: Chandigarh, Islamabad, Brasilia. Third, the very expansion of city size, partly through jobs that pull people in, raises the urban k: 'cost [per person] of providing water, sewage, urban transport, and fire and police protection rises after a critical city size.'[24] Fourth, the disparities between urban and rural investment/population ratios are — while less readily available than between agriculture and industry — probably even higher; for example, the Second Pakistan Plan (1960-5) allotted 68 per cent of water and sewerage facilities to Karachi, Dacca and Chittagong (with 3 per cent of the population) and 27 per cent of road transport investment went to Karachi alone (with 2 per cent of the population).[25]

REFINING THE K-CRITERION

A further group of objections accepts that the efficient allocation of capital between agriculture and the rest of the economy is a sensible focus for enquiry in LDCs. They assert, however, that something a good deal subtler than a quotient of 1 is required to equate the marginal social value of output on and off the farm. The assertion is valid, but for 'subtler' read 'lower'! These refinements imply pushing a share of investment into agriculture not just greater than at present, but greater than would be needed to bring the quotient down to 1, even at scarcity prices (p. 189) or indeed at scarcity investment prices and 'just' output prices (p. 199).

Complementarity

Clearly fertiliser output assists farming. If we were to count investments in fertiliser-plants, etc., as being 'in' agriculture, its share in total investment would seem higher, and the quotient lower. However, if investment in fertiliser plant is 'agricultural' because it ultimately raises the output associated with farm capital, investment in irrigating cotton is 'industrial'; for it similarly raises the output of spinning and weaving plant.[26] There is nothing 'one-way' in the impact of all this on the quotient as we have measured it. Nevertheless, comparisons of the extra output associated with investment *in* a sector can be misleading if that investment does not overlap with investment producing output *for* a sector.

Actually this misleading effect, while extant, is usually exaggerated. First, either fertilisers or cotton may be imported. If a planner decides to allocate investment to fertiliser factories instead of to agriculture because fertilisers are needed to raise farm output, he needs to show that domestic fertiliser output is 'better than imports'—that imports are subject to falls in quality, rises in real cost, or interruptions of flow, in a way that domestic products are not. It is absurd to say that investment in a fertiliser factory is 'really' in agriculture, and helps to raise farm output, if it means only that farmers use domestic instead of imported fertiliser. Such a switch, indeed, often harms agriculture, because new domestic fertiliser producers usually persuade the government to restrict imports, so that the farmer pays more for less reliable deliveries than before (chapter 13).

Second, there remain some non-farm investments that yield products useful to agriculture and not easily imported. Typical are investments in generating electric power to run tubewell and pumpset motors. However, even here the output of such investment usually has importable substitutes (diesel oil in this case). Investment in irrigation is counted as agricultural in this book, because its output—water—has no importable substitutes.

Third, in practice the mass of costs of non-importable infrastructure—helping produce output in other sectors but not assignable to them (for example, transport, education, power)—have been incurred for the urban sector. Even where they have not, rural users have usually bought such services, and paid 'non-agriculture' for them (as is also true for non-imported fertilisers). The value of 'non-agricultural output benefiting agriculture' to this extent materialises as a yield to industry, where it reduces sectoral k and is thus already allowed for in calculating the quotient; it should not be taken into account again as a 'complementarity'.

Fourth, LDCs do not feature much 'vertical integration' (ownership of raw-material and processing production by the same firm). Hence advantages from extra output in one sector are unlikely to be 'passed on'. They have to be retained in that sector, for example, by prices charged to buyers in other sectors, unless the producer is to lose out.

Finally, the sort of investment that produces non-importable services benefiting other sectors in LDCs is usually in agriculture, though rather subtly so. Much industrial spare capacity in LDCs is caused by lack of foreign exchange to buy raw materials, spare parts, or wage goods for workers. If there is no chance to raise imports substantially, more farm output — with its low import cost and (unlike electricity generation or luxury production) its propensity to substitute for unavoidable imports — is normally the cheapest way to release foreign exchange, and hence to enable industry to get moving again. As a stick for industrialisers to throw at agricultural investment, complementarity is a boomerang; for it is their deficient complement of farm investment that regularly aborts long-run strategies of industrialisation.

Delays in yield

The second attempt to refine the k-criterion involves trying to take into account 'gestation periods'. Non-agricultural capital is supposed to take longer, both to construct and once constructed to overcome its teething troubles, than agricultural capital.[27] We are invited by some industrialisers to conclude that, because non-agricultural capital takes longer to show a return, the k-criterion is somehow unfair on it: that we should compare the return of non-farm investment only after several years, or even not till 'capacity outturn' has been attained and learning completed. However, investment yields what it yields, not what somebody imagines it should yield at an undefined 'maturity'. If agricultural capital yields sooner than other capital — because it is built, or used effectively, with less delay — then that is an advantage to be credited, not an unfair windfall to be deducted, in comparing the merits of investments. Ideally, the expected output of each project over its lifespan — from the date of commencement of construction until the equipment is worn out — should be estimated, counting the production costs of the equipment as negative output, and valuing output more highly the sooner it occurs.

In fact, the normal way of estimating each sector's k tends, in a growing economy, to underestimate agriculture's advantage in getting rapid output from extra capital. To estimate a sector's k, we usually divide its average increase in capital stock, over a period of years, by its average increase in output over the same period. That way, non-farm projects in the period are 'credited' with much extra output that actually comes from the delayed maturity of projects commenced in earlier periods, while little farm output comes into this category because most farm capital matures more swiftly. Thus non-farm projects are not penalised for their delay in coming onstream, but in effect credited with their predecessors' delayed results. The method used in table 8.2 actually increases this understatement of agriculture's advantage; for investment is there measured from 1959 to 1964, and divided by extra output from 1960 to 1965, in effect delaying by a year the need for projects to show output at all — a delay that understates k more for non-farm than for farm projects. If farm investment nevertheless attains high quotients, advocates of non-farm investment who plead its long gestation periods are badly briefed. Incidentally, the failure of non-agriculture's k to fall (table 8.2) suggests that its gestation period is not falling either. Stubbornly long gestation periods aggravate the drawbacks of the high non-farm k; to use them as an argument to scale that k down suggests they are an argument in its favour!

Idle capacity

Another attempt to credit non-farm investment with its vices is concerned with capacity utilisation. Such investment is often used below rated capacity, partly owing to delay in coming onstream, and to shortage of the complementary raw materials or wage goods that higher agricultural output might have supplied.[28] Just as we are told that we must wait until the moment most favourable to non-farm investment to compare its productivity 'fairly' with farm investment, so we are invited to consider only those rare periods in the life of non-farm investment when it is functioning most efficiently.

Non-farm investment has an enormous advantage in achieving rated-capacity output: independence of the weather, and hence (at least potentially) of both seasonal and year-to-year fluctuations in domestic supply conditions bearing upon utilisation of equipment. A farmer must be ingenious to find off-season uses for irrigation channels, pesticide sprayers, even draught power. Yet it is industrial activities in LDCs — notably steel, power and heavy engineering — that have experienced large and on balance rising spare capacity, even when domestic demand is high.

If this were about to change in an LDC, then the plea for measuring k in terms of rated-capacity output rather than actual output might be less weak. As things are, it recalls the boy who, having murdered his parents, blames the poor implied return to his moral education on the fact that he is an orphan.[29]

Correcting past investment misallocation

Deeper and more serious objections, against arguing from a high quotient to a shift of investment to agricultural uses, are Mirrlees's argument from irreversibility and Srinivasan's argument from risk. The former rightly points out that, once a mistake has been made in a process, it may be best not to correct, reverse or allow for the mistake (three different treatments, by the way), but to push ahead along the course already begun, even if a better one would earlier have been available. Thus to react to past quotients above 1, by stepping up the share of agricultural investment, may inefficiently push *future* quotients below 1. On the other hand, to push ahead with non-farm investment could create learning effects, reduce spare capacity, and enhance complementarity among branches of industry, so that the quotient was brought closer to 1 than would be possible by a more agriculture-oriented route.

This points to an interesting logical possibility, but seems implausible. 'More of the same' has long been the treatment in most LDCs for the ills of non-farm investment (though the label on the bottle now often reads, oddly enough, 'Top priority for agriculture'). If 'more of the same' *were* a cure, both the quotient and its attendant symptoms (spare non-farm capacity, etc.) would long have begun to decline; but this has not happened in most LDCs. Also the link between apparent agricultural underemphasis and the size of the quotient (chapter 8, note 7) suggests that perseverance with the former will not cure the latter.

Irreversibility arguments rest partly on the belief that growth and 'development' are solvents of error: that they make up any deficiencies in supplies or markets for industrial plants initially built too big, or with too few technicians, or in the wrong place. However, it is *farm* investment that can more readily produce many outputs in many ways, and that is thus more adaptable to growth and change. Irrigation, pest sprays, even seed research laboratories can be switched, almost yearly, among many food, pasture, export, and domestic-raw-material crops according to the requirements of growth. Steel mills can produce only steel; and — even if growth provides the skill or the demand to obviate their initial design errors — the process, the type of steel produced, and above all the scale of production can be obsolete in a manner not curable as simply as, say, by switching an irrigation project between wheat and cotton.[30]

Farm investment too risky?

Planners, as well as individuals, prefer safer investments. Even if agriculture's k were persistently below the rest of the economy's, should its susceptibility to disturbance from the weather count against it in investment allocation? This argument is supposed to apply with special force to a planned economy; disturbances inter-act, so that the safety, 'plannability', and ultimately investment and output of low-risk sectors are damaged by undue concentra-tion upon high-risk investment, the uncertain products of which are inputs — and the uncertain incomes yielded by which create demands — for the rest of the economy. Once more, the argument usefully makes a valid logical point, but one that correctly inter-preted strengthens the case for agricultural investment.

First, agricultural output has not always shown greater fluctua-tions in LDCs than non-agricultural output; indeed, for the very few (five) LDCs in which trend values of real farm and non-farm output were available for a longish period (1953-66), yearly fluc-tuations about the trend were in every case larger for non-farm output![31] Second, agricultural output fluctuations, when due to bad weather, are likely to be accompanied by price fluctua-tions in the opposite direction, so the destabilising effect on in-comes is not concentrated on producers, but is shared between them and their customers. Third, the relative flexibility of farm investment more readily permits its users to respond to a prolonged recession — in demand or yield itself — by changes in their output pattern: Bangladesh's jute smallholders switch to rice when the jute market turns down, but Malaysia's tin mines have nowhere to go but tin.

Above all, the argument from risk assumes that the safety of a sector's output is unaffected by the volume and type of investment in it: that if production is riskier in agriculture than outside, so is investment. But this is simply false. Many agricultural investments (irrigation, storage, pest control) *directly* reduce the risk to output: indeed, for a risk-averse planner, this should supplement their higher yield as an argument in their favour. Others (fertiliser distribution, research into new seeds) *indirectly* reduce the risk to output, because they are heavily concentrated on irrigated areas where risk is low; thus they raise not just total farm output, but also the proportion of it that is relatively risk-free.

On the other hand, by increasing the strains on an integrated supply-demand system involving power and transport as well as industry, rapidly accelerated non-farm investment normally increases output risk. Moreover, except in such rare LDCs as India and Brazil with substantial non-agricultural diversity and experience, most non-farm investment involves operating at the frontiers of effective knowledge of production—and especially of marketing—thus increasing the proportion of total non-farm output subject to very high risk. The risk-averse planner should be concerned, not to invest in sectors with little past variability of output, but to select new investments reducing the variability of total output, and (where the components of total output are interdependent) of sectoral outputs too. That directs investment towards agriculture, not away from it.

SCATTER SCEPTICISM

What capital/output ratios?

There is one other sort of attempt to kill the quotient-hydra, not by decapitation but by machine-gunning with 'scatter-scepticism'. This has been brilliantly applied by Streeten[32] to the following, rather naive but once standard, approach to planning: decide the total extra 'output' wanted; multiply it by 'the' national capital/output ratio; treat the result as the 'required' investment—as though the capital requirement, per unit of extra output, were independent of the amount and type of that output, of *initial* levels of idle capacity, of the workers and administrators operating the capital, and of the policy environment; and then slide from required, through planned, to expected investment for plan fulfilment. Thanks to Streeten's exposé, this sequence of 'reasoning' can be stated like that, and its fallacies become obvious.[33]

A slide that Streeten does not warn against (though he does not make it) is from the demonstration that *overall* national 'capital'/'output' ratios are almost useless tools of planning, to the incorrect belief that the k-criterion—the approximate equalisation of (properly modified) *sectoral* incremental capital/output ratios as a rough indicator that investment finance is being allocated efficiently — is similarly useless. Plainly, the weakness of overall ratios in no way damages the k-criterion. Still, it is useful to look at one influential application of scatter scepticism to that criterion. Hirschman first published his critique in 1954, but republished it in 1971 and presumably still believes in it.[34]

Can it be done?

First, he argues that 'the calculations relating Output to Investment are either not possible or far from conclusive in the type of social overhead capital (transportation, power and water supply, irrigation) [that the planner] is likely to deal with.' While few calculations in planning are 'conclusive', surely these are 'possible'. The extra output, made possible by extra investment in an irrigation project, is tangible, measurable after the event, and—subject to risks of error that can be calculated and that diminish with experience—predictable before it. The use of social cost-benefit analysis, not only in 'transportation, power and water supply' but even for more dubiously measurable areas such as health and education, has become increasingly common in both the appraisal of planned projects and the evaluation of implemented ones; while far from perfect, such techniques allow us to correct for price distortions due to monopoly power, and to give special emphasis to benefits accruing to poor people.[35] The alternative to such techniques is the abandonment of economic appraisal in favour of arbitrary hunch.

Sectors and hunches

Hirschman's second argument, indeed, explicitly advocates that alternative. Such claims as that 'the last million pesos of scheduled expenditures on education will [raise output about as much as the last million spent on] transportation', while essential 'if national development and investment programs are to have *any* validity from the point of view of economics', nevertheless 'cannot be validly made'. Hence *'the determination of the proper share . . . will be made* intuitively and *arbitrarily'* (my italics). The planner must decide 'whether the change in the [transportation] environment intended to change the people should take precedence over [educational] attempts to change the people directly'—a decision where 'economics can supply no answer'.

Admittedly, social cost-benefit analysis is usually confined to comparing the *efficiency* of capital among projects with *similar* sorts of output: different sorts of secondary schools, rather than a secondary school and a bus route. This self-restraint makes for simplicity; it avoids the need for two sets of data (about buses and schools); it acknowledges that ministries of transport and of education hire micro-economists separately; but it does not indicate any high principle that projects should be compared within ministries rather than across them. In particular, it is false that 'complementary' investments cannot be compared by the *k*-criterion or its cost-benefit analogues. Even if it were true, it would not mean that such comparisons made more sense among projects within a sector than between sectors: the products of different types of secondary schools are at least as complementary with one another as with bus routes.

A rival high principle to Hirschman's is that the yields of (say) transport and education cannot be compared without total economic models. This is at best half-true, and anyway irrelevant to the k-criterion (or cost-benefit refinements). Such total models produce revaluations of the types of capital and of output associated with roads and schools, factories and farms, but do not invalidate the k-criterion for choosing among sectors for investment to produce outputs, once both outputs and investments have been properly valued. If the alternative is the abdication of economics in favour of 'arbitrarily' made choices within crude metaphysical dichotomies (changing 'the people' or 'the environment'), we had better stick to the k-criterion! It is indeed possible, by comparing places or times otherwise similar—by Mill's Method of Differences, or by modern statistical refinements of that method—to see whether the last million pesos, of properly valued outlay on various educational and transport uses, are yielding roughly similar additions to properly valued output. Possible; difficult; essential.

Comparing the known and the unknown

Hirschman argues that 'the heterogeneous character of figures included in the investment budget' precludes useful comparisons of the yield from 'an expenditure which is known in all its details' with that 'from one whose nature only is given'. That would rescue much heavy urban investment from embarrassing comparisons with higher-yielding, but less specified, rural schemes. However, the tracing of past, or expected, extra outputs from a project or sector need not be made easier or more reliable by the detail in which we know the make-up of its extra outlays. Lack of such detailed knowledge might, in principle, conceal the fact that the *higher*-yielding sector's outlays cost society much more than they appear to do, relative to those of the lower-yielding sector; and this could make the 'higher' yield illusory. In practice, however— as this chapter has shown—the reverse normally holds when the higher-yielding sector is agriculture (or the rural sector) and the lower-yielding sector everything else.

If we don't know the make-up of outlays in the *lower*-yielding sector, the low yield *may* be caused by their poor composition rather than by their having been pushed to an excessive level; but a reduced level is itself a goad towards a better composition. Anyway the make-up of outlays is usually better-known (and hence presumably likelier to be put right in advance, and less likely to be responsible for an unduly high k) outside agriculture than inside.

It is strange to penalise a low-k sector, such as agriculture, for our ignorance about *why* past investment in it has been successful, by using that ignorance as a stick to beat the k-criterion and thus to beat down future farm investment. Investing in successful sectors, and meanwhile doing the research to reduce our ignorance about the causes of success (so as to generate even higher-yielding investment later), must make better sense.

Overemphasis on allocation?

Hirschman believes that shortages are less likely to stem from inadequate investment in a sector than from 'faulty sector planning' and 'the great difficulty in properly carrying out well-designed sector plans' without 'steadiness of purpose, stability in administration, and other qualities in short supply' in LDCs. This is a false dichotomy. Capital should be so allocated as to equalise true sectoral k's, on reasonable assumptions about the relative impact on yields from administrative problems in different sectors; one reason for high non-farm k's is that it is outside agriculture, and especially in infrastructure and heavy industry, that the gravest impact can be expected from administrative under-development.[36] (Indeed, Hirschman points out that these problems are worst 'in fields such as electric power, where the time-lag between planning and execution is particularly long', but does not conclude that the implicit, chronically high, k justifies lower investment in such fields — an omission dangerously close to the 'gestation-period fallacy' of pp. 205-6).

It will not do to write off 'shortages and bottlenecks' due to bad intrasectoral policy as 'unavoidable concomitants of the process of accelerated development' if some sectors — those with high k's — are especially prone to such ills, yet consistently get huge capital endowments.[37] Furthermore — though to do so requires retraining, as well as new incentive structures — steady and purposeful administrators, good sector planners, etc., have to be allocated to equalise their marginal yields, just as much as capital has.[38] Not only is extra non-farm output particularly costly in terms of these men; the more of them that sit in underused steel mills and marshalling yards, the fewer are left to run the rural credit schemes, agricultural extension services, etc., where the yield of *efficient* extra administration is so great, and its relative scarcity so marked.

The sector-project problem

Many LDCs are short of prepared projects. Hirschman argues that the economist using the k-criterion, 'unless he can produce projects in a state of readiness-to-be-undertaken similar to the one

he attacks, . . . *should not* be listened to' (his italics). This is unacceptable, because the main reason why projects achieve that
blissful state is not their probability of economic success but the
extent to which they will benefit people with relevant (that is,
urban) political influence and power. As soon as possible, it makes
sense to tackle this by better rural project preparation; but good
rural projects cannot wait that long. Meanwhile, the fact that
'readiness-to-be-undertaken', rather than the best currently available estimate of potential social yield, influences project selection bears much of the blame for the driving-out of promising
but — thanks to urban bias — underprepared agricultural outlays
by dud but detailed heavy-industrial and infrastructural projects
that should never have been 'undertaken' save by the under-
taker.

Statics and dynamics

Hirschman's approach sometimes seems to suggest that outlays
demonstrably inefficient now can be justified by vague appeals
to dynamic efficiency later. 'Frequently . . . investment in public
utilities . . . [has] an igniting effect on development throughout
the economy and . . . must therefore be undertaken in spite of its
[high k].' Furthermore, 'to achieve balanced progress in agriculture and industry it may often be best to promote first industries
and particularly those industries which, while relying initially on
imported materials, are potential mass buyers of potential domestic crops.'[39] Igniting effects, balanced progress, and potential
potentials are rather vague defences of economic activity that has
long remained socially unprofitable owing to its high k. Such defences, between the publication of Hirschman's paper in 1954 and
its republication in 1971, sheltered much wasteful equipment —
made profitable to rich men by high levels of protection — in the
name of 'import-substituting industrialisation'. The inefficiency
of installing machines to assemble motor vehicles in Latin America
— machines that produce cars available on world markets for less
than the landed cost of the imported inputs — is an extreme case,
heavily supported by subsidised public services.

However, the inequities perpetrated in the name of balance,
igniting, etc., are even more serious than the inefficiencies. Food
literally 'ignites' the work-power of the rural poor; urban high-
ways ignite only social envy (whether expressed as fury or
misplaced admiration) and imported petrol. 'Balanced progress'
requires, not overinvestment in urban plant half-idle for want of
food for workers and raw materials for machines, but sufficient
farm investment to supply such wants, either directly or through

exporting, to provide the foreign exchange to import them: and agriculture is unlikely to achieve this without earlier mass, small-farm development. The k-criterion, for all its crudity, usefully illuminates these truths.

Scatter scepticism: conclusion

Scatter scepticism about the k-criterion—often, as here, linked to a defence of non-farm investments with high k—frequently includes arguments discussed earlier (pp. 192-209). The danger of scatter scepticism, unless handled with Streetenesque subtlety, is its swift movement from one argument against the k-criterion to another. The reader, left breathless, asks not whether each argument against it stands up, but whether the criterion itself (being assailable by so many arguments) can do so!

Why should Hirschman, one of the subtlest and most perceptive of development economists, attack the k-criterion in this rather light-headed fashion? His deep concerns, I believe, are three: the view that it is not new inputs but progressive changes in attitudes that generate development; a distrust of benefit/cost analysis as mechanistic and crypto-ideological; and above all—to cite the title of his 1971 collection of papers—'a bias for hope', for structural transformation of poor countries through industrialisation. There is much force in these three concerns, but I believe it is misguided to turn them against the k-criterion, and hence explicitly or implicitly against agricultural emphases.

First, the impoverished rural sector does not have, because it cannot afford to have, anti-economising, non-innovating attitudes. Subject to the need to avoid risk—and hence to preserve a securing social structure until an alternative appears—local rural traditions are surprisingly modern,[40] and may be expected to respond quickly and efficiently to new inputs, if their risk is not very high, and if relative prices permit a profit (chapter 13). Conversely, to impose large amounts of 'modern' urban investment and techniques—capital-heavy and for a long time dubiously profitable without such crutches as subsidy or protection—on a culture with a traditional, because capital-starved, rural base is likely to discredit appropriate industrial attitudes, not to foster them. If improved rural attitudes *are* needed, they depend partly on radical redistribution of rural income and power, but partly, too, on better prospects, education, extension, techniques, and above all water-controlled security. All are to some extent linked to, or embodied in, new farm capital.

As for Hirschman's second concern, much benefit/cost analysis indeed replaces socio-economic thought by mechanical comparisons among projects. And the k-criterion among sectors, at best, substitutes incompletely for benefit/cost analyses among projects, though, as we have seen, its pro-agricultural conclusions would be strengthened by such analyses. Verbal comparisons based on pure hunch, however, can be as unimaginative, or as mistaken, as any cost/benefit analysis—though the unimaginativeness and the mistakes are easier to disguise. While one cannot exactly calculate the true social value of the output of a primary school, I am sure that planners in an economy with scarce building materials and a big educational programme must make some shot at estimating it; that, by deciding as they do, they act as if it was just worth building the last primary school and would not be worth building another, that is, they *imply* an estimate that follows the k-criterion; that an estimate is no better for being wordy, informal and vague; and that this applies, too, to comparisons between agricultural and other outlays.

Finally, it is not a rejection of Hirschman's 'bias for hope' to follow out the k-criterion, and to conclude: small farms and mass rural development with labour-intensive investments first, a switch to capital-intensive rural development later, urban-based industrialisation later still. Hope deferred maketh the heart sick: but the above 'k-programme' involves less deferment than do industrialisation-first policies that, of their nature, repeatedly run into the sand. Almost every successful industrialisation has required prior agricultural transformation. It is courting disillusionment, not hope, to put the car before the horse.

9 The myths of urbanisation

If people in less-developed countries fare so much worse in villages than in towns, will villagers 'vote with their feet', by migrating townwards, until the gap between rural and urban expectations is removed? If such *urbanisation* happened, major rural-urban inequalities could not persist. This chapter examines why it happens so surprisingly little — and whether policy-makers should seek to increase or decrease it. Can really poor villagers react to their poverty by moving to the town? How far can such a process increase the proportion of persons in poor countries who gain, instead of losing, from urban bias?

Over-simple readings of the data have in most LDCs led to gross exaggerations of the rate of genuine urbanisation — permanent movement from village to town, net of movement the other way. Most of the rise in urban populations is due to natural increase — not only directly but also by pushing communities over the rural-urban borderline, and by making towns expand and 'eat up' nearby villages. Most migration in LDCs is intra-rural or intra-urban; and much of the residual migration from village to town is temporary, or in other respects does not represent a real urban commitment. As for true, permanent townward migration, it activates powerful processes, demographic and economic, limiting its capacity to raise the urban share of national population: processes already apparent in the recent population counts of such major cities as Calcutta and Colombo.

Thus urbanisation has been insufficient to reduce urban bias. Moreover, its structure has tended to increase urban-rural inequalities, for two reasons. First, urbanisation is 'epidemic', as people learn from other migrants about urban prospects. Thus villages near cities, and rural families with urban members, are the likeliest to seize on any potentially beneficial further townward migration. Such villages and families are often semi-urban before these further benefits accrue. The successful migrants who remain in the city, even before they moved, were richer and better-educated than their fellow-villagers; if the really poor villager moves at all, it is usually temporarily, to a job in the urban periphery, or even to no job at all — to crime, beggary, prostitution, all the currently romanticised delights of the 'informal sector'. Second, the villages, and especially their poorest members, also lose from the drain townwards of resources of skill and leadership.

Nor is the picture even lightened by substantial *net* remittances from urban migrants to their rural kinsmen. While there is no case for opposing urbanisation as such — still less for preventing it by force — it cannot cure the depressed conditions of the rural poor, except perhaps in the very long run.

VOTING WITH THEIR FEET

The idea of an equilibrium mechanism

Though primarily a sociologist, Hoselitz is in a major tradition of marginalist economics (chapter 4) in arguing that voluntary migration from village to town must cancel out any serious inefficiencies or inequities arising from urban bias. Suppose a townsman's material advantages over the villager exceed any net 'psychic income' from rural life. Will not the villager then do better (at the same level of capacities and effort) by becoming a townsman? If he does so, he reduces the pressure on land and the competition to get jobs in the village, and thereby improves the position of those who remain there. He also increases the number of workers struggling to get urban jobs, and the competition for housing and other amenities in the city, so that the benefits to city dwellers decline. The process of migration, runs the argument, will go on until both villager and townsman know that nothing is to be gained by moving. That can happen only when the rewards for work, requiring the same effort and ability and conscientiousness, are the same in village and town — allowing for the risk of being out of work in either place,[1] differences between urban and rural living costs (chapter 5, note 4), and any possible net 'psychic income' from living in a village rather than a town. On this reasoning, any substantial urban bias must cause urbanisation, which continues until any inefficiencies caused by the bias have been removed.

This argument, typical of neo-classical economics, assumes that people have the information and the resources to respond swiftly and rationally to any chance for advantage, and that they do so within a system with few obstacles to such response. If political and market power are not too unequal, and if access to information and training is widespread, then swift response within a fluid economy can plausibly be expected to steer it towards equilibrium and thereby enhance both efficiency and equity.

In developed countries, the argument is powerful. The reduction of regional and racial inequality in the USA, as Southerners have moved west and north since 1930, is a good illustration of it.

Even in such favourable conditions, however, the march to efficiency need not do much for equality, or do it swiftly. The better-off seem frequently willing to bear 'costs of discrimination':[2] to suffer absolute economic costs in order to retain *relative* status advantages over others upon whom they inflict greater costs. Among worse-off groups, moreover, even in rich countries, it is the more literate, informed and dynamic who migrate or are otherwise 'creamed off', leaving the mass of their colleagues with even less chance to advance. And it is part of the definition of an underdeveloped economy that the poor can move about to get richer (for example, by voting with their feet) only sluggishly, if at all.

Chasing the rainbow

Indeed, the cumulative forces making the townsman better off — political and economic pressures analysed in this book — are in most really poor countries increasing the disparity much faster than townward migration can reduce it. The slowness of 'equilibriating' urbanisation has two causes: the constraints preventing the very poor from leaving the village, and the obstacles presented by the socio-economic system to their effective and lasting settlement in the town.

In poor countries, the worst-off villagers can seldom move permanently to the town. First, they are often bound to the village, by law or custom, to work off old family debts they cannot repay. In 1950, some 10 per cent of Indian families, dependent mainly on agricultural labour for a livelihood, were 'attached', and frequently, in effect, bond-slaves;[3] Latin American peons are similarly immobilised. Even if they defy law or custom and go, their relatives may be penalised by loss of land or jobs, so the poorest class of villagers as a whole gains little. Second, most poor countries, especially in rural areas, are far from enjoying universal schooling; and the poorest villagers are the most likely to be ignorant of urban chances, or unable to exploit them because they are illiterate.[4] Third, a migrant, while looking for an urban job (or receiving urban education) instead of working in the village, needs money from someone — usually from his father or brother in the village; to support a migrant like this, a rural family must be well-off enough to have something in reserve. Fourth, as this shows, a family decision to 'urbanise' a member is usually a sacrifice of definite income now for possibly greater income later; the very poor can seldom afford either risk or the reduction of their slender current incomes; nor can they often meet such costs by major extra borrowings at reasonable interest rates.

Hence the poorest villagers are unlikely to be able to react to urban bias by massive, permanent townward[5] migration — except in a rich country, where they are not all that poor, and enjoy widespread schooling, social security in the event of unemployment, and no bond-slavery. In a poor country such as Ghana, the villager who moves to the town is usually a man who has *already* half-succeeded in joining the urban elite: 'the propensity to migrate increases with closeness to a large town, population size of the [village of origin], economic well-being of the rural household, number of relatives in the urban area, [and] the individual's level of education.'[6]

To the characteristics of poor villagers impeding their urbanisation — characteristics derived partly from the socio-economic system that cuts their prospects of earning (or borrowing) money — must be added 'immobilising' features of the system itself. These may involve deliberate restrictions on townward movement, in response to pressures from big farm employers who (because they provide the city with most of its food and raw materials) must be listened to; the very different forms of 'influx control' of Russia after 1861 and South Africa today exemplify that response.[7] The system of most LDCs, however, restricts townward movement more subtly. Transport from village to town is often poor, infrequent, and too costly for the poorer villagers. Barriers of dialect, and in many countries of language (India has thirteen major languages, Papua several hundred), impede movement, and are often reinforced by the retention of colonial or 'mandarin' languages for official and commercial matters. Information about job prospects seldom reaches rural areas; labour exchanges are usually confined to bigger towns.

Policy towards the urbanising response

All these explicit and implicit barriers suggest that the reduction of urbanisation is an aim of urban-biased policy-makers, as indeed seems natural: a big net inflow of rural migrants would compete with (and drive down the rewards of) organised urban workers, congest urban roads, and render smaller, less competitive and hence costlier the supply of products to towns from rural areas.

Yet, in a sense, urbanisation — at least of the skilled, educated, better-off and hence more mobile villager — is a *response* to urban bias. Indeed, my earlier work on urban bias has been taken, by a sympathetic reader, as suggesting that poor countries are 'over-urbanised';[8] an 'excessive' share of development spending in the cities must, almost by definition, pull 'excessive' numbers of people into them. However, any attempt to cure 'over-urbanisation' by locking the villager into his village, so as to impede the urbanising response to urban bias by such villagers as may be mobile, would be the ultimate urban-biased assault on rural rights.[9] The hypothesis that LDCs are 'over-urbanised', merely because their populations contain larger urban shares than did NRCs (now-rich countries) at comparable stages of development, is curiously ethnocentric, and anyway refuted by the statistical evidence that urbanisation is closely related to industrialisation in LDCs (but not in rich countries) today.[10]

The issues can be clarified by making three distinctions. First, what is wrong with rapid urban population growth in LDCs is not that it damages the successful migrant: at existing levels of rural and urban living, the drawbacks of urban expansion have been much exaggerated, and after all it continues to show the preference of the migrants. What is wrong is that it aggravates the bias against the villager, despite the theoretical expectation (pp. 217-18) that it would correct such bias. Second, the remedy is not to confine the artificial advantages of city life to the present beneficiaries by rendering urbanisation difficult, but to remove the arbitrarily assigned advantages that render urbanisation artificially attractive: to neutralise the pricing, investment, educational, medical and other policies that are currently transferring income from villages to towns, and encouraging the ablest villagers to follow. Linking these two distinctions is the third: many poor countries are 'over-urbanised' not in the sense that cities become undynamic or outpace industrialisation,[11] but in the sense that urban economic dynamism confers less and less welfare (partly because its cost rises and partly because it chokes off immigration later on), increasingly takes place at the expense of rural areas, and is linked with an output structure — in building as well as in industry — that employs few, benefits mainly the well-off, and rests on arbitrary price and investment advantages conferred by public policy and secured by private monopoly.

FALSE AND TRUE CASES AGAINST URBANISATION   Recent surveys of slum-dwellers and squatters in South and South-east Asia are surprisingly optimistic. Laquian sums up that 'they seem to be [quite] closely integrated with the economic and social system', to have 'many opportunities for saving and capital formation', and to reveal 'economic mobility' and 'high social and political participation'. McGee points out that 'for the Indian rural migrant about to move to Calcutta, the city is identified as a city of "hope" for the future', and asks, 'Why else would he move?' — though the limited numbers that do move, and (as we shall see) the high proportions that return, are significant here. Nor should one too readily accept that a city is too big for further expansion of industry to remain economic: 'industry continues to expand in these centres, showing that many industrialists themselves still think that the major concentration retains numerous advantages.'[12] It is the facts that these trends *do* eventually choke off urbanisation and urban industrialisation — and that much of the latter is made privately 'economic' only by socially uneconomic, urban-biased policies — that are worrying, not the natural urbanising response of migrants and businessmen to mistaken policies.

Urbanisation increases inequalities, both intra-rural and rural-urban. As both Marshall and Kautsky realised (chapter 4, notes 41 and 84), it selects out those who could lead the village away from poverty. Successful townward migrants stay in the urban area and reinforce its pressures for extra resources. Meanwhile, they set up economic and demographic forces rendering further migration increasingly difficult, so that the villagers left behind — especially if unrelated to the early migrants — have little chance to benefit from the urban bias that early migration accentuates.

DAMMING THE FLOW   There are far too many unknowns for a policy of artificially damming the urban flow to be justifiable on efficiency grounds (quite apart from the inequity of compelling even the mobile villagers to stay at home and accept urban bias). First, though the growth of urban unemployment (not mainly among immigrants) renders doubtful the case for urbanisation as a source of labour supply, it does not render 'irrelevant'[13] the argument that if rural labour shifts to the towns it will contribute more to national output; towns in poor countries are still dominated by underutilised capacity, by actual labour shortages in unskilled manual jobs spurned by the educated unemployed, and by a generally greater output/labour ratio. Past urban overinvestment there does justify heavy labour-inputs, now, to make more of this urban capital. If the disparities of table 7.1 justify raising the rural share in capital, they also justify lowering the rural share in labour, especially as man/land ratios rise. It suits urban trade unionists and businessmen to go for capital-intensive techniques, confining the benefits of urban growth to existing gainers (plus a few relatives), and persuading the politicians to adjust taxes and subsidies so as to make this profitable (chapter 12); but it is better, for development, employment and equality, to reverse these priorities.

Second, urbanisation could be needed for both low-cost industrialisation and rising levels of administrative capability.[14] The case for small-scale and rural industry often smacks of special pleading. The worst duplication, overcentralisation and administrative confusion in early development are frequently rural, especially where agriculture, irrigation and other ministerial fiefdoms overlap. Both the high cost of rural industry and the low capacity of rural administration spring partly from urban-biased pricing and investment decisions; but to rule out the possibility that the high costs of dispersed rural activity bear some of the blame, and to delay urbanisation accordingly, would be to push policy far ahead of what can be inferred from the available research.

A third argument against preventing urbanisation is that — to counter the threat to rural jobs, incomes and nutrition from rising man/land ratios (especially where water shortages preclude major agricultural innovation, 'green-revolutionary' or other) — one must pursue two paths. One is suggested in this book: much more investment in the intensification of farmland use, especially through irrigation. But the path of labour-intensive industrialisation must be followed too, and probably in the towns if it is to be efficient. Poverty means both 'over-urbanisation' and 'over-ruralisation' — both town and country have too few resources, given their distribution and use, to provide the residents with adequate living standards.[15] Hence (while slowing population growth and accelerating the creation of resources of skills and capital) policy should seek to place more of each sort of resource where it yields most: capital in rural areas; labour, up to a point, in urban areas. Of course, urbanisation of labour through urban-biased incentives is not justified by this argument.

URBAN RESPONSES TO THE COSTS OF URBANISATION   It is noteworthy that many city-dwellers have sought to artificially restrain further urbanisation. Their arguments rest heavily on the conditions of filth and disease, congestion and deprivation of privacy, transport noise and transport costs, above all of the poorest and most recent arrivals (largely rural floaters rather than true migrants). Such conditions must indeed depress humane observers. But why should they constitute a practical or a moral case for stopping urbanisation? Practically, they cannot form direct costs to the urban leadership, and do not give their victims any political power. Morally, they are after all preferred to village life by the migrants. But they do mean that urbanisation imposes, upon the settled urban community, external costs that are high and rising.

The costs are *external* in that they arise out of the actions of A, but are borne by B; if A moves to an already overcrowded area, in or near which B already lives, much of the extra unpleasantness is transferred to B and his like. The costs are *high* because, if existing townspeople are to be spared damage, many facilities (health, drainage, police) have to be granted to the newcomers. The cost per migrant is *rising* because each extra person or vehicle, using a congested facility, increases congestion more than proportionately.

To protect already-resident townsmen against such costs, the city acts against the migrant in several ways. Its elite refuses to raise local taxation for spending on 'foreigners', or compels migrants to bear the costs of their own contribution to pollution and disease by limiting the zones where they may reside. Or it organises political parties against them, such as Bombay's Shiv Sena, which was directed mainly against South Indian immigrants. Or it prevents their entry as best it can — difficult even in a totalitarian state (Stalin did badly at it), but eased if migrants have skins of different colour, as with influx control and the associated Pass Laws in South Africa.[16] Or they just stop providing the job chances that attract the migrant.[17] The understandable eagerness of city elites to restrict urbanisation should caution us against seeing such restriction as a cure for urban bias.

THE FACTS OF PSEUDO-URBANISATION

This section shows how little urbanisation has taken place in the really poor countries of the world — those of Africa and South and East Asia. Much of what has happened (after demographic 'optical illusions' are allowed for) is temporary, or in other ways fails to change the migrant's life-style in ways that prepare him for modern industrial development. Furthermore, several mechanisms limit the impact, on the shared population in urban areas, of such townward movement as has happened.

Before demonstrating these facts, we must recall that historically the vast mass of townward migration has not been caused by rural 'push' or urban 'pull',[18] but has been involuntary, a response to physical threats against life, limb or land. These are the great disaster treks, such as that following the partition of British India in 1947. As rural man/land ratios rise with population growth, refugees will find it increasingly difficult to find jobs, land or welcome in rural areas. The townsman is in practice unable to put up the shutters against such disaster movements, and they outweigh in importance any *voluntary* urbanising migrant response to urban bias.

In any event, the latter is not substantial. A cross-section comparison of agriculture's share in the labour force, in LDCs at different income-levels, led Kuznets to expect an observed decline in that share accompanying the income increases of the 1950s;

the actual decline was a good deal less.[19] If we take all the pairs of years between 1950 and 1967 for which estimates of that share are available in the same country, we find in Africa six cases in which it has risen, six in which it has fallen and three in which it has been static; in East and South Asia, there are four cases each of rising and falling agricultural population shares, and one static share. Only in the richer parts of the Third World, where immobilising constraints on the rural poor matter less — West Asia and Latin America — are falling shares of farm population clearly predominant.[20] For India, 'it appears fairly certain that the final [1971] Census estimate will show a rise in the [proportion of workforce in] agriculture . . . between 1961 and 1971'.[21] The close link in LDCs between urbanisation and industrialisation suggests that if the latter has been slow the former has also; and so it turns out.

Urbanisation: a demographic illusion?

From 1950 to 1960, the share of rural persons leaving for urban areas was 0.3 per cent yearly in South Asia, 0.6 per cent in East Asia, and 0.7 per cent in Africa — far less than rural population growth.[22] In the poorest regions of the world, South Asia and Africa, the urban share in population rose far more slowly than is generally believed (from 16 to 18 per cent and from 14 to 18 per cent of total population respectively). In China, it proved impossible to sustain the rapid rise in the urban population share during the 1950s with surpluses of food — perhaps the last frontier that constrains urbanisation; the urban share of population actually fell from 19 per cent in 1960 to 12-13 per cent in 1971. The proportion of people in urban agglomerations (over twenty thousand persons) rose much more slowly in poor countries than in rich ones, both in 1920-50 and during the 1950s. Urban population growth has slowed down in the very places that, not long ago, were thought to pose the most uncontrollable threats of 'megalopolitan' congestion, explosion or decay: throughout 1951-71 'the rate of growth of population in the Calcutta urban agglomeration was considerably lower than in rural West Bengal'.[23] A marked decline in urbanisation rates in poor countries began in the 1960s and is expected to sharpen in the next two decades.[24]

The number of true, permanent urban immigrants is itself habitually and grossly exaggerated. Ashish Bose has provided a valuable picture of this for India. In 1961 one Indian in three was born outside his or her place of residence. But most of this migration comprises village brides, moving to their husbands' villages; only 4.2 per cent of Indians were rural-born townsmen. If we deduct the 1.1 per cent who were urban-born but lived in villages, we find that *net* townward migration covered only 3.1 per cent. Half of these at very least — more probably two-thirds — were 'turnover migrants', staying in urban areas for less than ten years before returning to rural life.[25]

Several demographic 'optical illusions' help to foster the myth of mass urbanisation. The commonest, that rising proportions of urban residents must mean *permanent* streams of net townward migrants, hardly needs refuting, but there are others. The first takes place when an expanding city comes to abut on a village. Usually the village's population (and its natural increase) thereafter is counted as 'urban', even if its pattern of life has scarcely changed: '[In] Kuala Lumpur, where such boundary extension incorporated genuine suburban development, [this means true] urban growth; [not so] in other cases such as the Chartered Cities of the Philippines (which often include large rural populations).'[26] Bombay and Delhi, as I have seen, also contain long-submerged, but still largely rural, villages. The phenomenon is little researched, but must account for significant parts of urban growth in LDCs, except perhaps in South America.

Another 'optical illusion' of urban townward migration is created by the expansion of areas across some nominal borderline into a technically urban status that again need involve no change in economic behaviour. Their population and its natural increase then overnight become urban by classification. This, combined with migrants' own natural increase, makes the increase in the 'urban' population share a very misleading indicator of urbanisation, especially over long periods. Thus in Peru from 1940 to 1961, while national population grew by only 61 per cent, the population in agglomerations of over twenty thousand rose by 220 per cent, suggesting massive urbanisation. Yet in reality the population in cities of over twenty thousand *in 1940* grew by 175 per cent only, and the population in places of over twenty thousand *in 1961* by 173 per cent. Hence about a quarter of urban growth was due to reclassification of places as cities because they crossed the urban borderline. A third of the rest (about 61 per cent out of about 173 per cent) was due to natural increase of the *1940* population, and at least another tenth to natural increase of 1940-61 migrants. In Iran from 1951 to 1961, at least one-fifth of the apparent 'growth' in the urban share of the population was due to the reclassification of thirty-nine places that crossed the five-thousand border line. Much of Ghana's urban 'growth' has the same source. The effect also created a substantial illusion of urbanisation elsewhere.[27]

These two effects — 'eating' of one community by another, and

'borderline-crossing' of a community owing to natural increase —
separately increase the *classified* urban population. The effects
can even combine; between censuses, two villages of three
thousand, each swollen to four thousand by natural increase, can
expand their built-up areas until they meet to form a single village
of eight thousand, which is classified across an urban borderline
(typically five thousand) — and, for some, this creates a statistical
illusion of eight thousand townward migrants!

A third, subtler, illusion is created by the changing age-composi-
tion of populations; here the figures do not mislead us about the
facts of urbanisation, but about the permanence of its upward
tendency. Many LDCs have long featured a life-cycle pattern of
temporary urbanisation of 10 to 30 per cent of rural males, for a
few years between the ages of fifteen and thirty. Between 1945
and 1955, malaria control, in one country after another, slashed
mortality rates, above all up to the fifth year of life. Hence rural
children, who in earlier generations would have died, are surviving to enter the age-group fifteen to thirty. This swells the proportion of rural people in the age-groups of the traditional 'life-cycle'
migrants — and this process will last from about 1960 (or 1945 + 15)
to 1985 (or 1955 + 30). Even with no increase in either the proportion of the fifteen to thirty age-group who migrate or their average
stay in the towns, the fact that this 'migration-intensive' age-group
is a growing share of the population will raise the urban proportion
of population. The rise in the 'migration-intensive' proportion of
rural people, however, will be reversed as more of those saved
from early malaria death pass into the post-migrant (and return-
migrant) age-groups; it indicates neither permanent urbanisation
nor a shift in preferences.

Impermanence of much remaining urbanisation
Not only is the high proportion of rural persons in 'urbanising' age-
groups thus temporary: many individual urbanising villagers have
no intention of staying in the cities, and of those who have, an increasing proportion is being driven to return by the growing shortage of urban job opportunities. Even if both these groups of
temporary migrants remained constant as *shares* of the total
population, the growth of that population would inflate the growth
of *numbers* of urbanising immigrants, and give a misleading impression at once of the permanent provision of new urban facilities
that was justified, and of the capacity of urbanisation permanently
to release villagers from the pincer grip of rising man/land ratios
and urban-biased policies. To put it at its simplest, if temporary
urbanisation is growing rapidly, both census data on urban

residents and survey data on urban immigrants overstate the extent of true urban settlement.

I have spoken of the life-cycle pattern of temporary townward movement. At the age of fifteen or so, young men go to the city, often to seek work in building or mining. They stay in the city, for the agricultural slack seasons only (quite long enough to get classified as permanent migrants in some surveys) or year-round; but the period of urban work, often to save up for marriage but sometimes to discharge traditional family obligations (for example, under the *gandu* system of Islam in West Africa), seldom lasts more than five years.

These people *are* in a sense urbanising, even though their behaviour does not indicate structural change, but only the persistence of a traditional pattern of cyclical movement. If their numbers grow, it does mean that more people gain, instead of losing, from urban bias. Indeed, many temporary migrants, returning to the village, could in principle spread urban benefits — income, yields from savings, knowledge — more fairly around it than a few permanent urbanisers. In practice, however, there are problems. First, failure to urbanise — to get a secure, reasonably satisfactory job — is an important reason for return to the village.[28] Second, most temporary migrants remain rural in loyalty, and participate little in urban advance. Third, the 'engulfed' villagers of p. 225, and the temporary fringe townsmen examined here, are literally peripheral to urban life, living in the outer suburbs;[29] indeed, in big cities, they may reside nearer to their villages of origin than to their workplaces (in Colombo, bus journeys of three hours between work and slum are commonplace).

Processes limiting the rise in true urban population shares

Urban-rural welfare gaps are unlikely to be reduced much by the neo-classical equilibrium mechanism, in which the rural poor are supposed to 'vote with their feet' until the gap is closed. This is partly because more powerful equilibrium mechanisms choke off such 'urbanising' responses to urban bias. Both the demographic structure and the economic impact of this migration are such that the urban share of population and workforce — and hence the proportion of the nation's people who gain rather than lose from urban bias — rises much less rapidly, and for a shorter period, than would be expected from superficial observations of the initial movements themselves.

DEMOGRAPHIC FACTORS Nothing is more certain than ageing. Hence the upward impact of malaria control on the proportion of rural people in 'urbanising' age-groups fifteen to thirty is certain to be turned into a downward impact as time passes. Bombay in the 1950s experienced 'heavy net out-migration at ages 35 and over, especially among males';[30] as the DDT generations, saved from malaria death at ages nought to four, age past thirty-five into these net out-migrating groups, the overall urbanisation rate (and *perhaps* the urban share in population too) must drop. That is the first of two powerful demographic equilibrium mechanisms choking off the increase in the urban population share.

The second involves sex-structure as well as age-structure. We need to look at fairly large countries (because in small ones the issue is confused by international migration[31]) but their census data for males per thousand females in childbearing age-groups, around 1957-63, are strikingly higher in urban areas. For the Congo (Democratic Republic), there are 1,204 in urban areas, 726 in rural; for Ghana, 1,176 and 895; for Kenya, 1,696 and 832; for Nigeria, 1,196 and 858; for South Africa, 1,315 and 779; for Egypt, 991 and 962. In Asia the evidence is similar: Ceylon, 1,265 and 1,057; India, 1,253 and 1,000; Indonesia, 994 and 905; Iran, 1,086 and 948; Pakistan 1,428 and 1,020; Turkey 1,426 and 931. (The gaps lead to excesses in rural birth rates far too large to be offset by shortfalls in urban death rates.) Richer countries—in Latin America as well as Europe—show the opposite pattern, with female dominance in towns; but in a really poor country the urbanising migrant streams convey to the city their own huge majorities of men,[32] who have hitherto proved unable to bear children.

These migrant streams, while not as big or as permanent as is often believed, have gone on for a long time. They thus, over time, convey to the cities numbers quite large compared to urban populations, but still small compared to rural populations (because most rural populations in countries of Asia and Africa outnumber urban populations by at least 4 to 1). Hence they cause big male surpluses in the towns, but small female surpluses, if any,[33] in the villages.

Now, while urban migration continues, so does its unbalancing impact on urban sex-ratios[34] and hence its downward pressure on urban — but not rural — birth rates. Selective male urbanisation, typical in Asia and Africa, slows the relative urban rate of natural increase; and hence is less likely to substantially increase the proportion of people living in cities. On top of this, higher levels of education (and of exposure to family-planning campaigns) may trim urban birth rates. The proportion of people living in cities, therefore, rises only slowly. Demographic factors alone make it hard for urbanisation to reverse the unequalising impact of urban bias.

ECONOMIC FACTORS   There are also economic mechanisms by which past migration makes future settlements more costly and hence deter them. First, many aspects of congestion involve rising cost: probably the cost per person of 'providing water, sewage, urban transport and fire and police protection rises after a certain critical size . . . has been reached'. These rising costs are often not felt by firms, whose average costs in India seem to fall steeply as city size rises up to 200-250,000 and to stabilise thereafter. They do, however, reduce the city's attractiveness to later individual migrants, who must both pay more for private 'fire resistan[ce] . . . water supply, sewage . . . night soil disposal', and tolerate standards of public provision driven down by past migration. For established urban communities—even those whose social concern extends little beyond preventing communicable disease— rising costs also mean that past migration renders future migration unpopular.[35]

Second, city expansion raises the price of land acquisition, further urban building, and amenities. The rising cost of urban life, relative to rural life, is supposed to be one of the processes by which migration brings urban and rural living levels closer together; how can it be presented here as something preventing such migration *before* the gap has been closed, rather than signalling the fact that the gap *is* closed and that further townward migration is uneconomic? Well, it must be so presented, since (at least for literates) urban-rural gaps in real wages do not seem to contract, even after rising housing costs have severely curtailed migration. Several things are happening. New migrants are being forced to accept increasing congestion and squalor. Rural escape is increasingly confined to those with urban relatives able to accommodate them. The high and rising cost of rents, both for land and for new urban building, together with the growing job shortage, is probably pushing recent migrants increasingly into the hands of high-interest urban moneylenders. And earlier immigrants with a formal job are obtaining both job security and higher wages for themselves, discouraging employers from taking on later migrants, who are therefore deterred from entering. All these factors accentuate the 'get on or get out' polarisation, by urban conditions, of recent migrants into those absorbed into the urban community and those who do not escape from the rural fringe, and are driven to return to the village.

Third, the growth of urban economic activity, as compared to expectations, has been perhaps slower, certainly more artificially structured, and hence probably less self-sustaining—particularly in any form that can continue to employ growing numbers of urbanising immigrants. There are many reasons for this, some connected with urban bias itself: shortages of wage goods from the countryside, for want of farm incentives and farm investment, have crucially constrained non-farm expansion; encouragement (for example, underpriced imports) for 'non-farm investment' has stimulated capital-intensive, ultimately uneconomic and for both reasons low-employment buildings and industries. But there is one direct equilibrium mechanism at work, at least in the 'formal' sector of urban work: in government, large industry and construction, and transport. The fact, and threat, of immigration drives existing urban employees to take various steps to prevent wage-cutting job competition: artificial apprenticeships; job definitions that require the learning of increasingly indispensable skills; use of special access to jobs via family or tribe or caste; formal or informal trade-union action; even political pressure against darker-skinned unskilled competitors, for example against the Tamil immigrants to Bombay by the Shiv Sena party, and against Dinka immigrants to Khartoum by Arab workers. Existing employees thereby acquire the power both to extract costly concessions and to impose costs of disruption on employers who hold out. Such employers therefore increasingly adopt growth paths that use machinery instead of new, possibly immigrant, labour — and (chapter 13) are well placed to obtain subsidies for such machinery. Hence the incentive to urbanise is once more reduced.

Some otherwise perceptive discussions of urbanisation blame it for evils actually caused — as it also is — by urban bias itself. For instance, Furtado attributes to 'borrowed technology' and 'over-mechanisation' the fact that Brazil's urbanisation of 1950-60 — when total population increased by 3.2 per cent yearly, but urban population by 6 per cent — proved economically unsustainable, in that the industrial labour force grew by only 2.8 per cent yearly as against 3.5 per cent in agriculture.[36] But why was technology borrowed, mechanisation excessive? Was it, in large part, because the urban labour aristocracy strengthened its union organisation against the threat of competition from immigrants; and because urban business could respond by getting the government to cheapen non-farm imports of equipment, and thus to obviate the need to employ much more labour?

THE IMPACT ON THE VILLAGE

If urbanisation is not very substantial or lasting — likelier to be ended by equilibriating forces than to bring them to bear upon rural-urban disparities—is its total impact on rural-urban and intra-rural relations small? Unfortunately, matters are worse than that. Urbanisation not merely fails to reduce the inefficiencies and inequities of urban bias; it actually increases them. It polarises the rural-urban distinction by singling out, for full absorption into the already advantaged urban system, a few villages and villagers that might otherwise have acted as a vanguard for the others; and by increasing the gap between urban (and urbanised) and the remainder.

Removing the rural leadership

The dynamism of international migrant groups—the Gujaratis in East Africa, the Chinese in Malaya, the Spanish Jews in Holland —has often been observed, and misleadingly racial conclusions drawn from it. Almost by definition, people who 'get up and go' have more 'get up and go' than those who stay behind. The same applies, to a lesser extent, to those who move from village to town. They are likely to be brighter and more go-ahead than those who remain.

Townward migration of the better-educated and more intelligent—for whom the urban-rural pay differential is greatest—imposes a variety of costs on villagers. First, they do not benefit from actual and potential skills, for the training of which they have often paid. Even if the family of the educated migrant benefits from his remittances, the *village* loses the social benefits of his greater capacity to reason and to innovate. Second, villagers must support, in the city, the migrant who needs further education. Such education predisposes him to reject manual work, whether on the farm or in the town, and to rely on the rural family again for income while he waits for a sufficiently elevated job.[37] Third, young educands, by moving townwards, further deprive the village during critical periods of the strongest and most skilful hands to work on the family farm. Above all, the selection-out of the brightest removes the potential leadership of the rural sector; the better-educated villagers dominate migrant groups (chapter 11).[38]

Townward migration tends to leave out the very poorest villagers,[39] for four reasons. First, they are unable to meet its short-run costs, and to acquire the necessary knowledge. Second, families often need them for farmwork—and can seldom meet the fees for preparatory rural and further urban education. Third, urbanisation spreads by contact with earlier successful townward migrants, with two effects: to concentrate success (and income) instead of spreading it; and to locate a major share of urbanisation in biggish, but not desperately poor, rural families, with the sons moving as they reach the age of fourteen to sixteen if the family can afford it—as richer families can. Finally, the family of the migrant knowingly incurs costs now, in the hope of greater returns later; but risks, and delays in consumption, can seldom be afforded by the very poorest, especially when he must borrow (if he can) at the village moneylender's rates.

All this does not mean that the richest rural families have the highest migration rates; big landlords and moneylenders usually remain, to exploit local advantages and guard their assets (though absentee landlordism does exist). The migrants come mainly from the fairly poor, but not desperate, rural families. The migrants— and their families, but for the safety-valve of urbanisation—are often people whose economic surplus, while small, might otherwise induce them to take the political risks needed to press for changes in the village structure favourable to the rural poor as a whole. The 'selection-out', by successful urbanisation, of the more educated (and educable) *among* the middling-poor severely damages the chance of the remaining rural poor to find effective leaders.

Urbanisation further increases the rural sector's share of disadvantaged people because unsuccessful migrants tend to return more swiftly, especially if they fail to get a job.[40] The retention by many migrants of rural property[41] implies an income drain from the village if the unsuccessful do settle in the towns, and a cushion for urban failure if they do not. The Indian data have led a leading expert to emphasise, not 'push' and 'pull' factors in urbanisation, but the presence of a depressed group of 'turnover migrants' who are pushed to and fro between village and town.[42] But the bases of such people—and the costs of supporting them in sickness and old age—remain rural.

Impact on scarcities and bargains

Townward migrant influences the distribution of power and income in three ways. First, remaining villagers gain cohesion as villager and townsman are polarised (despite the effect of turnover migration in increasing movements between them). This is partly because the would-be urbanising villager is segregated in a growing urban periphery, engulfed village, 'informal sector' or whatever. Second, the urban sector is strengthened in its relations with the rural sector. Third, inequality in the village is probably increased, although this may be modified in Asia and Africa by net improvements in the position of rural women as a result of selective male migration.

URBAN-RURAL POLARISATION   We have seen that towns attracted the better-educated, and not the very poorest, villagers — and that it was the less successful who tended to return to the village. This is not the only way that urbanisation produces polarisation. It has 'epidemic' qualities; it is the villager who knows existing town-dwellers (usually earlier urban migrants) well, and who can rely on them for information and initial help, who is likeliest to move. Hence the families, and even more the villages, that first 'catch' the urbanising germ are likely to spread it to other members. Villages with many families already sending out migrants are likely to send out more; sometimes 'family and village ties are sufficiently strong to create an obligation upon the successful migrant to help sponsor new entrants to the city',[43] so that it is *successful* migration for longer-term settlement that is likely to concentrate upon the villages that initiate it, and draw them into a sort of quasi-urban sector. Such villages are likely to be physically as well as mentally nearer to the town.[44]

At the urban end, surprisingly, the large number of 'potentially temporary' migrants, retaining rural links, probably *increases* rural-urban polarisation. To some extent they are polarised on arrival, by their motives for migration, into 'bright youths with both the drive and the facility for rapid urban assimilation' and rural 'have-nots' who 'build for themselves within the city a replica of the culture they have left behind'.[45] The latter group is itself being polarised, into the decreasing proportion that settles into the desired secure job and becomes fully urban, and the growing proportion that returns to the village almost empty-handed. Even physically, the new immigrant communities live on the urban fringe; among townsmen they are nearest to the villages (on which they often depend for income until, and unless, they find work) and furthest from the centres of decision and employment. Doubtless the recent emphasis on the community sense and internal economic logic of migrant slum and squatter communities is right and needed; but such communities are, and are seen by immigrants as, temporary transit camps, either to successful urbanised status[46] or to a premature and rather shamefaced return to the village. It is time to warn against the growing 'idyllisation' of life in the slum; all the talk of the sense of community and the warmth of the informal sector is depressingly reminiscent of similar vicarious veneration, often in pastoral mode (chapter 4), of the impoverished village (and of 'traditional' medicine and education) by people who would seldom accept such conditions themselves. In any event the urban 'informal sector' is a transit camp towards rural or urban status, get-on-or-get-out, not a mediating unit with permanence. Its existence in no way refutes the hypothesis that conflict and polarisation between urban and rural *classes* is the 'leading contradiction' in most poor countries.

URBAN-RURAL POWER BALANCE   If it is those with a better education and some economic surplus who are pulled from village to town, and if the successes stay while the rest return, the strength of urban areas in bargaining with rural areas is bound to be increased. (That is one reason why one cannot infer, from the presence of numerous rural-based representatives in the parliaments of the Indian states, likely pro-rural action by such parliaments.) It is the impact on subsequent resource allocation, between village and town, of the town's success in capturing many of the village's most progressive people that tips the balance against such judicious, but falsely dichotomised, appraisals as Zachariah's: 'Cityward migration in India deprives the villages of the better educated and may be an important reason why the villages have not shown more social and economic advancement. On the other hand, the talents and skills of these persons might well have been *wasted* in the rural areas. Migration may thus have helped in bringing skills to areas where they could *most profitably* have been utilised and in contributing to a *better* utilisation of the human resources of the country as a whole.'[47] For it is disproportionate urban power—reinforced by, and encouraging, the 'cityward migration . . . of the better educated'—that (via public investment allocations and price manipulation) creates a situation where rural 'skills' are 'most profitably' used in the urban production of air-conditioners and sub-acute psychiatric services. However scarce, for the rural poor, coarse foodgrains and worm-treatment services may be, their rural provision would indeed appear, at market prices, to 'waste . . . talents and skills'—but only because it is rendered artificially *un*profitable through investment allocations and price manipulations by urban elites, including the 'better educated' rural migrants.

Even without policy pressures from educated migrants and others, the better-off and growing urban sector would absorb a disproportionate share of resources in a market system, because it could afford them; but the politics of urbanisation accentuates the unfairnesses. In what sense is it 'better' for more and more doctors, and potential doctors, to migrate from villages to towns already enjoying ten or twelve times the rural sector's levels of medical provision (table 11.3)? And is it not clear that, once they go, they will strengthen the pressures towards medical services benefiting the urban rich: kidney transplant machines rather than clean rural wells?

INTRA-RURAL IMPACT Is the fact that urbanisation probably worsens rural-urban inequality — and, as with doctors, inefficiency of resource allocation — offset by beneficial effects on income distribution within the village? Will not the bargaining position of the poorest, who usually stay in the village, be improved by the urban movements of their slightly better-off neighbours, since the competition for land and jobs will be softened? Unhappily this is not likely. If the migrants were on balance employers, lenders, or renters-out of land, the consequent concentration in fewer hands of credit, village land for renting out, and the power to hire labourers, will strengthen the power of the village elite — the bigger employers, landlords, moneylenders, who more seldom migrate — to pay low wages and get high rents and interest rates. If the migrants come from the better-educated families among the groups of small tenants and landless labourers, the benefits to such groups (from reduced competition to find land and jobs) are likely to be outweighed by the loss of competent leaders in negotiation or struggle with village elites.[48]

Urbanisation may improve the status of women in the village. In the village where I worked in 1965 in Western India — typical of Asia and Africa in respect of its selectively male migration — it was becoming less rare to see women running farms which their elder brothers, or occasionally husbands or (if the father was dead) sons, had left to seek urban work. This access to managerial positions must improve the status of village women. Whether, by impelling village families to call on the largely untapped energy and intelligence of women, the process substantially reduces the damage done by 'rural skill drain' is less clear. The gain is that migrants are replaced by women, instead of by men less dynamic than themselves. The loss is that women, as farm managers, may command little respect among workers and traders in traditionally oriented villages, especially Moslem ones.

Anyway, the benefits to women are limited. First, it is often men who take over the migrants' land. Even in rural Asia and Africa, where most of the townward migrants are men, they are usually young, and often have living fathers or elder brothers to work the land. (Indeed, it is the younger brother in a 'middling-poor' family, which has too little land for sensible subdivision but just enough resources to give him some clerical education, who is perhaps most prone to migrate.) Second, if the migrant returns, he resumes cultivation and the woman loses her entrepreneurial role. Third, in Latin America (except the Andean region), it is mainly women who migrate to the town; given the social constraints on their rural advance, and the values of *machismo,* their rising rural 'scarcity value' cannot help them nearly as much, in the quest for equality, as the chance to manage the farm would do, and that chance they rarely get.

Urbanisation and financial flows between town and country

It is widely believed that large sums of money are remitted by urban migrants to their families in the villages. If this were so, it could counteract much of the damage done to the village by urbanisation, and perhaps revive one's faith in its alleged power to reduce rural-urban inequalities. However, the scanty evidence —mostly Indian—suggests that remittances are not very large.

In Ranchi, India, around 1961, 86.1 per cent of migrants remitted nothing, and only 3.0 per cent sent home 16 rupees a month or more (enough to raise the income of their rural households of origin by perhaps 15 to 20 per cent). Moreover, while we hear much of the money remitted to the village by these urbanisers who succeed (probably a falling proportion of migrant streams), we hear far less of the cash flows with which villagers must support their migrant relatives while they seek jobs or acquire education. Work on ten villages in Tamilnadu (Madras) State, India, suggests that, at least in the 1950s and early 1960s, these 'reverse remittances' roughly balanced the cash flows from town to country. For the rural family, the burden of reverse remittances must be met months or years before direct remittances flow in return, often involving costly loans. These rural burdens are certain, but the later rural benefits are not; there is no guarantee that, even if he becomes self-supporting, the migrant to the city will keep up his remittances.[49]

Nor do remittances, both ways, exhaust the impact of rural-urban migration on the flows of cash between the two sectors. Apart from indirect effects on bargains between city and countryside the better-off migrant is likely to take with him savings from rural activities, and to use them in the city—either as investment to make more money, or to be used up in buying a house and furniture. This sort of transfer has precisely the effects analysed by Kautsky (chapter 4, note 81). The migrant also often embodies costs of education, both on fees and in work foregone, to his family —with the benefits accruing largely in the town. Finally, the migrant tends to go home during illness or pregnancy, thus throwing the burden on the rural family, a tendency lauded by some (p. 64) as reducing the costs of industrialisation to the urban sector.

This is a bleak picture, and there are exceptions to it. Many 'urbanisers' bring back information and innovations to their rural base (but would they have done the same if they had not gone to live in the city?), and there are income flows from migrants to villagers, though net of reverse flows they may be small or negative. Above all, some villagers still *choose* to try their luck in the town. Governments, to reduce the social costs, should remove the artificial disadvantages of rural life and agricultural activity, not bar the victims of these disadvantages from trying, even futilely, to escape. The village must be made less artificially unappealing; the villager must not be further assaulted by urban 'influx control'; but hopes that urbanisation will correct urban bias are misplaced. Urbanisation remains the hope of the hopeless, the outlet of the occasional exceptional villager, but the opium of the development expert.

10 The need for savings

We have considered three sets of arguments for squeezing the rural-agricultural sector. Firstly, the damage done to efficiency and equity by the squeeze might be put right automatically, as its rural victims move to the towns to become beneficiaries instead; in practice, however, that makes matters worse. Secondly, development might normally have been accompanied, or accelerated, by the squeeze in the past; but there is little historical evidence for this. Thirdly, elites or populations in poor countries might seek economic structures emphasising investment or industrialisation or both; but the evidence suggests that a squeeze on agriculture as tight as prevails in most poor countries today will achieve neither objective quickly, let alone efficiently or equitably. We now consider the fourth argument for the rural squeeze: that industrial investment is better for future savings than is farm investment. This is the most persuasive and important argument for urban bias; but it owes much of its power to faulty logic and incomplete evidence.[1]

The argument goes like this. Growth—a necessary condition for development — depends on two things: the extra output obtained from scarce resources such as capital, and the economy's capacity to *save* the incomes paid to the producers of such output, thereby permitting further capital accumulation. High yields on capital, unless saved, are a once-and-for-all boost to incomes and do nothing for sustained growth; this is the effect of farm investment. Low yields, saved to permit more investment, may mean less 'efficiency' now, but much more growth later; this is the effect of industrial investment. If farm investment benefits the rural poor, they will spend almost all their extra incomes. Big farmers will do a little better, but even they can use their unspent incomes most profitably, not by saving to finance investment, but by lending at high interest rates to boost consumption by the rural poor. Extra industrial production, however, uses lots of equipment and little labour — the opposite of farming — so that most of the incomes corresponding to it go to the owners of capital[2] as profits, not, as in farming, to the family farmer or the labourer.[3] Saving is a much higher share of profits than of wages (and in urban areas even employees can usually save something). Thus the proportion of extra income *saved,* and hence made available for further investment and growth, is higher in a city than in a village, in industry

238

that in agriculture; and this soon outweighs, as a contribution to development, the effects of higher yields in rural areas or on farms.[4]

TWO INAPPLICABLE COUNTER-ARGUMENTS

Savings for growth?

To this *savings argument* there are two fashionable but faulty objections. First is the argument that savings to finance investment for growth may not matter much, because growth is not development, and because even growth depends on much more than savings and investment, notably on the skill and health of the working population. This is true but irrelevant, because — especially in poor economies — growth is certainly necessary (though not sufficient) for development, and conventional capital investment is needed both for growth and for other desirable changes. Furthermore, the wage-goods used up by the 'non-investment' supporters of development — doctors, educators — are diverted from supporting workers who could make extra consumer goods, just as surely as if those wage-goods were used up by such 'conventional' producers of investment goods as workers building factories or dams.

Growth is needed for development in three senses. First, even if a really poor LDC distributed its food and schools absolutely equally, everyone would remain ill-fed and under-educated. Second, the resources for material and intellectual development must come from somewhere. Third, the political leeway for development targets other than growth — equalisation, jobs, dignity, a weakening of the old constricting hierarchies of caste and tribe — can come only from growth of income sufficient to compensate some of the more powerful losers from such changes.

In poor countries growth requires extra physical capital. 'Investment in human capital' is useless without the utilised capacity to provide jobs for the educands, as India's growing army of unemployed engineers is learning to its cost. Certainly in many LDCs, notably in Africa, big outlays on training are needed if new capital investments are to be properly run and efficiently worked; certainly also, especially in Asia, the bad health of many agriculturists makes doctors a desirable complement to dams. This, however, does not make savings unimportant; it merely means that savings must not be limited, either in definition or in direction, to the financing of bits of physical capital.[5] Saving is necessary to pay a man who designs or builds a bridge — and to pay a doctor who cures farmers of worms, or a hydraulic engineer who keeps a dam going. In each case funds have to be diverted from paying people who make consumer goods such as food or clothing; hence, if economic balance is to be maintained,[6] incomes have to be diverted from buying such consumer goods, whether to private purchases of health or education, to payments of tax, or even to hoarding under the bed.[7]

Whether we call such diversion 'saving to permit investment' or (in older and more rigorous terminology that echoes both Senior and Marx, and therefore Ricardo) 'abstention to finance an economic surplus'[8] matters little. If the poor and the rural cannot spare extra income to save in the narrower sense, neither can they spare much for the wider gamut of non-consumption activities to enhance income in the future.[9] At least *prima facie*, there is still force in the belief that only a small part of extra rural income from investment will be used to swell the economic surplus—after the poor have met some of their outstanding consumption needs, and the rich have profitably re-lent to meet others.

Many types of capital?

A second attempt to remove the props from under the savings argument is the claim that physical capital is not one thing but many. The planner has indeed to allocate (or persuade private individuals to allocate) 'capital' as desired. But 'capital' is not one big blob of uniform jelly, usable to produce many different things but always in a unique undifferentiated activity called 'productive investment'. Rather capital comprises many resources — pig-iron, steel, ball-bearings, concrete, doctors — which cannot be substituted for one another by users, and which are not alternative lines of production to which one may direct a particular batch of workers or equipment. Often these sorts of capital are specific to one sector of the economy (tractors, machine-tools). Thus 'investment allocation', for yield or savings or anything else, is allegedly misconceived as a single problem. Rather, it is claimed, there are two linked sets of problems: to allocate a wide range of resources among the production of investment goods, and to allocate each of the many investment goods available (after production and foreign trade) among lines of production. Any attempt to allocate global investment according to a single criterion, whether yield or savings, means (one is told) failing to discriminate among numerous decisions requiring, possibly, distinct procedures.

In this extreme form, the attempt to stop planners making general rules is absurd. The economy is not *that* inflexible. Even in the short run, dollars can be used to import lathes, tractors, lathe factories or tractor factories (chapter 7, note 14); or a country can stop exporting iron ore and make it into steel instead; or the unspecific skills that less-developed educational systems tend to overproduce (lawyers, accountants, even general engineers) can be pushed or lured from one line of activity to another.

Moreover, planners' horizons are not *that* short. In one year, the allocation of new investments is indeed tied down by the initial structure of the economy, and unlikely to make much impact on the bundle of machines available, or therefore of items producible. But poor countries usually invest each year to the value of over 4 per cent of their capital stock (some of which has to be set against the wearing-out of the old plant). Hence about a fifth of the capital stock at the end of a five-year plan was not there at the beginning. There is no economically determined reason why the structure of this stock, and notably the proportion in agriculture, cannot alter substantially between start and finish of a plan; if it does not, and should, then the reasons are political.

However many sorts of capital goods exist, and however numerous the types of industrial capacity needed to provide them or of lines of production they can support, they have one thing in common. To increase their quantity, they have to be paid for, either by saving at home or by persuading foreigners to lend and permit an import surplus. Thus investment *finance* is allocable, even if 'investment' is not. And the savings argument, that total investment will produce yields *saved* to a greater extent if concentrated outside agriculture, is just as good—or just as bad— if used as a guide to the allocation of global investment finance, or of a particular type of investment goods already produced. The latter are seldom all that specific: some ball-bearings can be used only in an ice-cream machine, but not many; and even here one can choose how much of total investment finance should be allocated to increasing, replacing, or even maintaining the ice-cream bearings or the machines that make them.

THE SAVINGS ARGUMENT EXAMINED
Having disposed of two attempts to dismiss the debate, we now enter it. The forthcoming attack on the savings argument may recall the man who, accused of returning his neighbour's kettle with a hole in it, replied that he had never borrowed it, that he had returned it sound, and that the hole had been there when the kettle was loaned.[10] A truer parallel, I hope, is with the defence against a charge of libel that the statement alleged was not made,

that if made it was not defamatory, and that if made and defamatory it was true.

It will be argued below that:

1   Food consumption has a greater effect on the productive efficiency of workers in agriculture than elsewhere; hence income lost to saving need not, in the farm sector, therefore contribute little to output; and the impact on yield of farm investment is not exhausted by valuation of the farm product itself.

2   Extra industrial capital, far from raising profits, can lower them and depress total savings; this is less likely (or less relevant) in agriculture.

3   Personal saving by farmers, even small ones, is much more than either official statistics or the savings argument allow — and they convert savings into investment by using their own plentiful labour, not scarce and subsidised imports.

4   The enrichment of small farmers forces moneylenders to use their incomes more productively, increasing *effective* saving.

5   Personal saving is the only one of three domestic components of investment finance (the others being savings by the public sector and by firms) that is at all likely to increase just because a bigger proportion of income accrues outside agriculture.

6   Even if total savings *were* benefited much more substantially by non-farm investment, this contribution to growth would be outweighed by the lower yield on such investment, since governments can later switch high returns on farm investment to pay for further investment.

7   Insofar as people prefer to invest in their own firm or farm, to allocate investment to a low-yielding part of the economy is to 'lock in' to it their savings-out-of-yield, and hence their future investment; hence the initial choice of an unproductive sector is very damaging, since it wastes future savings on that sector too, especially if it is industry.

8   Most fundamentally, if I spend income, that is not the end of the affair; the producers of the items on which I spend my income can save or spend, the persons 'receiving their spending can do the same, etc. If the beneficiary of farm investment saves little, therefore, that saving is not lost, but only delayed. The cost of delayed saving, while real, is less than the cost of lost saving; and its weight, as an argument against farm investment, is correspondingly smaller. When we further consider the leaks into imports in the successive 'rounds' of spending, the savings argument begins to look totally unconvincing.

THE PRODUCTIVITY OF CONSUMPTION
In the US or Britain, where most people are overweight, extra food consumption probably reduces both the output per hour of work, and the number of hours put in. In poor countries, more food consumption can often mean more work at higher productivity.[11] During the food shortage in Bihar in 1967, villagers were too weak to dig or even maintain wells. In the Sudan, I have seen the difference made by hunger to workers picking cotton. These effects damage both quantity and quality of labour. The effects on quality are the more damaging. One might think that most poor villages had so much spare labour that waste did not matter. But (apart from the psychological effects, and the desirability of conserving effort in hot, wet climates) the presence of spare or unemployed labour does not make up for the damage if dirt is mixed with long-staple cotton and numerous bolls are left unharvested. Even reductions in the *quantity* of effort (often due to lack of food) reduce output, because at the peaks of work requirements in agriculture there is usually little or no competent spare labour, especially at harvest time.

It is agriculture that produces food, and lost food output is unlikely to be offset completely by higher imports or lower exports. Therefore, resources or incentives to agriculture — especially food-growing agriculture — produce outputs that can be productively consumed, offsetting the fact that, compared with other parts of the economy, less of the corresponding income is saved.

Moreover, there are several reasons to expect extra income to be used for productive, body-building consumption of food if the income is generated rurally, for example by farm investment. First, spending per person — including the value of consumed output from the farm — is lower in rural than in urban areas (pp.148-52); therefore, in rural areas more food needs remain unmet, and there is a greater chance both that extra income will be used to buy food and that such food will be needed for productive energy. Second, distribution of current (and probably extra) rural income is in most poor countries less unequal than in towns (Introduction, note 5); thus, again, a bigger share of extra income will go to those likely to spend on, and needing, extra food. Third, the typical rupee's or peso's worth of output is made with more capital and less labour in the city than in the countryside; hence the cost of replacing or duplicating labour that is inadequate because hungry is a smaller share of output; also it is more readily obtained, because in LDCs towns (unlike villages) usually have labour-exchanges and year-round jobless. Above all, the seasonality of farm production renders many workers short of food just when they need energy to work effectively; such shortages can be eased if more rural investment provides more rural income, and thus increases both supply and effective demand for food.

Rural peaks of effort are likely to be required when food is scarce and expensive. Especially in a single-crop economy, by the time weeding and harvesting have to be done, the rural family has exhausted its grain stocks — certainly if it has no land of its own and lives from labouring for others, and quite probably even if it is a small farm family, driven to sell much of its crop immediately after harvest to repay debt. Unfortunately, this period of hard work and scanty food is also the rainy season, which increases the breeding rate of numerous insect pests, and thus further expands food needs by increasing the village family's requirements for protection against disease. Many village studies confirm this unhappy coincidence of a peak in the need for food with a trough in its availability.[12] Hence more food, or more income to buy it, can — by being well timed — add a good deal to rural output; there is no analogous timing impact in cities.

Non-farm investments, moreover, often mean more overtime, and/or higher-paid (because more productive) work, for already employed urban workers; these are unlikely to be short of food initially, so that the extra output caused by their better nutrition — even to the extent that they spend extra income on food — is usually negligible. If non-agricultural investment actually creates employment for now unemployed urban workers, it will raise their productive capacity, not just by giving them a job but also because they can eat better, and thus work better when employed than when unemployed; but this effect is clearly stronger in rural areas, where extra output uses more labour and less capital.

The direct effect of food consumption (and also perhaps of better clothing, water supply and shelter) on agricultural and industrial labour input and labour efficiency is a scandalously neglected research topic. Certainly it shifts the balance somewhat in favour of rural investment: extra rural income is relatively likely to provide food; rural workers are worse fed; and at low calorie intakes more food means higher productivity. This gives rural (but probably not urban) consumption out of extra wages an important productive role. Two indirect arguments, however, need consideration.

First, 'You can't eat steel.' The fact that much industrial output is a form of forced abstention from consumption is often used as an argument in its favour. Conversely, however, insofar as extra output comprises food; some of which goes to the hungry worker, it too is an input into future production.[13]

Second, the hunger of rural workers is not caused only by lack of food, but also by a special sort of maldistribution of power to buy food. This familiar curse of poor rural people is the 'debt spiral'. A wedding or a bad harvest forces them to borrow; when the next harvest comes, they must sell much of it at rock-bottom prices to repay; therefore, well before the harvest after that, the food has run out and a new, bigger loan is necessary; and so it goes on.[14] If the income level in villages can be substantially raised overall — even better if it can be done selectively, so that the really poor gain most, and gain when they would otherwise have to borrow — this vicious circle can be broken; and with it a major reason why so many small farmers, just before harvest, are too badly fed to work properly or sufficiently.

We know far too little about how, or how much, dietary improvements help working efficiency. But the relationship is a powerful argument for using investment to grow food, and for not being too miserable, even as growthmen, if the incomes paid to *grow* food are used to *buy* food[15] instead of being saved. There is little reason to accept the assumption behind the savings argument, that the yield of income helps create future output only if it is saved; in what follows, we do so only to expose more basic fallacies in the savings argument.

INVESTMENT, PROFITS AND SAVING

Industrial workers may save a slightly bigger share of their income than farmworkers, or even small farmers, but the effect is small. The real thrust of the savings argument is that industrial investment, because it produces output by using much plant and equipment (capital) per employee, generates much profit income relative to wage income. Profit-receivers, being fairly rich and seeing investment prospects in their own firms, save much higher proportions of income than wage-earners. Hence there is an *a priori* argument for putting investment where it yields profit income rather than wage income.

To use this argument to advocate industrial rather than farm investment, however, is over-simple. Suppose we want to get the share of profits in income as high as possible. By investing in industry, which uses lots of capital, we certainly boost the volume of capital owned (publicly or privately) relative to the number of wage-earners. But the *amount* of profit depends on the profit *rate* per unit of capital, as well as on the number of such units. And, by increasing the volume of industrial capital, one diminishes the profit rate upon it in several ways: by picking increasingly unpromising sites or industries (the better ones having been used already); by increasing the competition among the suppliers of the products of capital; and by boosting industrial supply while one denies oneself, through failure to expand agriculture, the benefits of mass demand.[16]

Profits can also be eroded by extra industrial capital through its impact on the industrial wage bill. Although few workers are employed in industry, the extra capital equipment supporting each one increases both his market value (since he adds more to output, an employer can afford profitably to bid his wage up higher, if need be, against other employers) and—more important—his bargaining power. Extra industrial equipment can easily reduce from 50 per cent to 25 per cent the share of a firm's costs comprising wages; then the workers know that the proportionate burden to the firm of a given wage rise is halved—and the cost of letting capital stand idle during a strike is sharply increased. In the restrictive union situation in industry in many poor countries, these benefits will largely go to *existing* workers;[17] but even if they all went to new ones—more jobs rather than higher wage rates—profits would still be eroded. Economics is complicated; we cannot be sure that more capital per worker means more profits per rupee of wages. Industrialisation *a l'outrance,* indeed, often means public or private investment that is likely to incur losses, for which the operators are compensated by state subsidy: not a situation helpful to savings.

DO FARMERS SAVE?

The savings argument against farm investment concentrates upon the relatively poor capacity of farmers, especially small farmers, to save. We shall argue that personal saving, out of family income, is only part of the story; but are farmers really that bad at it?

The belief that they are has two sources. One is statistics of national income, which seriously understate such non-monetised activities as farm saving embodied directly in investment — for example, time spent by a small farm family in desilting its own field irrigation channel.[18] The other is the view that poor people simply cannot save much — which overlooks both the special incentive to plough back into one's own concern, and the fact that the farm family's ample off-season leisure can be diverted to do-it-yourself investment, such as desilting that channel, without reducing the farmer's sparse consumption (as would happen if workers were hired to do the desilting investment, or if the farmer did it while he might be weeding his rice).

Careful estimates of agricultural saving, whether indirect (by seeing how much investment, on or off the farm, it finances) or direct (by enquiries at farm or village level), reveal rural and agricultural propensities to save much higher than those calculated from national income figures. Indirect estimates suggest that agriculturists in West Pakistan were privately saving a good deal of their disposable income in 1964-5;[19] indeed urban savings were 8 to 9 per cent of income as against 12 to 13 per cent in the rural sector,[20] though this owes much to the emergence of a capitalist farm sector making heavy and not altogether efficient calls on the imports and investment made possible by that saving. Nevertheless, the surprisingly high farm savings ratios have echoes elsewhere: Thailand, 15 per cent in 1963 (as against 10% of farm income invested in the agricultural sector, not all of it home-financed);[21] India, between 5 and 8 per cent in 1967-8.[22] These indirect data contrast with estimates based on national incomes of only 2 or 3 per cent; but direct micro-studies reveal even higher savings. A survey of Indian evidence in the 1950s suggests that rural savings rates were running around 12 per cent.[23] The current work in progress in India's nine Agro-economic Research Centres, into the use of extra farm incomes generated by the 'green revolution', looks like showing even higher rates. Colin Clark provides a different sort of evidence, showing that small-farm savings sufficed in several poor countries to provide more capital per acre than most big farms enjoy.[24]

The evidence refutes the claim that farm investment will generate incomes of which almost nothing is saved. What *is* true is, first, that some rural saving is drained off by price twists to finance socially low-yielding urban investment (ch. 13)—but this is part of urban bias, not a defence of it; second, that farmers would have more incentive to save, and to embody their savings in farm investment, if its returns were not artificially depressed by policies turning the terms of trade against agriculture (chapter 13); and, above all, that *at a given income rural people save more than urban people*. The main reason why rural people do not save still more is that urban bias keeps them poor! For example, in India in 1961-2, rural households with Rs. 4,800-7,200 yearly saved 19 per cent of income; urban households with Rs. 6,000-10,000, though richer, managed only 11.4 per cent. Rural savings were low because fewer than 7 per cent of rural households got above Rs. 3,000 yearly -- a level below which urban households had *negative* saving! — as against 14 per cent of urban households.[25] The savings effort of the rural not-so-poor was all the more remarkable in that (1) though poorer than comparable urban groups they supported larger households (see chapter 12, note 29), (2) they faced higher costs of living (see chapter 12, note 32).

The 'farmers don't save' argument owes such force as it retains to distortions produced by urban bias itself. Even in an economy thus distorted, the argument is questionable. In one freer from urban bias, it would be negligible.

MAKING MONEYLENDERS PRODUCTIVE

The 'debt cycle' diverts the savings of the rural rich — lucratively to themselves — away from financing investment towards supporting 'dissaving' (consumption in excess of income) through usurious loans to the rural poor. Rural investment, to raise incomes all round, is politically essential to alleviate this. Legal restraints on interest rates are a waste of time and paper, so long as thousands of lenders want to do business at higher market rates, and millions of borrowers are prepared to pay.[26] Even killing the moneylenders is useless, as it will *worsen* the shortage of consumer credit. Only a richer rural mass can reduce the demand for such credit; and only such reduction can drive private money-lending incomes to support investment, or indeed assure banks that their rural loans will be used for investment purposes.[27]

Credit cooperatives are sometimes seen as cheap methods to break the rural debt cycle and increase savings capacity, without the cost and effort of massive investment to raise rural incomes. These palliatives seldom work, superficially for organisational reasons (corrupt secretaries, etc.), but really for two more fundamental reasons. First, the rural power structure ensures that the big landlord-employer-moneylender controls most of the resources of most village cooperatives;[28] where will the farmer who fights him get his next job, or *consumer* loan, when he needs it?[29] (And urban bias involves steering resources to big farmers anyway — see p. 289.) Secondly, the basic shortage of consumer credit — and the encouragement that the consequent high interest rates provide to wealthy villagers to lend for consumption, rather than to save for investment — can never be met by organisations geared to producer credit alone.[30] The only way to free the poor villager from the debt bind — and to force the rural moneylender to use his savings to buy (or lend for the purchase of) investment goods instead — is public investment to benefit the villages: investment big and well-distributed enough to raise mass rural incomes, and thus to reduce the need for crisis borrowing.

DE-EMPHASISING 'PERSONAL' SAVING

Even to the extent that an extra rupee of farm income is less likely to be saved by its recipient than an extra pound of non-farm income, the total impact on the nation's capacity to save is not necessarily affected. Rich countries, as a rule, do save a higher proportion of income than poor ones; but the difference is due much more to higher *company* savings than to distinctions in family thrift.[31] The development path of now-rich countries tells the same story: in the early period extra plough-back by companies was the main source of extra savings. Even if we define 'savings' more widely as contribution to the economic surplus, family thrift is not the main thrust; it is *State,* or *de facto* community,[32] support for education and health that distinguishes rich from poor countries — and in some cases that marked the run-up to the beginning of accelerated development process, notably in Bismarck's Germany and in Tokugawa Japan.

Family saving is often earmarked for dwellings. It is hard to find cases where private saving, out of personal disposable income, provided the main financial support for the early stages of development investment.

How, then, does an extra rupee of farm income differ from an extra rupee of non-farm income in its impact on *total* saving? A crude statistical test, for India, shows no clear difference.[33] More investigation is needed. Is the difference so small in poor countries other than India? What is the effect on savings *next* year of extra farm or non-farm income this year? However, the above finding should survive such enquiries. Government saving benefits in obvious ways from extra farm incomes: when farmers do well, the government need not spend on relief works, and finds it easier to collect taxes on farmers. Moreover, the capacity of companies making fertilisers or transistor radios to save and plough back profits increases when farmers and farmworkers have more money to spend on such products — indeed, a high rural tendency to spend extra income on domestic output could thus even *help* savings.

ARE SAVINGS EFFECTS ENOUGH TO JUSTIFY EARLY INDUSTRIALISATION?

Will all this reduce the difference in impact on a poor economy's savings capacity, as between extra farm and non-farm income, enough to emasculate the savings argument — so that we can safely rely on the fact that farming, and especially small farming, shows yields higher than other activities as a justification for raising farm investment? It helps to translate the 'yield-savings debate' into simple algebra. The rate of growth of an economy (extra income this year as a proportion of last year's income), written *g*, must equal two items multiplied together. The first is the proportion of income ploughed back to finance new investment (savings last year as a proportion of income last year), written s. The second is the extra income associated with that extra saving-and-investment (the marginal output/capital ratio), written v. The relationship of g, s and v can be expressed as an identity, $g = sv$, for

$$\frac{\text{extra income}}{\text{last year's income}} = \frac{\text{saving-for-extra-capital}}{\text{last year's income}} \times \frac{\text{extra-income}}{\text{extra capital from saving}}$$

The key question is: will the fact that non-farm investments, over the years, generate a bigger s outweigh their smaller v? In most LDCs, farm investment has a dramatic advantage in v, out-performing non-farm investment by at least 2.5 to 1 (table 8.2). That is in spite of price distortions making investment cheaper to industry than to agriculture, and undervaluing farm output relatively to non-farm output (chapter 13). Moreover, if urban bias did not direct so big a part of farm investment to large farmers, who do not support it with as much productive effort as small farmers (but who do market more of their output, largely to the cities), the farm sector's advantage in v would be even higher. To put the true advantage in yield of the farm sector — in prices reflecting real scarcity values, and assuming efficient allocation between big and small farmers — at 3 to 1 over the non-farm sector is to be conservative for most poor countries.

So if v in agriculture is about three times v in non-agriculture — if the farm sector is thrice as good at turning extra capital into output as the non-farm sector — then the non-farm sector needs to have an s at least three times as high as the farm sector, that is, to be *very* much better at ploughing back its benefits into saving, if present investment allocations are to be justified from the standpoint of growth.[34] There is no evidence of such big differences; if we are considering the effect on *total* national saving, a difference of 1.3 to 1 between the results of an extra Rs. 1,000 of income in non-farm and farm sectors is probably an overstatement.

All this illustrates two principles of policy. First, three-quarters of damn-all is damn-all. A massive urban project, misconceived in the heat of a premature industrialisation programme and standing half-idle, is likely to yield so little that, even if three-quarters of its yield were saved, the total saving would be small. Had the equipment used for the urban project instead been diverted to a minor irrigation network, the yield could have been four times as high; even if only one-quarter were saved, one-quarter of four is more than three-quarters of one, so the rural project generates more savings to finance later investments.

The second principle is that policies can be switched. Industrialising governments might do best to increase incomes first, through 'going for yield' by investments in the farm sector, and *later* milking those higher incomes for savings to support non-farm investment. There will then be more to milk than there would have been to support premature industrialisation; and the savings fund will then support a larger number of mutually complementary non-farm investments on a decently large scale. Paradoxically, the fact that many Indian industries have been set up in too small-scale plants[35] owes much to premature industrialisation; high-yielding farm investment is neglected, so there is not enough national income to provide the savings that would finance large, efficient factories in the required sectors. 'Going for yield' first, via carefully chosen farm investment, would later release much more finance for industrial investment — by the well-timed injection of a smaller *share* of a larger savings *fund*. (This argument is strongly analogous to Wicksell's point that 'if by sacrificing 50 crowns . . . now I can receive in return 100 from a one-year production process, but 150 from a two-year one . . . I ought to choose the *one*-year alternative, even if I intend to wait two years for my returns, because by repeating the one-year production process the next year on double the scale (since I then have 100 crowns at my disposal) I will obtain 200 at the end of the second year instead of 150.')[36]

THE 'LOCK-IN' EFFECT

It is especially important in poor countries not to steer investment to low-yield sectors or firms, because the yield from such investment, if saved, is likely to finance reinvestment in those same sectors. Where sophisticated methods of financial control are scarce, a man will often be prepared to make big sacrifices of yield expectation (and hence of the social efficiency of investment)[37] in order to keep an overview of the uses of his savings. Also capital markets are imperfect — businessmen in one line of activity know less about prospects in other lines in Pakistan or Kenya, than in the USA or the USSR.[38]

In poor countries the vast majority of businesses are family-based farms, small family-run concerns giving urban services or retailing, and so forth. Organised financial channels — banks and stock markets — lack the local knowledge, decentralisation of outlets, or capacity for small-scale organisation to lend to these small family concerns. These, in turn, know more about their own prospects than about those of big firms, and avoid administrative costs (and other people's management fees) by investing their savings in their own concerns. Therefore, a small farm or firm tends to 'lock in' savings to finance its own investment; and so does the non-farm sector as a whole. Low yields — or high — thus tend to get reinvested where they first materialise, and to perpetuate themselves.

Often the 'lock-in' effect goes further. Governments characteristically encourage banks to lend below market rates of interest to stimulate investment by approved (that is, usually, industrial) customers. There is seldom enough money to satisfy all potential borrowers, and rationing takes place, for example, by the allocation of a bank's loans to firms whose directors are represented on its board,[39] and which keep any liquid funds in the bank. Apart from this, difficulties of communication, knowledge and even dialect keep funds within a district or even village of origin; and extended-family, tribal or caste loyalties further reduce the capacity of funds to circulate in search of a high return.[40] All these lock-ins — especially that in the family farm — are strongest where risk is most feared; a Western shareholder will reduce his risks by 'spreading his portfolio' over different sorts of company, but an Indian or Nigerian farmer with a small surplus is usually more concerned with the risks from ignorance, and is likely to keep his cash at home and 'spread his portfolio' indirectly by growing a larger variety of crops, purchasing irrigation facilities, or otherwise reducing the impact of risk upon his own firm's saving-and-investment.

Hence, to justify a choice of industrial investments for our *initial* savings because of their high s (and despite their low v), the planner in an LDC usually needs a bigger s-advantage than might appear. That is because an investment, once committed to a high-yield or low-yield sector, tends to 'lock in' its savings there. There is little to be said for generating lots of savings if they are destined for low-yield activities.[41]

Admittedly one sometimes does not know, or owing to future price changes cannot anticipate, the returns to investment when making a choice between sectors. However, if mistakes have been made, the 'unlocking' effect, needed to lure farm savings to support industrial investment later, is surely smaller than the 'tide-reversing' effort needed to lure industrial savers to invest in farms. Dramatic technical progress in farming can do this, but cannot be relied upon. So uncertainty, and the implicit need to keep flexible, strengthens the case against 'lock-in' in the non-farm sector, from which later extraction is likely to be especially difficult.

THE BASIC OBJECTION

Suppose all our previous objections to the savings argument are unfounded, in other words, that:

1   Only the *saving* out of extra income helps future growth; extra consumption makes people fatter, not fitter to work;

2   Farmers really do save a very small part of the extra income from any investment benefiting them;

3   Extra capital in industry raises the *amount* of profit in an economy, and hence the *amount* of personal saving, more than it would in agriculture;

4   It is *personal* saving, not government or company saving, that provides the main source of development capital;

5   Even if small farmers get richer, moneylenders do not find much of their cash diverted from consumer loans towards investment finance;

6   Relatively to farm investment, the savings advantages of in-dustrial investment are more important than its comparatively poor yield;

7   This is not outweighed by the tendency of returns from invest-ment to be reinvested (if at all) in the sector where they initially accrued — and thus 'locked into' initial yield levels.

Even if we accept these seven unlikely propositions, there re-mains a basic objection to the savings argument.

The objection is that *cash spent is not spent for ever.* If farmers spend most of their extra income, it is received by the workers and capital-owners who make the goods those farmers buy, and who may well save much of these receipts. Even if they do not, by spending they enrich a further set of consumer-goods producers, who may be more thrifty. It can be proved that: 'In a *closed*[1] eco-nomy, if *extra initial income is provided*[2] to any group or groups, the *ultimate*[3] *cash*[4] value of extra saving is *normally*[5] the same as the extra initial income, and hence independent of the savings behaviour of the groups.'

The italicised words are explained below; but this statement means that normally, however spendthrift the villagers, and how-ever thrifty the townsfolk, investment initially enriching *either* group by £1,000 will eventually mean just £1,000 of total saving.

1) By assuming a 'closed' economy, we assume away foreign trade, so that income cannot be spent on imports. This simplifies the argument, but does not affect its substance.

2) There are several ways in which extra initial income can be provided, to be saved or spent by recipients, and if spent to be further spent or saved by the second 'round' of recipients, etc., in what economists call a *multiplier* process. Usually we think of initial income as accruing to people for work on investment goods — for example, to build a factory or a dam. In this context — where we are comparing the fate of a given volume of money

benefiting rural or urban workers—we could just as well consider the 'extra initial income' as £1,000 worth of *benefits* from extra production due, respectively, to a dam or to a factory. Even if the government provided the extra initial income by printing the money, so that it had to choose to give it to villagers or to townsmen, the statement would hold and the analysis would be the same.

3) By 'ultimate' value, we mean the value towards which total saving tends, after a large number of rounds of spending-and-saving have occurred. To take a simple case, if *everybody* spends four-fifths and saves one-fifth of extra income, an extra initial income of £1,000 produces an ultimate value of savings of just £1,000. At the first round, £200 is saved. The other £800 is spent, and its recipients save another fifth of it, or £160, and spend once more the remaining (£800−£160) or £640. Of this, once again, one-fifth is saved . . . and so on. Ultimate saving is £200 $(1 + (4/5) + (4/5)^2 + (4/5)^3 + . . .)$ which adds up to £1,000.[42] However, saving soon pays for growth soon; there is a cost in delaying saving—the benefits do not accrue until later on. There may be a further cost of delay, viz:

4) 'Cash value' means that no guarantees against inflation are on offer! If saving is delayed, inflation may erode the value of the equipment and machinery that it finances.

5) 'Normally' is included only in order to rule out a wildly unlikely, indeed pathological, case, as we shall see below.

The statement is repeated below for convenience. We then give two surprising examples of its validity, both for a simple economy with only two 'groups', in Agriculture and in Industry. This is followed by an analogy to show why it works (a formal proof requires a little matrix algebra and is relegated to the appendix at the end of this chapter). The section closes with a discussion of the policy implications of the fact that 'In a closed economy, if extra initial income is provided to any group or groups, the ultimate cash value of extra saving is normally the same as the extra initial income, and hence independent of the savings behaviour of the groups,' and of possible modifications in a real-life, 'open' economy, with foreign trade.

In the first example, we suppose that Agriculturists save none of their extra income, spending nine-tenths of it on products of other Agriculturists and one-tenth on the products of Industry. In Industry *all* extra income is saved. Superficially, that looks very favourable to investment benefiting Industry, on the savings argument. But what happens? If £100 of income initially benefits Industry, it is all saved, and savings rise by £100. If the £100 benefits Agriculturists, they spend one-tenth (£10) on Industry where it is saved;

they spend the other £90 on products of the Agriculturists, who spend one-tenth (£9) on Industry where it is saved, the remaining £81 being spent on products of further Agriculturists; the latter spend one-tenth (£8.10) on Industry where it is saved . . . and so on. At each successive 'round', extra farm cash income is nine-tenths of the addition at the last round, and of that nine-tenths, one-tenth is spent on industry and saved by recipients. Hence *total* saving is $[£100 \ (\frac{1}{10} + \frac{1}{10}(\frac{9}{10}) + \frac{1}{10}(\frac{9}{10})^2 + \ . \ . \ .)]$ or £100. This is the same as when the income went straight to Industry (though it is delayed).

But perhaps this is because of the 'leak' from Agricultural spending to Industrialists, and hence to saving? Very well; in the second example, we plug the leak. This time, suppose Agriculturists spend nine-tenths of extra income on the produce of other Agriculturists, and save the remaining tenth; in Industry, as before, all extra income is saved. As before, £100 benefiting Industry goes straight into saving. The £100 benefiting Agriculture goes nine-tenths into spending on Agriculture (to create new farm income), one-tenth (£10) into saving; of the £90 spent, one-tenth (£9) is saved at the next round; of the £81 again spent, £8.10 is saved at the round after that; and the series builds up as before. Ultimate cash saving still totals £100.

So there is no difference in the total, ultimate cash value of saving—it is the same as the cash value of the initial benefit—whether we allocate all that benefit to (1) an industrial sector that saves everything, (2) a farm sector that saves nothing, spends one-tenth of any extra income on industrial products, and spends the rest on farm products (first example), or (3) a farm sector that saves a small proportion of extra income and spends all the rest on farm products (second example). In the Appendix at the end of this chapter, we prove that the savings generated will exactly equal the initial benefit, irrespective of the benefiting sector, *unless* one sector (or group of sectors) saves none of its extra income *and* uses none of it to buy from any sector which does (a pathological case to which exceptions are indeed 'normal'!).[43]

This can be made intuitively plausible by analogy. Consider a large, cuboid water container, with waterproof sides, divided into many water cells of cubic shapes. Each water cell has a plug in a hole at the bottom, and partitions at the sides to separate it from each of the other water cells. The plugs and partitions may or may not be perfectly waterproof, but they are not absorbent. Under the entire container is a very large tub, which will catch any liquid flowing out of the container through the bottom set of plugs. Now suppose that ten gallons of cold water ('investment') are poured into the cells. All this water must *ultimately* find its way into the tub below (as 'savings')—no more, no less—unless some of it was initially poured—or finds its way—into at least one cell ('sector') with a perfectly waterproof plug ('no saving out of extra income') *and* separated by perfectly waterproof partitions, directly or indirectly, from any leakage of water into any other cell with an imperfectly waterproof plug or partition (that is, 'no spending on products of any sector in which the producers *do* save some extra income, *or* spend any part of it on *any* products of any sector which saves some extra income, or which spends. . . .').

What happens in an 'open' economy, where extra income can leak abroad (by being spent on imports) as well as be saved? Let us try and adjust the analogy. The water must still normally all leak out of the water container, but this time it can find its way into either of two tubs underneath: 'saving' and 'imports'. The ultimate cash value of saving-plus-imports will be the same (normally) as the value of the initial set of incomes. What matters is to keep the real value of saving high relative to imports. In the extreme examples earlier in this section, where the industrial sector saved all its extra income, the criterion would turn in favour of that sector (which would have the maximum saving-to-import ratio possible, infinity). But this story is not complete, because 'lock-in' effect means that industrial saving tends to finance further industrial investment, which has a high import content. Nor is it realistic, because even in the non-farm sector as a whole in a poor country the wage share is unlikely to be less than half, of which a substantial share is spent on imports, while even some of the profit share is used for luxury and largely imported consumption. While in agriculture both the share of labour income and its beneficiaries' urge to spend may well be higher, such spending is much likelier to be on domestic rather than imported products. Of the ultimate saving-and-imports (equal to initial benefits, irrespective of the group receiving them), the share claimed by imports will probably be higher if the initial benefits are enjoyed by a typical urban group, than if they go to the rural sector.

So the savings argument is stood on its head. In a 'closed' economy, long-run cash savings are not boosted by steering initial benefits to (industrial) savers, because all those benefits normally leak into cash savings ultimately. More dramatically, moreover, in a real-life 'open' economy, it is savings *plus imports* that ultimately mop up the total cash value of those benefits; hence, to finance high levels of interest, it is the proportion of savings-plus-imports going to imports that needs to be kept down;[44] and the efficient way to do that—to keep 'ultimate saving' high as a proportion of the constant sum of 'ultimate-saving-plus-ultimate-imports' — is to steer initial benefit not to high savers but to low importers; not to city but to village; not to industry but to agriculture.[45]

Investment that benefits low-saving, high-domestic-spending, rural groups has its dangers. The low savings *delay* growth, because extra domestic investment cannot be paid for until the leak into savings ultimately happens (though if the initial benefits were placed in high-yield sectors, foreign loans might well be possible to tide over the delay). Moreover, only *cash* saving is ultimately unaffected by the direction of initial benefit; *real value* is likely to be eroded before 'ultimacy' happens.[46] The trouble with high-spending beneficiaries is that they bid up the price of the consumer goods that they buy with their extra income. This makes the production of such things more profitable. People trying to make such profits, therefore, bid up the prices of the investment goods that make the consumer goods. This reduces the value of the equipment that can be financed by the saving, when it ultimately materialises.

But this is one of those 'long chains of reasoning' in economics against which Alfred Marshall warned us. The government can try to snap the links at several places. It can try to ensure that 'inflation' in consumer goods is felt in the formation of queues rather than in price rises; it can steer imports towards capital equipment, increasing its supply, and protecting it against the pressure of inflation; or, as savings materialise, it can encourage savers to switch towards financing types of investment less affected by price inflation (yet desirable on other grounds). In any case, the task of policy becomes to keep inflation away from investment goods,[47] thereby maintaining the real value of saving even when delayed; not to push initial benefits, whether from supplying equipment or working with it towards a low-yielding, well-off, albeit high-saving, industrial sector.

APPENDIX

For any closed economy, let C be the non-singular[48] matrix (m by m) of marginal propensities to consume. Then the jth element in the ith row, C_{ij}, is the proportion of extra income in the ith sector which is spent on products of the jth sector. Any row sum, $\sum_{j=1}^{m} C_{ij}$ for each value of i, must lie between zero (representing a marginal propensity to save or MPS $= 1$ in the ith sector) and unity (an MPS of zero in i).

Now impose, on the spending pattern represented by the matrix

C, a set of extra initial incomes (such as those created by investment demands) for sectors $1, 2 \ldots m$. This set can be represented by a column vector D with m elements, such that (for any i between 1 and m) d_i, which may be positive or zero, is the extra income created in the ith sector by the initial investment. Now when the income-receivers in the ith sector receive d_i, they will spend $c_{i1}d_i$ on the products of Sector 1 and create that amount of secondary income there; $c_{i2}d_i$ in Sector 2; and so for all sectors. This applies to all values of d_i from $i=1$ to $i=m$. Hence, if primary income was D, secondary income is identical with first-round spending out of D and is CD. Hence first-round saving is the sum of the elements of $(D-CD)$.

The new column vector, this time of secondary spending, CD, has to be pre-multiplied by the C-matrix of marginal propensities to consume in just the same way. Hence tertiary income, which is identical with the secondary spending out of CD, is C^2D; and hence aggregate second-round saving is the sum of the elements of $(CD-C^2D)$.

The process continues through numerous rounds, and the value of *total* final saving tends to the sum of the elements of S, where

(1) $S = (D-CD) + (CD-C^2D) + (C^2D-C^3D) + \ldots$

or

(2) $S = (D-CD)(I+C+C^2+\ldots)$

or, since $0 \leqslant c_{ij} < 1$,

(3) $S = (D-CD)(I-C)^{-1}$

or

(4) $S = D(I-C)(I-C)^{-1} = D$.

In words, if all the above operations are legitimate, total saving *ultimately* equals the cash value of total investment, irrespective of the distribution of that investment among sectors.[49]

Can the above argument go wrong? Only if some group of sectors uses *all* its extra income to buy its own products, saving nothing *and* buying nothing more from the rest of the economy; only if C is capable of being block-diagonalised and contains at least one block in which each of the rows adds up to exactly unity.[50] In this case, the decomposable submatrix of wholly independent, zero-saving sectors obeys its own (infinite-multiplier, hyper-inflationary) laws. But if even one-millionth of its extra income is either saved or used to buy products of the 'normal' economy, all is well.

11 The rural skill drain

Loyal to the economistic dogma that what cannot be counted does not count, most discussions of rural-urban resource flows have concentrated on the more easily measurable sluices: the volume of rural taxation and rural public outlay, the net flow of agricultural private saving and investment, the intersectoral terms of trade. We shall turn to these later. However, crucial, perhaps larger, flows result from the use of the system of education, together with subsequent assignments of, and incentives to, educated persons.

In most poor countries today the process of rural education and its aftermath is a huge sieve, through which the ablest young people pass to the cities, there to help the urban elite. The content of rural schooling is largely irrelevant to rural needs; and, by being enabled to retain its intelligent young leaders for agricultural development,[1] *the rural sector in almost every poor country would benefit from the termination of rural education.*

That is not recommended here. It would restrict both personal opportunities and the training of whatever elite poor countries need; and it would hurt the more talented village children, and their parents — who gladly make sacrifices for their children's urban future, sometimes out of family feeling, sometimes in the hope of remittances (against which they do not set the lost contribution of their children to other villagers' welfare). But the italicised statement, while not a guide to action, does dramatise the predicament of a rural sector whose education is moulded by, and for, urban hands.

TOO LITTLE AND TOO MUCH

Both efficiency and equity suggest, oddly enough, that the rural sector is receiving both too little and too much education. Too much, given the scarcity of rural opportunities — itself largely the result of urban bias — which compels many educated villagers to seek work in the cities, further draining the rural sector. Too little, because people are being unfairly and inefficiently denied life-chances by the accident of rural birth; in India, the child born in a community of more than five thousand persons has seven and a half times as good a chance of receiving a university or college education as the child born in a small (rural) community.[2] This disparity is much less than in most poor countries. At least half the educational resources devoted in poor countries to teaching urban-born undergraduates could, with higher returns, be used to teach rural-born undergraduates instead.

The share of education allotted to the *rural-born child* is *not enough* either to give him[3] a fair share of the chances of personal development available in his country or to allocate educat*ing* resources efficiently; yet, given the excessive incentives and directives for educated persons to work in cities, the share of education allotted to the *rural sector* is *more than enough* to harm both its prospects of development and the efficiency with which educated resources are allocated. To increase the educational prospects of the rural child will increase, more than proportionally, the drain of capable persons from village to town. The point is illustrated in table 11.1.

At each educational level, the role of the rural sector is (1) *lower* than its role in the relevant age-group, producing both unfairness to rural children and misallocation of teaching resources; (2) *higher* than its prospects of retaining, as rural workers, educated persons from that group,[4] producing both a brain-drain out of the villages and — we shall argue — a misallocation of skilled persons. To increase rural educational chances alone, while making (1) better, would make (2) worse. A remedy for the inefficiencies and inequities of (1) *and* (2) would need simultaneous efforts to make rural work more attractive (and urban work less attractive)[5] to educated persons, and to carry through a rural education drive.

How does the rural skill drain work out in practice? First, we give a crude valuation of the cost, to the villages, of transferring skilled people to the cities of India. Second, we look at the example of Delhi University. Third, we examine the distribution of *educating* and of *educated* persons in a number of poor countries, with special attention to doctors.

THE VALUE OF THE SKILL DRAIN

The extra income enjoyed by educated persons is not a true measure of the return to education,[6] but does provide a minimum estimate of the value transferred from village to town when such persons migrate. Having enhanced their earning capacity by education, they then transfer this extra capacity to the town; the 'extra' is their direct impact on average urban income. The estimate is a minimum because it leaves out the indirect effects of education that are 'urbanised' by migration: effects on the migrant's well-being not reflected in his wage (for example, that he can read a

newspaper), and effects on other people of more educated neighbours (literacy and numeracy are especially important here).

On this basis, the minimum estimate from table 11.1 is that,
around 1964-5, the value in India of the services of educated people
born in villages, but resident in towns, was about £100 million,
or 2.3 per cent of total rural income in that year.[7] Moreover, almost all the indirect benefits must have accrued to the urban sector.
Nor would these educated migrants have been useless to the village; education helps villagers to use existing resources more
fruitfully, and to assess new resources more accurately.[8]

A DRAINING UNIVERSITY AT WORK

A survey of Delhi University students showed that in 1957-8 only
3.8 per cent came from farm families, and as few as 1.1 per cent
wished to return to agriculture. In this survey 22.2 per cent came
from rural areas;[9] a roughly comparable study suggests that at
most 7.5 per cent return there,[10] so that at least two-thirds of
Delhi University's rural-based students ($22.2 - 7.5$, as a proportion of 22.2) were 'drained' to urban areas as a concomitant (and
in many cases surely as a result) of university education. Incidentally, the fact that a first-rate and rurally-aware university like
Delhi had only 22 per cent of students from rural areas, as against
34 per cent for all Indian places of higher learning (table 11.1),
reveals a hidden component of urban bias in educational provision: facilities substantially used by rural educands are usually
inferior to comparably graded facilities used mainly by their urban
counterparts.

BAD SCHOOLS FOR IGNORANT RUSTICS

The rural child seldom gets even half the town child's chance of an
education. Moreover, the villages are still often strongholds of
rote learning for recitation from Bible, Koran or Gita. Also inadequate, in quantity and quality, is the village educand's share of
teachers. This is both a cause and an effect of rural skill drain: a
cause, since it compels many bright children to urbanise if they
seek adequate secondary or even primary education, and this is
often the first step towards permanent settlement in the city; an
effect, because if more of the able teachers of rural origin worked
in the villages the problem would be less serious. In India in 1961,
there were just over twice as many teachers (of all types),[11] per
person of teachable age, working in urban areas as in rural areas.
Moreover, the disparity increased as the level of schooling rose; at

secondary level, there were *seven*[12] times as many teachers per potential pupil in urban as in rural areas. When analysis of the 1971 census is complete, it will show a similar picture.

This difference is echoed in Argentina, though the differences between village and town are less marked at primary level. The Argentine urban primary school child seems to enjoy twice the prospects of *secondary* education of his rural counterpart; for every hour of primary-school teaching the capital city enjoyed 3.7 hours of secondary teaching, as against only 1.4 hours in the rest of the country.[13] In most poor countries, too, the turnover rate of rural teachers is much higher, and the quality of their buildings and equipment much lower, than in urban areas — leading to very high drop-out rates among rural students, as a Nigerian survey shows.[14]

Figures alone cannot convey the inappropriateness of rural schooling. Textbooks often identify urbanisation with success. Competent training for farming is very rare. Drop-out is worsened by bad timing of vacations — in India's biggest state, school examinations coincide with a peak harvest season![15]

LITTLE RURAL EDUCATION — BUT FEWER RURAL EX-EDUCANDS

The relatively low rural literacy rate, apart from measuring the shortage of schools for villagers (and the reluctance of the schooled to remain villagers), reflects the understaffing of the farm sector by people who can fully and swiftly grasp new techniques.

In all cases, agriculture's shortage of educated workers increases as we go up the educational scale. This suggests that the Indian evidence of 'rural skill drain' (pp. 260-1) has counterparts in other poor countries. Many of the educated urbanisers are rural literates, trained, and attractively rewarded, only for urban work.

Much of the urban-rural income differential, moreover, is due to the fact that the village under present policies offers poor job prospects to trained persons, so that (apart from a few idealists) the rural-born ex-educand who returns home is the failure. In India in 1960-1, one in eight matriculates and graduates living in rural areas was jobless, as against about one in sixteen in the towns.[16] Once in work, the matriculate might expect to earn over 43 per cent more in urban than in rural areas, and the urban graduate over three times more — as against only 25 per cent for the uneducated, barely enough to cover the extra transport and housing requirements of urban life, on top of the 10 to 15 per cent higher urban prices.[17] In Sri Lanka (Ceylon), the median urban

unskilled worker earns only 11 per cent more than his rural col-
league, while for clerical and allied workers the difference is almost
80 per cent.[18] In Eastern Ghana, a clear urban advantage in real
income emerges only above middle-school level.[19]

Thus an uneducated man, or one who fails to acquire a city education, loses little by going back to the village. But any educated
and competent person, with skills usable in either rural or urban
sector, will prefer the latter, unless he is extremely idealistic. Even
people with high-level skills apparently specific to agriculture find
it pays them better to exploit low-level skills in industry; in Argentina in 1959, out of every twenty agronomists, five were employed
in industry and only two in agriculture![20] The *failure* — the
drop-out from city education, or the graduate who cannot hold
down his urban job — is the most likely educated migrant to
return to the village.

This partly explains the big urban-rural gaps in educated persons'
prospects of pay and employment, and the association for skilled
people of rural work and low status. The rural sector in general,
and agriculture in particular, enjoys staggeringly small endowments of skilled persons (and those they retain are *either* no good
or rare idealists). In India in 1961, 13 per cent of the urban workforce, but only 1 per cent of the rural workforce, were matriculates;
in agriculture alone, the corresponding figures are 2 per cent[21]
and 0.4 per cent; 73 per cent of rural workers, but only 42 per cent
of urban workers, were illiterate. In rurally based farming, eight
out of ten Indian workers were illiterate.[22] At higher skill levels,
the differentials are even wider. And tables 11.2 and 11.3 suggest
that India is less urban-biased than most poor countries, especially
undemocratic ones.

THE BIAS AGAINST RURAL RESEARCH

The educational system, then, at once provides villagers with few
prospects for advancement, and funnels townwards those few
who are bright and driving enough to overcome that bias. Hence
it is not surprising that higher education produces relatively few
people able and willing to do research, or indeed any work, relevant to rural needs.

It would be absurd to argue that *all* research, even in a very poor
country, need be 'relevant' to anything. In search of dignity, an
'emergent' nation rightly seeks areas of theoretical excellence,
where its scholars compete in the global intellectual ranking. In
furtherance of a national culture, too, activities are justified that
a Philistine might regard as useless. Even *per se*, any intellectual

community needs to augment those scarce commodities, sweetness and light. What is really frightening is the notion that 'relevant' research, especially in agriculture, somehow cannot attain the highest levels of theoretical interest and challenge. Moreover, these high ideals are mocked by urban bias: by the masses of mis-trained, unhappy and increasingly unemployable general-arts graduates pouring out of the universities of the Third World; and, in a different way, by its architects and engineers designing air-ports, sports stadia and luxury houses, while the rural masses live as they do.

No is the case for 'redirection towards relevance' refuted by the need to specialise. Of course, not every small country needs its own agricultural research institute. But can this justify the tiny scale of agricultural research and training in almost all poor coun-tries; the chronic shortage even in India of able workers in locally applied rural 'R and D'; the scandalous lapse of 15-20 years be-tween the end of the Second World War and the seed improvements of the 'green revolution'; or the fact that *even now* most research on such matters takes place in foreign-funded institutions, while domestic universities proliferate lawyers to oppose each other, doctors to cure neuroses in Northampton, and liberal arts graduates to become unemployed?

Anyway, the proportion of higher educands studying for qualifi-cations in agriculture is small enough; time taken to complete the course is longer, and drop-out rates are higher, than for most other courses in poor countries; and hence the proportion of *graduates* who have specialised in agriculture is terribly low. Many over-whelmingly agricultural countries, by 1967, still had none. Some were quite large (Congo, Libya, Malawi, Morocco, Paraguay, Jordan) and some had avowedly rural ideologies (Tanzania, Zambia), though it was former French territories that dominated this catalogue of neglect -- Dahomey, Mali, Senegal, Somalia, Haut-Volta. Countries with under 3 per cent of graduates spe-cialised in agriculture included India, Pakistan, Mexico, the Philippines, Argentina, Cuba (!), Nicaragua, the Lebanon, Malay-sia and Ceylon. Only a tiny handful of poor countries trained more than one in ten graduates in the skills needed to advance the wel-fare of the farming masses -- apart from mini-states, only Liberia (14 per cent), UAR (15 per cent) and Honduras (38 per cent)![23]

We saw that in Argentina few of the trained agronomists worked in agriculture; in most poor countries the picture is similar.[24] The reluctance to specialise in this vital field, and having done so to practise it, is unsurprising in view of the pay offered. In Nigeria in the mid-1960s, among graduates and those with comparable professional qualifications, 31 per cent of agricultural specialists earned less than £720 a year (as against under 5 per cent of all qualified persons); only 7 per cent (as against 44 per cent) earned over £2,000.[25] In India, at the 1961 census, 50.4 per cent of the agricultural specialists with *post-graduate* qualifications employed in the public sector earned under Rs. 300 (then about £23) monthly, and their median income was Rs. 299; for physicists the comparable figures were 33.2 per cent and Rs. 370.[26] Under these conditions, we must anticipate a growing gap between requirements and availabilities of skilled personnel in developing agricultures.

DOCTORS AND OTHER EXPERTS

If specialists are neither trained nor well-rewarded for rural work, we may expect severe biases against villagers in the provision of facilities requiring skilled people. We have seen something of this already in education itself, where the self-validating and self-perpetuating nature of urban bias in status, reward and provision is clear; rural teachers long to get back to the city, away from the poor pay and conditions they currently endure, and they impart their preferences to their pupils.

In other fields of professional specialism too, the process works in three ways. Firstly, few and inferior facilities and specialists are allocated, or attracted, to the village. Secondly, these specialists are trained for, and eager to return to, the city; commitment is low and turnover high. Thirdly, neither facilities nor research priorities come to grips with rural problems. It is perhaps in the medical field that this is clearest (table 11.3).

Even in rich countries, there are disparities in medical provision, though urban slums are at least as likely to suffer as remote rural areas;[27] but the disparities do not approach those in poor countries. The townsman has nine times as good a prospect of medical attention as the villager in India, eleven times in Ghana, thirty-three times in Ethiopia. The poorer, the larger in area, and the less densely populated a country is, the greater in general is this disparity, partly because such features worsen urban-rural communications, and separate the rural doctor (and the doctor's spouse) more decisively from the bright lights, the company of the elite, and the prospects of lucrative private practice.

As with education, so with health: the numbers in table 11.3 understate the maldistribution of facilities. 'Most rural physicians cluster in the provincial capitals, and beyond, in the truly rural areas, there is one physician for more than 200,000 people' in most of Africa.[28] Moreover, as with education, the quality of rural specialists is lower. The data in table 11.3 refer only to 'Western' (allopathic) doctors, from whose useful services rural people are often diverted by other forms of medicine; in South Asia most rural physicians are 'ayurvedic' (herbalist) doctors.[29] While traditional medicine is often staunchly defended by members of the national elite — and even by visiting non-medical 'experts' — few use it themselves; it is good enough for the villagers. Moreover, lady doctors — a crucial constraint in family planning programmes — are especially loth to work in rural areas.[30] The four-fifths of India's population living in rural areas have probably received under half the family-planning outlays, and most other poor countries show more severe disparities.

The *types* of health facilities provided almost rule out adequate emphasis on villages. 'In . . . Zambia, 250 health centres, enough for the entire population, could be built at the cost of the new teaching hospital in Lusaka. . . . [In Pakistan the 1965-6 Annual Health Report] devoted 22 of its 92 pages to the "Jinnah Post-Graduate Medical Centre" and exactly five lines to "Rural Health Centres" [for which] total expenditure [was] Rs. 16.5 million [as against Rs. 43.5 million for the Jinnah Centre in Islamabad of which Rs. 10 million was the architects' fee] . . . [Most] health care planning in Iran is based upon hospital building.'[31]

Nor is it the case that, as often claimed, villagers use urban facilities to any great extent. Work in India, Kenya and Uganda shows that, as a sufferer's distance from the source of medical help increases, the chance that he will seek treatment decreases at a much faster, increasing, rate — the 'patient gradient'; transport is too costly and unpleasant, especially for the poor and ill (it is noteworthy that the 'patient gradient' is even steeper in rural India than in better-endowed areas within rural East Africa).[32] As for hospitals, in Ghana in 1966, 80 per cent of in-patients at the five major hospitals came from 'the same urban area as the one in which the hospital is situated' and only about 15 per cent from rural areas, where 77 per cent of the people live.[33] In most poor countries, referrals of the rural sick to urban hospitals do not happen on any substantial scale.[34] Nor could they; even if urban doctors did go and work in villages, the major problems (except for tuberculosis and leprosy in some areas) are not touched by the urban systems of sophisticated curative medicine. These major problems are childbirth and its complications;[35] ante-natal and infant protein-calorie deficiency; dysentery; worms; and in some areas bilharzia, trachoma and filariasis. What is required is, first, a massive effort at *preventive* medicine — insect and parasite eradication, improvement of water supplies, ante-natal care; second, *social* medicine quite beyond the usual scope of the physician—concentrating on nutrition, hygiene and family-planning campaigns; and third, an array of simple treatments (for dysentery and various worms) that a competent para-medical assistant can administer.[36]

In short, it is a question of retooling attitudes and structures, as well as 'resources', to the needs of the rural poor. If one tried to measure the drain of medical resources by valuing the extra 'urbanised' income from the bright or well-to-do children who come from village to city to learn to be urban doctors, the result (while doubtless large) would be a gross underestimate. Whenever the terms of exchange are turned against the villager, so that he cannot afford to feed his children properly; whenever resources raised by rural taxation are used to provide tapwater in government offices, while villages lack clean wells; whenever free 'Western' medicine is allocated by city elites to themselves, or their employees, while the rural masses are left to pay for private mumbo-jumbo remedies[37] — in all these cases, rural skill drain damages the health of rural people.

The scapegoats of chapter 3, the foreigner and the private entrepreneur, have been popular also as whipping-boys for anti-rural medical distortions. As usual, there is more than a grain of truth in the accusations, but the real causes lie much deeper.

Certainly the hospital specialisms that Indian doctors learn in Britain, in order to improve their prospects by selecting less popular branches of health — notably geriatrics and traumatic surgery — render them even less suited to rural care in India than before;[38] but few of these ambitious migrants would have worked in rural areas anyway. One may note the almost identical numbers of Indian-trained doctors serving the 480 million rural Indians and working abroad; or the virtually complete absence from rural practice of native doctors with experience abroad who returned to Ghana, Trinidad, Kenya and Malaysia.[39] But it is not foreign practice that causes the drastic misalignment of medical services (table 11.3). Such practice undesirably transfers to rich countries the benefits of medical training carried out at the expense of poor countries, and such doctors as return are often specialised irrelevantly to the health needs of their own countries. But one cannot therefore blame the rural-urban misallocations and brain-drains *within* poor countries upon analogous phenomena *between* poor and rich countries. After all, why does not the government of a poor country impede overseas medical migration,[40] or adopt the rather modest adjustments of terms of service or incentives required to get more doctors to rural areas, or combine both objectives by ensuring that medical training is geared to preventing and curing the mass debilitating diseases of rural areas — as has been attempted in Tanzania — instead of the urban neuroses of Nottingham or Nairobi?

This question brings us to the second scapegoat, private medical practice. It is often argued that rural people in poor countries get so little medical care largely because there is seldom a well-developed public health service,[41] so that doctors are not only free to treat urban patients irrespective of need, but are almost compelled to do so to make a living; the rewards of urban practice are much higher in a free market, and the costs to the doctor lower.

While scarce health resources in poor countries should be, and (as shown in Sri Lanka as well as China) can be, rationed by need and not by ability to pay, and while state control is necessary to achieve this, it is not sufficient. For 'the State' is not a faceless body of social optimisers, but the embodiment of powerful interests, especially the interests of the city. Its officials are primarily concerned, in poor countries, with *urban* health: their own, that of their employees and customers, and (with regard to infectious diseases) that of their neighbours. Sharpston's work in Ghana, like much of Gish's evidence, reveals clearly the overwhelming urban concentration even of doctors in government services.[42]

Even 'statist' and egalitarian governments, in countries where there is no private medicine, do not escape. In Cuba, well after the revolution, Havana was four times better served with doctors than the rest of the country (table 11.3). The Chinese authorities rightly boast that they have got one-third of their doctors into village work,[43] but that is for over 80 per cent of the people, so the urban population remains *eight times* as well served with doctors as the rural population, almost as big a disparity as in India.

Neither wicked foreigners nor wicked capitalists can be blamed for much of the misallocation of medical resources towards cities in poor countries. 'The State', if it could be neutral, could deter doctors from using their training, received at public expense, to relieve rich nations of the need to expand their own medical schools. 'The State', if it were concerned to maximise social benefit, could build rural health centres with the money now used (in one recent West African case) to equip its main (urban) hospital with extremely costly kidney transplant facilities, for which the only demand came not from patients but from a surgeon trained to use them.[44] Why does 'the State' not do these things? Not because it is wicked, but because it consists of human beings under natural pressures. The doctors who desire New York incomes are the sons or nephews of ministers and civil servants; so are the rich city-dwellers who clamour for, and can afford, attention. Villagers just have the wrong relatives. In a less-developed country 'the executive of the modern State is but a committee for managing the common affairs'[45] not of the bourgeoisie but of the towns-men: not of a bourgeois state but of a burghers' state. That the bonds are those of family, propinquity and personal concern, rather than of 'class solidarity', makes them all the stronger.[46]

It is not hopeless, though. Once a man understands how his biases damage others, he can begin to correct them; only if he refuses to do so must he be fought, peacefully if possible, otherwise violently. Much cant is talked about the justice of violence to counter hidden state violence, and about the identity of poverty, exploitation and violence; but it is not cant to stigmatise as violence the diversion of health resources to kidney machines, while villagers suffer infant-mortality rates as high as one in five for want of the simplest medical care.

12 Tax policy towards the rural sector

TAX POLICY: NON-ISOLABLE, SMALL, BUT SIGNIFICANT

In many poor countries, it is through taxation in excess of current outlays that governments seek to make up for deficient private savings—and to obtain investible resources to be moved among sectors in accordance with policy. However, one should not consider tax policies towards the rural sector in isolation from other policies affecting it. A comparison of several poor countries suggests that 10 to 15 per cent of farm income is taken away from the farm sector and transferred to the rest of the economy, just by policies raising the prices of what farmers and farmworkers buy and lowering the prices of what they make and sell.[1] Even this takes account only of the transfer effect of price twists, via their impact on the value of what is actually bought and sold. But they cause two further sorts of income 'transfer' from countryside to city: the extra *output* and income that higher prices encourage the non-farm sector to work for, as against the reduction in *output* and income that price disincentives induce in the farm sector; and the inducement to savers to finance (output-yielding) investment in the non-farm sector, instead of in the farm sector, because price twists have made the non-farm emphasis relatively more profitable. If we include these two effects, price twists—in an LDC with output divided about fifty-fifty[2] between farm and non-farm sectors—could easily cut the income of farmers and farmworkers by 15 to 20 per cent, and raise the income of others in the economy by a rather smaller[3] amount.

Major non-tax transfers among sectors confuse the analysis of tax policy towards the farm and rural sectors, for three reasons: dwarfing, inclusion and overlap. First, few governments in poor countries *collect* as much as 20 per cent of total income in taxes of all kinds,[4] so that a transfer of 15 to 20 per cent of income among sectors (by price twists) will dwarf any *transfer* via tax effects.[5] Second, the price shift is brought about, in part, by taxing exports—which are primarily agricultural—and by industrial import controls, which enable the non-farmer to sell his products more expensively because they nobble the foreign competition; the net impact on the balance of resources, between farmers and others, from taxes applying to prices in the shops can be included in the price twist or the tax shift, but not both. Third, there is a blurred area of public policy that is sometimes considered in discussions of 'who pays the tax', sometimes not: operations of marketing boards, price policies of nationalised industries, and other related matters greatly affect the transfer of benefits between town and country, whether through the prices each pays or through the incomes each can earn, but it is not clear whether these are tax issues. This blurring is found not only in economics but also in budgets: not only articles in learned journals, but also finance ministers' statements, in analysing whether tax burdens are properly distributed between townspeople and villagers, sometimes include and sometimes exclude the impact of railway charges, marketing-board profits, and local rates.

All this is important, because 'much of the literature argues that agriculture is not being taxed heavily enough in most developing countries',[6] without trying to put taxation into its (usually very small) place in the context of the total burdens borne, and benefits received, by agriculture and other sectors. Kaldor's objection to a 'burden of taxation . . . insufficient on subsistence agriculture'[7] ignores non-tax transfers—including the huge price twists. Even more misleading is the result when, to a standard analysis of taxes and outlays affecting sectors, an author adds some but not all of the other items affecting the distribution of burden and benefit between them. Thus Ved Gandhi, having been criticised by S. R. Lewis for ignoring non-tax policies in arguing that Indian agriculture was undertaxed, subsequently adds a rather arbitrary selection of non-tax items: concealed subsidies to farmers via price support, cheap inputs and loans, etc., are considered, but analogous (and much larger) subsidies to industry are ignored; some of the cost to farmers from compulsory procurement of grain is allowed for, but not the greater cost of the offloading of PL 480 grain imports (chapter 13).[8]

Even some straight taxes on agriculture, if informal and subject to administrative direction, are often left out.[9] On the evidence of those few poor countries with available data, agriculture and the rural sector are *over*taxed, relative to the rest of the economy, by all the criteria that can be sensibly applied to tax policy. However, the data are often doubtful, and the criteria controversial and highly 'interpretable'. Even if, for some LDCs and/or some criteria, the arguments that follow do not suffice—even if there is *under*taxation of agriculturists or villagers—it is small by comparison with the excess burdens they bear on account of public policy regarding prices, investment allocation, and the distribution of administrative and technical skills.

Despite the relatively small impact of tax policy, it must be looked at in any assessment of governmental intentions towards developing agricultures. First, tax burdens (and current outlays) represent conscious and integrated public policy more clearly than do the mass of largely *ad hoc* governmental decisions on prices and investment — even if these decisions more substantially affect the balance of advantage between town and country. Second, fiscal policy-making is usually concentrated into annual budgets, which provide convenient foci to examine administrative, legislative and executive decision-procedures on the farm- nonfarm balance. Third, the tax/income ratio, and hence the role of fiscal policy, increases during the development process.

WHO SHOULD PAY THE TAX?

There are four main determinants of where a tax burden of a given size should fall in a poor country — and of whether agriculture, or the rural sector, is paying too little or too much. They are administrative feasibility, growth, stability and equity. First and most obviously, taxation should involve — and should be in forms that will continue to involve — low collection costs, both in money and in political stress. Second, taxation has to make the largest possible net contribution to growth and development: in other words, it should be raised from people who if untaxed would have used the money in non-developmental ways (or developmentally but at low rates of return), and should encourage productive activity. Third, taxes should be so chosen as to enable both governments and taxpayers to plan: that is, both the yield[10] of total taxation to the government, and the income of taxpayers, should be made more stable, as a result of the taxes paid together with the decisions induced by them. Finally, the incidence of tax should be fair (in a sense to be defined), both between taxpayers at similar levels of income and welfare and between taxpayers at different levels ('horizontal' and 'vertical' equity respectively).[11] These four criteria are complex and may conflict; but on all of them, in most poor countries, the proportions of tax paid by the rural sector, and by the farmers, are probably too high.

COLLECTION COSTS IN THE WIDER SENSE

Normal collection costs are likely to be higher, per pound of tax collected, in rural than in urban areas.[12] Rural collection is from many dispersed households, with bad communications between communities; taxpayers are often illiterate and seldom have records of transactions; and the average taxpaying unit has a smaller income (and hence pays less tax) than in the town, although the cost of making contact and obtaining the tax is greater. Where taxes are paid in kind because a village is largely non-monetised, further costs are involved in collection, valuation, transport and storage. On the other hand, a larger proportion of townspeople are regularly paid employees in government offices or large factories. Taxes on income can be collected on a pay-as-you-earn basis; taxes on consumer goods can be collected through a few large, relatively easily supervised urban shops and markets. These administrative considerations clearly justify a greater emphasis on urban, as against rural, tax-gathering than would be implied by growth, equity and stability considerations alone.[13]

However, there is more to 'collection costs' than that. Governments seek to avoid costs of 'political stress'. In a referendum-based democracy—one person, one vote, one value (the last implying equal pressures both on and by each voter)—such costs would be minimised by imposing equal tax *burdens*[14] on everyone, irrespective of economic sector. The urban localisation, and intra-urban concentration, of power and wealth, and their ease of access to (and interpenetration with) governments, however, produces a divergence between the policies that would minimise stress in such an 'ideal' democracy, and the policies that do so in a real-life LDC. The greater literacy, articulateness, and 'adult-maleness' (chapter 9) of urban populations increase that divergence. In almost all poor countries, immediate political stress can be reduced by taxing the many, the dispersed, the weak—the rural people—more heavily, compared to the townspeople, than would be the case if political stress were determined by an egalitarian or democratic balance of influences. However—to mix clichés—the easy way out stores up trouble.

For the politics of stress avoidance and the economics of administrative costs have a point of contact. Both stress and administration become costlier, if taxes have to be changed repeatedly during growth and development. Moreover, as countries become less poor, taxpayers' demands upon the government—and their capacity to finance its activities—grow.[15] Thus, to avoid the costs of constant change while increasing the government's capacity to meet the requirements of development, a tax system should be income-elastic—should show a yield that grows more than in proportion to national income.[16] That depends on the make-up of the tax system, and in particular on its comprising particular taxes with yields that are themselves income-elastic. Taxes on agricultural incomes (and on rural incomes, which largely comprise agricultural incomes and almost wholly depend on them) feature yields that usually grow slowly when their recipients' incomes grow: agriculturists are poorer and less unequal than others, so that extra income does relatively less for their capacity to pay tax; their extra incomes often take the form of better harvests, consumed by the farm family before the taxman arrives; and the difficulty of assessing and collecting taxes on farm income often induces governments to impose poll tax, acreage tax, etc., which are wholly unresponsive to income growth.[17] Moreover — even with no urban bias — income, population, and income per person would grow somewhat more slowly, during development, in agriculture (and in rural areas). Therefore agricultural and rural taxation is likely to grow more slowly than agricultural and rural income, and much more slowly than national income.[18] Great reliance on rural taxes therefore imposes on governments repeated political and administrative costs of changes in the tax base, or increases in tax rates, if the total tax is to grow faster than national income.

TAXATION AND DEVELOPMENT IMPACT OF INCOME FOREGONE

Efficiency

Suppose a government has settled on the desired amounts of taxation and expenditure. The developmental impact will now depend mainly on the answers to two questions. First, what is the difference in the share of the taxed resources that (1) would have been devoted to developmental purposes by the taxpayers had they not been taxed, and (2) will be so devoted by the government after the tax? Second, what is the difference in the developmental yield of the resources so devoted, according to whether it is government or (potential) taxpayer looking after them? The first is the problem of comparing the *savings-income ratios* of the government and of different classes of taxpayer, such as rural and urban, out of extra income. The second is the problem of comparing the *efficiency* of the investment in which government, townsman and villager embody such extra savings. Of course 'savings' and 'efficiency' must be interpreted not literally but liberally: if farmers, factory-workers or ministers divert cash from consumption outlay so that children may benefit from an extra teacher of engineering, that is developmental even if it is not 'saving' in the narrowest sense; and a transfer of income by taxation, if it means that investment benefits a different proportion of poor people although the cash value of the total benefit is unaltered, changes the 'ethical' even if not the strictly economic efficiency of investment.

Advocates of a high tax burden on agriculture are impressed with the higher savings ratio outside agriculture; they claim, despite the arguments of chapter 10, that taxation on the village cuts its private *spending* and benefits public saving and investment, whereas non-farm taxation is often at the expense of private *saving*. They believe that 'it is shortage of resources . . . which limits the pace of economic development', rather than inefficient resource use. But this policy is made more expensive by the farmer's extreme price responsiveness; taxes making farmers' purchases dearer (or reducing the reward to farm labour) will reduce farmers' and farmworkers' effort. It is no longer possible to argue, as it was in 1963, that 'economic incentives do not operate in the same way in the subsistence sector as elsewhere . . . a rise in the price of locally produced food may . . . *decrease* the amounts offered for sale'. So far from 'compulsory levies on [agriculture reliably increasing] the supply of food for sale', both African and Indian experience show that such levies—in effect price cuts—reduce its production and its sale.[19] Flat-rate levies avoid the damaging effect on incentives—but not the harm done to the farmers' capacity to invest and to buy current inputs of fertilisers and pesticides. This is especially important during a 'green revolution' when the returns to such purchases are rising, and when farmers' output response to changes in profitability is increased by their new-found capacity to adjust productive inputs, especially fertilisers.

The disincentive effect of urban taxation is probably less serious. First, townsmen are better off; if I get 50p an hour, a 10p tax both makes less difference to my welfare and leaves me with a higher hourly wage than if I get only 20p, and is hence less likely to stop me cutting my input of work. Second, price twists and input shortages in many poor countries are such that there are substantial excess profits, taxable without much effect on incentives, for each unit of industrial output that businessmen can get the input to produce: in Pakistan in the 1960s, their time was better spent in obtaining a licence to acquire scarce imported input, than in raising even further the profit per unit of such input by increasing their efficiency.[20] Third, the numerous would-be employees waiting for jobs in government and industry—and the frantic efforts of the employees' unions to prevent 'dilution' and keep wages up—suggest that urban wages, as well as urban profits, could be taxed more highly without serious disincentive effects in most poor countries.

However, the main impact on efficiency of the choice of 'whom to tax' probably does not lie in incentive or disincentive effects, but in the rate of return on the investments that taxpayers would have supported, out of the part of their income that they would have saved if it had not been taxed away. Clearly, if taxes on agriculturists are paid with money that they would otherwise have saved and 'locked into' farm investment, then—even if such taxes are invested elsewhere by the state—resources are shifted from high-yield to low-yield sectors of economic activity even at prevailing prices, and more so at prices reflecting real value (table 6.3). Moreover, the pressures against excessive public spending on low-yielding show—airports, sports stadia, overstaffed diplomatic missions—are reduced if such spending is financed by the dispersed rural poor rather than the articulate urban not-so-poor.

Savings

Chapter 10 showed why, in allocating investment, 'saving from yield' is less important than yield itself. Similar arguments apply to taxation: the yield that a private individual's earnings would have obtained, had they (1) remained untaxed and (2) been used instead to finance investment, matters more than the proportion of such untaxed money that they would have spent, at least on home products, since the makers of such products themselves save part of their extra incomes. However, here too, savings do matter: some spending is on imports, and some of the rest bids up prices. Can rural taxes be justified on the grounds that they cut back private savings less than urban taxes?

There are two arguments. The first is that rural people, because they are poorer, save a smaller proportion of income than urban people; that this also applies to the proportion of any *change* in income, due, say, to taxation, which the 'taxee' meets with a change in saving instead of in consumption; and that therefore rural people should bear the brunt of taxation because, being poor, they do not have much savings to reduce as a consequence.[21] That argument—apart from its dubious basis in fact (chapter 10) —would, with equal force, justify concentrating the tax burden on *any* group too poor to respond by saving less: the unemployed, children, even cripples. Such Pharaoh-like elevation of aggregate savings over interpersonal equity could be acceptable only if alternative methods of financing development were even more disastrous.

The second 'argument from savings' for rural taxation—that at the *same* income level a villager saves a lower proportion of income than a townsman, and should therefore be taxed more heavily—is ethically acceptable but empirically false. Despite the lack of reliable savings institutions in rural areas, and despite price twists against the profitability of the rural investments into which much rural saving is locked, the proportion of average income (and even more of *extra* income, due, say, to tax reduction) saved by rural people in poor countries is surprisingly high (chapter 10)—higher than that of savings by townspeople at the same level of money income per person. There are several reasons for this: higher living costs may leave the townsman with less to save; there are more rich neighbours to emulate; and often migrant men use extra incomes to buy consumer goods for the rural family which is later to follow them townwards.

On the other hand, even a staunch advocate of rural taxation reports a whole series of studies showing a high propensity to save out of extra rural income[22]—that is, a lot of private saving to be lost if that income is taxed away. In Pakistan in the late 1960s, rural people clearly saved a higher share of extra income than urban people at similar income levels.[23] Indian evidence confirms this impression (chapter 10, note 25). If the savings argument for rural taxation means that rural (and other poor?) people should be taxed heavily because saving is little affected by taxation because they are poor, its premises are intolerable; if it means that they should be taxed heavily because they save little given their poverty, it is false.

The marketed surplus and monetisation

There is a group of related arguments for rural taxation that also mingles logical conclusions from intolerable premises with the ethically neutral but false. This time there are three strands. It is argued that the share of national income outside agriculture will rise, if agriculture is taxed to the bone and the surplus transferred to the rest of the economy: that is true enough in the short run, but such a policy would damage both equality and growth. It is argued that marketed surpluses can be obtained by taxing agriculture: except for once-for-all requisitioning in kind (and even that reduces marketings later), that is false. It is argued that a subsistence sector is best induced to become monetised by being compelled to acquire money to pay its taxes: that is confusing, inequitable, and incompatible with any consistent monetary policy.

The 'doctrine of surpluses' strand of the argument is discussed elsewhere in this book (ch. 4). Its influence on advocates of high rural taxation is clear. Thus S. R. Lewis writes, 'Since agriculture is the predominant sector and since the non-agricultural sectors will grow relative to agriculture. . . *a priori* . . . investment resources for [them] must come in the first instance from it,'[24] and he goes on to advocate rural taxation. We have seen that the *a priori* appearance in fact camouflages an illogical argument, but it is quite logical for Lewis to argue that, *if* industrialisation requires early and major financial transfer from agriculture, then rural taxation exceeding rural public outlay is one way to achieve that goal. Kaldor's argument that taxes on the 'subsistence sector' should rise to support growth in the 'market sector' is identical (note 7). However, while robbing the poor to pay the rich may raise the share of national output in 'growth sectors' (or raise the savings/income ratio), such a policy should be advocated openly, not in the neutral guise of an intersectoral transfer. Since 'growth sectors' started prematurely are low-yielding and often self-choking for want of agricultural inputs, to finance them out of agricultural taxation is inefficient as well as inequitable. The 1970s feature mounting concern that, in poor countries, (1) accelerated development has done little for mass welfare, yet (2) efficient growth does seem a *necessary* condition for major increases in welfare. In that climate, tax policies seeking structural change *per se* — despite lost welfare and retarded efficiency — seem inappropriate.

The arguments that rural taxes compel monetisation and that they increase marketings are linked. Due argues that direct rural taxes, in particular, 'must be paid in money and therefore force the subsistence farmers to sell produce or labour services'.[25] Even in Africa (the main topic of Due's paper) this sharp subsistence-marketing distinction hardly applies. 'Subsistence' farm families already obtain much of their cash by outside work for commercial farmers, by seasonal migration, or by borrowing at high interest (increasingly from urban sources or, if from traditional moneylenders, from those whose loanable reserves are swollen by urban activities). Increases in such activities by subsistence farmers, if indeed induced by higher taxation, need not increase marketings. Even if they do, extra marketed crops can be sold to rural merchants, or to people who escape tax, or pay it in cash; hence *townward* marketings need not rise because of direct rural taxation. If Due's process *does* work, it is by compelling poor subsistence farmers to sell more of this year's crop, though it drives down the price.[26] Apart from hurting the poor, this discourages production next year.

Subsistence food output, consumed by hungry mini-farmers, is not an evil, to be extirpated by tax policy in the name of development. However, one might advocate taxes on the subsistence sector to bring it into the cash economy. The desirability of this as an end in itself is not obvious. Even if it is desirable, many taxes — especially taxes on output, such as 'tithes' of grain — are not collected in cash. Moreover, taxing to secure monetisation is likely to be inconsistent with another very common policy in development finance: the support of public investment by 'permissible' levels of money-printing, which are decided by estimating how many people will enter, or enter more fully, into the money economy in the plan period. The cash these people will, at a typical moment, want to hold, since it is taken out of circulation, can be replaced by extra printed money to pay for some government activities — if other things are equal. But they are not equal if the government is itself inducing the monetisation, taxing and re-spending the cash as people begin to hold it, and thereby reducing their willingness to save.

Development and taxes on kulaks

If taxes are imposed on *better-off* farmers, the equity and efficiency case for taxation is much stronger — they can afford to pay, and they probably would get lower returns than small farmers on the investments they would make if untaxed, because they have fewer family workers per acre to provide cheap labour in support of such investments.[27] The arguments from enhanced marketings, savings, etc., for taxing subsistence farmers of course no longer apply, but they are dubious anyway. Most big farmers pay too little tax, partly because of the high administrative costs (and easy avoidance) of agricultural income tax; but some caveats are in order.

First, even rich farmers are frequently taxed more, in relation to taxable capacity, than non-farmers with the same income. Second, although poor villagers face lower prices than poor townsmen, rich villagers probably face higher prices than comparably rich townsmen (chapter 5, note 5). Third, price twists on the output side probably bear specially heavily on rich farmers, though input subsidies do so too (chapter 13). Fourth, it is on the bigger farmers that the 'green revolution' strategy for low-cost agricultural breakthrough has chiefly, if often mistakenly, relied; to reduce their incentives (and cash resources) for the heavy purchases of new inputs required by that strategy, especially in its early stages, can be risky. Above all, we seldom know who, in the farm sector, actually feels the *impact* of tax whose initial *incidence* is on big farmers. Much of their spare cash still circulates in the village, employing otherwise jobless people; will they suffer when that spare cash is mopped up by a tax? If the tax is on a farm input, can it be shifted forward as price rises, perhaps for a coarse grain eaten mainly by the poor; or shifted back to landless labourers, as cuts in employment and/or wage rates?

None of the above is meant as a general case against taxing big farmers. It does, however, suggest that the emphasis on mopping up, for urban development, the often modest 'gains' of the 'green revolution' may be misplaced. One would be more convinced that governments, seeking higher taxes on big farmers, were concerned with greater equality—rather than with knocking poor old agriculture once again—if they also implemented land reforms, and increased taxes on high *urban* income and wealth.

EQUITY

Taxable capacity

In most poor countries, tax payments per household are smaller in rural than in urban areas. However, the difference is not sufficient, for three reasons: the requirements of growth in respect of savings and efficiency, discussed above; the relative under-provision of tax-financed public services to rural areas; and the extent to which urban and rural tax payments stand in differing relations to capacity to pay (or to public benefits received), and thereby impose disparate burdens on urban and rural households.

All this is often ignored or obfuscated. In 1971, for instance, the Pakistan Taxation Commission alleged 'inadequate taxation of the agricultural sector' because it 'claims about one-half of the GNP' but contributes only 27 per cent of taxes. In fact, in the last two years for which data were available to the Commission (1968 and 1969), agriculture produced about 46.3 per cent of the value of output, to sustain some 67 per cent of the population. Agricultural income per person thus averaged only 42.5 per cent of non-agricultural income per person. If a person could just keep alive on 30 per cent of Pakistan's income per person in 1968 and 1969, average taxable capacity in agriculture would thus stand to that of other sectors as $(42.5-30)$ to $(100-30)$, that is, as 1 to 5.6; if 35 per cent were needed, as is more likely, the ratio would be 1 to 8.7; yet tax *payments,* on the Tax Commission's own figures, were in the ratio 1 to 5.5 (27 per cent of tax being paid by the 67 per cent inside agriculture, and the other 73 per cent by the remaining one-third of Pakistanis).[28] Hence, contrary to the Commission's statement, agriculturists in Pakistan were clearly *overtaxed* in the late 1960s. This takes account only of capacity to pay, not of the urban concentration of benefits (see chapter 8, note 25), nor of the greater maldistribution and hence taxability of intra-urban incomes, nor of the non-tax drains on agriculture via pricing (p. 270).

This list of omissions underlines the fact that greater 'average' poverty is not the only reason why rural households in poor countries have lower capacity to pay tax than urban households. Rural income is usually less unequal (Introduction, note 5) and hence produces proportionately fewer households with substantial tax-paying capacity. Rural households on average possess less capital than urban households, and it is harder to realise for a spendable — and therefore taxable — gain. Like income, capital in most LDCs is distributed less unequally in rural areas than in urban areas, creating fewer concentrations of great and obvious 'taxability'. Moreover, rural households invariably (owing to adult migration and child mortality) comprise a greater proportion of children;[29] that reduces the taxable capacity of the rural household, first by imposing greater costs for child-minding, infant food preparation and education, and second by preventing mothers and elder siblings from earning extra income to pay tax. The large amount of costly rural moneylender credit means not only that interest payments reduce the villager's capacity to pay tax,[30] but also that higher tax payments worsen his debt position further. Finally, the fluctuations over the year of agricultural seasons — and hence of earning prospects and food prices — compel most rural families to 'lock up' savings in the form of stocks of grain for later consumption in the household, once again reducing taxable capacity.

Furthermore, although urban prices exceed rural prices in poor countries by 5 to 20 per cent (chapter 5, note 4), this particular upward impact on real rural *average income*, relative to urban, of that price advantage does not mean an upward impact on rural taxable *capacity*. This is because taxable capacity is heavily concentrated on the highest income groups,[31] and these actually suffer a price *dis*advantage by virtue of living in rural areas. In general, rural products are dearer, but urban products cheaper, in urban than in rural areas; most of the value of consumption in poor countries (food, cotton, wood) is produced rurally; hence the price index for the average purchaser is higher in towns, because the many rural goods bought dear by townspeople outweigh the few urban goods bought dear by villagers. But the rural rich — the repositories of most rural taxable capacity — are not 'average' purchasers. Like the urban rich, they spend large parts of their income on *urban* goods: so large, in fact, that they pay more for total purchases than they would in the city. Hence the rich, potentially high-taxpaying, consumer is worse off — less able to pay tax — in country than in city, not only because rural average income is lower; not only because the rural rich enjoy a smaller increment above rural average income than do the urban rich above urban average income; but also because, *for the set of goods rich people buy,* rural areas are more expensive.[32]

Not all these factors could be allowed for in my estimate of rural and urban taxable capacity in India (in each year from 1950-1 to 1961-2).[33] This was obtained by calculating—for the richest, second-richest, third, fourth and fifth 1 per cent groups of rural households, the second-richest 5 per cent, and then the other 10 per cent groups down to the poorest 10 per cent—(1) income per household member, *minus* (2) flat-rate subsistence requirements per household member,[34] *plus* (3) one-tenth of the value of capital and land per household member (assumed to be the maximum realisable gain). This calculation was then repeated for the urban sector. Several considerations raising urban taxable capacity—more easily realisable capital, fewer small children to prevent family members from earning, less onerous credit, less need to carry stocks—were omitted for want of data. On all other matters, I chose assumptions that raised rural, and cut urban, taxable capacity as much as was compatible with common sense. Nevertheless, on a criterion for tax progressiveness that seems generally acceptable,[35] India's rural sector was paying more tax than the urban sector, relative to taxable capacity, in every tax year from 1950-1 to 1961-2. The measured excess of rural tax payments over 'equitable' levels was small — only 1 to 2 per cent of rural income. The actual excess must be larger, given my numerous (unavoidable) omissions and assumptions, all tending to bring it down. Above all, it is in addition to numerous non-tax burdens imposed on the rural sector.

Three considerations strengthen this conclusion, and broaden its applicability. First, since the early 1960s (except in 1967-9 when wheat was procured from farmers at prices above world market levels), the total tax and non-tax share of India's rural sector in bearing the costs of development is unlikely to have fallen, while its share in national income — though not in population — has. Second, as a lively democracy, India was likely to have a tax structure less urban-biased, by comparison with equity norms, than most other poor countries, whose rural masses lack effective votes, but whose elites are at least as urban-oriented. Third — perhaps surprisingly — there seems to be more evasion (as a proportion of tax due) in city than in country;[36] its reduction, automatically raising the urban tax share, would right a major inequity (*viz.* inequality before the law) and would prevent nominal tax rates from exaggerating, as they do at present, the townsman's share of the tax burden.

Tax burden and benefit

The rural sector's share of tax burdens has in most LDCs probably been too large, by comparison with its capacity to pay. A different way of looking at taxation is to ask whether the rural sector has paid more or less than the benefits it has received from public outlays. Just as the 'capacity to pay' question gives an incomplete answer (because resources are transferred out of rural areas through *non-tax* state action), so does the 'tax-benefit balance' question (because state action, by making urban investments more attractive relative to rural, induces private individuals to embody rural savings in them). Nevertheless, just as the rural sector pays too large a share of taxation relative to 'capacity' even if we ignore non-tax burdens, so in most poor countries does it probably pay out more in taxes than it receives in public benefits, even if we ignore the outflow of private benefits induced by public action.

Admittedly, information on these matters is scanty. Table 8.1 showed that typically only 18 to 25 per cent of national investment has gone to agriculture; but this does not tell us how much public expenditure has gone to the rural sector — the key issue. FAO's periodic surveys of development plans suggest that *planned* public expenditure in agriculture is seldom above 15 to 20 per cent of the total, even in poor countries with 70 to 80 per cent of populations in agriculture,[37] and plans have usually been more seriously underfulfilled in the agricultural sector than elsewhere. There is of course extra spending on social services and infrastructure that partly benefits agriculturists. However, since the agricultural population in most LDCs probably pays at least as high a share of tax relative to its size elsewhere as in India and Pakistan (where it is 25 to 30 per cent of tax for 75 to 80 per cent of people), it is unlikely (though not impossible) that the rural sector has received more than it has paid.

The picture is complicated by aid. Aid outlays have been especially skewed against agriculture, and home-financed public expenditure rather less so. Ought one really to compare the proportion of taxes on rural areas with the proportion of public spending, from resources raised *domestically*, that benefits them? There are three drawbacks to such a procedure. First, the fact that less than 12 percent of aid has gone to agriculture[38] — and that almost all 'infrastructural' aid to education, health, power, transport and so forth has benefited urban residents[39] — is in part due to the preferences and pressures of recipient governments; it could reasonably be argued that a government raising one-third of taxation from the rural sector should, in equity (and efficiency considerations reinforce the argument), see that the rural sector receives at least one-third of the total benefits from all public outlay, whether financed by home taxation or foreign aid.[40] Second, most aid comes as foreign exchange; this is worth more (relative to local outlays) than relative prices suggest, because governments deliberately underprice it (chapter 13); therefore aid deprivation costs the rural sector more than it seems to do, so that excluding aid benefits from the assessment of the rural-urban balance would be even more unsatisfactory. Third, it is quite possible to use local outlays to redress any anti-rural bias induced by the structure of available foreign aid. Hence the comparison of rural shares of taxation and of total public outlay seems appropriate.

There are very few direct attempts to compare the rural sector's share of taxes paid with its share of benefits received. For India in 1958-9, taxation of the farm sector exceeded *current* government outlays benefiting farmers— including relevant outlays on health, education, transport, power, etc. — by rather over 4 per cent of farm income.[41] That is well in excess of any plausible estimate of government capital outlays to benefit agriculture — even including those that were aid-financed. In Pakistan in the late 1960s, some 27 per cent of all taxation comprised direct taxes on agriculture alone;[42] its share in *total* taxes must have been well above its share in public-sector outlays.[43] Finally, Sabot has shown that the government of Tanzania, for all the sincerity of Mr Nyerere's rural and egalitarian emphases, has produced 'a rural-to-urban income transfer'; 35 per cent of monetary GNP in 1969-70 was urban, and a still smaller share of government revenue, while 44 per cent of the total development budget benefited urban areas totally or primarily.[44]

RURAL TAXES AND STABILITY

Many facts and arguments, though disappointingly few available figures, suggest that the rural sector bears too high a share of the tax burden in most poor countries from the standpoints of efficiency, equity and ease of collection. Our fourth criterion, income stability for taxer and taxed, points in the same direction. Income can fluctuate because of varying demand for one's products, or because of one's varying capacity to supply them. All producers, and hence all taxpayers, in poor countries as in rich ones, are at risk of demand-induced instability in their incomes: foreign buyers' requirements for rubber or tin, as ragards the quantity they will absorb or the price they will pay, vary from year to year; and the needs of domestic demand management, especially in view of shortages of foreign exchange, can compel the government to take measures that lead to instability.

Such demand fluctuations do not obviously damage agriculturists, or rural residents, more or less than others. Subsistence producers are by definition immune, but dairy farmers and growers of export crops are particularly vulnerable. If cereals are unlikely to be cut back in demand as sharply as buyers' income, the opposite is true of milk, fruit and (in a really poor country) cotton.

Yet, although rural and agricultural incomes fluctuate somewhat less for reasons of demand, they are more prone to variations in supply, especially climatic variations in the sub-tropical savanna and monsoon areas where most of the world's poor live. Supply is harder to manipulate than demand, and agricultural supply hardest of all: it is quite easy to smooth demand by varying government purchases for central stocks, more difficult to manipulate imports of raw materials to ensure smooth supplies to industry, and very hard, except in the long run, to immunise agricultural supply against poor rains. On balance, the resident in the farm-based rural sector, and especially the poor and 'unirrigated' farmer, is especially prone to income fluctuations — and, being poor, tends to lack reserves (of body-fat or of savings) to help him cope with them.

Under such conditions, rural-based taxation (unless implausibly flexible and sophisticated) makes things worse. Falls in income for a subsistence farmer, during a bad harvest, will be that much more serious if the taxman takes away a set proportion (or worse still a set amount) of his grain or milk. The damage to an urban worker is less: partly because he is less poor and thus less damaged by a given fluctuation; partly, perhaps, because his income fluctuates less. Moreover, government revenues — and hence public capacity to finance development — will be less stable and 'plannable' if they rely on taxing a weather-dependent farm sector, especially one growing only a small number of crops. Hence both developmental and equity arguments suggest that income fluctuations justify a low share of tax burdens at least for pest-prone, unsurely watered parts of agriculture — and for the rural areas chiefly dependent on them.

The case for much higher overall taxation in most poor countries is powerful. Their great internal inequalities, and the high levels of sumptuary expenditure by the rich, show that extra taxes can be paid; the developmental requirements in the public sector are glaringly obvious; and historical experiences as diverse as Japan's in 1870-1900 and the USSR's after 1917 suggest that the developmental gains outweigh the possible damage through disincentives.

Agriculture and the rural sector, in the *absolute* sense that they also have their wealthy and their wastrels, are also undertaxed. But agriculture and the rural sector are also poorer, more equal, more vulnerable to instability, and more efficient in their use of untaxed resources than the rest of the developing economy. *Relatively* to it, therefore, farmers and villagers are already overtaxed; and the pressures to tax them further are both causes and effects of urban bias.[45]

13 Price twists

The distinction between removing resources from the farmer, and turning prices against him, can be artificial. For instance, if the government procures one-fifth of a given amount of marketed farm output without payment, that is equivalent to causing the price of all marketed farm output to be reduced by one-fifth. Yet there is a broad distinction between physical, 'direct' controls acting on outputs, and 'indirect' controls to influence prices. Often one type or the other is seen as superior ideologically: physical controls are allegedly 'socialist', price policies 'liberal'. This is absurd. Price policies are often used deliberately by left-wing governments, and physical controls have usually served such right-wing ends as the extraction of tribute to maintain a court. What matters is why particular sorts of control are used, and, even more, what they do.

This chapter begins by examining how various types of prices can be turned against the farm sector. Next, it considers the intended and actual impact — on the amount and efficiency of farm and non-farm output, and on income distribution — of such price movements. In this section we ask whether they have transferred resources out of the rural sector to a substantial extent; and to what degree they are due to the special power of urban business and labour as well as to government action. Third, we look at the links between policies depressing farm prices — relative to the prices of farmers' inputs, and of consumer goods bought by villagers — and policies affecting other sorts of price relationships. The latter policies, defensible in their own right, incidentally damage agriculture and benefit industry. Since that effect is seldom compensated by other action, it is intended by, or at least acceptable to, policy-makers.

The anti-agricultural thrust of past government price policies, and the predominance of relatively well off and inefficient urban interests among those groups with power to influence such policies, does not imply that LDC governments should in future intervene less in price formation. Governments are urban-biased largely because of the pressures on them of powerful urban interests. Governmental withdrawal would not remove urban bias in price formation, but merely enable powerful urban monopolies to impose it without governmental mediation. The need, therefore, is to increase awareness, among governments and social thinkers, of the biases produced by the balance of pressures upon them; in social analysis as in psychoanalysis, insight is usually a necessary condition for improvement. However, just as great efforts of will are usually needed to transform self-awareness into mental health, so improvement of the price balance, between agriculture and other sectors, will require *more* government action.

This chapter is about how and why the relative prices received and paid by agriculturists — and by the rural sector — are different from the prices that *would have* prevailed if the government had not taken (or had prevented private persons from taking) the actions that altered prices. At times, it will ask *what* prices would then have prevailed. We need not, however, argue metaphysically about ideal price systems; it suffices to show that different — we argue higher — agricultural prices would be desirable, and are being prevented.

Nor need we decide if the terms of trade have 'moved against' agriculture — that is, whether a unit of farm sales commands more or less farm and farm-household purchases than previously. This is an arbitrary exercise, because its outcome depends on when 'previously' is. Moreover, even if a 'normal' year, with average climate and no price twists, could be found, any subsequent trend in agriculture's terms of trade could not be interpreted without more information. For instance, a fall in the power of a unit of farm output to purchase a unit of non-farm output (in the 'terms of trade of agriculture') might be due to the acquisition of new skills in farming, so that (in a competitive situation) farm output became relatively cheaper; or to import-cost increases affecting the non-farm sector; or to rising incomes, leading to a much larger expansion of demand for non-farm goods than for farm goods. The first of these three changes could leave farmers better off; and none of them would permit us to blame farmers' 'worsening terms of trade' upon outside action (monopolistic or governmental) damaging their bargaining power *vis-à-vis* their suppliers or customers. It is on such action that this chapter concentrates.

TYPES OF PRICE TWIST

Current farm input prices

At first glance, any allegation that current inputs[1] are made costly for farmers in poor countries seems both contrary to fact and inconsistent with a thrust towards industrialisation. Are not the subsidies to farm inputs clear from dozens of critical reports in the early 1970s: on Sri Lanka (Ceylon), with irrigation water

supplied free to farmers at great cost to the public, and with subsidised tractors; on Bangladesh, with free pesticides, half-price
fertilisers, and subsidised tractor maintenance; and so on, for
almost every country in the Third World? And would not a farm
input, if made too costly, be little used, thus cutting the output of
cereals and raw materials for urban consumption, raising their
price (and thus the wage demanded by urban workers), and choking off the industrial profits to finance future expansion?

The actual administration of input subsidies, however, invali-
dates both these criticisms; for it usually makes inputs *dearer* to
the mass of farmers, and confines subsidies to the big farmers,
who are responsible for most sales to the town. They are best able
to overcome the complex bureaucratic obstacle course of licences,
approvals, credit applications and form-filling that separates subsidised inputs from the soil. They have contacts, knowledge, power
and money to exploit any corruption or nepotism. And, sometimes,
only they want to buy even subsidised inputs. Small farmers are
often tenants paying 30 to 60 per cent of output as crop-share rent,
and having to borrow at 25 to 50 per cent annual interest. Such
farmers often lack either the resources or the incentives to use new
inputs, especially if outputs are risky. Furthermore, such inputs
as tractor-hire and weedicides replace labour and are therefore
less attractive to small farmers, who have idle household labour
but little cash. Also, because many operations with subsidised
inputs (especially fertilisers and weedicides) must be precisely
timed, the purchases — and for the poor man the acquisition of
credit — must be swiftly and accurately synchronised. All in all —
unless administrators are determined and independent — the
bigger, literate, relatively knowledgeable farmer, with his own
cash or bank account, gets most of the subsidised inputs[2] and uses
them to produce the outputs needed for urban consumption.

If this were all, it would be unfortunate, but the pricing of current
farm inputs would hardly induce a twist *against* agriculture. However, these subsidies are usually applied to inputs that, even at open-
market prices, are hard to come by. So even the big farmers who
get nominally 'subsidised' inputs in fact have to pay rake-offs to
intermediaries — distributors, managers of cooperatives, or local
civil servants. Together with the costs of queues and delays, these
rake-offs can easily raise the price well above the market level.
Just as Prohibition in Mississippi was effective, not in reducing
drinking, but in enabling the state government to transfer to
drinkers part of the cost of policemen's pay, so fertiliser subsidies
in Bangladesh affect mainly the distribution, between government
and farmers, of the cost of 'paying' officials.

If fertilisers are scarce already, more will not be got into the field by subsidising them.[3] Also, unless administrators are both well paid and fearful of detection, human nature will ensure that nominal subsidies do not greatly lower effective input prices. But how can they induce a price twist against agriculture? Four methods are at work.

Most important, because scarce subsidized inputs are acquired more easily by big farmers, input scarcities for small ones are greater, and prices higher, than they would be if subsidies were absent. (For example, in Bangladesh in early 1973, import prices suggested that a maund — about 80 lb — of the nitrogenous fertiliser urea would have cost Rs. 40 on a free market. The 50 per cent subsidy should have cut that to Rs. 20. I found that big farmers paid about Rs. 35 to 40 including all rake-offs, while those small farmers whose special conditions rendered it worthwhile competed for the remaining urea at Rs. 55 to 65 — about 50 per cent *above* market prices.) Second, farm input subsidies, even nominal ones, help industrialisers — and industrialists — to argue for lower prices for the *products* of the (apparently) subsidised inputs. Third, if inputs are available to a nation's own farmers more cheaply than to its neighbours' (or to its foreign-owned plantation sector), nationals acquiring such inputs may well sell them abroad for a quick profit rather than use them to farm, especially if the latter is made less attractive by high risk, crop-share rents, or interest rates; if subsidised inputs leak abroad in this fashion, unsubsidised inputs become more sought after and costly on the 'free' or 'black' markets where small farmers in particular usually have to buy.

Fourth, a national penchant for subsidies on current inputs normally benefits the non-farm sector. First, that sector uses more current inputs, relative to gross output; to produce £1,000 of net output, a farm might typically use land and labour to convert perhaps £200 of seed, manure and fertilisers into £1,200 of gross output, whereas a factory could well be converting £2,000 of current inputs into £3,000 worth of gross output. Second, a larger proportion of the non-farm sector's current inputs are 'subsidisable' — the farm itself provides much of its own seed, animal manure, water, draught power, etc. Third, state-owned firms comprise a much larger share of both the value of purchased inputs supplied to, and the productive capacity in, the non-farm sector than is the case with the farm sector, so that the enforcement of subsidised sales to the non-farm sector is easier (though of course if everything is 'subsidised' nothing is[4]).

These arguments do not refute the case for farm input subsidies under all circumstances (though they will seldom help small, poor farmers much if rural power remains with big, market-oriented farmers). If the government wants to make it worthwhile for farmers to adopt an unfamiliar or risky input, or one with a social benefit substantially above its benefit to the individual (for example, rat poison, the success of which depends on *general* adoption), then initial subsidies will usually make sense. They are often introduced in just such conditions of deficient farm demand for a worthwhile input that will be welcomed once it is well known; but they are then often continued long after the innovation has 'caught on'. If effective, they then intensify, by lowering the price, a demand that cannot be met. Without the well-paid and well-supervised administrators that few poor countries can afford — or will allocate to agriculture — this policy of 'subsidy plus scarcity' means corruption, misallocation, unwanted disincentives (not least to directors of publicly-owned firms making fertilisers, which often can record sales in their accounts only at subsidised rates), and — for most farmers — in the long run fewer and dearer farm inputs.

Subsidies, whether or not they actually turn input prices against farmers (and hence against the whole rural sector — p. 154), are applied not to free-market prices but to prices actually charged to farmers. The chargers frequently enjoy import licences conferring effective monopoly or cartel powers. Sometimes they are domestic producers enjoying heavy protection. A subsidy, like a sale, giving '30 per cent off' means little if the initial price was 75 per cent on.

Three sorts of information help us, as nominal 'subsidy' data do not, to assess the impact of public and private manipulative action on farm input prices: estimates of benefit/cost ratios of extra input use; international comparison of input prices relative to other prices; and time-trends of such relative prices, and of crude input prices too. Benefit/cost ratios measure the ratio of extra outputs to extra inputs, both (often very crudely) at the cost that the nation has to pay for them (and with future yields, and costs, discounted by appropriate interest rates). If such costs and yields are reflected by market prices, then any input associated with a benefit/cost ratio substantially exceeding unity will be bought, because the buyer will gain significantly more by selling the output than he loses by buying the input.

To put it another way, a farmer will go on applying a fertiliser — if he can get it, and if the risk is not too great — until the expected value to him of the extra crop yield from another pound has been pulled down (by diminishing returns) fairly close to the price of that pound. If value and price fairly closely reflect social benefit and cost respectively, the (social marginal) benefit/cost ratio of applying extra fertilisers at that point will not be much above 1. If it is, and for a wide range of outputs, we may suspect that the true, delivered price of the input is being made so high as to discourage farmers from using as much as social benefit/cost considerations would indicate.

Yet FAO estimated the ratio for an extra pound of typical fertiliser mix in 1962 to be 2.8 in South America, 4.4 in Africa (south of the Sahara), and 4.7 in Asia and the Far East; even by 1975 the ratios were expected to be as high as 1.9, 3.3 and 4.5 respectively. The benefit/cost ratios for extra pest control in India in 1966 were even bigger: extra insecticide produced 3.6 times its value in extra sugar cane, 2.3 times in cotton and 4.6 times in rice; for extra outlay on chemical seed treatment, the respective multiples were 10.0, 34.4 and 44.6.[5]

Plainly, there are many factors other than high input prices—low output prices, input inaccessibility, risk, ignorance, share-cropping, high interest—discouraging farmers from applying enough inputs to push the social benefit/cost ratio of further applications right down to 1; but ratios this high certainly suggest that the effective prices paid for inputs (if not the official or listed prices) were excessive.

Direct evidence confirms this suggestion. In the mid-1960s, in the seven poor countries studied by the US Department of Agriculture, the amount of rice or wheat required to buy a pound of typical fertiliser mix—its 'real price'—was much higher than in most rich countries. Evidence from elsewhere confirmed this[6] (though despite the very high benefit/cost ratios cited above, the contribution to yield was lower[7]). The big, diverse, potentially autarkic LDCs, India and Brazil, featured exceptionally high 'real prices' for fertilisers, and those more successful in agricultural development (Mexico, Taiwan and Greece) lower ones. In 1970-1, whereas in developed Japan farmers received 1.43 times as much for a kilo of paddy as they paid for a kilo of fertiliser, in nine poor countries of South-east Asia the ratios ranged from 0.96 (South Korea) to 0.12 (Burma), averaging around 0.4.[8] As for wheat, all three very poor countries (income per person $250 per year or less) were in the bottom eight of the seventeen countries with available data in 1970-1 for the price ratio of 'wheat sold by farmers' to 'fertilisers bought by farmers'.[9] Things may recently have been getting worse. After some years of stable fertiliser prices, the uptrend in India in 1964-8,[10] and again in 1972-5, outpaced the index of agricultural wholesale prices. As oil and petrochemicals get more expensive, the favourite whipping-boy in many LDCs appears to be fertilisers—though they are complementary with many other non-oil-using inputs, so that agricultural production as a whole needs far less oil per pound's worth than industrial production.

Farm output prices

It is above all by cheapening farm outputs that both private and public powers transfer savings capacity from agriculture to the rest of the economy. Only goals of 'anti-agricultural' resource transfer and output restructuring as ends in themselves could justify the prevailing low levels of farm-gate prices in poor countries. The balance of *private* power would suffice to tilt the 'price-fixing balance' in favour of modern urban industry: one or a few big suppliers of fertilisers or soap, able to influence total availability and (via advertising) demand for their product, are able to affect its price, as thousands of isolated and competing farmers are not. Moreover, the industrialising preferences of historically 'developing' governments have often led them to transfer resources out of agriculture by cheapening food.[11] But the urban concentration of governmental power and support, and the underlying planners' ideology, are nowadays stronger than ever. And the private power balance and governmental preferences interact: being nearer the city and more unified, industrial interests have secured a bewildering variety of measures from governments, ranging from the distribution of subsidised food to the mulcting of farmers through marketing boards, all tending to keep down the prices at which farmers (and their employees) sell output to the substantially richer and less efficient urban sector.

The treatment, by governments of LDCs, of free or subsidised agricultural imports is an extreme example of how farm output prices are forced down. This 'PL480' aid—mainly from the USA under Public Law 480, though also from Australia and Canada—has been mostly wheat, with some maize and cotton. Obviously LDCs, with chronic food shortages and little foreign exchange, cannot afford to turn down such gifts and subsidies.[12] But there is no need to handle them in a way permanently damaging to the farm sector. Initial damage there must be, since the supply of imported grain rises, so that the price to farmers falls;[13] but such damage can be offset, for example by special taxes on the non-farm sector.

Instead, LDC governments have often increased the damage to the farm sector: first, by using the receipts from selling PL480 commodities to finance development programmes benefiting mainly *non*-farmers; second, by selecting times and amounts of PL480 marketings that neither stabilised food prices (instead of forcing them down) nor built up safe levels of government stocks;[14] and third but foremost, not content with the downward pressure on prices from normal releases of PL480 imports, by heavily sub-sidising such releases to consumers. These subsidies, ostensibly aimed to help the poor, reach mainly the settled urban employees, who can obtain ration cards and get to 'fair price shops' more easily than other people.

India has been the largest recipient of PL480 aid. A rough esti-mate of the *immediate* losses to Indian farmers, through price cuts on their wheat sales caused by the releases of PL480 food grains, was 1.9 per cent of total farm income in 1957-63, 7.7 per cent in 1964-7, and 1.2 per cent in 1968-9.[15] Nor is that the whole story; each extra ton of PL480 grain, imported and released steadily every year, through disincentive effects on domestic farmers re-duces their output of (and income from) grain by about one-third of a ton per year.[16] The farmer can make good some of that loss by planting other crops instead of wheat, but his return is smaller[17] (else he would have planted them before the days of PL480); any switch from grain often transfers profitable processing activities from villages to cities; and anyway even total farm output falls when (because PL480 grain releases cut *grain* prices) its *average* price falls.[18] S. R. Lewis sums up that PL480 causes extra re-leases which, unless compensated, are 'in effect a tax on these commodities. If there is a response [to price] of production or marketing . . . the "tax" on agriculture . . . may harm general eco-nomic progress.'[19] There is; it has.

Output is also often procured from farmers in *ways* that depress its price. Procurement by the private sector is increasingly so organised as to enable urban purchasers to use market power to lower the farmer's prices, especially if he is a small farmer forced to undertake 'distress sales' at harvest time to repay debt (these small farmers often lose again to townsmen, when they are forced to buy back grain, at higher prices, several months later). The involvement of Latin American, and increasingly Asian, landlords and rural moneylenders in urban activities, by causing their rental incomes to be spent in the town instead of the village, intensifies these anti-rural effects of private procurement, as Kautsky ex-plained in the context of Austria-Hungary in the 1890s (chapter 4). Moreover, as share-cropper populations increase and land gets scarcer, crop-share rents rise, so that the proportion of crop sur-rendered to this increasingly urban landlord class itself increases, effectively reducing the *average* price the tenant-farmer receives for the crop not retained in his household.

Upon these private transfer mechanisms are superimposed

public interventions in procurement. In Indonesia, for instance, 'the price of rice has long been kept below the world market price by prohibiting exports and through open-market sales of imported rice by the government [. . . which] has been even more successful in reducing the rupiah price of rubber and other export crops.'[20] Around 1967-8, about a quarter of Indian cereal marketings were publicly procured, at prices about 25 per cent lower than were obtainable, in the market, by sellers better placed to select the time and place of sale.[21] In the 1970s compulsory procurement of wheat, while not fully enforceable, has been used by the government of India to hold farm-gate prices while world prices rose sharply. There is of course nothing wrong, except to a dogmatist, with state grain trading; what is wrong is its use to turn the terms of trade against rural producers. Rural people do not even gain as consumers, though government intervention in food pricing has been overwhelmingly motivated by cost-of-living considerations;[22] procured grain is steered to low-price grain stores located overwhelmingly in cities, and rural buyers can find themselves paying more than before, because procurement has reduced rural food supplies. In India and Bangladesh, this is familiar; in Thailand, 'outside metropolitan Bangkok there is no cheap rice distribution'.[23]

Government procurement, at low prices either through compulsion or through timing, has been substantial enough to depress farm prices. It accounted for 36 per cent of milled rice output in Burma, 39 per cent in Ceylon and 29 per cent in Taiwan as long ago as 1956;[24] proportions are generally higher today. And the sheer revenue pressure on governments to procure at low prices is enormous—especially since they are also pressed to sell cheap, above all by articulate urban interests.

If the procured grain is at once the main staple and a major export crop, food procurement merges into marketing-board activities, and the two can combine to turn the depression of farm output prices into a major source of government revenue. The State Agricultural Marketing Board in Burma provided 46 per cent of it in 1955;[25] from 1950-1 to 1967-8, its official purchase price for rice ranged from 25 per cent to 52 per cent of the price at which it resold rice for export, averaging 46 per cent, and except for a two-year period 'farmers . . . had little opportunity to obtain . . . better than official prices'.[26] The activities of marketing boards are especially important in West Africa, and have been the source of much controversy.[27] In principle, they can stabilise producer prices; in practice, given the balance of pressures on governments and the temptations of easy revenue, they tend to become sources of systematic downward pressure on such prices. Irritatingly enough, this argument about rural people's right to a decent life has, like many of its companions, been submerged in a dogma-ridden debate about the role of government in the development process.

Compulsory procurement, subsidised import disposal, marketing boards: these are three of the many methods used by governments in poor countries to keep down farm output prices. Most rural people probably lose from this process (pp. 318-19). It is, however, part of a sincere if misconceived attempt to transfer resources from agriculture by a Preobrazhensky-style price squeeze. That attempt has other aspects.

Pricing of non-farm inputs and outputs

The management of foreign exchange in most poor countries cheapens non-farm inputs, and makes non-farm outputs more costly (chapter 3, note 6). For example, textile firms wanting to export cotton buy foreign exchange at far below its real value to the economy; this cheap imported cotton drives down prices and wages for cotton-growers at home. Both cloth and garments are heavily protected against competing imports in the name of industrialisation; the price of clothing is thus forced up.

Ricardo argued that the resulting excess profit in textiles would eventually be eliminated, as new businessmen were attracted into the industry (chapter 4, note 11), but 'eventually' is a long time; delays and restrictions in the licensing of investment make it longer still; and when it does arrive the farmer is little better off. The price he gets for his cotton still cannot rise above what amounts to a subsidised import price, and the price he pays for his clothing cannot fall below a level including substantial import duty. The movement of new suppliers into the textile industry, by reducing average profit there, may reduce farmers' envy; it will also ultimately stem the outflow of rural savings into urban textile investment; but by then damage to agriculture will have been caused by that outflow.

The *direct* transfer of rural resources townwards, to pay the high prices 'created' by foreign-exchange policies for non-farm inputs and outputs, is familiar enough. The *indirect* harm to farmers on capital account — as such policies pull saving off the farm, into the non-farm investment which they make artificially profitable — is less familiar but perhaps more serious.[28] Among domestically produced non-farm inputs, organised energy and transport are usually supplied by state-owned firms. These face considerable pressure to price their outputs at below commercial levels and even to carry losses to this end. That, in effect, subsidises power and transport, and thereby selectively benefits industry and construction; as compared with agriculture, they feature higher ratios of purchased inputs to net output, of power and transport to purchased input costs, and of organised (and subsidisable) power and transport to total power and transport use. Power and transport loom large in industry, both directly and as parts of the cost of other purchased inputs. Agricultural power and transport are more often human, animal or otherwise unsubsidisable. Public-service alternatives—buses or electricity—are often not 'on tap' for rural users, and thus cannot be 'switched on' if subsidies render them attractive.

Hence input subsidies, financed by taxes on all, produce overwhelmingly industrial benefits. They also brush off onto subsidised consumer services special to the town, notably buses and home electricity. Their attractions once again help urban workers by raising real benefits, and urban employers by cutting the wages needed to provide a given level of real benefits, but not the rural resident even though his taxes help to pay for them.

When villages receive electricity or roads and buses, they too enjoy subsidies. And the non-farm sector loses something because it contains the public utilities that are compelled to subsidise power and transport; their profitability and cash flow, and hence incomes and reinvestment in 'their' part of the non-farm sector, are set back by compulsory underpricing. However, general taxation, levied on village and town alike, greatly reduces this compensation to the farm sector; and the provision of subsidised inputs is enormously skewed towards the towns. This applies even more strongly to such 'quasi-inputs' as the health and educational standards of workers (chapter 11).

Prices of ancillary services—credit and marketing

An exception to the urban thrust of research in poor countries is that we hear more of rural and agricultural credit and marketing than of their urban and non-agricultural counterparts. This is because the nature of rural enterprises, production processes, products, disposals, and communities — all overwhelmingly agriculture-based — generate special problems, largely absent in cities. These problems make credit and marketing critical for the extraction of rural surplus for urban use.

The farm *enterprise* is usually smaller than the urban enterprise, and united with a family to generate a set of borrowing and marketing needs which, unlike those of the biggish firm, must usually be met from outside. The agricultural *production process* (like village crafts, such as carpentry and milling, linked to it) shows clear seasonal patterns in which peaks of input (and credit) requirements alternate with peaks of output (and marketing);[29] such a process does not permit the enterprise to set aside fairly constant parts of its resources as liquid funds or as a marketing division, as an industrial enterprise can do, so that special seasonal needs for borrowing, transport and storage make themselves felt. Most farm *products* have high weight/value ratios, and are more prone to seasonal and annual price fluctuations than are most non-farm products. As for *disposal,* the storage of most farm products is more costly (per unit of value) and more risky (as regards both decay and price decline) than that of most non-farm products; per ton of output marketed, the average distance travelled is probably greater for farm than for non-farm products, and (given the small scale of transport and the high weight/value ratio of products) the transport cost per pound's worth of output is certainly greater. Finally, rural *communities* often generate customs that keep out many outside suppliers of credit and marketing services, and hierarchies that assign the right to supply such services to particular persons or groups; the two features easily create high monopolistic prices, especially in remote villages. All these factors render rural people especially vulnerable to underallocation or exploitation in credit and marketing; but they also mean that the rural provision of such services is costly.

Over and above this, however, the balance of monopolistic and governmental actions and omissions in most poor countries makes rural borrowing and marketing dearer, and their urban counterparts cheaper, than can be justified in economic or social terms. Here as elsewhere, this illuminates not any particular lack of wisdom or morals in poor countries, but the urban bias of their power structures.

In 1973 the president of the World Bank, Mr Robert McNamara, called attention to the very low proportions of institutional credit that were advanced in rural areas of poor countries—below 10 per cent of credit in Bangladesh and Iran (as against, respectively, 82 per cent and 46 per cent of the workforce); below 15 per cent in Thailand, the Philippines and Mexico (76 per cent, 70 per cent and 47 per cent of workers); and below 25 per cent in India (68 per cent). Indeed, these proportions are much *lower* than the rural areas' share in national output, despite these areas' unusually *high* producer and consumer credit needs (relative to income) caused by the marked seasonal fluctuations in agriculture. Work in progress by Dr Szczepanik of FAO confirms this view. According to the Burrows Report, in Kenya 'commercial banks direct their funds [30 per cent of gross domestic savings] from rural to urban areas . . . [depriving agriculture] of one of the necessary conditions for accelerated growth.' The authors did argue that there is no 'unsatisfied effective demand for credit in agriculture', but rightly added that 'easy loans to large, credit-worthy clients in the towns [leave] no incentive to tackle the much harder job of getting credit to the small-scale farms'.

In Kenya and most other LDCs, if demand for agricultural credit is low, it is largely because urban bias keeps down the prices of the extra goods that credit-financed farm investments can produce; if ineffective, because urban bias keeps the rural sector relatively poor and unable to translate its needs into viable loans; and if less 'easy' than urban lending, because urban bias subsidises large non-farm investments and ensures that they produce outputs at artificially high protected prices.[30] As with rural education (chapter 11), so with rural credit: a policy to supply more, without a policy to render its rural utilisation relatively more rewarding, would do little or nothing to remedy the present unfair and inefficient situation. Obviously a limited supply of rural credit, relative to demand, would raise its price; and both aggregate and specific policies do tend to limit the supply of credit going to the villages, despite official statements to the contrary. In aggregate, the installation of government (and the encouragement of private) non-farm investment, and price measures that reward levels of such investment that exceed what is socially profitable, naturally encourage lenders to advance their cash to urban enterprises and consumers. Specifically, many LDC governments do nothing to stop banks from welcoming directors with major outside individual or family interests, almost always urban enterprises; in India in the late 1960s (and almost certainly elsewhere) the banks openly gave low-interest lending preference to such enterprises. Neither formal bank nationalisation nor government instructions seeking rural 'priority' will greatly affect the natural loyalties of, or deals within, what are in effect integrated production-and-credit urban family enterprises.

The counterpart of confining subsidies and banking specialisms — private, governmental and foreign—largely to modern urban enterprise is reducing the quantity and quality of institutional credit in rural areas. This raises its price: directly through shorter total supply; indirectly by failing to challenge the frequent monopoly powers of the village moneylender, or to provide properly run large-scale alternatives to his localised and small-scale, and therefore high-risk[31] and high-cost, activities. This effect on the price of credit is camouflaged, as with other inputs (pp. 288-91), by 'subsidies'. These, unless creamed off by administrators, go to big farmers, who often relend them to swell the flow of moneylender credit. If they get to the small farmer, he often sensibly uses them in partial repayment of moneylender debt. In either case, inadequate agency credit actually underpins the 'debt cycle' (p. 248).

The failure of institutional credit in poor countries to cheapen productive borrowing for the rural poor epitomises the impact of urban bias, via the relevant agencies' lack of funds, shortage of good administrators, and preference for surplus farmers. The rules of successful rural lending are well known; yet it is the moneylender who observes them, while the underfinanced, politicised and maladministered rural agencies, cooperative or state, usually neglect them. I am spelling out the rules here, in order to show that clear-cut alternatives do exist to urban-biased policies. The rural lender must be both liberal and tough, if he is to succeed in reaching the small borrower and in generating a large and growing flow of credit. Liberality involves:

1 *Avoiding insistence on 'productive' use of the loan.* Such insistence merely drives many an illiterate, fearful or super-honest borrower to more expensive lenders. It often fails, because one can borrow for a stated 'purpose of loan'—or even accept a loan in kind—to cover an outlay one would have undertaken anyway.[32] Nor would successful 'productive tying' necessarily be desirable, since borrowers rightly seek loans for purposes yielding most to them.[33] A loan from the cooperative, used to pay off the village moneylender by saving the borrower the difference between interest costs on the two sorts of loan (typically 25 to 40 per cent and 8 to 15 per cent)—may well increase the borrower's prosperity, and hence his capacity to repay the cooperative, more than would any conventional (productive) investment. The same often applies to a loan to buy food, needed anyway, at cooperative rather than merchant interest rates.

2 *Accepting a wide range of securities.* Village moneylenders typically accept forward sales of crop or labour services (both usually at very low prices, raising the true interest burden), jewels, houses, and much else as security; rural banks and cooperatives usually insist on land, or (rarely) forward sales of one of a small number of crops, usually with precisely graded and timed deliveries. The agencies' preferred security is very terrible, yet not fully credible (what would they do with the land?). Hence small farmers are discouraged from borrowing, yet once they have borrowed not convinced they must repay: hardly a recipe for a healthy, growing cash flow in the agencies. Moreover, tenants—let alone landless labourers—cannot borrow against the security of land.

3 *Being prepared to extend loans.* Much moneylender credit is loaned in the knowledge that the capital will never be repaid. Agencies are unprepared to make such loans overtly. Hence the supply of such 'irredeemable' credit is often locally monopolised and thus very expensive (25 to 50 per cent). Yet a loan at, say, a real rate of interest of 16 per cent for ever on sound security is not contrary to good banking practice—only to the shibboleths of credit administrators whose timidity, by preserving the limited cheap institutional credit for the cities, suits powerful urban interests very nicely.

Yet a lender must also know when to be tough, and this involves:
4 *Maintaining realistic interest rates.* Much rural lending by cooperatives and state-supported banks has been at rates too low even to keep up with inflation—that is, loans, even if fully repaid, have been in part gifts to borrowers! That sounds like a subsidy to the rural sector; but it is not so simple.[34] All loans involve a risk of default. If the agency lender charges a real rate of interest too small to make up for (that is, less than the proportion of) defaults, his funds decline, and so does his yearly lending and his chance of pushing down moneylender rates. Moreover, agency loans at very low rates—like subsidised fertilisers—will go to those able to use their influence to get them: to big farmers, frequently also moneylenders, who thus acquire the capital to jump in with extra lending capacity as agency credit declines (or, as commonly, disappears through backruptcy). The village poor, faced with moneylender credit at 25 per cent, would do far better with competing agency credit at a realistic 15 per cent — enough to permit its lending to expand despite some defaults—than at 8 per cent, dwindling to a trickle and throwing borrowers back on the village moneylender.[35]

5 *Insisting on repayment.* In several languages, 'government loan' is translated by the same phrase as 'aid' or 'gift'; in none is 'moneylender loan' so rendered. Yet unless agency lending is backed by recoveries *using the force of law* (except in limited cases of genuine hardship, defined in advance), it is doomed to dry up. The pre-electoral writing-off of rural defaults has in several poor countries, notably Ceylon,[36] become a regular event. Such happenings are concessions not to the rural poor, but to the rich farmer-moneylender, who supplies the town with its food and raw materials, gets the scarce subsidised agency credit—and, often in return for being excused repayment, mobilises the rural votes. In both Ceylon and Bangladesh there are reports — which I may not quote but which are supported by recent evidence[37] — showing conclusively that it is big farmers who borrow to relend and

will not repay, not small lenders who borrow from need and *cannot* repay, that feature the highest default/loan ratios. As the venal priest says in Buñuel's film *Viridiana*, 'Go on, go on! The more you sin, the more you have to be forgiven!'

These five 'rules', observed by the largely successful[38] rural moneylenders, neglected by their largely unsuccessful institutional rivals, are obvious (to anyone who has lived in a village, anyway), familiar — and generally disregarded, in lending practice if not in the quasi-theoretical disquisitions with which government documents preface their rather scant lending plans for the rural sector. That is not due to malice or stupidity, but to the pressure on governments from the urban interest, and to their genuine belief in rapid industrialisation. Both induce them to ensure that (1) scarce money-to-lend is steered towards 'modern', urban, usually industrial activities; (2) what is left for the rural sector finds its way chiefly to big farmers, who use it to increase marketings for the towns; (3) rural moneylenders, who are anyway increasingly induced by the pattern of incentives to reinvest their surpluses in urban activities, are not seriously threatened (let alone impoverished) by successful rural competition from agency credit; and (4) scarce talents for financial administration serve mainly urban and industrial development. These four aims are compatible with observed governmental actions in poor countries regarding rural credit. They are honourable aims; unfortunately they are misguided, and compatible with a mystifying warm bath of 'goodwill' towards rural credit that has lulled most commentators into ignoring the actual policies.[39]

Marketing can be more briefly dealt with; for verbal concern for rural needs has been similarly matched with practical concentration on urban requirements. Roads from village to market induce more rapid rural growth,[40] but come far behind inter-urban and especially intra-urban transport, which are clamoured for by more powerful (and concentrated) voices. That can be seen from the splendid main roads of the capital cities in some of the world's poorest and most 'transport-starved' agriculture-based countries, such as Ethiopia. Within agriculture, emphasis on (and subsidies for) tractors used substantially for inefficient haulage — and concentration of animal development on rich men's foods rather than poor men's draught-power — means that advances in marketing tend to benefit big farmers producing cash crops for the towns, rather than small men selling in nearby village markets. Furthermore, while concentration of transport and storage upon rapidly perishable goods — fruit, milk, vegetables — has some justification, it selects the sector of agricultural marketing least relevant to rural nutrition, and especially to the rural poor. Even more clearly than credit, marketing is a case where rural deprivation is due less to intra-rural exploitation[41] than to urban priorities and urban neglect.

Capital goods prices

Farm inputs are made costlier, relative to non-farm inputs, by policies that make capital goods artificially cheap. Given agriculture's low capital/labour ratio in production, that is one way of using pricing of capital goods to discriminate against agriculture. Another is a credit policy effectively reducing agriculture's share of loans (pp. 297-300)[42] A third is foreign-exchange and domestic policies making capital goods for agriculture more expensive, relative to other forms of capital goods, than they would have been with neutral (or no) policies on this issue. It is symptomatic of past policy biases that one naturally thinks of tractors and even combine-harvesters as examples of 'agricultural capital', and — in view of their labour-replacing effect, their tendency to enrich only the big farmer (and the lucky licensee who buys them with cheap foreign exchange), and usually their lack of contribution to output — these items are too cheap in most poor countries, especially those with plentiful labour and little land. But perhaps even tractors — and certainly tubewells and pumpsets, seed drills and iron ploughs, draught animals and wheelbarrows — while absolutely too cheap, are too expensive *relative to non-farm capital:* to machine tools, lorries and ball-bearings.

The price of non-farm capital is reduced by all sorts of open and concealed subsidy: allowances to pioneer industries, initial and investment allowances against tax, tax-holidays, etc.[43] Above all, the underpricing of foreign exchange (often available especially cheaply for imports of capital goods) favours the parts of the economy producing output with heavy inputs of capital, and importing large parts of capital goods and current inputs: industry, transport and modern construction. These sectors' requirements are made cheaper by comparison with the more frequently home-made (and often solely labour-using) capital requirements of agriculture. Furthermore, where foreign exchange is artificially cheap, it has to be rationed; and urban businessmen are best placed to secure the import licences that serve as ration cards.

Since public policy, private monopoly power and their interaction all make *farm* capital relatively dear — as well as relatively hard to borrow for, and productive of relatively underpriced outputs — the discrimination against farm investment is great. One wonders how much politicians realise this when praising the 'green

revolution', for its techniques succeed best when combined with
on-farm investments in water control, while price policy encourages
farmers to steer their savings towards urban capital goods instead.

Price twists — the total situation

Though I believe that the evidence in this chapter shows what I
claim, I am not happy about many individual items; for it is hard
to assess the total effect on farmers of these different sorts of price
twists, but dangerous to isolate them. For example, can one isolate
the fact that, in Pakistan in the late 1960s, farmers received 54
per cent *more* rupees per ton of wheat than they would have done
had they been able to export it and then to swap their dollars for
rupees at official rates?[44] To do so is misleadingly to reverse
the true direction of the price twist. First, official rates understated
the rupee value of these dollars by 80 to 150 per cent.[45] Second,
non-farmers received much more than 54 per cent (indeed over
100 per cent) *de facto* rupee subsidy over world prices (thanks to
protection discriminating against agriculture)[46] so that the rupee
price of farmers' purchases was boosted much more than that of
their sales. Third, to compare the cost to Pakistan of a domestic and
foreign-grown ton of grain, we must use the *delivered* prices to
domestic markets, including internal transport costs, which boost
imported prices between dock and housewife more than domestic
prices between field and housewife; for domestic grain fields, in
a mainly rural country, are usually nearer than the docks to the
final consumer. Hence more appropriate comparisons, also for
Pakistan in the 1960s, show that farmers would have received
about 50 per cent *more* non-farm goods, had they been able to
trade at world prices, than they enjoyed at 'twisted' prices.[47]

Dantwala's Indian estimates confirm that partial data are hard
to use impartially.[48] He too claims that Indian farmers received
produce prices above world levels in 1962-9. But his claim is
helped along by five unacceptable procedures. He compares (for
example) the *wholesale* wheat prices at Mega, Punjab, with the
US *f.o.b.* (free on board), export price to *ports* on the *Persian Gulf*,
converted to rupees at *official* exchange rates, and concludes that
Indian farmers were being paid above comparable world prices. But
Indian farmers receive procurement prices that are below wholesale
prices; India does not buy US wheat f. o. b., but c. i. f. (inclusive of
carriage, insurance and freight); grain procured in India is used
by consumers (not just at ports) and for them is supplemented by
a smaller average internal transport bill than imported grain from
docks; the relevant docks, anyway, would be in India, not the Gulf,
usually raising international transport costs; and the rupee price

of dollars on the free market — admittedly itself pushed up by Indian policies on foreign exchange, but a fair reflection of what the Indian government, *given its policies overall*, has to pay for non-aid wheat imports — in 1962-8 averaged 53 per cent above the official price.[49] The inappropriateness of paying farmers so much less than the world value of their grain is increased by the fact that, owing to industrial protection, they must pay well above world prices for their purchases of non-farm goods.

We should try to assess the total impact on the farm sector of price twists, in view of the traps of not doing so — although this chapter has shown that each of the key types of price seems to be turned against agriculture. There are two central problems: (1) What might farmers receive and pay, if 'things were different' in some defined way? (2) What is the total impact upon their welfare of receiving different prices?

1   We have rejected a metaphysical search for 'just' prices in favour of assessments of the impact of particular actions on actual prices. However, most serious attempts to estimate 'price twists' compare the non-farm goods purchasable, per unit of farm goods, (a) at domestic ('twisted') prices and (b) at world prices. While world prices are not God-given, they do measure what a country could expect to earn (or save) if it had more of a particular product, so that it could export more (or import less).

Moreover, the ratio, at world prices, between a country's agricultural and non-agricultural products yields *minimum* estimates of the 'proper' price ratio between them. First, the prices of traded agricultural goods are themselves depressed by governmental and monopoly action: by excessive, underpriced releases of (in itself desirable) food aid;[50] by import restrictions that, unlike those industrial products, largely escaped the trade-freeing deals of the 1960s; and by the enormously greater cartel and monopoly power of industrial sellers — companies and countries.[51] Second, if income distribution were more equal, so that demand more closely reflected need, the demand for food and fibres — and hence the relative world price of farm products — would be higher. Third, the world price of products, per unit of labour embodied in them, means far lower rewards per unit of farm labour than per unit of non-farm labour. Hence, the 'world price ratio' of agricultural to non-agricultural products is below the 'free market' ratio, the 'egalitarian' ratio and the 'labour valuation' ratio; for market liberals, social democrats or socialists respectively, the world price ratio thus represents a minimum estimate of the value of farm goods relative to non-farm goods.[52]

2   There is more than one way of approaching the question:

what is the cost to the farm sector of having to buy its non-farm products dearer than at world prices, and sell its farm products cheaper? The cost is overstated by table 6.3, which shows the difference between agriculture's share of GNP at domestic prices and at world prices, because in most poor countries agriculturists, and even more rual people as a whole, consumer a large part of total farm output, and for this part their income is not *directly* reduced because of artificially low market prices.[53]

Hence we must estimate the direct effect on farmers of the underpricing of the goods they market. In Pakistan around 1956, the value of farm marketings in effect extracted 'free', by underpricing (as compared with world prices) relative to farm purchases, was about $400 million, which is some 13 per cent of total farm output. In Argentina in 1958, some 29 per cent of farm output was being 'stolen' by just one of the many methods in use. In Kenya in the late 1960s, the small farmer or his employee – had he been able to sell his output on world markets and buy his consumption needs, instead of being forced to accept local prices manipulated against him – would have been able to consume 14 per cent more, and the large farmer or his employee 22 per cent more.[54] Such total calculations are not available for many poor countries: PL480 sales alone cost India's farm sector about 2% of its real output in 1957-63, 8% in 1964-9, and 1% in 1969-70. In 1964-72 rice prices were 7% to 55% below world levels![55]

This direct loss on what they buy and sell is only part of the impact on farmers of underpricing of their product and overpricing of their purchases. Such pricings also induce them, as we shall see, to produce less. There are thus *four* income-reducing effects on the farm sector of actions against its relative prices: the direct price loss on the surplus product it sells to non-farmers; the lost extra output it would have produced and marketed, had prices been more attractive; the interaction between these two effects (the extra output would have fetched a higher price too); and – for a poor and underfed peasant sector – the lost impact of higher income on the capacity and will to grow more corn for family consumption.

These four effects can easily double the direct price loss inflicted on the farm sector. That is, if the farmer, because he exchanges his marketed surplus for town goods at domestic instead of world prices, loses 5 to 10 per cent of his real income – not high estimates for most poor countries – the indirect impact via disincentives to production could easily raise the proportion to 10 to 20 per cent. And if farmers are poorer and town producers richer, this shifts consumer demand – and hence increases in employment and wages—away from rural craftsmen and suppliers, towards their bigger urban counterparts (normally producing each unit of output with more capital and fewer poor workers). Moreover, some of the price twists — notably in interest rates — are not reflected directly in the farm sector's terms of trade.

The damage to those who work the land is not confined to surplus farmers. Much of the income loss appears as reduced employment and wages of those who work on their land—landless labourers and deficit farmers; moreover, like the rural craftsmen, they are often paid in kind, and will often find that a low food price costs them more (through reduced and cheapened work) than it gains them. Among surplus farmers — 60 to 80 per cent of rural communities in most of Asia and the Nile Valley, 80 to 95 per cent elsewhere in Africa — the smaller and poorer suffer most from a *given* worsening in relative farm prices, because for them even greater poverty is especially likely to compel sale when and where the buyer chooses. And trends in relative farm prices may be *worse* for the small farmers and the rural poor, than for the better-off, larger surplus farmers.[56]

THE IMPACT OF PRICE TWISTS

The deliberate raising of non-farm prices, relative to the prices of farm goods, is directed at structural transformation of poor economies through industrialisation, first by forced savings transfer, second by price incentive. Agriculture is forced to save and to transfer its savings to the rest of the economy: for agriculturists receive less than the value of their product; and non-agriculturists can therefore purchase more than the value of theirs. While there is no guarantee that non-agriculturists will use these gains to purchase productive assets (or that agriculturists would not have saved the extra income they would have enjoyed if prices had not been twisted against them), a government can induce the embodiment in non-farm investment of the urban sector's gains, either by accumulating them itself (as profits on the operation of marketing boards) or by incentives to investment. Price twists, indeed, create such incentives; both funds and temptations for off-farm investment are made more plentiful, and for farm investment less so. Price twists also directly encourage workers, managers, educators and suppliers of allocable inputs to switch out of agriculture.

Does this work? Of course, the very fact of price twist leads to measurement biases that overstate its success in inducing industrialisation; non-farm output is valued more, and farm output less, than at untwisted prices, so that the share of total output outside agriculture is overstated. Price twists are part of a conscious strategy to secure industrialisation both by forced savings transfer and by incentive switchings.[57] The aim is good; poor countries are unlikely to overcome poverty without substantially reducing their reliance on agriculture. However, price twists (like investment biases) are part of a strategy of *instant* industrialisation that is self-defeating. Their disincentive effects dry up the growth of specific farm outputs, of total farm product, and of marketed surpluses from agriculture — the very springs of industrialisation. Their converse incentive effects, on non-farm output, seem small. Meanwhile equity as well as efficiency is damaged: to seek to hold farm and food prices is to attack inflation through the incomes of the weakest; the incorporation (by marketing boards and other means) of price twists into the often questionable processes of farm price stabilisation also damages the rural sector. In general, cheap-food policies in predominantly agricultural countries, contrary to appearances, damage more poor people than they help.

The structural intention

'One means of providing such capital [for "developing the non-farm sector"] is through a change in the terms of trade against the agricultural sector, thereby raising profits in the nonfarm sector as a basis for saving and investment. Thus a policy for raising agricultural prices may well be inconsistent with more basic objectives of development,' writes the author of the standard current text on agricultural development;[58] indeed, it is the standard view of the development literature that, if prices begin to move in favour of agriculture, something has gone wrong. Industrialisation, however inefficient or premature, is not to be deprived of command over resources, however scarce (or productive in agriculture), and however great the price distortions needed to shift such resources! Yet many successful past development paths were different. During Japan's 'take-off' (1877-1905), farm product prices rose 31 per cent faster than farm input prices from non-agriculture: yet seventy years later, all ten South and East Asian LDCs whose food price policies were surveyed by FAO used them to 'stabilise the cost of living', that is, to *cut* food prices![59] Experience suggests this retarded growth; theory supports experience, because such price policy shifted both capacity and incentive to invest towards parts of the economy using new capital less efficiently. Income distribution probably suffered too; in all the ten LDCs, about half the economic agents were farmers and another quarter were their employees, so that depressed food prices mean the transfer of resources to a not-so-poor minority: urban food consumers and their employers. S. R. Lewis concurs that 'the literature on growth and structure of the low income countries . . . suggests that terms of trade relatively favourable to industry would aid substantially in the growth of the nonagricultural sector.'[60] The aim is often, explicitly, to enable industrialists to pay workers less by keeping their food cheap; this was the case in Taiwan,[61] though the rate of extraction from agriculture (mainly through the fertiliser-rice barter system) was well below that of most poor countries. Krishna documents how, in many countries, 'development policy [has sought] to keep bread and raw materials cheap for the growing industrial sector'; he is convincingly scathing about the impact on farm incentive of this 'negative price policy', but his evidence that things have changed since the mid-1960s rests too heavily on the existence of 'support prices' (which are often very low) to be equally convincing.[62]

When we add the theoretical biases in both neo-classical and Marxist traditions (chapter 4) to the practical experience of price policy, there is little doubt that its aim is to raise the share of output outside agriculture.

The impact on total farm output

That can be done in two ways, however: by raising the growth rate of non-farm output or by lowering that of farm output. The former is desirable, the latter not. In an interdependent economy, the latter may prevent the former. Two general observations seem relevant. First, prices giving optimal 'signals', or incentives, to economic agents encourage them to maximise output from given resources; the further one pushes price signals away from the optimum, the more one must expect to reduce output.[63] But, even without government help, the greater market power of non-farm producers would enable them to obtain higher prices, relative to the farmers, than would be optimal. Therefore government-sponsored price twists enhance an already-present distortion, move prices further away from the optimum, reduce real output, and hence must cut the real value of farm output more than they raise that of non-farm output.

Second, it would contradict this sequence if, as was believed until recently, farmers in poor countries were unresponsive to price changes: slow even to switch from one activity to another, and very unlikely to increase total output because it becomes more profitable to do so.[64] This is sometimes alleged to be because of 'conservatism' or 'subsistence mentality' or 'primitive affluence', leading to 'target income' behaviour[65] such that higher rewards per unit of effort encourage some farmers to *reduce* effort and maintain income, thereby offsetting the responsiveness of other farmers. Sometimes unresponsiveness is traced not to the farmers' alleged psyches but to their shortage of resources, especially land, which may be so densely cultivated as to leave little scope for acreage expansion in response to price rises (or anything else).

It is easy to resolve this contradiction. The second set of arguments, alleging that farmers and hence total farm output are in general unresponsive to price, is not supported by fact; the first set, claiming that farmers' responsiveness implies serious output loss from actions that worsen the system's built-in tendencies to underprice farm output, is so supported. There are three theoretical reasons for expecting that it should be. First, the poorer an economic agent is, the more he responds to extra earning chances (and the more unwanted leisure he has, the less likely is it that he will respond to them by working less and resting more);[66] the small farmer, who is responsible for most farm output in most poor countries, is extremely poor (and for much of the year unemployed. Second, this poverty often makes family farmers and farm labourers so hungry that they work less, or less effectively, than they wish to do; higher farm prices (and hence more incentive for big farmers to provide extra work for small farmers and the landless, sometimes bidding up wage rates) can permit them to eat properly and hence to do the effective work that physical weakness formerly prevented; that supplements the incentive effects on output. Third—given the unpleasantness of much physical labour—successive *identical* cuts in its lowly rewards will *increasingly* reduce the amount of it that workers are willing to perform—especially if they have the alternative of even more intensive self-employed work on their own 'cabbage patch', albeit at a very small return. The higher monopoly power of urban producers already pushes relative farm prices down, so that further reductions through price twists—or the reversal of such reductions—can be expected to have quite major, and 'normal', incentive effects on farmworkers' behaviour.

What of the traditional doubts about farmer responsiveness? Very densely populated farm areas, indeed, seldom have extra land to sow to a crop whose price has become attractively higher; but, as they are usually irrigated, farmers can respond to new projects for double-cropping, more intensive fertilisers, and other labour-using ways to raise output—if prices justify it. Elsewhere, farmers can shift from grazing to arable, can shorten fallows, and can shift to more valuable but more time-consuming crops—again if prices justify it. As for psychic objections, small farmers in poor countries are indeed conservative. They have to be: the margin of survival is too close to encourage gambling. This can delay the response to risky innovations; but there is little reason why conservatism in this sense of aversion to risk should impede price responsiveness. Farmers in general commit fewer fertilisers, pesticides, acres of marginal land, man-hours, etc., than they might if they were strict profit maximisers, because the inputs (and their costs) are gone for certain, while the outputs (and returns) are subject to risk; but if the returns go up or down, as price twists are relaxed or intensified, there is nothing in the nature of human reactions to risk to prevent inputs from going up or down in response. Certainly 'target income' behaviour would so prevent them; but there is now evidence against the existence of such behaviour on any large scale, and in favour of some positive response of total farm output to farm prices.

Krishna usefully summarises the evidence that total farm output in poor countries rises in response to increases in its price.[67] He further notes that the evidence is strengthened by many of the 150 to 200 findings that acreage or yield of a *particular* crop so responds, since they refer to areas that grow little else, so that if that crop responds total farm output does well.

Some of the reasons adduced for expecting total farm output to respond more swiftly to price in rich countries[68] in fact suggest the reverse. 'Greater opportunity for a flow of labour resources back and forth between the agricultural and the non-agricultural sectors' in fact prevails not in rich but in poor countries, with their variable seasonal return migrations of semi-urbanised workforces,[69] and with many family farms including substantial reserves of labour that can be switched between village craft products and farming according to attractiveness of relative prices.[70] 'A rise in returns to labour will encourage labour at the expense of leisure' more strongly and swiftly in poor and severely (albeit seasonally) underemployed rural communities, than in wealthy ones with a long working week. And, while 'the agriculture of high-income countries is much more dependent on purchased variable inputs such as fertiliser,' awareness and usage of such inputs has expanded greatly, since Mellor wrote, in many underdeveloped areas (alongside new, more fertiliser-responsive varieties of crops). That situation may well render adoption rates, and hence outputs, more responsive to improvements in farmers' terms of trade than in developed agricultures, where very high levels of fertiliser usage have pushed the return to extra doses down much further.

The response of total farm output to price, especially in densely farmed areas, is likely to take longer, but to be less reversible, than the response of particular crops. That is because of two distinct, though insufficiently distinguished, aspects of producers' response to price changes. When crop prices rise, I am *encouraged* to substitute crop production effort (for example, second weeding) for other activities (including leisure), and to divert expenditures into crop inputs, such as fertilisers: the 'incentive effect'. I am also *enabled* to undertake new long-term farm investments, out of my higher profits or by extra borrowing against the security of a crop that will now be worth more: the 'investment effect'. The investment effect is bound to take longer to generate extra output, and the results may be diffused—for example, though it is higher crop prices that yield me extra profits, it can still pay me best to use them to produce not more crops but more milk, for example, by purchasing mature shade trees for cattle.[71] But the new investments will yield extra outputs much less sensitive to reduction if prices fall later than are extra outputs responding to simple incentive effects. The latter effects are less important parts of price response for total farm output than for specific crops, because in the latter case responses are possible without investment, by switching given amounts of labour and land among crops. The relatively more important consequences of these investment effects, while delayed and diffused and hence hard to pick up in statistical work, certainly boost the long-run price responsiveness of total output—and the permanence, and hence policy importance, of such responsiveness.[72]

Specific key outputs

Planners may well be concerned, not with total farm output, but with one or two key crops, urban staples or export products. For specific crops, the evidence of positive price responses—rapid, perhaps too rapid[73]—is overwhelming.[74] But we know little about the exact size, causes and effects of such responses. I feel much surer about the need for higher overall farm prices, for both incentive and investment effects, than about advising governments to tamper mechanically with specific, isolated supply prices in the hope of calling forth specific output levels of a crop. There are several reasons for this.

First, several aspects of responses to a price rise of a particular crop—timing, size, impact on other crops—are uncertain. They depend on the presence or absence of spare land for the crop whose price has risen, and of workers to sow and reap it without clashing against existing peaks of labour requirement; on the extent to which extra output of the crop would replace other crops that are fixed parts of a rotation, or mixed with other crops, and on the viability of satisfactory alternative rotations or mixtures; on the proportion of a crop normally grown for family consumption; on whether the crop is grown largely on land that can grow nothing else, or by individuals who can reallocate land to it; on whether the crop is largely confined to certain lands, on which over a wide range of prices it clearly earns more than anything else (for example, tea), or 'spreadable' into marginal land according to prices;[75] and on whether the crop occupies a small part of total land area, so that a decision to devote another small part to it results in a huge proportionate rise in its output.[76] Often the timing of the price announcement, and the spread of rapidly changing farm techniques, are critical. Measures of responsiveness for particular crops in particular places, while almost always positive, show remarkable instability over time.[77] With tree crops, which take a long time to mature and then usually occupy the land for decades, the lag between the price change and (almost invariable) positive response of output can be five or six years;[78] between incentive and response the environment of farmers (and the aims of policy) can change drastically.

'Social engineering' in agriculture, permitting predictions (for instance) that a 20 per cent rise in the price of rice will after two years call forth an output rise nearer 5 per cent than 10 per cent, is probably far off in most poor countries. Even further off are reliable predictions of which other crops will 'give' to grow the extra rice.[79] The now overwhelming evidence that peasants respond to prices, therefore, can seldom be safely used for 'fine-tuning' attempts to achieve precise expansions of output of *particular* products. An overall increase in farm prices relative to non-farm prices—while less immediately palatable to the urban interest—has output-raising consequences which, although longer-term, are more certain.

Marketed supply

The impact of manipulating agricultural terms of trade—or, if other prices are unaffected, farm prices—on marketed supply is a central question of development policy. It is wrapped in two confusions, which happen to be very comfortable for the short-term urban interest. The first is the logical confusion between the correct observations that (1) urban growth requires growth in rural marketings to urban areas and (2) urban savings are enhanced by turning relative prices against the farmer, and the incorrect observation that (3) the latter process assures the former. The second is the empirical confusion between the correct observation that (4) the share of its output, that a peasant household does not retain immediately after the harvest, may well decline when agriculture's relative prices improve, with the incorrect observation that (5) the volume of rural output marketed to the urban sector, net of the volume later bought back from it, is also quite likely to decline. Out of this ripe mixture, sadly typical of much of 'development studies', have been drawn the usual anti-rural conclusions.

Adam Smith argued that the growth of urban output depended on the growing transfer of food from rural areas for the increasing urban workforce. Attainable urban output indeed increases when there is extra food for the towns (that is, with more food output or imports, or less rural consumption or food exports); simple algebra shows this (p. 95). But it also proves that the constraint, placed by the growth of townward food marketings[80] on the growth of urban output, can be relaxed by (1) increases in output per member of the urban workforce; (2) reductions in the proportion of income that he spends on food; (3) rises in food prices, so that a constant share of urban money wages, spent on food, requires a smaller volume of townward food marketings; (4) falls in the urban wage rate, which have the same consequence.

Now (3) and (4) are different sides of the same coin, and its name is 'improvements in agriculture's relative prices'. Hence such improvements increase the urban workforce that can be supported by a given volume of food marketings.[81] So the *facts* that low relative agricultural prices transfer savings townwards, and that urban growth is constrained by rural marketings to the urban sector, do not imply the *fallacy* that governments, by turning relative prices against agriculture, relax the constraint on urban growth presented by the supply of marketed food. They tighten it. The use of low farm prices to force out savings for the town involves the internal contradiction that such prices, because they imply cheap food and a large share of national income for urban wages, automatically raise urban demands for food.

This is why Preobrazhensky's advocacy of the 'price scissors' to force out rural savings, when implemented, had to lead through compulsory procurement to (inefficient) directed farming (chapter 4); and this is why poor countries cannot finance urban growth out of such savings, if they are unable or unwilling to take this brutal path. Because farmers respond to the operation by producing less, the contradiction is sharpened. Worst of all, both Soviet experience (chapter 4) and recent evidence suggest that it is marketings townwards (net of buyback) that farmers subject to the severest cutbacks, when the urban goods that such marketings can purchase are reduced by pressure against relative agricultural prices.

Many enquiries into peasant marketing avoid the central policy question:[82] to what do townward marketings, *net of rural buy-back,* respond, and how? Many rural marketings are 'distress sales' by mini-farmers, mainly to meet debts. Such sales could well drop when farm prices rise, because the money to meet a given debt can be raised from a smaller volume of sale. However, since these poor sellers seldom grow enough food for their family's needs, they buy back at least as much food from the market as they sell;[83] hence, if such sales drop when food prices rise, that proves nothing about the response to such price rises of net townward marketings. (Indeed, the associated retention by small farmers of more of their own food output implies that they require to buy back less food later.)

The mass of net townward marketings (though not always of gross total marketings)[84] comes from the larger farms, for which they dominate total output; hence the known price responsiveness of total output (see pp. 309-12 above) almost guarantees that of net townward marketings. Second, the larger a farm's total output, the larger its net marketings;[85] since total farm output rises with price, this suggests that rising farm prices also induce more marketings. Third, some direct evidence links growth in net townward marketings to favourable movements in the farmer's relative prices. An Indian study suggests that a 10 per cent improvement in the farmer's terms of trade will induce him to raise his net townward marketings by about 10 per cent also, and recent work shows that 'all the statistical tests indicate *positive* [responses of marketings to] prices . . . between 1957 and 1972' — confirming earlier evidence from Pakistan and the Philippines.[86] Fourth, villagers are less able and less willing to buy back if food prices are high — so that more food remains available for the town.

Non-farm output

Thus cheaper farm output, or dearer inputs to grow it, or dearer consumer goods to buy with revenues from its sale, will reduce specific farm outputs, total farm output, and net farm surpluses marketed townwards. Will there be a compensatory rise in non-farm output, as its producers respond to the incentive created for them by better relative non-agricultural prices? There is no evidence on the response of non-farm output to favourable internal terms of trade, except in the very general sense that, if it were really dramatic, industrialisation would have been more of a success in the many poor countries that have turned prices against agriculture. There are, however, some theoretical grounds for expecting at least the modern and commercialised part of the non-farm sector to find it harder than do farmers to respond to higher output prices with greater output.

First, agriculture features 'variable factor proportions', that is, it is almost always possible to raise output by increasing the input of one or two production factors, even if the others stay constant. Labour alone, which is usually available outside peak seasons, can raise output by extra weeding, water-control or bird-scaring — if the price of extra output makes it worthwhile. Outside agriculture, however — and especially in *modern* industry, construction, power and transport — 'fixed factor proportions' are more common. In a blast furnace specific amounts of coal, of iron ore, of several chemicals such as sulphur, and of labour-time from several types of technician are essential to produce a ton of steel; petrol, driver and lorry are essentials of haulage, and more of just one or two is useless; and so on. Hence — while farms can usually respond to price incentives just by using extra family or hired labour — many modern enterprises can do so only by increasing their purchases of many inputs in similar proportions. Especially in countries short of foreign exchange for imports, such synchronised increases will often be ruled out by 'bottlenecks' — especially if many industrialists are seeking similar extra inputs at once.

Second, the modern sector's response to high output prices is also slowed down and reduced by the organisation of labour. Despite massive urban unemployment, workers in the modern sector restrict competition, partly by acquiring genuinely needed skills and partly by trade-union organisation, and can thus ensure that higher non-farm prices benefit them substantially — thus reducing the profit incentive, to businessmen, in responding to higher prices by producing more, especially as they must often do so through over-time rather than through extra employment at normal rates. Neither in the family farm, nor (except in some large plantations) outside it, are such incentive-reducing effects important in agriculture.

Third, the impact on enterprises in one sector of a change in its prices relative to other sectors is greater in proportion as such enterprises buy a large part of their purchased current inputs from other sectors. The proportion of *purchased* current agricultural inputs coming from non-farm enterprises — fertiliser, pesticide, etc. — is large,[87] boosting the impact of changing relative agricultural prices on farm profitability. The non-farm enterprise buys a much larger part of its purchased current inputs from other non-farm enterprises, diluting its gains from a general rise in non-farm prices.

Fourth, an analogous effect operates at individual level. A worker or businessman gains little from better relative prices for products of 'his' sector, if he uses most of his income to buy its products, which are getting relatively dearer. The farm family certainly uses up, by value, a large part of income to consume food and other farm products; but it is seldom a large net buyer of them, instead obtaining them from the family farm, from wages in kind, or from grain payments for petty lending or renting. Of the farm family's cash outlay — that is, of what changes its real value when *relative* farm prices change — much comprises non-agricultural purchases. The opposite is true of the non-farm sector: its workers and businessmen spend a large and growing share of their income on each other's products, and a declining, though still large, share on farm products.

These last two effects, combined, mean that the impact on the accounts of a firm or a family from a fall in relative farm prices is more substantially negative in the farm sector than it is positive in the non-farm sector. The first two effects — the non-farm sector's organised workforces and fixed factor-proportions — render it less *able* to respond to a given impact than the farm sector. Two further considerations relate to the *will* of individuals in sectors to respond to price impacts.

First, employed workers and businessmen in the non-farm sector, being richer but less endowed with leisure than their agriculturist compatriots, are more likely to respond to rising rewards per hour by reducing effort instead of increasing output: not very likely, but more likely. Second, if farm prices fall and non-farm prices rise, the extra profits accruing to a non-farm enterprise increase its operating surplus, and thus create an investment fund *slightly*, but usefully, cheaper than urban credit sources; but the corresponding reduction in the farm's operating surplus (1) throws the farm upon *much* costlier sources of rural credit if it wishes to maintain its level of investment, and (2) since the farm usually has a smaller initial volume of investible funds (relative either to total sales or total purchases), produces a larger proportionate cut in them.

I do not wish to push these arguments against *non-farm* responsiveness too far. Non-farm output as a whole, I think (there is no real evidence), does respond positively to favourable relative-price effects, incentive and 'enabling'. But there are strong *a priori* grounds for believing that the value of extra output generated by such response falls short of the value of output lost through the corresponding, output-reducing, response of farmers to unfavourable movements in farm prices. The shortfall is larger if 'correctly' priced than in the artificial prevailing prices at which it is normally measured, since these boost the value of non-farm output and understate that of farm output. Moreover, as the structure of protection attests (pp. 321-4), much of the extra non-farm output induced probably ought to be imported, and much of the (larger) value of farm output lost is probably needlessly imported. Extra non-farm output induced by manipulation of the internal terms of trade — whether via incentives or via the forced transfer of rural saving to lower-yielding urban investments (chapter 8) — usually involves large and unfruitful losses of efficiency.

The distributional impact

Many governments in poor countries genuinely see measures to depress prices to the farm sector as protecting the very poor by keeping down food costs (chapter 13, note 22).[88] However, first, most of the very poor are in, or dependent on, the farm sector, and they probably lose when farm prices are kept down. Second, the beneficiaries of low food prices are, selectively, the urban not-so-poor, who have easiest access to 'fair price' shops. Third, price-depressing measures damaging farmers are neither confined to food nor concentrated on poor men's foods such as maize, millets, pulses and root crops. Fourth, food prices could be kept down by taxpayers, through subsidies financed from government revenue; a preference for forcing the farmer to accept less constitutes an attack on the living standards of rural people, who on average are much poorer than urban people; moreover (since large farmers partly escape through selective subsidies), the poorer rural farmers suffer most. Only the first point requires explanation.

It is natural to assume that most of the very poor gain from cheap food. In India, Bangladesh, Pakistan, Sri Lanka and probably Indonesia, some 20 to 25 per cent of workers engaged in agriculture belong to households that neither own nor rent any farmland, and another 15 to 20 per cent to households that own or rent holdings so small that some members must take outside employment, at least part-time. In rural Latin America more extreme inequality offsets greater average income, and generally the proportions are at least as high. They are probably lower in most of Africa, though not in Ethiopia, Kenya, or overpopulated riverain areas like the Nile Valley. But if, in most poor countries, say 25 to 40 per cent of agriculturists are net *buyers* of farm products, it is natural to suspect that the very poor in rural areas *gain* when such products are made artificially cheap.

Usually, however, this suspicion is wrong. First, much of the income of the very poor is in kind;[89] its value to employees rises as food prices rise. Second, as the farmer grows more output when its price becomes more attractive to him, farm employment rises too — especially since much is generated by the fertiliser-intensive 'green-revolutionary' techniques of raising output. Third, the extra demand for labour can pull up real agricultural wages, especially at harvest time — and particularly if, as in Kerala in South India, labourers organise to demand a share in benefits. Fourth, many a deficit farmer will be pulled into surplus by the 'incentive effect' of higher food prices, and will then gain from them by net crop sales. Above all, better agricultural prices, relative to non-farm prices, will raise both the income that surplus farmers can spend, and the proportion of their saving that, they find, it pays to use for rural reinvestment; hence demand for, and income and work in, a whole range of petty rural crafts and services will increase, generating subsidiary income for many desperately poor people (such as 'ex-untouchable' Indian castes of cobblers and rope-makers) with little or no land. Cost-of-living arguments are thus no counterweight to the commonsense view: deliberately to turn relative prices against the farm sector, which is poorer (and in most poor countries internally less unequal) than the non-farm sector, worsens the distribution of income.

Stabilisation and support

Two sorts of price policy towards agriculture are commonly mis-read as evidence against price twists. Government action to stabilise farm prices often tends to reduce them, and to increase the year-to-year variation in farmers' income. The benefits of guaranteed 'support prices', below which the farmer's price for a commodity is not allowed to fall, are usually restricted to the big surplus farmer, and to years of glut.

To be against stability is like being for sin; but a farm family gains only if its *income* is being stabilised, preferably around a rising trend. The stabilisation of the *price* at which it sells farm produce is likely to make income less stable under most circumstances. This is because — in the absence of price stabilisation — produce prices are low when good harvests increase the supply of market-ings, and high in years of bad harvest. In other words, for most farmers, price instability usually compensates for output instabil-ity to some extent, and thus makes cash income — price times marketed output — more stable, not less. If public policy stabilises prices in good years and in bad, the typical farmer in a poor coun-try — suffering high climatic risk to his crop but normally selling a small surplus — no longer gets a better price when the harvest is poor, and thus in the matter of risk fares worse than before.[90] Of course, the farmer who can afford reliable control of water and pests — usually a biggish surplus farmer — suffers little output risk and therefore does find that income is stabilised by the removal of price risk. Security makes him more likely to invest, and the extra capital raises his future production and his townward marketings.

This increase in supplies is one reason why price stabilisation in agriculture usually goes hand in hand with price reduction (for which only the big surplus farmer is likely to be compensated by his extra sales volume). Another reason is that, by the gap they set between purchase price and resale price of farm goods, governments usually make farmers bear the administrative costs of stabilisation,[91] which are especially high if it is achieved by 'buffer stock' policies,[92] because huge stores have to be moved and protected.

The main reason why stabilisation usually cuts average farm prices — especially when (as often) it is achieved through the major role played in procurement, and hence in price-setting, by marketing agencies or boards — is that these experience intense pressures to keep down the resale price of the commodity to consumers and processors. These consumer subsidies are usually paid for — through low procurement prices — out of the farmers' pockets rather than from general taxation. Worse, marketing agencies are seldom content to stabilise prices, or even to subsidise buyers; they push farmers' prices down further still, so as to earn revenue for the government by running large operating surpluses.[93] These can be achieved by making the growers accept lower prices, because the board is virtually the only regular buyer. As with PL480 (chapter 13, note 17), the growers' losses do not end there; lower prices discourage production, so that potential extra sales are lost as well. And it is the tea, rubber or sisal smallholder — not the big plantation-owner — who suffers, as he often can neither wait nor manoeuvre, but must take the marketing agency's low price.

As for price support, such 'fixation of a floor reduces the risk of buying [a] package'[94] of approved inputs for some farmers only. Normally, the 'floor' is descended to only in glut. For the small farmer, who does well in a glut because he eats more (even if his few residual sales earn him less cash), support prices *increase* the variation in welfare between glut and scarcity. They stabilise the income only of farmers who *lose* from a glut — big surplus farmers who would gain nothing (except weight) by eating the extra crop, and who would have to sell it even if prices tumbled. As with stabilisation, so with price-support schemes: the running costs tend to be imposed on the farmers themselves, through low support prices, and price-cutting sales of publicly held grain when the glut is over.

Support prices can usefully speed the uptake of innovations on bigger farms — the maintenance of wheat prices in India in 1968-71 is a case in point — but are not meant to be paid often, any more than a floor is for frequent falling upon. Price support seldom compensates farmers for twists in average prevailing prices; price stabilisation often involves further twists. This does not render such policies undesirable, but they seldom reduce price twists much. Moreover — though farmers do respond to lowered income risk by increasing their farm inputs, and hence their output[95] — such response is relevant only if these schemes really reduce income risk. For the poor and risk-prone farmer, who fears risk most and is thus most responsive to its diminution, they do not.

OVERALL PRICE POLICY: THE IMPACT ON THE FARM

In poor countries, prices are turned against farmers through many channels; and the industrialising impact on output *structure* is small, often self-defeating, and outweighed by the damage to the *size and distribution* of output. But how much of all this is related to the direct impact of public and private power on relations between farm and non-farm prices? Poor countries feature many price 'distortions', sometimes fully or partly justified from the viewpoint of equity or growth; is the fact that such 'distortions' damage the farm sector more than an unhappy side-effect? Should we seek a general explanation of the relative prices of products (and productive agents) in poor countries, from which relationships between farm and non-farm prices would follow, rather than — as here — examining the specific types of price received and paid by farmers?

Imports, exports and foreign exchange

Most governments of poor countries manage their foreign-exchange positions by a combination of two policies; it could be described as 'balanced' or 'contradictory' according to taste. First, their central banks are instructed to buy and sell foreign currencies more cheaply than open-market rates suggest; that means, overall, that imports are rendered cheap and attractive, and exporting — since one gets so little domestic currency for one's marks or dollars — less profitable. Second, since few poor countries can borrow enough to support the resulting balance-of-payments deficits, access to this 'cheap' foreign currency is hedged around with numerous conditions: import licences, bonuses for specific exports, multiple exchange rates, and above all extremely high rates of protection, especially for processed industrial goods. The second set of policies usually succeeds in reversing the impact of the first set on imports, but not on exports. Thus most poor countries feature totalities of policy, towards foreign trade and foreign exchange, that encourage substitution for processed imports (for example, assembly, instead of import, of cars) and — partly because resources are pulled towards such import-substituting activities — discourage exports.[96]

This combination of policies may seem unwise; but decisions persisted in by eighty or more poor countries stem from stronger imperatives than unwisdom. One piece of logic underlying them is sound enough. Many a poor country has a large share of world markets for an item like tea or jute, with limited demand, so that greater production for export could drive prices right down. For example, a rise in world tea export supply of 1 per cent means a price fall of around 5 per cent. Sri Lanka (Ceylon) markets about one-third of world tea exports. A rise in Ceylon's tea exports of 3 per cent (that is, in world tea exports of 1 per cent) would thus cut prices by 5 per cent, leaving Ceylon worse off than before.

Much of the case for exchange-rate policies that favour import substitution and disfavour exports, however, is less sound. Even before the oil price explosion, there was no long-run trend in international prices against poor countries' exports as a whole.[97] As for the volume of such exports, the success of some countries and of specific commodities suggests that sluggishness elsewhere is not God-given, or even demand-determined. Rather it is the result of suppliers' policies and preferences, and these are themselves largely created by the incentive structure generated by governmental policies: a structure unfavourable to exports. Not that the incentive structure can be left to 'the market': that has produced trade-led growth only in a few small, well-aided countries. Moreover, 'the market', especially in the foreign-trade sector, consists largely of a few big firms, often owned abroad and repatriating profits thither, and able to influence the price and output structure, rather than responding passively to it in the socially optimal fashion that some textbooks suggest.

The case against the foreign-exchange and trading policies of most poor countries' governments, then, is not that such policies have distorted a market that would otherwise have functioned beneficially, but that they have strengthened the already harmful market power of privileged groups of big monopolistic firms and their organised employees. That is natural, because 'the State' is not neutral, but is influenced by the powerful, the organised, the wealthy, and — under urban bias — the near. On relatively esoteric issues of foreign-exchange management, the voice of the villager is likely to be especially weak.

A policy of balance-of-payments management has therefore been shaded first towards import substitution; then towards import-substituting *industrialisation* (as if foreign exchange spent on agricultural imports did not count);[98] and finally into a network of licences, quotas and tariffs that provides the modern urban sector with cheap imported inputs, and heavy protection against imports of competing outputs, for import-substitution (and recently also for export promotion) even at very low levels of efficiency — while agriculture, or at least that part of it not oriented mainly to supplying urban demands, pays for its imports through the nose, or is denied them altogether. Naturally foreign-trade and foreign-exchange policies have damaged agricultural prices;[99] but the root cause is not 'mistaken' levels and structures of protection, but the power of urban interests, which press for these socially 'mistaken' but privately profitable policies. Wrong diagnoses have led to soft options: instead of switching the emphasis to agriculture, poor countries are now encouraged by some economists to switch from heavy protection against competing non-farm imports to artificial incentives for non-farm exports!

Overvaluation of the domestic exchange rate, as Trotsky realised (chapter 4, note 111), is a powerful weapon for squeezing agriculture. In Argentina, just before the 1959 devaluation, agriculturists were losing about $500 million yearly to the rest of the economy — about 29 per cent of their total income! — for this reason alone.[100] This 'works' because farmers usually import a much smaller share of production and consumption requirements than others, and thus lose to non-farmers when imports are artificially cheapened. As for exports, agriculture's share in their value — for instance, in Argentina, not only exported cattle, but also that part of the value of canned beef that is produced by cattle-farmers and not by canners — is usually bigger than its share in output for domestic sales. Domestic currency overvaluation therefore also harms agriculture (and causes resources to be shifted out of it) by rendering exports less rewarding to home producers and/or less appealing to foreign consumers. Crudely, the farmer is the exporter, and gets too little for the dollars he earns; the industrial producer is the importer, and pays too little for the dollars he uses.[101]

Undervaluation of foreign currencies — selling dollars and marks too cheap — creates excess demand for them, and this is kept down by several devices. Unfortunately, these devices — protection, licensing — far from correcting the 'overvaluation bias' against agriculture, usually worsen it. First, levels of protection are usually much higher than they seem to be[102] — effective rates of 500 per cent are quite common — and protection is largely confined to industry. Second, the more 'processed' an item, the higher is its level of protection in most cases, which plainly disadvantages the farm sector. Third, where scarce and underpriced foreign currency is 'rationed' by licensing, industry usually gets priority for imports. To issue licences for restricted imports of finished goods does not keep down their price to farmers, because — unless the importer is the same firm as the final user, which is rare *for farm inputs* — such licences are merely ways to allocate the monopoly right to add such profits as bring up the total price to its full scarcity level; that price the farm purchasers still have to pay.[103] Moreover, the complex procedures for issuing import licences (in Mexico the Ministry of Commerce uses thirty-seven criteria and handles thirty thousand applications monthly, accepting one-third[104]) handicap farmers, and even suppliers of farm inputs, who are often far from the point of decision and for climatic reasons unable to wait long for approvals.

The prices of consumer goods

These are affected in two main ways by government action in poor countries. Relative to what they would otherwise be, the prices of consumer goods are pushed *down* by measures that, in effect, compel their domestic producers to sell cheap — PL480, compulsory procurement, price policy of public monopolies of rail transport and household electricity, etc.[105] If nothing were done about it, this would discourage investment in producing consumer goods. To stop this happening, prices of consumer goods are pushed *up*, relative to the prices of investment goods, by a great variety of subsidies to businessmen installing new capital equipment.

As with currency overvaluation and the measures correcting its impact on the foreign balance, so with cheapening of consumer goods and the measures correcting its impact on the businessman's choice between spending and ploughing back: both the initial effect on prices and the measures to offset it damage agriculture to the advantage of the urban sector. Most consumer goods come from agriculture, so that if producers are forced to subsidise consumers it is principally farm sales that are 'taxed'.[106] And the ratio of capital goods to total output is in today's LDCs much lower in agriculture than elsewhere (table 7.1) so that a subsidy on investment again involves a relative advantage to non-farm activities.

As with protection, so with the relative pricing of consumption goods: policies systematically transferring resources from agriculture to the rest of the economy are based, not on unwisdom, but on the pressure and concentration of urban power. In both cases, it is useless to say 'stop intervening and leave it to the market': not only because this has seldom produced development in the past, but also because the same pro-urban distortions, achieved by private power through pressing for particular *government* price policies, would in a 'market' situation be achieved instead by using *monopoly* buying and selling power to rig prices. Urban power is basic; subsidies to labour-replacing imported capital, and hence to unemployment and foreign deficits, are a secondary consequence. This is not to say that nothing can be done. One can try to overthrow the power structure, to change it, or to work through it. But to ignore it — simply to assert (or, worse, to deny) that foreign currency, or domestic capital, or urban food, is 'too cheap' and to express wide-eyed wonder that governments thus cause agriculture to develop so slowly — is to indulge in an apolitical economy that will indeed ensure that nothing is done.

'Explaining' government pricing decisions —
the examples of capital-goods and public-sector products

Why do many economists seek to explain pervasive decisions on relative prices in poor countries by 'mistakes' special to those decisions, rather than by the power structure that influences them? Partly this is a relic of a bad old tradition that led some marginalists to see 'uninfluenced' market prices as neutral and fair, and all outside attempts to shift such prices as wrong.

That view cannot be defended. Some products, like cars, are supplied by a few big firms with great influence on supply and thus price; others, like millet, are supplied by many small firms. Again, unequal income distribution pushes the demand (and hence the price and the apparent 'value') up for cars and down for millet. In a poor country especially, governments can sensibly render it both cheaper to buy millet and more profitable to grow it (by subsidies in the short run, by investment and research in the long), while rendering car purchases dearer and car sales less profitable by taxation. Intervention in pricing, to correct for (and to correct) maldistribution of income and power, is not a 'mistake'. But given the maldistribution of power, the forces pushing the interveners in the wrong direction — towards accentuating instead of correcting inequality of income and power, usually in the urban interest — are strong.

Symptoms of biased price intervention attract great attention (to the point of being confused with causes) because they are so clear and so damaging. High and ill-structured protection shifts poor countries' resources into making things they could import more cheaply, and away from promising export lines. The empiricist tradition of social enquiry, suspicious of searches for motive, tends to blame the trade failures on the protection-dominated pricing policies, and to leave matters there. Similarly, it is easy to show that, if farmers bear the costs of cheap-food policies, they will grow less food. In each case, the really interesting question is why such policies are persisted in. The common feature, advantage to the powerful and articulate urban sector, also seems to explain other pricing 'errors' by governments in poor countries.

Consider, for example, the failures in many poor countries of large parts of the public sector's production activities, combined with the continued expansion of those activities. A few dogmatists dismiss this as an inevitable concomitant of the 'inefficiencies of socialism'; but a substantial minority of success stories, and the fact that the Third World's nationalised industries — both successes and failures — are not very 'socialist' (egalitarian or under popular control), gives this the lie. Another approach, more typical of economists today, is to blame the failures upon underpricing of outputs; upon the retention of more workers than can usefully be employed; and, nevertheless, on the selection of techniques requiring much costly equipment and little of the amply available labour. Once more, most of this is true; but why is it true? Are not outputs underpriced to satisfy urban users of power and transport, workers retained to appease urban trade unions, capital equipment purchased because (for reasons explained already) urban interests see that it is kept artificially cheap? And if, as seems likely, the much greater degree of public-sector involvement outside than inside agriculture is partly responsible for agriculture's deprivation of capital and human resources — while these are showered on ailing industries — what explains this differential public activity? Entirely the small, dispersed, family nature of farm production — or, in part, the greater capacity of the organised urban sector to secure intervention in its own favour?

A final instance of mispricing conveys the same moral. Most poor countries have huge, idle reserves of labour most of the year. Yet they install artificially 'cheap' capital equipment to replace labour: luggage loaders at stations and airports, tractors and threshing machines and even combine-harvesters on farms, tower cranes on building sites. Price systems are permeated by direct and indirect subsidies to such import-using, labour-displacing decisions. Moreover, policies toward the structure of production generally tend to concentrate capital in units that can cheaply get money for labour-replacing innovations, but that find it costly to use workers instead.[107] The International Labour Organisation's 'employment missions' to Colombia, Sri Lanka and Kenya spelled this out in detail, and certainly that can assist local understanding. But is it really understanding that is at fault? We should be asking: who imports the tractors, who controls the unions, who gains from artificial cheapening of heavy capital imports? As an impeccably neo-classical economist observed at the 1973 Bellagio Conference on the theory of agricultural development, the real question is: who runs the country?

14 What can be done?

The main job of the social scientist is to describe and analyse the interplay of human actions to produce social outcomes. Secondly, he can try to show that more generally acceptable outcomes are available if some actions are modified. Thirdly, he can offer advice about how such modification is to be secured. This book has concentrated on the first two tasks. I have tried to show that the rural sector has not obtained (owing to its own weakness and the strength of others) sufficient shares of resources to meet generally accepted criteria of efficiency and equity. However, the rich and powerful benefit from the results of urban bias, at least in the short run; people usually act in their own interest, and in poor countries with high discount-rates often in their short-run interest; and, because people with similar interests combine to advance their group, any 'invisible hand' that might harmonise their *individual* wishes never gets near the conductor's baton. This is firmly held by the urban elite. So what can be done?

The social scientist's capacity is to analyse; he has, usually, no special talent for administering governments or revolutions (or even university departments). But he can assess whether, in particular situations, particular means of correcting the evils he diagnoses are likely to succeed. In this case, what is needed is simple: a much larger share of all sorts of developmental resource — savings, aid, brains, dollars, administrators — for rural areas and agriculturists; and, within these, concentration of resources on the poor, weak and efficient, not on those whose main socio-economic 'virtue' is to transfer their spare food or savings to benefit the urban sector.[1] But how is this to be brought about, given the new reality of development: the combination of extreme urban concentrations of power with overwhelmingly rural concentrations of people, poverty, and prospects of efficient use of scarce resources?

Two extreme cases can be mapped out: the persuasive and the revolutionary. In some poor countries—India may have been an example — the openness of society, the freedom of discussion, and the growing self-awareness of the rural poor might allow the weight of reason and argument, combined with growing political pressures, to cure urban bias on their own. After all, the returns on extra farm investment would be higher than on other investment; should grow faster, in the wake of the 'green

revolution' and the oil price explosion; and could ultimately remove the brake on non-farm expansion hitherto applied by lack
of wage goods. Farsighted members of the urban elite, especially
planners, want this too — and are coming to realise that 'a squeeze
on agriculture' cannot achieve it. Moreover, even in the short
run, if less urban bias means more total output, some of the benefits can be so used that the urban sector is compensated for losses
as urban bias is reduced: probably not fully compensated (for
that might fully restore its political capacity to secure the pre-
existing scale of urban bias) but, given growing rural pressures
also, at least persuaded to accept the new situation.

In any case, even in poor countries without free debate and
enquiry and without effective organisation of the rural poor, the
power of argument should not be underrated. Even some dictators
have been convinced of the need for major resource diversion
to attack mass rural improvement. Not all urban power centres
are shortsighted and selfish all the time; and few are monolithic.
Nevertheless, substantial reduction of urban bias by 'peaceful
persuasion' *alone* is not likely in many poor countries. The chronic
failure of agriculture's shares in investment, brains or administrative attention to rise — despite much talk of 'green revolution'
and of priority for agriculture — speaks for itself.

At the opposite extreme to a 'light of pure reason' approach is
the view that only revolution can substantially improve the access
of the rural poor to income and power. In some poor countries,
this is true, but social scientists are not qualified to advise them.
How to make revolutions, how to ensure that they benefit the
rural poor — social scientists neither know these things, nor have
the right to sacrifice human life to their ignorance. If they are concerned with relieving mass rural poverty, therefore, they should
refrain from advising, or otherwise assisting, such countries.

There remain many — probably most — poor countries in which
improvements in the share of the rural poor in income and power,
and the associated gains in both efficiency and equity from concentration on labour-intensive small farming, are neither impossible without revolution nor inevitable given persuasion. Suppose
one wishes to bring about improvements there, what should one
do? It depends who 'one' is. I shall briefly examine priorities for
peasant movements; labour movements; businessmen; national and
local politicians and planners; researchers, domestic and foreign;
and finally overseas developed countries and international organisations concerned with trade, aid and private investment. In each
case I shall try to separate strategic priorities — concerning what
one does first, and where one is going in what order — from tactical

issues concerning how support can be mobilised and opposition reconciled or weakened.

WHAT THE RURAL SECTOR CAN DO —
'PEASANT MOVEMENTS'

Peasant movements in poor countries are generally directed against other peasants. The targets may be farmers of a different tribe, caste, region, religion, or language. In the case most favourable to increased efficiency and equity, the target is the rich landlords, but such peasant movements for land reform are rarer than one might imagine from the concentration on them in the literature. Even *their* targets are rural, except that some of the huge landlords attacked by Latin American peasant movements are substantially urbanised absentees. Moreover, a movement representing specifically a peasant interest is unlikely to do much for the rural labourer (save as a transient matter of tactics); indeed, the 5-acre tenant is concerned to push down rents and wages. Without some sort of theory — or ideology — to guide it, a 'peasant movement' is likelier to divide rural people among themselves than to confront the urban sector that exploits them all.

Can these twin problems of peasant movements — rural divisiveness and lack of challenge to the urban elite — be solved? Rural divisiveness can be reduced if two conditions are met: adequate land, of sufficient quality, to permit a politically plausible reallocation of land to provide both the mini-farmer and the landless labourer with a holding that can support his family; and gross inequality of landholding, so that only a tiny number of giant landlords needs to be deprived of land (with or without compensation). Latin America contains several of these extreme, ideal cases for rural unity, notably in Ecuador.[2] Most poor people, however, live where land is scarcer and inequality less extreme. Peasant movements seeking access to land rights, therefore, have to obtain land from many not-so-rich 'medium farmers'. Even if they succeed, the land acquired can seldom provide a viable holding to the masses of both small farmers — the staple of peasant movements — and landless labourers.[3] In the Indian state of Kerala, landless labourers probably lost as a result of the distribution in the late 1960s of land from large farmers, who hired most of their workers, to small family farmers who did most of the work themselves. Other measures of *rural* redistribution, benefiting mini-farmers at the cost of medium and big farmers, often have similar effects.

Land scarcity, and the resulting conflicts over rights, must exacerbate the familiar conflicts of caste, language, region and tribe that render peasant movements so hard to keep together over long periods, or in large countries.[4] It will not do to dismiss these internal conflicts as side-effects of 'false consciousness', unless one can specify a focus for action by the rural poor that will both reduce them and identify a route to common gain. Such a route does exist, but it unites *rural* people rather than *poor* people. The splitting of the countryfolk can be remedied to the extent that they campaign *together* for better relative prices, greater public investment and lower taxation for villagers, a larger share of properly qualified administrators and teachers and doctors, and so forth. This strategy involves the leaders of the rural poor in alliances with some landlords, merchants and moneylenders; but much of the benefits of rural (as of urban) growth can then leak toward the local men of power and wealth.

These unpleasant truths perhaps explain why most leaders of peasant and rural-labour movements have felt themselves compelled to ostracise the *kulak* interest. So cut off, they are unlikely to succeed. The dangers of collaboration are real enough, but urban-rural inequality usually contributes more to the poverty of the rural poor than rural-rural inequality, which it also sustains and reinforces. Given the desperate land scarcity of Java, Bengal or the Nile Valley, even complete rural equalisation would leave the rural poor very poor indeed, whereas removal of urban bias would not; and the best path to intra-rural equalisation may well be first to weaken the urban forces that rely on rural inequality to obtain surplus food, savings and educands from the village elite.

Peasant movements are seldom inspired by an urge to get, from the towns, a more just and efficient share of the nation's resources. It may be ethically desirable, and it is probably tactically necessary, for them to reorientate themselves in this direction — especially where land scarcity otherwise divides mini-farmers, both from landless labourers and from a substantial group of middle farmers, as regards their attitudes to purely rural redistribution. Peasant movements, however, are locally led and attuned to specific situations, and thus unlikely to take general outside advice. What, if any, is the scope for those in urban life — in governments, universities, business, or labour movements — who sympathise with this approach, to work with or help peasant movements?

There are hints from past experience, but they generally concern the behaviour of urban groups seeking to advise the rural poor of their rights against the *rural* rich. Sometimes the attempts are highly instructive, as when Paulo Freire imparts literacy to Brazilian peasants by teaching (as it were) not 'the cat sat on the mat' but 'the landlord sat on the peasant'.[5] More often they are well-meaning but over-simple, as with the 'emissaries' proposed in 1972 by the Ethiopian Ministry of Land Reform to inform the tenants of their rights under the (abortive) draft land reform law; the Ministry seems to have realised neither that such emissaries would need armed guards, nor that the real problem of enforcement lay in legal and political machinery dominated or subverted by landlords. But neither the successes nor the failures teach us much about the prospects of informing rural people about their rights, claims and powers *vis-à-vis* the *urban* interest.

The question of 'spontaneity versus outside education' in political movements is old and complex. However, there are special reasons why outside education may be needed to make rural people in a poor country aware of (and organised against) urban bias. They tend to be isolated and dispersed; the pressures of the rural rich against each group of rural poor are local and immediate, while the urban exploitation of the whole rural sector (of which these pressures are often the consequence) is national, remote, and often subtle. For example, when prices disappoint the farmer he is apt to blame a local glut or a rapacious merchant, not deliberate but obscure policies made in a remote city. Moreover, purely local peasant movements are often led by separatists, populists or golden-agers. Either Marxism or marginalism, properly developed, can explain urban-rural relations and can be simply but honestly presented to villagers; but only an inverted snob would pretend that these complex forms of organised thought were likely to be applied in villagers' meetings, without help from outside. Nor will villagers' normal contact with the city, in itself, help much: usually the successful townward migrant is captured by the city, the failure returns frustrated to the village, but neither becomes an agent promoting rural awareness of urban exploitation.

Urban politicians, teachers, students and thinkers—if they are sympathetic to rural advance and can to some extent detach themselves from dispositional urban bias—should involve themselves directly in rural life, by visiting and learning and explaining, not by using villagers as 'blind, inert force' (chapter 4, note 139). Sympathetic townspeople will thereby help the villager to understand the forces that keep him poor, and that create a common rural interest in counteracting them. It is not being suggested that urban Visiting Experts lead rural revolutions! The dichotomy between an organised movement to enforce objectives, and persuasion and debate to achieve them, is false: both happen together. Few townspeople, doing well out of urban bias, will abandon self-interest: but some will think long, will realise that rural consciousness is one powerful weapon against the urban bias that ultimately threatens urban as well as rural progress and tranquillity, and will seek to help, without paternalism, to inform and unite the rural movements that express that consciousness.

LABOUR MOVEMENTS

Rural labour movements suffer similar drawbacks to peasant movements: dispersion, rural divisiveness, lack of visible and localised urban targets. Agricultural trade unionism developed late in Western Europe and the USA, and is still none too successful. In poor countries, there are remarkable isolated success stories of rural labour organisation for higher wages, for example in Kerala: but population growth, and urban-influenced foreign trade policies that cheapen labour-replacing innovations like tractors and weedicides (chapter 13), weaken rural labour, and thus its movements' prospects of lasting success. Also rural workers may need the beginnings of income growth before they can afford the costs, risks and delays of organised action. Rural labourers, and their organising capacities, would often gain more from (anyway efficient and equitable) increases in the share of 'labour-enhancing' resources allocated to agriculture, than from direct attempts at rural unionisation in advance of such increases.

Can urban trade-union leaders, without sacrificing their own interests, reduce urban bias? It largely depends on whether they take a conservative or an expansionist view of those interests. Usually they concentrate, 'conservatively', on improving wages and conditions for their *existing* employed membership. Such improvements, especially if non-agricultural growth is supported by subsidies and by artificially large allocations of public investment, can be obtained by steady increases in capital per worker in the unionised part of the economy. (That way, too, clashes with urban employers are reduced, because wage rates and the volume of profits can rise together.) But if an urban trade-union leader interpreted his interests in 'expansionist' fashion, he would seek to increase the number of employees he represented, and hence his voting, striking, demonstrating and bargaining strength. The 'conservative' strategy builds a wall around the privileged urban employee elite: villagers can move townwards, can join the 'informal sector' to be enthused over by the sociologists of urban pastoral, but cannot readily get unionised urban jobs. They are often forced back to the village; the prospects of executing a rural strategy of improved incomes via equilibriating townward migration (chapter 9) stay bad; and, lacking urban alternatives, rural people also lack bargaining power.

Now suppose that urban trade-union leaders took an 'expansionist' view of their interest, and sought to increase their membership with slowly growing wages rather than to keep membership constant with rapidly growing wages: an expanding army rather than a walled garrison.[6] More villagers could settle in urban jobs; remittance flows to the village (chapter 9) would become clearly positive on balance; there would be less temptation for urban employers to secure labour-replacing equipment with subsidies (chapter 13), or infrastructural support through cheap power supplies, because workers could be engaged instead.

But could urban trade-union leaders in poor countries get away with such a strategy, or would their existing membership drive them out? Certainly, the expansionist strategy has high risks, though also if successful high rewards, for the leadership—and the members—in terms of real political 'clout'. However, the conservative strategy carries, in the medium term, at least comparable risks, without comparable prospects of reward. For it confirms capital-intensity in industry, neglect of agriculture, and industrial pressures towards the policies rendering such choices artificially profitable; and the real growth in output produced is small. In particular, shortfalls in wage goods (1) prevent the real value of urban wages from rising substantially, and (2) compel periodic cutbacks in non-farm production and employment. Hence the conservative strategy cannot for long 'deliver the goods' in terms of real wage increases even to the existing membership.

Urban trade-union leaders in poor countries might therefore try a strategy of membership expansion (clearly explained to their existing members) in the reasonable hope that it will set in motion forces which, though favourable to agriculture, will in the medium term raise *real* wages for their members faster than a conservative strategy of membership protection. The latter raises money wages, and maybe relative wages, for the organised urban sector: but if very slow growth in members' real wages is the price (quite apart from damaging effects on the nation as a whole), it may be too high even for the urban trade-union leadership.

BUSINESS

Small farm enterprises, especially family farms, are major losers from urban bias, but can do little about it. Large farm enterprises are bought off (pp. 97-8, 114). What about the town-based firms? Big and small, public and private, they own in a typical poor country over 80 per cent of business capital. Being on average larger than rural firms (especially farms) and less dispersed, such town-based firms have even greater shares of 'business power'. The extent to which their power supports urban bias depends on how actively, if at all, they back the government's urban policy, and on how far they respond to it by locating their own activity in urban areas, and/or by reinvesting there any income earned from rural activities.

The problem is not a lack of available self-interested courses of action by urban firms to benefit the rural sector. Rather the problem is that the gains from pressing for urban-biased policies — and from responding to such policies with locations of business activity even more urban-oriented than strict profit maximisation would suggest — are familiar, rapid, short-term, and hence cumulative. Even if greater gains were available by other means, the existence of quick, safe and habitual gains, created by urban bias in public policy and in private response, leads businessmen to repeat that response, and to press for 'more of the same' policy. Why the attraction of the quick, safe and habitual, as opposed to the profitable? *Is* a more rural orientation of business potentially more profitable? What can be done to make it more attractive — and how should businessmen begin?

Quick returns are particularly attractive in poor countries. The uncertainty of the future, the scarcity of credit and the smallness of much business combine to make rates of interest high. Ironically, despite the long gestation periods of much of non-agriculture, business expects its returns there to be relatively fast, given the 'pioneer' subsidies for urban investment and the general ignorance of rural prospects. Risk aversion typifies owners of small, new enterprises that are anyway risk-prone. Familiarity with urban activity, combined with government policies inducing relatively rapid increases in urban output, reinforce the desire of the 'footloose' sector of business to concentrate on urban investment; moreover, the physical expansion of towns 'captures' some formerly rural-based concerns as villages are swallowed.

Yet there may well be a much larger section of currently urban enterprise that is 'footloose', as regards both what it does and where it does it, in poor countries than in rich countries. The share of net output from such activities as grain milling, which can reasonably be carried on at the rural or the urban end, is large; fixed capital assets play a smaller role in production; multi-product enterprises are a longstanding tradition, whose origins still survive in the thousands of craftsmen who are also small farmers; conversely, business families committed to hundreds of years of making a particular non-agricultural product are, by virtue of the recency of accelerated development, rarer. But does it really pay footloose firms to go to, and to reinvest yields in, rural areas? And does it pay urban savers to lend to—or to become—rural firms?

If the answer is 'no', there are two mysteries: chronically high rural interest rates, and the big divergences between farm and non-farm marginal capital/output ratios (chapters 8 and 13). Neither is strictly incompatible with a lack of profitable investment outlets in rural areas. High rural interest rates might be caused not by competition to borrow for profitable production activities, but entirely by intense demand for consumer loans with great risks of default. A high value of extra agricultural output, per unit of extra capital, signifies largely that family farms saturate extra capital with their own labour, and only to a small extent that the owners of the capital—even if distinct from the farmers who work it—can enjoy a high rate of profit.

Yet even these explanations suggest remedies. If small farmers are used to paying high interest rates to moneylenders for consumer loans, that will make them readier to pay to borrow the extra cash to finance low-risk productive investment, which will later enable them to escape from the moneylenders' clutches. If extra farm capital, to produce a lot of extra output, needs to be saturated by family labour, then urban investment in the purchase *and improvement* of land, for subsequent renting or resale in small units, should offer attractive returns. In both cases—urban lending for farm investment, and direct urban investment in farming—it will be the job-creating, labour-intensive additions to capital stock that produce the highest social returns; but, unless such misincentives as subsidies to tractors and weedicides distort the picture, such activities will be privately profitable also.

All this has no undertones of 'capitalism' or 'socialism'. Irrespective of the economic system—whether the urban 'firms' be one-man carpenters, big private companies, nationalised industries or cooperative banks—rural[7] direct investment, or lending to rural undertakings, can in most poor countries be very profitable, both socially and to the firm; as it can be to plough back the profits into further rural investment. The great majority of urban firms, however, do not undertake such investments. They prefer safer, more familiar, urban investment and lending; and they rely upon pressing the state for infrastructure and subsidies—upon urban bias in public investment allocations and in pricing—to render such activities profitable.

This account suggests some politically acceptable remedies. First, and simplest, up-to-date and specific information about the prospects and profitability of rural, and especially agricultural, lending and direct investment can be much more widely diffused. Second, banks (public, private or cooperative)—apart from helping to spread information — if they have urban as well as rural branches, can use funds and trusts to spread the risks of rural investment; why should not the publicly or privately owned urban firm, or indeed the urban worker with rupees to spare, acquire an equity interest in the 'green revolution' rather than a low-yielding post office savings certificate that finances, for the most part, the (even lower-yielding) heavy-industrial side of government investment? Third, inasmuch as business avoids rural and agricultural investment because—though the 'gestation period' between investment and *output* is relatively short—unfamiliarity and 'teething troubles' delay *profits,* financial policy has a part to play: short-term, 'pioneer agriculture' loans, perhaps at somewhat subsidised interest rates but non-repeatable, could be made available to urban firms undertaking new rural ventures.

One way to tackle these tasks is through a *Rural Finance Corporation* (RFC) with major responsibilities for research and information as well as lending. That could help to solve the problem of a chronically insufficient share of investment in rural, and particularly agricultural, activities. In so doing, it would avoid urban hostility; for its *method* of dismantling urban-biased structures of institutions and incentives would render safer, as well as more comprehensible and quicker-yielding, those rural lending and investing opportunities that could show higher internal yields to those who seized them, as well as higher social returns, than the urban opportunities they replaced. Where price twists are very severe, some compensatory subsidies to an RFC might be needed, but its operations should be confined to the stimulation of investment in, and of lending to, rural undertakings showing high rates of social return.

The main aim of the RFC should be to get capital moving into good rural projects. This can be achieved by helping rural, as well as urban, people to place cash or activity in rural instead of urban areas. Most villagers living fifty miles from Calcutta, but many hundred miles from the 'wheat revolution' of the Punjab, have much better knowledge (and cultural contacts) in the former, though private as well as social profitability indicates investment in the latter. An RFC could help villagers to seek lending and investment outlets in other villages, not just in the nearest city.[8] Again, there is nothing specifically capitalist about this idea. It is applicable whoever the savers are, whoever owns the firms they work for, and however the rural production units in which they invest directly, or to which they lend, are owned or managed.

Business, then, can profitably press less for, and respond less to, urban bias—but through new institutions[9] that will change business preferences, rather than through new actions in the existing framework. Until that framework changes, it may not be too useful to advise urban, or rural, businessmen about how to advance their own interests by expanding rural activities. Already too many extension officers have persuaded gullible *farmers* to attempt unprofitable, or even physically impossible, patterns of farm activities; and the investment choices of army officers in Pakistan, and urban businessmen in the Indian Punjab, during the 'wheat revolution' of 1964-71 reveal a willingness to undertake new rural activities when they appear sufficiently safe as well as profitable. However, in general, urban business could be advised: devote less of your political pressure to securing incentives for urban activities, and more to removing the disincentives —and the barriers (risk, lack of information and slowness of realised returns)—impeding you from undertaking rural activities.

POLITICIANS AND PLANNERS

Of course the 'bourgeois state' exists. Planners and politicians are not merely influenced by class and other group pressures; they are often members of the very groups that exert those pressures. But politicians and planners are not monolithic, and nor is pressure. Many of them, out of idealism or long-run self-interest, do seek to remove identifiable biases against the rural sector and agriculture, and thus to assist equity, growth and development. If the share of investment and public expenditure in irrigation, agricultural research, rural health, etc., should rise; if rural people's share (though not their total) of savings and tax burdens should fall; if price twists against villagers should be corrected—how can a non-neutral government with a non-neutral state machine, under urban pressures, in practice approach these tasks?

Style

Often, powerful urban interests that would lose from a diminution of urban bias cannot be overthrown. Often they dominate the government that should confront them. In such cases, the more enlightened planners and politicians gain nothing from sham confrontations ('top priority for agriculture'). Instead, they should seek genuine—if often indirect or half-hidden—shifts of resources and prices towards the rural sector. Meanwhile, the more powerful urban losers should be offered a form of compensation that, while socially profitable, encourages them so to manage their own affairs as to create external benefits in rural areas.

A second aspect of the requisite changes in the manner of government—and this may sound naive—is to change the life-style of the political and administrative urban elite. This is not a matter of showy sacrifices: below a certain point, lower pay and worse working conditions for politicians, civil servants and planners will damage the quality of recruits and induce officials to take bribes. The wealth of many Third World politicians, however, has a form, an ostentation, that destroys their contact with the rural poor, who are already more remote from them (in distance, potential, and aspirations) than the urban poor. In this sense a Swiss bank account, or gold under the bed, is less damaging than a presidential palace, or civil service business conducted (on the basis of overseas higher education) in French or English.

But the issue of 'life-style' goes beyond accessibility. Most urban elites have forgotten how rural people live. In a poor, would-be-democratic country, where the rural 70 to 90 per cent of the people are governed by an urban elite, should all the members of that elite spend a few weeks of each year *incognito*, helping with farmwork at peak seasons? This Gandhian (and Maoist) ideal of *shramdan*—work-gift—should be taken seriously, not because a Permanent Secretary, MP, professor, or visiting 'expert' from the UN or the World Bank is likely to be any good at ploughing (though he probably needs the exercise), but because chairbound decision-makers need to be directly acquainted with the conditions of the masses for whom they decide.

Alienation of rich from poor, of government from governed, is world-wide; it can be limited but not removed, even in China or Tanzania. What is special to 'developing countries' since 1945 is an extreme additional alienation, of urban elite from rural mass. In the rich world today, governments and their staffs contain much knowledge—gained from personal experience, contact, report and observation—of the working situation of the largely urban masses they administer. When most rich countries began to develop, they did so with elites somewhat more rural, and masses already more urban, than do most developing countries today: the imbalance, in knowledge and origins and commitment, between urban elite and rural mass was therefore less extreme. Moreover, the imbalance was not yet sanctified by the convenient ideologies of urbanism (chapter 4).[10] All in all, ruling groups in today's developing countries, to maintain contact with and understanding of rural life, need special help, such as might be given by prolonged periods of direct work in rural areas:[11] a truth that both Gandhi and Mao intuitively grasped.

Organisation

More subtle approaches to urban pressure groups; demonstrative changes in life-styles to improve contact with rural people: to some extent these are the politics of gesture. Gestures matter, especially to enthuse rural people by driving out their memories of opposite gestures: arrogant and ignorant officials,[12] showy urban affluence, talk of 'hewers of wood and drawers of water'. But gesture without content, a new round of breastbeating about 'top priority for agriculture' (agriculture gets priority, towns get resources[13]) is useless. What policies might, with some chance of pacifying or overcoming urban opposition, steer resources towards rural areas, especially small farmers, and thus assist efficiency and equity alike? What follows is skeletal: details will vary enormously among poor countries, except those lacking significant urban bias (for example, perhaps, Taiwan and China) or significant rural sectors (for example, Hongkong, Singapore). I deal first with governmental organisation.

Gradually, the balance of recruitment, pay and career structures of the public services—teaching, medicine, perhaps police, as well as the civil service—should be changed. The need is, at the same time, to generate confidence between government and rural people, and, within the government services, to turn the sections operating in rural areas into the *corps d'élite*. Promising measures include:

1 Extra pay for rural postings, especially remote ones;

2 A consequential freeze on urban-oriented dearness allowances, city compensatory allowances, etc., especially where, as is usual, the beneficiaries actually obtain many goods more cheaply in urban than in rural areas (chapter 5, note 5);

3 Incentives within rural branches of the public service, to reward good rural performance—for example, higher command areas under irrigation schemes—despite the risk of corruption and misreporting (the risks might be reduced in some cases by assessing performance by a vote of affected villagers);

4 Longer postings to the same rural area (so appointees stay long enough to be useful), combined with provision of family facilities, and pay that renders such postings relatively more attractive;[14]

5 Coordination of rural services (notably agriculture, irrigation and general rural development), usually not by the customary and

unsuccessful method of knocking together heads — and ministries — in the capital city, but by decentralising responsibility to one officer at local level, and requiring him to work with local elected representatives (steps can be taken to reduce the risk that many of these will be *kulaks*);

6 As a counterpart of this, helping to end the almost universal problem that agriculture's share in development outlays is smaller than planned, by initiating—probably in the Prime Minister's office, at least in countries with half a dozen conflicting agro-rural ministries and two-thirds or more of the population in agriculture —an adequately staffed monitoring, troubleshooting and implementing arm of the planning machinery, with exclusively rural responsibilities;

7 In order to raise the share of public outlays in agriculture and in rural areas, assignment of appropriate personnel, especially economists skilled in project identification, away from central banks and planning commissions and nationalised industries, towards crop research institutes, expansible irrigation (especially groundwater) projects—and evaluation teams to help local officials to prepare and monitor sound projects;[15]

8 In order to assist in 'ruralising' good civil servants, to establish a career structure by which promotion into higher administrative grades can be achieved by good performance at rural executive level,[16] and not principally by formal qualification, subsequent examinations, or presence at the centre at moments critical not for rational development but for 'office management';

9 For those who first enter the public service by qualifying examination, an automatic assignment of most of the best entrants to home rural branches of the services concerned (see 1 above).

The package would vary among countries, not only with the field situation but with the balance of power within the urban sector, both among ministries and as between government, urban business and union pressures. Also the package would not have immediate effect, not only because it would take time before new administrators had been educated to the new priorities and promoted to positions of influence. But the very announcement of such a package—preferably, for maximum impact, all at once— would help create incentives and institutions that would both obtain some immediate results and encourage training institutions to reorder their own priorities accordingly.

Policy

Administrative change is only part of the story. What is to be administered? What *measures* can raise the share of resources going to the rural poor, while the *men and institutions* to implement such measures are still weak, but are being improved and encouraged? Again, only a skeletal list is given; again major concerns are to contain adverse reaction from the powerful urban elite, and to mobilise favourable reaction from the rural areas. These measures aim at 'the best result possible, not the best possible result'.[17]

1   Powerful indirect measures to redress the rural-urban balance, without too serious open affront to existing urban power, could concentrate on the composition of *output*. Currently, Major changes in the composition of agricultural output are usually influenced by planners with a view to matching the likely patterns of extra demand out of expected increases in group incomes. That means emphasis on the demands of the urban rich for fruit, dairy products and so forth. Nutritional efficiency would suggest shifting emphasis to crops with high calorie yield[18] per acre, grown and eaten by the rural poor: to maize, millets, cassavas, yams, and perhaps potatoes and pulses — crops chronically neglected in development plans.[19] Also the composition of non-farm output, especially in building and construction, could be moved in a more 'rural' direction.

2   Most governments, seeking to survive in face of mass discontent and elite pressure, have (since losers tend to make more fuss than gainers) limited capacity to change *income distribution* directly. More of that capacity should be concentrated on urban-rural redistribution—desirable as intra-rural redistribution (land reform) or intra-urban redistribution (ceilings on house property) are in themselves. Measures reducing the most extreme anti-rural price twists—because of their damaging impact on the efficiency of total output, and hence on governments' capacity to compensate the more powerful and vociferous losers—are among the most promising here.

3   Rural access to education should be improved, but only *pari passu* with the opportunities and rewards available for trained workers (especially medical personnel, mechanical and engineering specialists at all levels, and accountants) in rural areas. While 'schools are universally treated as cable-cars up to the modern sector it is useless to try to inject new knowledge and research capacity into agriculture via the school system';[20] the people injected, naturally responsive to wage incentives and prevailing values, will use their qualifications—however agricultural the exams—as passports to the city. Thus incentives, values and educational emphasis have to be put right together, in step.

4   In order to make greater emphasis on rural development

generally acceptable, the facts are the best propaganda. The sheer inequality between village and city, in terms of access to health and education, transport and electricity, is seldom widely realised and often wholly unresearched. Governments can ease their task, if they seek to reduce the urban bias of the systems they control, by spreading the necessary knowledge.

5   A subtler form of hidden fact is the true rate of return over cost for major projects in agriculture and elsewhere. It has been suggested[21] that the mere act of estimating and publicising such true rates of return in 'accounting prices', reflecting the true scarcity of inputs used and outputs made, would ease the task of shifting towards rural activities. This is desirable, but even such rates of return understate the advantage of rural and agricultural projects, partly because unequal societies produce structures of market demand that undervalue food and hence render its 'scarcity value' artificially low: therefore 'adjusted accounting prices' allowing for this fact should be used. Such calculations could well improve resource allocation in the public sector; but private persons—deciding where to put their talents or their cash—look at private rewards at market prices actually prevailing, and they will be more moved by changed structures of incentives.

6   Clear, annual and attainable targets for the share of public expenditure, public investment and (with appropriate incentives, disincentives and controls) private investment in agriculture, and for the share benefiting rural activities, should be set and monitored. (These targets should make realistic estimates of the — usually low — share of outlays on defence and public buildings benefiting rural areas.) Typically, in a country with 70 per cent of its population and workforce in agriculture, it would be reasonable to expect the share of public investment there to rise, from currently normal levels around 20 per cent, to 35 to 45 per cent in five to ten years. This sort of 'deliberate speed' would permit adjustment, and—given typical growth rates—would prevent declines in the absolute volume of public non-farm investment (and probably permit the continued rise of private non-farm investment[22]). The pressure to publish and defend the shares of public activity benefiting agriculture and the rural sector could well produce improvements in itself.

7   There is at least one exception to this gradualist policy. Most poor countries could and should increase, over the period 1976-81, public outlay on applied agricultural and linked rural research at least tenfold, in constant prices. Part of this increase should be spent on improving the pay, training and hence quality of agricultural and rural research workers at all grades. Since

trainable research capacity is scarce, this would mean less research into other matters. Hence some of the costs, direct and indirect, would be borne by sectors of the economy depending on research into roads, steel, nuclear energy, soap advertising, kidney transplants and other things — unimportant and important — but less important than agricultural stagnation and mass rural misery. (Naturally, without increases in the relative pay and incentives of trained field officers, better training will achieve little; but nor will improved financial motivation without more, and more useful, knowledge.)

8   Within agricultural spending on education and research, more public emphasis should go to mini-farmers with, say, ¼ -1½ acres of irrigated, or ½ -4 acres of unirrigated, arable land. Research steered towards non-irrigated farming, or cheap small-scale irrigation (for example, bamboo tubewells), or other non-transferably small-scale technology (for example, in storage), or towards 'poor man's crops' — though it will have limited value without redistribution of rural and therefore (pp. 97-8, 114) rural-urban power — tends to benefit small owner-farmers, and is thus a relatively promising way to help liberate them from reliance on the favours of the rich. Such liberation can seldom be effectively achieved through isolated sections of government directed at providing inputs, extension or credit to such small or marginal farmers; even if these sections received enough finance, the power structure — within rural areas, and through urban demand patterns and political pressures — would still misdirect many of its benefits towards large surplus farmers.[23] It will remain difficult to carry out the measures — above all, land reform — required to direct the benefits of rural growth to the rural poor, because a real urban interest, in acquiring plentiful marketed surpluses, is affected in the short run. Anything, notably higher agricultural efficiency, that directs that urban interest towards a longer view, and makes it less fearful for marketed surpluses, will help reduce its obstruction of intra-rural redistribution.

RESEARCH PRIORITIES

What can researchers and research administrators, in university, business and government, do to increase the proportion of their efforts devoted to studies likely to improve the lot of the rural poor? And what can be done to render more effective a given financial and human effort in this direction? The questions are linked; for the inefficiency and maldirection of most rural research is both cause and effect of its underendowment. Today, few trained agronomists practise their profession (chapter 11, note 24); the results of existing rural micro-research (notably farm management studies) remain uncollated, unanalysed, and hence largely unread and almost wholly unapplied; key policy issues in agricultural economics and rural sociology take second place to fashionable angels-on-a-needle pseudo-theory, Marxist and marginalist alike. All this naturally seems to weaken the case for more outlay on agricultural research. Yet, while such research receives little prestige, attention or cash from the centre, the information needed to improve matters will be inadequate, and the temptations to do what is safe and familiar will remain strong.

Many universities in poor countries already include applied agricultural components in their training in biological or social sciences. Even for graduates, however, these are usually short, general, low-prestige projects. Those few universities (such as, in India, Nagpur and Jabalpur) that emphasise intensive village studies for social-science graduate students usually provide too little supervision (and too small a proportion of student time) to turn such studies into genuine training for field research. Indeed, they often confirm bright students' views that such applied rural research is 'cow-dung economics', conceptually and analytically second-rate.

In fact, such research requires exceptional skill, as the huge gap between the insightful best and the average makes clear. It is essentially an interdisciplinary exercise, involving at its best several social and several natural sciences; and it requires the time, concentration and humility needed to understand why villagers make the choices they do. All this implies that training in applied rural research should come near the end of a course of university studies (since one cannot communicate with other disciplines until one has, at the requisite level, an understanding of one's own). It should also test limited and manageable hypotheses; and should receive a good deal of supervision from senior researchers.

Training for research is the crucial constraint, in most poor countries, on high-quality and useful applied work in agriculture. That is so for two reasons. First, many agricultural researchers in poor countries are trained to perform unapplied and inapplicable research. Libraries of agricultural universities, often replete with books on the care of the dog and on the proper conduct of social surveys in US cities, illustrate the problem. Academic career structures, set up to reward the imitative 'theorising' in which their administrators were themselves skilled, confirm it.

Second, students, though overwhelmingly urban, often appreciate the problem intuitively. The best students tend to drift from research and from agricultural studies (biological, economic and social) as 'soft options' for poor students. This shows that higher education in these matters in poor countries usually fails to develop students' capacities and to crystallise their ideals.

It is easier to suggest neglected topics for rural research than to specify how the researchers should be recruited, trained and retained in such research: to identify ways to expand research budgets at high social rates of return, than to break the human constraints on such expansion. First, despite the above critical remarks, even *conventional* agricultural research showed very high rates of return — at least in India — well before the 'green revolution' appeared on the scene.[24] Second, much of that genetic breakthrough could have probably been achieved sooner, and certainly exploited sooner once achieved, with appropriate research emphases in the poor countries themselves. Third, its side-effects — from agronomic problems (such as the increased risk of wheat-rust mutations specific to the new and genetically undiversified new varieties) to socio-economic issues (such as the development of varieties suitable to the risk-aversion, labour-timing and cropping patterns of mini-farmers) — demand and repay further research. Fourth, especially as high-yielding varieties approach a growth plateau while population grows remorselessly on, new research requirements appear: the location of buried groundwater, together with analyses of the size *and distribution* of costs and benefits from tubewells to reach it and cropping patterns to exploit it, is the highest priority in many poor countries.

Expanded agricultural and other rural research faces barriers of dispositional, rather than of allocative, urban bias. The sums of money, even the numbers of first-rate brains, required are relatively small; and the most hardened instant-industrialiser will welcome innovations raising the food output per unit of investment.[25] The difficulty, even after the spotty successes of the 'green revolution', is to convince people that applied agricultural research, in biological as in social sciences, deserves the attention of first-rate brains and offers a high return. Yet this is an area where relatively inexpensive amendments to salary and career structures, and to training methods, can have an enormous impact.

WHAT CAN FOREIGNERS DO?

Many people in rich countries are coming to believe that they have an interest in helping poor countries to raise the share of resources devoted to agriculture. Until recently, neither in aid nor in trade have rich countries helped much. The rural sector, especially agriculture, has received an even smaller share of aid than of domestic resources; and gifts and near-gifts of food and cotton have constituted anti-aid to agriculture (chapter 13, note 16). Trade concessions to poor countries have favoured their manufactured exports, and have anyway been few.

Yet agricultural success in poor countries is in the interests of rich countries. This is not, as some people fear, to ease the path of neo-imperialism by preventing poor countries from industrialising and competing. It is because, on the contrary, efficient growth in poor countries, followed by expanded and selectively industrial specialisation and trade with rich countries, requires the prior conversion of agriculture from a drag into a booster; because the inflationary implications for rich countries of world food shortage, intensified by the oil-based rise in fertiliser prices, are both alarming and (probably) most cheaply curable through mass agricultural take-off in poor countries; and because flows of scarce capital to poor countries, whether as aid or on private account, are hard to justify if their concentration on urban-industrial development impairs both their yield and their contribution to the elimination of poverty.

But, if even the best-intentioned governments in poor countries cannot overcome urban bias without changes in style and organisation, the same applies even more strongly to foreigners, especially aid donors and international organisations. If the blinkers of Delhi and Nairobi shut out the facts of the rural hinterland, so do the blinkers of Washington, London or Moscow.

An illustration of the problems is the aftermath of the World Bank's sincere and determined attempt, since 1972, to raise the share of its lending that goes to agriculture, and in particular the share that benefits the rural poor. The World Bank is not yet so organised as to perform this task competently. Decisions are centralised in Washington, a very urban place. The few 'field' missions in poor countries operate in capital cities, and usually 'have no time' for prolonged visits to any one rural area (Brazil and Malaysia are striking exceptions). Concentration on large, easily monitored and hence mainly urban projects is a natural outcome of incapacity to monitor a sample of, say, storage bins on small farms, or tubewells, or farms using new pesticides. Such monitoring activity need not conflict with—indeed, could normally be undertaken by—national ministries, with appropriate funding and technical assistance. But there is no substitute for direct and *prolonged* acquaintance, by representatives of donor agencies, with specific field conditions and rural communities.

The World Bank's 'Bangladesh Office' in Washington in 1973 contained photographs of a low-lift pump and a deep tubewell operating under field conditions: 'for those who write about them all day but do not know what they are', as the caption drily explained. The first-class people in the Bank's Dacca Office know what they are and how they work, and they have seen the problems at field level. Hence they constantly press Washington to concentrate on helping the government of Bangladesh to improve the field maintenance and command areas of these irrigation devices. But the pressure out of Washington is for more projects: hence the 'visiting experts' sent briefly to Dacca seek to evaluate and initiate the new projects. Such experts usually lack the local knowledge needed to improve the performance of old ones. Moreover, even 'field' missions lack the time, capacity and local contacts to monitor the field performance of specific 'bits' of aid, let alone to undertake baseline and follow-up surveys to compare villages receiving them with *otherwise* similar 'control' villages. Yet Bangladesh contains one of the World Bank's most serious operations; and the World Bank is among donors exceptionally enlightened and research-oriented.

Agricultural aid, then, tends to amplify the remote, centralised, 'gigantistic' patterns set by much domestic agricultural investment. In spite of this, its returns are likely to be higher than on non-agricultural aid. However, donors who want to understand the forces that direct even rural investments towards the satisfaction of urban and rich-farmer interests, or who want to help the recipient to obtain better and more equitable returns from such investments, will have to study rural communities, and at the same time get involved in direct overview of at least a sample of rural aid projects. That involves decentralisation—of experts, control and cash—from donor countries to aided countries, and from the offices in capitals to 'the field' in the real sense. Younger and more empirically minded staff are needed, fluent in local languages and able to communicate with farmers, labourers and extension officers, rather than at their ease only with Permanent Secretaries; new staff, eager to live and work in rural areas, will thus have to be recruited. The priorities and attitudes of the best individual members of the US Peace Corps and British Voluntary Service Overseas movements must be implanted into the monitoring of the impact on output and equity of rural aid, if such aid is to have the desired effect. That does not mean lower pay and worse conditions for field staff; it does mean a different way of life: different priorities, lodgings, meals, friends.

A problem, concerning the relation of donor to recipient government, is that some recipient governments have no intention of raising the share of total investment in agriculture. More rural aid merely enables such governments to pare their own rural outlays even further. Several African ministers have responded to donors' efforts to aid agriculture by such remarks as, 'We know you want more rural projects here—so you work them out!' This attitude suggests lack of concern for agriculture. A necessary condition for effective agricultural or rural aid is that the programme should, in essence, be designed by the recipient government, not forced down its throat by the donor agency (though technical assistance in project preparation is perfectly proper). Donors might consider, when they raise the proportion of aid going to agriculture, the 'matching grant' principle in a new form: that extra sums for the sector will be made available only to the extent that the recipient government, by raising agriculture's *share* in domestically financed investment, indicates that it, not the donor, is setting the rural priorities.

Perhaps the most important obstacle facing aid donors, and to a lesser extent other public and private investors, is what I term the 'sector-project problem'. Despite theoretical and empirical evidence that productive outlays in labour-intensive small farming show high returns, the World Bank in particular has found difficulties in identifying good projects within that sector, or, when evaluating past projects there, in demonstrating satisfactory yields. There are several reasons for this; each implies not any reneging on the shift towards rural and agricultural emphases but a remedy in the area of project identification or execution. First, urban-biased polities will generate *urban* projects that are relatively carefully selected, prepared and administered. Second, foreign donors do little to discourage that preference by national targets for agricultural aid tending to replace, rather than to support, an appropriate sectoral policy by the recipient. Third, and perhaps most important, complementarities are more important within rural and agricultural activities than within other sectors: a combination of several types of rural activity (for example, irrigation, seed research, credit, extension) is often needed to attain high yields. Fourth, donors (like ministries and even businessmen) tend to split such activities into 'projects' and to evaluate them in isolation and thus unfavourably, and, in general, to define 'project' rather narrowly and tightly: large numbers of ½-ton storage bins for small cereal farmers may show high social returns, but seldom get considered as projects, since the hardware is dispersed and hard to identify; where there is no hardware, as in a rural lending or crop-insurance scheme, a proposal has even less chance of getting itself considered. Fifth—a linked issue—lenders and bankers, even in the aid agencies and even in the post-McNamara enlightenment, often require that a potential project have identifiable beneficiaries, from whom interest and capital can be recovered, before it can be evaluated—excluding many promising projects, notably in irrigation. Finally, market prices (and price policies) influenced by inequality (pp. 178-9) tend especially to cut rates of return, even in accounting prices, on projects to expand small farmers' output of 'poor men's crops'—especially for their own families' consumption.

As in other parts of this chapter, all this unsolicited advice is directed to those individuals and interests who wish to reduce urban bias—in this case, people in donor countries and agencies who wish to raise the share of aid going to agriculture and the rural sector, without inducing corresponding cutbacks in recipients' own efforts there. However, two donor counter-pressures exist. First, donors are industrialised countries; commercial pressures, for aid to obtain export orders for investment goods, will therefore come principally from producers currently satisfying the investment needs of industry.[26] Second, insofar as such commercial pressures do come from firms in rich countries seeking to sell to 'developing' agricultures, the goods involved are usually those produced for the agricultural sectors of rich countries, which take up the bulk of such firms' production. Hence donors often press for unsuitable agricultural aid, notably labour-replacing inputs, such as weedicides, tractors, and even combine-harvesters (which make sense in the labour-starved countryside of the USA or the UK, but not with labour as under-utilised as in India or Ethiopia), and for types of fertilisers and pesticides unsuited to the soil, humidity or transport conditions of poor countries. Such pressures towards non-agricultural—or, if agricultural, misplaced—aid, however, are resistible. They usually operate against the pressures, self-interested or humanitarian, that originated the donors' movement towards more agricultural aid in the first place.

Aid is only a small part of foreigners' impact on poor countries. On average, it supplies (net of capital and interest repayments of past aid loans) about one-tenth of foreign exchange receipts, and a roughly similar proportion of investment. Almost all the rest of foreign exchange, in poor countries taken together, comes from export earnings; and almost all the rest of investment is financed by domestic saving. (Private foreign investment—except in the mineral countries of Africa—probably sucks out, as repatriated profits, somewhat more than it puts in as new investment flows.) Thus, though urban bias is not induced *primarily* by 'foreigners' (chapter 3), any consideration of their impact on it must go beyond the role of private or aid capital. The question of what, if anything, they can do about agricultural exports from poor countries—and in general of the impact of rich countries' trade policy on poor countries' urban bias—must be raised.

Most agricultural exports from poor countries comprise sugar, beverages (tea, coffee, cocoa), jute, sisal and cotton — the last three often 'embodied' in exported textiles. Such exports face various types of restriction on their entry to rich countries. Sugar, textiles and some other farm products from poor countries (fruit, vegetable oils) compete directly with powerful and relatively inefficient farmers in rich countries—farmers 'temperate' in their agricultural climates, but not in the protectionist pressures they apply to governments. Tropical beverages face little competition from domestic production in Europe or North America; but for that very reason governments can cut demand for them by ever-higher sales taxes, without either facing angry domestic producers or seriously eroding tax revenues.[27] One can estimate fairly accurately the types of agricultural product for which freer entry to 'Western' markets will do most to reduce mass poverty in the producing countries;[28] the creation, redirection and enlargement of funds (such as the EEC's 'European Social Fund') to compensate losers in Western countries (whether competing producers or chancellors) by transferring to them some of these countries' gains in efficiency from freer trade with poor countries, should therefore concentrate on 'losers' replaced by this especially beneficial form of trade liberalisation.

Such liberalisation would also benefit the 'overdeveloped' countries by reducing pollution, since agricultural chemicals would be concentrated on production in countries where their addition to output, per unit, was high, and their environmental damage low. Nor is there any real reason to believe that opposition to such liberalisation is greater (as against being better orchestrated, for instance by the giant beet-sugar farmers of Normandy) than in manufactures. Yet such trade concessions as rich countries make to the poor are typified by their lists under the UNCTAD scheme for 'preferences on *manufactured* exports', lists that (in conjunction with other trade policies) effectively exclude most exportable manufactures with the greatest agricultural content, notably textiles and processed foods. Rich trading nations could certainly do much to adjust the structure of their trade 'concessions' so as to help poor countries seeking to reduce urban bias.

But this is only a small part of the answer. For one thing, the crops involved in international trade are not, for the most part, the income sources or calorie sources of the rural poor. For another, the problem is lack of resource allocation to, and prices turned by public action against, *already profitable* domestic farm activities — not any imagined success by rich countries in rendering such activities unprofitable. In general, the control of urban bias is in the hands of the governments and people of poor countries themselves. Foreign scholars, usually comfortably removed from the policy dilemmas, command little respect when they preach either that all is well — that industrialisation is going splendidly — or that only revolutions (made by others, suffered by others) can put matters right. Our duty is to attempt to make the policies of our own countries more helpful to poor people in poor countries; and, as regards those countries, not to preach, but to analyse, to sympathise, and to warn.

Guide to abbreviated
references in notes

Notes

Tables

Index

Guide to abbreviated references in notes

Balassa: B. Balassa et al., *The Structure of Protection in Developing Countries*, IBRD/Johns Hopkins, 1971.

Blaug: M. Blaug, R. Layard and M. Woodhall, *The Causes of Graduate Unemployment In India*, Allen Lane (Penguin Press), 1969.

Breese: G. Breese, ed., *Urbanisation in Newly Developing Countries* Prentice-Hall, 1966.

Burrows: J. Burrows et al., *The Second Decade: a Basic Economic Report on Kenya*, Report no. 201-KE, Annex 3 (vol. 4), 'Key Issues in the Private Sector', IBRD, Washington, 1974.

Capital: K. Marx, *Capital*, vol. III, Foreign Languages Publishing House (Moscow), 1959.

Ceylon Report: ILO, *Matching Employment Opportunities and Expectations: a Programme of Action for Ceylon*, Geneva, 1971.

Chenery: H. Chenery et al., *Redistribution with Growth*, Oxford (for the World Bank and the Institute of Development Studies), 1974. Unless otherwise stated, reference is to M. Ahluwalia's paper, 'The Dimensions of the Problem'.

Colombia Report: ILO, *Towards Full Employment in Colombia*, Geneva, 1970.

Connell: J. Connell, B. Dasgupta, R. Laishley and M. Lipton, *Migration from Rural Areas: the Evidence from Village Studies*, report to the International Labour Organisation, 1975.

EJ: Economic Journal (Cambridge).

Engels: F. Engels, *The Condition of the Working Class in England* (1844-5), in *Marx and Engels on Britain*, Foreign Languages Publishing House (Moscow), 1953.

Epstein: T. S. Epstein, *South India: Yesterday, Today and Tomorrow*, Macmillan, 1973.

EPW: Economic and Political Weekly (Bombay).

Fanon: F. Fanon, *The Wretched of the Earth*, MacGibbon & Kee, 1965.

FAO/P: Food and Agriculture Organisation, *Production Yearbook* (Rome).

FAO/S: Food and Agriculture Organisation, *The State of Food and Agriculture* (Rome, annual).

FT: Financial Times (London).

V. Gandhi: V. Gandhi, *Tax Burden on Indian Agriculture*, Harvard, 1966.

Gish: O. Gish, *Doctor Migration and World Health*, Bell, 1971.

Habakkuk: H. J. Habakkuk and M. M. Postan, eds., *The Cambridge Economic History of Europe*, vol. VI. pt. II, *The Industrial Revolution and After*, Cambridge, 1965.

Jakobson: L. Jakobson and V. Prakash, eds., *Urbanisation and National Development*, Sage, 1971.
JDS: Journal of Development Studies (London).

Kautsky: K. Kautsky, *Die Agrarfrage*, Dietz (Stuttgart), 1899.
Krishnaswamy: K. Krishnaswamy, in A. Peacock and G. Hauser, eds., *Government Finance and Economic Development*, OECD, 1963.
Kuznets: S. Kuznets, *Economic Growth of Nations*, Belknap (Harvard), 1971.

Lehmann: D. Lehmann, ed., *Agrarian Reform and Agrarian Reformism*, Faber, 1974. Unless otherwise stated, reference is to the paper by M. Lipton, 'Towards a Theory of Land Reform'.
Lenin: V. I. Lenin, *The Development of Capitalism in Russia* (1899 and 1907) Progress Publishers (Moscow), 1964.
Lewin: M. Lewin, *Russian Peasants and Soviet Power*, Allen & Unwin, 1968.
Lewis: S. R. Lewis, *Pakistan: Industrialisation and Trade Policies*, OECD/Oxford, 1972.
Lipton: M. Lipton, *Assessing Economic Performance*, Staples, 1968.
Little: I. M. D. Little, T. Scitovsky, and M. Fg. Scott, *Industry and Trade in some Developing Countries*, OECD/Oxford, 1970.
Luxemburg: R. Luxemburg, *The Accumulation of Capital* (1914), Routledge, 1953.

Marshall: A. Marshall, *Principles of Economics* (8th ed., 1903), Macmillan, 1961.
Mellor: J. Mellor, *The Economics of Agricultural Development*, Cornell, 1966.
Myrdal: G. Myrdal, *Asian Drama*, Allen Lane (London), Pantheon (New York), 1968.

Papanek: G. Papanek, *Pakistan's Development: Social Goals and Private Incentives*, Harvard, 1967.
Preobrazhensky: E. Preobrazhensky, *The New Economics* (1924), Clarendon, 1965.

Reynolds: L. Reynolds, ed., *Theory of Agricultural Development*, Yale, 1975.
Ricardo: D. Ricardo, *Works*, ed. P. Sraffa, vol. 1 *The Principles of Political Economy and Taxation*, Cambridge, Royal Economic Society, 1951.

Robinson: E. A. G. Robinson and M. Kidron, eds., *Economic Development in South Asia*, International Economic Association/Macmillan, 1970.

Seers: D. Seers and L. Joy, eds., *Development in a Divided World*, Penguin, 1971.
Shand: R. T. Shand, ed., *Agricultural Development in Asia*, Australian National University Press and Allen & Unwin, 1969.
Shukla: T. Shukla, ed., *Economics of Underdeveloped Agriculture*, Vora, 1969.
Smith: Adam Smith, *The Wealth of Nations* (1776), ed. J. S. Nicholson, Nelson, 1884.
Southworth: H. M. Southworth and B. F. Johnston, eds., *Agricultural Development and Economic Growth*, Cornell, 1967.
Streeten: P. Streeten, *The Frontiers of Development Studies*, Macmillan, 1972.
Streeten/Lipton: P. Streeten and M. Lipton, eds., *The Crisis of Indian Planning*, Oxford, 1968. Unless otherwise stated, reference is to M. Lipton's paper, 'Urban Bias and Rural Planning: Strategy for Agriculture'.
SW: K. Marx and F. Engels, *Selected Works*, 2 vols., Foreign Languages Publishing House (Moscow), 1951.

Taylor: M. C. Taylor, ed., *Taxation for African Economic Development*, Hutchinson, 1970.

UN (Bangkok): *Development Prospects for the Coming Decade: Report of the Fifth (Bangkok, 1969) Interregional Seminar on Development Planning* (UN ST/TAO/SER.C/133), New York, 1971: paper by M. Lipton, 'Transfer of Resources from Agricultural to Non-agricultural Activities: the case of India'.
UNA: UN, *Yearbook of National Accounts Statistics* (New York).
UND: UN, *Demographic Yearbook* (New York).

Wolf: E. Wolf, *Peasant Wars in the Twentieth Century* (1971), Faber Paperbacks, 1973.

Yaffe: D. Yaffe, *Soviet Industrialisation: Planned Economic Development and the World Economy*, Institute of Development Studies (mimeo), Brighton, 1972.

Notes

INTRODUCTION

1 The UN target was a 5% yearly rate of 'real' growth (that is, allowing for inflation) of total output. The actual rate was slightly higher.

2 Net aid from the donor countries comprising the Development Assistance Committee (DAC) of the Organisation for Economic Cooperation and Development (OECD) comprises over 95% of all net aid to less-developed countries (LDCs). It fell steadily from 0.54% of donors' GNP in 1961 to 0.30% in 1973. The real value of aid per person in recipient countries fell by over 20% over the period. M. Lipton, 'Aid Allocation when Aid is Inadequate', in T. Byres, ed., *Foreign Resources and Economic Development*, Cass, 1972, p. 158; OECD (DAC), *Development Cooperation* (1974 Review), p. 116.

3 L. Cooper, *Radical Jack*, Cresset, 1969, esp. pp. 183-97; C. New, *Life of Henry Brougham to 1830*, Clarendon, 1961, Preface.

4 See the mounting emphasis in his *Addresses to the Board of Governors*, all published by IBRD, Washington; at Copenhagen in 1970, p. 20; at Washington in 1971, pp. 6-19, and 1972, pp. 8-15; and at Nairobi in 1973, pp. 10-14, 19.

5 M. Ahluwalia, 'The Dimensions of the Problem', in H. Chenery et al., *Redistribution with Growth*, Oxford, 1974 (hereafter cited as Chenery).

6 See K. Rafferty, *Financial Times* (hereafter cited as *FT*), 10 April 1974, p. 35, col. 5; M. Lipton, 'Urban Bias and Rural Planning', in P. Streeten and M. Lipton, eds., *The Crisis of Indian Planning*, Oxford, 1968 (hereafter cited as Streeten/Lipton), p. 85.

7 F. Muir and D. Norden, 'Common Entrance', in P. Sellers, *Songs for Swinging Sellers*, Parlophone PMC 1111, 1958.

8 Streeten/Lipton; Lipton, 'Indian Agricultural Development: Achievements, Distortions, Ideologies', in *Asian and African Studies* (Israel Oriental Society), vol. 6, 1970; and 'Transfer of Resources from Agricultural to Non-agricultural Activities: The Case of India', *Fifth UN Interregional Seminar on Development Planning* (Bangkok, 1969) (UN ST/TAO/SER. C/133), UN, 1971 (hereafter cited as UN (Bangkok)).

9 M. Arnold, *'Porro Unum est Necessarium'*, in *Culture and Anarchy* (1869), Prose Works, vol. V, University of Michigan Press, 1965. See also G. B. Shaw, *The Doctor's Dilemma*, Act 1, and T. Carlyle, 'Morrison's Pill', in *Past and Present* (1852), in *Works*, vol. II, Chapman & Hall, 1891, book 1, chapter 4.

10 Nobody who, like myself, has worked in Bangladesh could miss the combination, not rare in Asia or East Africa, of (1) extreme poverty, especially in villages; (2) a responsive peasantry 'raring to go' with improved techniques; (3) a system that steers 70 to 80% of scarce

savings, skills and political energy into a tiny, inefficient but influential urban sector. Even a total cure for urban bias — given the momentum of outgoing projects — could not efficiently slash this proportion *at once* to, say, 40 to 55 per cent. But clearly movement towards a cure is the first requirement.

11 More complex and specific objections to the 'urban bias' explanation of persistent poverty — the possible interlocking of rural and urban outlays, the alleged shortage of truly viable rural schemes, the possible need for industrial income as a source of savings — are dealt with below: see especially pp. 204-5, 349-50; and ch. 10.

12 Alec Nove, *An Economic History of the USSR*, Allen Lane, 1969, pp. 125-7, 132-3; P. C. Mahalanobis, *The Approach of Operational Research to Planning in India*, Asia, 1963, esp. chapter 3; E. Preobrazhensky, *The New Economics*, Clarendon, 1965 (hereafter cited as Preobrazhensky); E. Domar, *Essays in the Theory of Economic Growth*, Oxford University Press (New York), 1957, pp. 223-61; and see below, pp. 124-30.

13 W. Beckerman, *In Defence of Economic Growth*, Cape, 1974, p. 220.

14 G. R Allen, 'Confusion on fertilizers and the world food situation', *European Chemical News*, Large Plants Supplement, 18 October 1974.

15 K. Nair, *Blossoms in the Dust*, Duckworth, 1961, pp. 184-8.

16 P. Streeten, in *The Frontiers of Development Studies*, Macmillan, 1972, p. 89 (hereafter cited as Streeten), tellingly cites Wicksell's discussion.

17 Of course, part of the trouble is that those who benefit from rapid general industrialisation are not those who suffer the pain. The Russian finance ministers, Vyshnegradskii and Witte, in the last decades of the nineteenth century, forced near-starving peasants (by taxation in kind, and other means) to produce for foreign markets, thus providing foreign exchange for industrial imports. Vyshnegradskii said 'We must export, though we die'; he meant, as Robert Cassen remarks, 'I shall export, though you die.' T. H. von Laue, *Sergei Witte and the Industrialisation of Russia*, Atheneum (New York), 1969, pp. 26-7, 107.

1 THE COEXISTENCE OF POVERTY AND DEVELOPMENT

1 T. Carlyle, *Past and Present* (1852), Dent, 1967, p. 5.

2 That absolute numbers have not fallen would be unsurprising, as populations have doubled in the last thirty years. Nor am I making the empty statement that the proportion below some 'poverty line', shifting upwards with growth, has not declined — that the poorest fifth remain the poorest fifth. I am saying that the poorest fifth have got no richer.

3 K. Marx, *Theses on Feuerbach*, XI (1845), in K. Marx and F. Engels, *Selected Works*, Foreign Languages Publishing House (Moscow), 1951 (hereafter cited as *SW*), vol. 2, p. 367.

4 Investment seems to account for about one-third of recent growth in LDCs, and aid for about one-third of that — 10 to 15% (G. F. Papanek, 'Aid, Foreign Private Investment, Savings, and Growth in Less Developed Countries', *Journal of Political Economy*, January-February 1973). Yet donors and recipients who do not understand why poverty persists can hardly steer aid towards activities that reduce it. Hence the disillusionment with aid; as a share of rich countries' gross national product, it fell steadily from its 1961 peak of 0.54% to 0.30% in 1973. (See Introduction, note 2.)

5 This is 'real' output (including subsistence output consumed on family farms) measured at prices of a particular 'base year' to get rid of increases due not to growth but to inflation. Figures are for *domestic* product growth; i.e., they include foreign business income even if sent back home after being derived from domestic product. Since such remitted profits grew quickly in the period, national product figures (for production yielding income to *nationals*) would give very slightly lower growth estimates than those in Table 1.1, but such figures are seldom available.

6 About 9% of the gross domestic product of poor market-economies is exported to rich market-economies ($26.1 billion f.o.b. out of $295.7 billion in 1965). From 1950 to 1970, the typical unit of such exports lost 17% of its purchasing power over imports from rich countries. Hence 17% of 9%, or 1.5%. UN, *Yearbook of International Trade Statistics 1969*, p. 20; S. Kuznets, in G. Ranis, ed., *The Gap Between Rich and Poor Nations*, IEA/Macmillan, 1972, p. 39; UN, *Monthly Bulletin of Statistics*, November 1965, p. xxvii, and December 1971, p. xxx.

7 In 1965, net transfer (gross aid *minus* repayments of both capital and interest on past aid loans) was $5.4 billion from the donor countries that supply data to the Development Assistance Committee of OECD, and which account for about 95% of all aid. Hence *total* net transfer was just over 1.9% of the 1965 GDP of poor countries ($295.7 billion). But OECD net transfer grew only to $5.8 billion in 1970, rather more slowly than GDP of poor countries. Hence 1.8%. World Bank/IDA, *Annual Report 1971*, p. 68; Kuznets, in Ranis, ed., *The Gap Between Rich and Poor Nations*. Aid was negligible in 1950: probably negative, net of colonial tribute.

8 P. K. Bardhan, 'Agriculture in China and India', *Economic and Political Weekly* (hereafter cited as EPW) (annual number), 1969. To 1975 this remained true (Dwight Perkins, work in progress).

9 Even during the epochs of slavery and serfdom, the 'bottom 10%' could hardly have survived on less; yet inequality was presumably greater under such systems, so that the 'top 50%' were on average receiving more. That would suggest income per person *lower* in 1950 than, say, in 1250. Furthermore, such savings made by the

rich in the forced-labour age were substantially embodied in religious and cultural hardware with little impact on growth.

10 S. J. Patel, *Essays on Economic Transition*, Asia, 1965, p. 49. See also G. Blyn, *Agricultural Trends in India 1891-1947*, Philadelphia, 1966, pp. 94-107; A. Bagchi, *Private Investment in India 1900-1939*, Cambridge, 1972, pp. 4, 75. For analogous evidence, see 1902 and 1948 figures in R. W. Hooley and V. Ruttan, 'The Philippines', in R. T. Shand, ed., *Agricultural Development in Asia*, Allen & Unwin, 1969 (hereafter cited as Shand), p. 219.

11 OECD (DAC), *Development Assistance 1971*, p. 116.

12 In principle, this diversion of resources for enlargement of the economic surplus could be a cause of near-stagnant levels of mass consumption (arguably a worthwhile sacrifice for future growth, especially if the rich made commensurate sacrifices). However, this is not a large part of the explanation. Even where the share of gross domestic saving rose very fast from 1950 to 1970, there would still be plenty left for extra consumption. If, in a country with 75% growth of income per head in the two decades (average for all persons in the LDCs), gross domestic saving had risen from 15% to 25% of GNP — a very big increase — consumption per head would still grow from (85% of 100%) to (75% to 175%) of 1950 GNP, that is, by 55%. Poor people's consumption has not grown at anything like this rate.

13 Indian National Income Committee, *Final Report*, Delhi, 1954; A. Rudra, 'The Rate of Growth in the Indian Economy', in E. A. G. Robinson and M. Kidron, eds., *Economic Development in South Asia*, IEA/Macmillan, 1970, esp. p. 40. However, if (as argued in chapter 13) LDCs systematically overvalue industrial output compared to farm output, then — since the former has grown faster than the latter — the growth in real value of GDP will be overstated. But the effect is probably small (I. M. D. Little, T. Scitovsky and M. Fg. Scott, *Industry and Trade in some Developing Countries*, OECD/Oxford, 1970 (hereafter cited as Little), p. 75, B. Balassa et al., *The Structure of Protection in Developing Countries*, IBRD/Johns Hopkins, 1971 (hereafter cited as Balassa), p. 34, and must be set against the substantial underestimation effects uncovered by Rudra.

14 For discussion of the issues involved in measuring development, see W. Beckerman, *International Comparisons of Real Income*, OECD Development Centre, Paris, 1966; *Journal of Development Studies* (hereafter cited as *JDS*), July 1972 special number: *Development Indicators*, ed. N. Baster; G. Myrdal, *Asian Drama*, Pantheon, 1968 (hereafter cited as Myrdal), vol. 1, pp. 540-1.

15 Or, indeed, to build up spare capacity for inefficient branches of production.

16 Little, pp. 43-4. They also summarise evidence of growing inequality in India, Mexico and the Philippines. For India, see chapter 5, note 20. Brazil cannot have done much better since 1950: see chapter 5, note 23.

17 ILO, *Yearbook of Labour Statistics*, 1971, pp. 553-63 and 661-9;
   Myrdal, vol. 1, chapter 12. Even in the heartland of the 'green revolution', the Indian Punjab, real wages of farm labourers showed little,
   if any, tendency to rise in the 1960s. T. N. Srinivasan, 'Wheat Revolution or Green Revolution?', mimeo, Indian Statistical Institute, 1971;
   and P. K. Bardhan, 'Green Revolution and Agricultural Labourers',
   EPW (special number), July 1970, pp. 1239-46.

18 To be more accurate, about eight-tenths as fast. The ratio of the
   proportionate change in food expenditure (at constant food prices)
   to the proportionate change in income is called the income-elasticity
   of demand for food, and can be estimated from a wide range of data
   at 0.8 when income per person is about $100, 0.5 at $500, and zero
   at $2000. J. Mellor, *The Economics of Agricultural Development*,
   Cornell, 1966, pp. 57-66 (hereafter cited as Mellor). See also US
   Department of Agriculture, Economic Research Service (Development and Trade Analysis Division), *Elasticity of Food Consumption*,
   Washington, 1965, p. 20; UNCTAD, *Research Memo, 48*, Geneva
   1974.

19 Food data from FAO, *Production Yearbook 1970*, Rome, 1971 (hereafter cited as *FAO/P*); income growth from table 1.1; 0.8 elasticity
   at $50-100 per person as above. The choice of years makes little dif-
   ference. The 1960s were worse than the 1950s; for 1950-58 alone,
   observed income-elasticity of demand for calories was 0.64 in India,
   less than the 0.8 which would have implied equal distribution of
   income-growth, but more than the 0.35 (14% ÷ 40%) for the whole
   period 1949-50 to 1968-9. In 1950-8 the Philippines figure was 0.44,
   also better than the figure below for 1950-68. Y. Hayami and
   S. Yamada, 'Agricultural Productivity at the Beginning of Industrialisation', in K. Okhawa, B. Johnston and H. K. Yaneda (eds.), *Agriculture and Economic Growth: Japan's Experience*, Princeton and
   Tokyo, 1970, p. 120.

20 *FAO/P 1970*; and table 1.1 sources. It should not be thought that at
   Mexican calorie averages, which are above requirement levels, extra
   calories do not matter—maldistribution means that many people
   are seriously below requirements. In any case, behaviour in calorie
   consumption as income rises is being adduced as evidence that
   rises are being maldistributed; not as an indicator of poverty.

21 Assuming a growth in private consumption capacity also around
   75%. The erosion of income growth by extra investment and public
   consumption (and worsening terms of trade) has to be set against
   the increase in aid and the slight reduction in average age and hence
   needs of family members.

22 Carlyle, *Past and Present*, p. 3; F. Engels, *The Condition of the Work-
   ing Class in England* (1844-5), in *Marx and Engels on Britain*, Foreign
   Languages Publishing House (Moscow), 1953 (hereafter cited as
   Engels).

23 E. Hobsbawm, 'The British Standard of Living 1790-1850', *Economic
   History Review*, August 1957, pp. 46-68.

24 M. Lipton, *Assessing Economic Performance*, Staples, 1968 (hereafter cited as Lipton), pp. 195-6.

25 See, for instance, A. Gerschenkron, 'Agrarian Policies and Industrialisation: Russia 1871-1917', in H. Habakkuk and M. M. Postan, (eds.), *Cambridge Economic History of Europe*, vol. VI, pt. II (*The Industrial Revolution and After*), Cambridge, 1965 (hereafter cited as Habakkuk).

26 Mahboob ul-Haq, *The Strategy of Development Planning*, Oxford, 1966; G. Papanek, *Pakistan's Development: Social Goals and Private Incentives*, Harvard, 1967 (hereafter cited as Papanek); and my review article in *Asian Review*, November 1967, pp. 51-6.

27 Hobsbawm, 'The British Standard of Living', *Economic History Review*, August 1957, pp. 46-68.

28 P. Samuelson, 'Interaction between the Multiplier Analysis and the Principle of Acceleration', *Review of Economics and Statistics*, vol. 21, May 1939, pp. 75-8, reprinted in M. G. Mueller, ed., *Readings in Macro-economics*, Holt, Rinehart & Winston, 1966. See also A. D. Gayer, W. W. Rostow and A. J. Schwartz, with I. Frank, *The Growth and Fluctuation of the British Economy 1790-1850*, Oxford, 1952, vol. 2, pp. 551-4.

29 Hobson argued that demand was created by forcing colonies to buy exports (J. A. Hobson, *Imperialism* (1902), Allen & Unwin, 1938, esp. p. 72). This is part of the explanation, for some Western countries some of the time: as a major explanation, for most Western countries most of the time, it will not do.

30 S. Kuznets, *Economic Growth of Nations*, Belknap, Harvard, 1971 (hereafter cited as Kuznets), pp. 11-14, 250-2. These datings correspond very closely with W. W. Rostow's in *The Stages of Economic Growth*, 2nd ed., Cambridge, 1972, p. 32. 'Outside agriculture' need not mean 'in *wage* employment', of course.

31 High wages (and 'rich-country' conditions of work) in the 'modern sector' in LDCs help businessmen and workers in rich countries, by lessening the competitive threat from LDCs' exports. They also help the LDCs' labour aristocracy—but discourage their businessmen from hiring their unemployed poor, and harm efficiency. Until the mid-1960s, given the pressures, international agencies and notably the International Labour Office naturally supported such a high-wage, low-employment set-up. Its recent change of view is much to the credit of ILO, and of the power of reason.

32 The exception tests the rule; the Indian state of Kerala has powerful trade unions in agriculture because its farmworkers are densely concentrated (in big villages or continuous quasi-urban settlements), often literate, and hence easily organised.

33 Nowadays the imbalances are usually inflationary, rather than deflationary as in 1929-35; but the problem remains the same.

34 Earlier, the workhouse system of 1795-1834 in Britain, harsh and inhuman as it was, provided an ultimate assurance against starvation that most of the world's poor now lack.

35 Notice the irrelevance of most such legislation, assiduously imitated in some LDCs, to the problem of mass development in the self-employing, largely self-financing small-farm sector.

36 H. F. Lydall, *The Structure of Earnings*, Oxford, 1968; Myrdal, vol. 1, p. 689; I. Adelman and C. T. Morris, 'An Anatomy of Income Distribution Patterns in the Developing Nations', *Development Digest*, October 1971, esp. p. 36, for the statistically important role of education in reducing inequality, and cf. chapter 11; Chenery.

37 The weakness of such pressures, and of the hopes they sustain, in 'segmental societies' means that 'those who are left out . . . will be convinced almost from the start of the process that the advancing group is achieving an unfair exploitative advantage over them.' Thus capitalist . . . development appears to be particularly ill-suited for highly segmented societies', though 'centralised decision-making typical of socialist systems is unlikely to function at all well' either. Segmented nationhood, for most of Asia and Africa, renders tolerance for unequal development short-lived, though it renders persistent inequality likely. A. O. Hirschman, 'The Changing Tolerance for Income Inequality in the Course of Economic Development', *Quarterly Journal of Economics*, November 1973, p. 554.

38 It is because capitalists, to enrich themselves, seek to enlarge the market — improving mobility and increasing the prospects of specialisation — that Marx was right, and Gunder Frank wrong, in seeing capitalism as an agent of development and not the cause of 'the development of underdevelopment'.

39 For a discussion relevant to the argument that capitalism cannot be equalising unless major 'feudal' relics have been destroyed, see R. Barrington Moore, *The Social Origins of Dictatorship and Democracy*, Penguin, 1969, esp. p. 417. (The argument is not confined to the conditions for a *democratic* path, however. In Russia the 1861 reform deprived the *pomeshchiki* of their serfs; in Japan the Meiji reform of 1868 deprived the feudal nobility of most of their fiefs.) On the reinforcement by 'capitalism' in LDCs of ascribed 'feudal' power, see T. S. Epstein, *South India, Yesterday, Today and Tomorrow*, Macmillan, 1973 (hereafter cited as Epstein), pp. 147-55; F. G. Bailey, 'An Oriya Hill Village: II', in *India's Villages*, M. N. Srinivas, ed., 2nd ed., Asia, 1960, pp. 135-9 and 142-6; and Papanek, pp. 42, 67-8. A brilliant account of a successful prior confrontation of 'feudalism' by 'capitalism' is C. Hill, *God's Englishman*, Weidenfeld, 1970.

40 I am grateful to R. P. Dore for this observation.

41 Kuznets, p. 294.

42 In democratic LDCs mass rural voting power might conceivably be a counterweight. But the rural poor are illiterate, divided and unorganised; the rural rich, helped by the urban alliance (pp. 97-8, 114). have powers over them — of employment, lending and renting — that preserve much political control; and access to rule still implies joining the urban elite.

43 At far higher effective levels than ever prevailed in most now-rich countries.

44 J. R. Hicks, *Theory of Wages* (1932), Macmillan, 1963, chapter VII.

45 In view of the initial proposition (p. 13) that poor countries feature a struggle between an urban and a rural *class*, it is worth pointing to the common interest of the rural sector in high farm prices (see below, pp. 67, 318). Engels, p. 295, writes that in England just before 1815 'the farmers had to sell their corn at low prices, and could, therefore, pay only low wages.'

2   WHAT IS 'URBAN BIAS', AND IS IT TO BLAME?

1 Either criterion will usually do, because we 'know from experience' (and can explain from general physical laws) that the object conforms to the rule if and only if its physical condition is appropriate. The observed behaviour of die or bowl usually shows whether it conforms to both criteria. If, 'n many throws, a die falls 'almost equally' often on each of its six faces, we can estimate the probability that it is unweighted; and either an 'adequately' undistorted pattern of outcomes, or an 'adequately' small probability (of weighting of the die) calculated from that pattern, is necessary and sufficient for us to say we are 'adequately' — say 99% — sure that the die is true. Where the criteria seem to conflict — usually because the agreed rule does *not* correspond to a physical uniformity in the object — arguments about bias are possible. Consider a game with rules such that the die, when thrown, is intended to have a slightly higher chance of showing six than any other face. Is such a die biased or true for that game? Would an unweighted die be true or biased? (Similar puzzles arise if investment is deliberately so allocated as to enrich poor villagers more slowly than richer and less efficient townsmen, *because* the latter allegedly save more; this is not clear bias, if the allegation is true and if it is a sensible aim of policy to maximise the proportion of income saved. See chapter 10.)

2 'Biased' is one of those words best understood by understanding its opposite, 'unbiased'; as with 'real', it is the negative term that 'wears the trousers'. J. L. Austin, *Philosophical Papers*, 2nd ed., Oxford, 1970, p. 87; and *Sense and Sensibilia*, Oxford, 1962, p. 15, esp. note 2.

3 Economic welfare, as affected by productive efficiency and distributive equity, is of course not everything. There are many other components of human happiness, from love through creativeness to security; but these are much more influenced by resource allocations than many people realise. (In many, perhaps most, poor countries the selective migration of males to cities damages the rural family; the trend of urban westernisation, often tourist-oriented, the rural arts; the relative obviousness of urban crime, the villager's chances of adequate police protection.) But the clearest impact of

the allocation of resources is on efficiency and equity, which is why we define our norms in terms of efficient and equitable allocations.

4 The curves and all the points marked on figure 2, except the end-points, will normally shift if the *total* amount of a resource available to the nation changes. If there are £1,000 million instead of £500 million a year to invest, the proportion for the rural sector likely to maximise efficiency, or equity, or urban or rural welfare, will change — partly because of complementarities (an extra sugar refinery may justify extra investment in sugar farming, but urban and rural invest-ment will not in general rise in the same proportion). So will the power balance as it affects actual allocations. Hence any given placing of the points in figure 2 (or figure 1) has to assume a given *total* availability of the resource.

5 In fact urban bias may be so severe in most LDCs that it impedes them from fulfilling even this minimal necessary condition for efficiency. Governments, by adjusting their own allocations (and their incentives to others) so as to shift some resources towards agri-culture, could probably raise farm output without lowering industrial output; for it would pay industrial employers to replace increasingly scarce capital with otherwise underemployed (but ready and able) labour. But it would be difficult to prove this.

6 Lipton, pp. 74-83.

7 In poor countries, too, governments are often big net borrowers from their people to cover capital (and sometimes current) outlays that cannot be met by taxation owing to mass poverty. Such net borrowing, by raising the demand for loans, pushes up 'market' in-terest rates even further — and leaves the 'social rate of time-prefer-ence' further behind.

8 Lipton, p. 103, for details.

9 *Ibid.*, p. 105.

10 Not 'from': we should add extra output (net of cost) *made possible by A*, and deduct output made impossible (for example, by causing factories elsewhere to go short of essential inputs). Similarly for *B*.

11 I.M.D. Little and J. Mirrlees, *Manual of Industrial Cost-Benefit Analysis*, vol. 2., OECD, 1968.

12 For an attempt at logical demonstration that equity requires a far more 'equal' distribution than normally prevails in rich countries, and at adequate definition of 'equal', see J. Pen, *Income Distribu-tion*, Allen Lane, 1971, chapter 7; Lipton, pp. 85-106; I. Bowen, *Acceptable Inequalities*, Allen & Unwin, 1970, chapters 2 and 9.

13 Some rural activities generate income in urban areas, and vice versa; and some income is transferred between town and country by remit-tances. These complications are dealt with on pp. 204-5 and 236-7, but any redefinitions they may suggest are most unlikely to invalidate this proposition.

14 A. C. Pigou, *The Economics of Welfare* (4th ed.,1932) Macmillan, 1932, chapters 8 and 9. See also Lipton, pp. 92-5.

15 See below, p. 167. Recent evidence suggests that this is now

true even in Latin America, despite rural areas dominated by very rich landowners. In India the evidence for greater intra-rural than intra-urban equality is clear, and this probably also applies to Pakistan, Bangladesh and Indonesia. Little is known for Africa, but tribal allocation of land (especially abundant land) is unlikely to permit great intra-rural inequality, whereas the income differentials within most African cities (and urban civil services) are visibly even greater than in South Asia. See Chenery, p. 21.

16 In practical political terms, of course, I am not recommending major reductions in urban income per head! The real question is whether resources should be allocated so as to concentrate more on *raising* income per head in rural areas, and less in urban areas, than in the past. This example is illustrative, and is presented in stark and static terms only to simplify the exposition.

17 Chapter 12 considers whether governments in less-developed countries have, in their own taxing and spending policies, departed in an urban-biased direction from *their own* equity norms. We still have to prove, of course, that the countryside is in fact worse off than the city (chapters 5-6).

18 Unless help is confined to the very poor, however, a shift from coarse grains towards wheat and polished rice—nutritionally damaging, and raising costs per pound of grain—is a risk.

19 There is one further issue, a complex one: that of employment. If the share of the rural sector in *output produced* increases at the expense of modern industry, employment is almost certain to rise substantially, helping the poor by enabling them to earn by productive work (pp. 54-5). If the share of rural (poorer) people in *income* grows, matters are not quite so clear: per pound earned, the rich employ directly more domestic servants, building workers, etc., than the poor can afford to do. On the other hand, and probably outweighing this, *indirect* employment, via consumer demand for goods, is more if income goes to poor people—they spend a larger share of it, and almost certainly on more labour-intensive products and fewer imports, than the rich.

20 Similarly, although demand for extra medical care means extra income for a doctor in any event, both efficiency and general welfare surely gain if that additional treatment is devoted to the largely untreated illnesses of the poor villager, rather than to the usually less serious and already relatively well-provided conditions of the townsman.

21 Alternative interpretations of the dimension of bias (ch. 3)—that systems are biased for or against capitalists or foreigners or the philoprogenitive—are really instances of this argument. We deal with the industry-agriculture version here, because of its substantial overlap with the urban-rural dimension of bias.

22 The family living on its farm, and the quasi-feudal giant estate, have little else in common except this almost total integration of workplace and place of residence!

23 Many census organisers recognise this by allowing local officials to vary the normal classification; for instance, the Indian Census of 1961 required 'towns' to show not only five thousand persons at a density of over two thousand per square mile and at least 75% of employed males outside agriculture, but also 'pronounced urban characteristics'. UN, *Demographic Yearbook 1970*, New York, 1971, (hereafter cited as *UND*) p. 162; A. Bose, 'The Urbanisation Process in South and South-east Asia', in L. Jakobson and V. Prakash, eds., *Urbanisation and National Development*, Sage, 1971 (hereafter cited as Jakobson), pp. 87-90.

24 *UND, 1962*, pp. 380-88, shows that the few poor countries that measure 'size of locality' by counting residents living in agglomerations (the relevant method here) generally have small proportions of the urban population (living in communities over five thousand) in possible borderline towns (population five to ten thousand): Panama 7.4% (1960), Venezuela 8.1% (1961), Greece 7.0% (1961), Turkey 15.5% (1955), Bulgaria 19.0% (1956). Ghana 26.2% (1960). Of course only small sub-groups, even of these percentages, can have lived in localities that were neither clearly urban nor clearly rural.

25 *UND, 1962*, pp. 159-65.

26 There is some evidence that small towns are losing people, resources and influence to big ones. Bose, 'The Urbanisation Process in South and South-east Asia', in Jakobson, p. 106.

27 Colin Clark, *The Conditions of Economic Progress*, 3rd ed., Macmillan, 1960, pp. 492 *et seq.*

28 An interesting attempt to make the relevant discriminations, and to develop a case for more government encouragement of appropriate parts of what he calls the 'intermediate sector', is D. Steele, 'Hindrances to the Programme to Encourage the Rise of African Entrepreneurship in Kenya resulting from the Theory of the Dual Economy', *JDS*, Oct. 1975.

29 B. J. L. Berry, 'City Size and Economic Development', in Jakobson.

30 This does not mean that the specially favoured nature of the capital city should be ignored where it exists. See the data for allocation of teachers in chapter 11.

31 *Census of India 1961*, vol. 1, pt. II-A (ii), Union Primary Census Abstracts, pp. 3-5.

32 Even such terms as 'underdeveloped' and 'underprivileged' suffer from these and other deficiencies. P. T. Bauer, *Dissent on Development*, Weidenfeld, 1972, p. 318.

33 The significance of agriculturists' part-time income from crafts is well discussed by F. Dovring, 'The Transformation of European Agriculture', in Habakkuk, pp. 607, 611 and 668.

34 W. A. Lewis, *The Theory of Economic Growth*, Allen & Unwin, 1955, p. 205-6; A. Ganz, 'Problems and Uses of National Wealth Estimates in Latin America', in R. Goldsmith and C. Saunders, eds., *The Measurement of National Wealth* (Income and Wealth Series VII), Bowes & Bowes, 1959, p. 230; P. N. Dhar and H. F. Lydall, *The*

Role of Small Enterprises in Indian Economic Development, Asia, 1961, p. 16. In the Indian Third Plan, anticipated ratios to extra output (1965 *minus* 1960) of net investment in 1960-4 were; agriculture 0.9, small industry 1.0, large industry and mining 2.6, housing 1.8 — and railways and communications 6.5. W. B. Reddaway, *The Development of the Indian Economy*, Allen & Unwin, 1962, p. 211.

35 Dhar and Lydall, *The Role of Small Enterprises in Indian Economic Development*, pp. 4-9, shows that barely 3% of India's workforce in 1955-6 could be attributed to 'modern' industry, even on a generous definition (factories with electric power, or over fifty employees, or both). The proportion has hardly grown since, as industrialisation has used extra capital rather than extra labour. And most poor countries are less 'industrialised' than India.

36 This of course begs questions about incidence (will more food benefit mainly urban workers?) to which we return on p. 56 — they matter less where much of the extra farm output is consumed on the farm.

37 C. T. Leys 'A New Conception of Planning', in M. Faber and D. Seers, eds., *The Crisis in Planning*, Sussex University Press, 1972, vol. 1, esp. pp. 60-6; and 'Political Perspectives', in D. Seers and L. Joy, eds., *Development in a Divided World*, Penguin, 1971 (hereafter cited as Seers, pp. 106-38.

38 The Poulson affair and *'l'affaire Aranda'*: for a single convenient source, see *Sunday Times*, London, 24 September 1972, including magazine supplement. A source for the Nixon *affaire* is hardly required!

39 For discussions of the logic of dispositions that I found very helpful in understanding urban bias as a state of mind, see G. Ryle, *The Concept of Mind*, Hutchinson, 1949, pp. 42-5, and chapter 5.

40 See, however, K. Marx, *Pre-Capitalist Formations* (ed. E. Hobsbawm), Lawrence & Wishart, 1964, and, indeed, the subtle class analysis of Marx's *The Eighteenth Brumaire of Louis Bonaparte.*

41 A. V. Chayanov, *Theory of Peasant Economy* (tr. B. Kerblay, ed. D. Thorner), Irwin, Homewood (Illinois), 1966.

42 Nowhere has this conflict been more brilliantly described and analysed than in K. Kautsky, *Die Agrarbrage*, Dietz (Stuttgart), 1899, (hereafter cited as Kautsky) especially pp. 208-21; see below, chapter 4.

43 A landless labourer is just a 100% deficit farmer.

44 As compared with the relative world prices prevailing, the price of industrial products was kept thrice as high relative to farm products. S. R. Lewis, *Pakistan: Industrialisation and Trade Policies*, OECD Oxford, 1972, (hereafter cited as Lewis) p. 65; see below, pp. 306-7, and pp. 124-30 for comparison with the policies subtly advocated in the USSR by Preobrazhensky, and crudely brutalised by Stalin.

45 In other words, 'antagonistic' and 'non-antagonistic' contradictions in both capitalist and socialist economies — while rightly *distinguished* by Mao Tse-tung ('On Contradiction', in *Collected Works*, Foreign

Languages Press (Peking), vol. 1, pp. 343-5) — are wrongly *identified*.
46 Conversely, however, intra-village conflict and faction are more serious, because the protagonists are weak *vis-à-vis* the city, and cannot settle their disputes at its expense. For an extreme but telling statement of the high barriers presented by factionalism to village development, see Baljit Singh, *Next Step in Village India*, University of Lucknow (Department of Economics), 1959.
47 See below, pp. 223-30. Another confirmation of the smallness of true, *permanent* rural-urban migration comes from Tanzania; see M. A. Bienefeld and R. H. Sabot, *The National Urban Mobility, Employment and Income Survey of Tanzania, 1971,* Economic Research Bureau and Ministry of Economic Affairs and Development Planning, Dar es Salaam, 1972.
48 Even when there are quinquennial elections and massively rural electorates, it is the townsmen who write the papers and put out the radio programmes (even a largely illiterate village usually has access to a radio), fund political parties, pick candidates, own or frequent 'political' coffee-houses and bars.
49 H. V. Richter, 'The Union of Burma', in Shand, pp. 159-63.

3   ALTERNATIVE EXPLANATIONS OF BIASED DEVELOPMENT

1 *Census of Pakistan,* Karachi, 1966, vol. II, pp. 11-16; Karachi, no date, vol. III, pp. 11-25.
2 *South African Statistics 1972,* Department of Statistics, Pretoria, 1973, pp. A11, A27, V13.
3 Merle Lipton, 'White Farming', *Journal of Commonwealth and Comparative Politics,* March 1974, and calculations from her forthcoming study. This paragraph owes much to discussions with her.
4 Theories claiming that human societies adapt effectively (Chayanov) or even progressively (Boserup) to population growth. A. V. Chayanov, *Theory of Peasant Economy* (tr. B. Kerblay, ed. D. Thorner), Irwin, 1966; E. Boserup, *The Conditions of Agricultural Growth,* Asia, 1965.
5 OECD (DAC), *Aid to Agriculture in Developing Countries,* Paris, 1968, p. 11. See also chapter 12, note 38.
6 Little, pp. 177-8.
7 K. Mark and F. Engels, *Communist Manifesto,* in *SW,* vol. 1. For India, see, for example, the papers in *EPW* since 1971 by A. Rudra, D. Thorner and U. Patnaik; the debate continues.
8 Growth of income per head, 1950-2 to 1964-6, from OECD Development Centre (Research Division), *National Accounts of Less Developed Countries,* Paris, 1968. Public and private investment, 1966, from IBRD Economic Department (Comparative Data Unit), *Comparative World Tables,* Washington, 1968.
9 FAO, *State of Food and Agriculture 1970* (hereafter cited as *FAO/S*),

pp. 228-57. Data for agricultural shares in population and in gross domestic product for 1965. Shares in gross *national* product would be preferable if they were available (p. 157). Different tax rates on agricultural and non-agricultural output should also be allowed for if income disparity is to be assessed. However, since these distortions apply to all the countries being compared in a non-systematic manner, they probably do not affect our results.

10 1952-4 to 1967-9 for food and agricultural output, from *FAO/S 1970*, pp. 268-9; 1950-7 to 1964-6 for total output (OECD Development Centre (Research Division), *National Accounts of LDCs*). The case for trying out food output is that deliberate policies to restrict crops such as coffee or jute, to avoid glutting export markets, are less likely with food.

11 *FAO/S 1970.*

12 Chenery, pp. 8-9, note 12.

13 Little.

14 B. J. L. Berry, 'City Size and Economic Development', in Jakobson, reports such views.

15 A. Bose, 'The Urbanisation Process in South and South-east Asia', in Jakobson, p. 85.

16 T. G. McGee, 'The Role of Cities in Asian Society', in Jakobson, p. 174.

17 G. Blyn, *Agricultural Trends in India, 1891-1947*, Philadelphia, 1966, pp. 94-107; M. Lipton, 'India's Agricultural Performance: Achievements, Distortions and Ideologies, *Asian and African Studies*, Israel Oriental Society, Vol. 6, 1970.

18 J. Nehru, *The Discovery of India*, 3rd ed., Asia, 1960, p. 300; but see B. N. Baden-Powell, *The Indian Village Community*, Longmans, 1896, and *The Original Growth of Village Communities in British India*, Swan Sonnenschein, 1899; M. Darling, *The Punjab Peasant in Prosperity and Debt*, 4th ed., Oxford, 1947; H. Mann, *The Social Framework of Agriculture*, Cass, 1968; F. Brayne, *Better Villages*, Oxford, 1937. See also the work of Gilbert Slater.

19 U. Lele, *Preliminary Report on the African Rural Development Survey*, IBRD, 1973, pp. 61-2. The failure of crop research stations to retain good personnel after independence in South Asia, and notably their loss of economists to central banks, are also typical.

20 H. V. Richter, 'The Union of Burma', in Shand, pp. 159-61, 151.

21 These indicators of economic 'openness' are crude, but nothing else is available for many LDCs.

22 About 15% of differences in the real *growth* of income per person among the forty-five LDCs is linked to differences in their initial *levels.*

23 Balassa, p. 71.

24 For the small differences in *completed* family size between rich and poor occupations and castes, see J. Stoeckel and M. A. Choudhuri, 'Differential Fertility in a Rural Area of East Pakistan', *Millbank Memorial Fund Quarterly*, April 1969, p. 193; and J. N. Agarwala,

A Demographic Study of Six Urbanising Villages, Institute of Economic Growth Occasional Paper No. 8, Asia (Bombay), 1970, tables
49, 50, 52, 53. For the dangers of reasoning from high family size
norms to larger families—of failing to allow for death rates—see
'Some Aspects of Human Fertility in Puerto Rico', 1951 Millbank
Memorial Fund Conference Report, New York, 1952; and F. Okediji,
'Socio-economic Status and Differential Fertility in an African City',
Journal of Developing Areas, April 1969, pp. 347-9. Evidence that
those prone to high child mortality have many children to ensure
a surviving son appears from the fact that four caste groups are rank-
ed identically in order of birth rates and of death rates in J. B. Wyon
and J. E. Gordon, *The Khanna Study: Population Problems in the
Rural Punjab,* Harvard, p. 251. (There is only one chance in twenty-
four that this is an accidental effect.) For the opening-out of rural-
urban differences in fertility rates—previously sufficient only to
make up for mortality differences—under the impact of an urban-
oriented family planning effort, see 'Preliminary Estimates of Fertility for Korea', *Population Index,* January-March 1971, p. 6.

25 Schofield, *Village Nutrition,* in press, MIT, 1976.

26 P. Hill, *Rural Hausa: a Village and a Setting,* Cambridge 1972,
chapter 3, indicates the complex trade-offs that must underlie any
economic decision about the desired family size.

27 The argument of this paragraph is based on one developed by
S. Kuznets, in a lecture at MIT in 1964, to refute the notion of a
'low-level equilibrium trap'—growth in income per person producing extra population increase sufficient to reverse that growth—for
an LDC as a whole.

28 Readers should be reassured that a death rate of 8 per 1,000 does
not imply that the rich live on average for $1,000 \div 8$ or 125 years.

29 For evidence that poor illiterate communities know and practise
contraception, see—among many others—A. Romaniuk, *La fécondité
des populations congolaises,* Mouton, 1967, pp. 280-96, esp.
pp. 292-5. Recent research confirms the alleged 'old wives' tale' that
further pregnancy is less likely during prolonged lactation. A. Berg,
The Nutrition Factor, Brookings, 1973, pp. 38-9.

30 R. Cassen, 'Population Policy', in Streeten/Lipton, for the high return to investment in birth control, and *The Population of India,*
forthcoming, on the impact on planned birth rates of anticipated
falls in child mortality.

4 IDEOLOGIES OF RURAL AND URBAN
DEVELOPMENT

1 J. M. Keynes, *General Theory of Employment, Interest and Money,*
Macmillan, 1936, p. 383.

2 I am doing this.

3 T. S. Eliot, 'The Metaphysical Poets', in *Selected Prose* (ed. J. Hay-
ward), Penguin, 1955; see pp. 115-20 and esp. p. 117.

4 David Hume, another major contributor to classical economics and a contemporary of Smith, was similarly all of a piece as philosopher, historian and economist.

5 It may seem odd that North-West Europe should be the ideological base for social-scientific thought about the development of Africa, Asia and Latin America. Possibly Aristotle and the *Artha-shastra* demonstrate sensibilities as integrated, and produce structures as capable of being developed to analyse urban bias in terms of classes *and* markets *and* ethics, as Adam Smith; I do not know. Perhaps because it was the original colonising and (in the modern sense) developing region, North-West Europe has in practice certainly played the dominant ideological role analysed here.

6 J. Plamenatz, *Man and Society*, Longmans, 1963, vol. II, esp. pp. 323-4, 330, 344, argues that, of the various senses of 'ideology' in Marx and Engels, the most interesting covers those ideas 'which serve the interests of some group, and also all the ideas or doctrines which are not scientific', but rightly points out that being unscientific, speculative or illusory is neither necessary nor sufficient (nor, one might add, helpful) for an idea that serves, or is used to serve, class interests.

7 Karl R. Popper, *The Logic of Scientific Discovery*, 6th impression (revised), Hutchinson, 1972, pp. 82-4. (An example of this stratagem, in the case of that significant minority of Freudians for whom the approach was hardened into ideology, is to so interpret a dream that is clearly the reverse of wish-fulfilment as to turn it into a 'success' for their approach, by attributing the dream to the operations of the 'censorship mechanism'.

8 See Paul Streeten's preface to G. Myrdal, *Value in Social Theory*, Routledge, 1958, pp. vii-xix.

9 That is, in a sense in which rural-agricultural growth does not depend on extracting any form of urban-industrial surplus.

10 The proportions of both in agriculture are today lower in the UK than in almost any comparable country, and lower than in several wealthier countries, such as the USA and Sweden.

11 D. Ricardo, *Works*, ed. P. Sraffa, vol. 1: *The Principles of Political Economy and Taxation, Cambridge*, Royal Economic Society, 1951 (hereafter cited as Ricardo), p. 317. Smith, however, saw that 'the inhabitants of a town, being collected into one place, can easily combine together [unlike] the inhabitants of the country, dispersed in different places'. Adam Smith, *The Wealth of Nations* (1776), Nelson, 1884 (hereafter cited as Smith), book III, chapter 1, p. 53.

12 Hence Ricardo is wrong to infer that, because the industrial profit *rate* (on his assumptions) gets cut back to the same level as the agricultural profit *rate*, selective protection of industry is 'no more injurious to the agricultural class than to any other part of the community' (Ricardo, p. 316). Agriculture's *share* in profits is cut. So is the wage of specifically agricultural (skilled) labour, relative to industry: for Ricardo's process, by raising the share of industry in the nation's capital, is bound to raise its demand for labour (and also its labour productivity) as compared with agriculture.

13　Ricardo, p. 317.

14　The 'level of protection' is equated among producers — in the sense of giving an artificial advantage to none — if, for every producer, the ratio of the *world price* of his value-added (that is, outputs *minus* material inputs) to the *home market price* is identical (Balassa, pp. 3-27).

15　Whether defined as a 'given' revenue loss from tariff cuts, as a 'given' value of extra imports of deprotected items, or as a 'given' reduction in the average tariff rate on the total bundle of imports.

16　P. Eckstein, 'Uniform versus Differentiated Protective Tariffs', *JDS*, July 1969. See also Smith, p. 279.

17　Smith, p. 155. Attempts to show that someone else (usually Cantillon) said this first are unconvincing: 'every great discovery has been made many times before, but by lesser men, who did not realise they had discovered anything.' As for Cantillon, he said something different: that the greatness of towns is 'limited by the product of the lands owned by the landowners who live there, net of transport costs', because this comprises effective demand for the series of urban craftsmen and labourers. R. Cantillon, *Essai sur la Nature de Commerce en General* (1755), ed. L. Salleron, Institut National d'Etudes Demographiques, 1952, p. 9. On p. 77 Cantillon hovers around Smith's key perception, but never really gets there. How could he? Smith was the first economist to have the advantage of interpreting a modern agro-industrial 'revolution' in progress around him. France's did not arrive till 1830-50.

18　Strictly this is a tautology — one could substitute 'whisky' for 'food'. Food is in practice the important constraint, partly because a really poor family spends 50 to 70% of *extra* income on it, partly because domestic food supply responds slowly, if surely (pp. 309-12), to rising prices induced by rising demand.

19　Assuming — reasonably (Mellor, pp. 73-6) — that the proportion of a given money wage, spent by a (poor) industrial worker on food, will be almost unaffected by a change in price, other than a monstrous one. We can probably neglect the risk that m, the productivity of *industrial* labour, will decline significantly for, say, a 5 to 10% fall in the food it can afford.

20　'What are the limits on wage employment . . .? . . . Wage goods to pay for their work. . . . The size of the agricultural surplus is the vital factor that limits the wage labour force.' (N. Kaldor, cited in R. Robinson, ed., *Developing the Third World*, Cambridge, 1971, p. 98.) Compare W. A. Lewis, 'Economic Development with Unlimited Supplies of Labour', reprinted in A. N. Agarwala and S. P. Singh, *The Economics of Underdevelopment*, Galaxy (New York), 1963, pp. 400, 432-4.

21　Smith, pp. 282-3; N. Kaldor, *Essays on Economic Policy,* vol. II, Duckworth, 1964, p. 180.

22　Smith, p. 3. He does not clearly separate this real *static* difficulty, of so dividing labour as to enjoy falling unit costs as the size of farm increases (even with a given technology), from the bogus *dynamic* claim that technical change — 'improvement of the productive powers of labour'— in agriculture 'does not keep pace with its improvement in manufactures. Ricardo also 'did not understand the distinction' (M. Blaug, *Ricardian Economics*, Yale, 1958, p. 15).

23 Strictly (1) is diminishing returns to a fixed factor when combined with a variable factor; (2) is decreasing returns to scale; (3) is neither. See my 'Population, Land and Decreasing Returns to Agricultural Labour', *Bulletin of the Oxford University Institute of Economics and Statistics*, September 1964.

24 Notwithstanding E. Roll, *A History of Economic Thought*, Faber, 1961, p. 197.

25 For Nassau Senior and John Stuart Mill, see Blaug, *Ricardian Economics*, pp. 157-8 and 179-80. See also K. Marx, *Theories of Surplus Value*, Lawrence & Wishart, 1969, vol. II, pp. 18-19.

26 Lewis, 'Economic Development with Unlimited Supplies of Labour' in Agarwala and Singh, *The Economics of Underdevelopment*; and R. Nurske, *Problems of Capital Formation in Underdeveloped Countries*, Oxford, 1953, pp. 33-6, are *loci classici* for the former views; see Myrdal, vol. III pp. 2041-62, T. W. Schultz, *Transforming Traditional Agriculture*, Yale, 1964, pp. 53-70, and D. Jorgenson, 'Testing Alternative Theories of the Development of a Dual/Economy', in I. Adelman and E. Thorbecke, eds., *The Theory and Design of Economic Development*, Johns Hopkins, 1966, pp. 45-60, for refutations. For a critique of the latter view; cf. Streeten/Lipton.

27 A. Marshall, *Principles of Economics*, 8th ed., Macmillan, 1961 (hereafter cited as Marshall), pp. 388-94, esp. p. 393. See also A. C. Pigou, *The Economics of Welfare*, 4th ed., Macmillan, 1932. p. 224. Their argument, that the consumption of items produced under decreasing returns should be discouraged by taxes (and under increasing returns, encouraged by subsidies) because their expanded production increases (decreases) cost of production and price for *all* persons, applies neo-classical methods to a basically classical proposition.

28 A concession of this sort is often made, to encourage larger loans with lower handling costs per pound.

29 Risk is a different matter; see p. 208 for the argument that investment in agriculture is riskier than in industry.

30 Dharm Narain's demonstration that in 1950 the Indian small farmer sold almost as big a share of output as the big farmer owes much to special conditions in that year, and hence was contradicted by a later enquiry (Usta Patnaik, *Capitalism in Indian Agriculture*, D. Phil. thesis, Oxford 1972). More basically, marketed surplus is normally measured to include produce temporarily sold (to pay debts or relieve storage problems), usually by small farmers, and later bought back by them. True marketed surplus *net* of buyback is obviously a bigger share of output on a 1,000-acre farm than on a 5-acre farm. It is with

this true surplus (available to the non-farm sector), and with favouring the big farmers that produce it, that urban interests are concerned.

31 Smith, p. 95. The Punjab (and Chilalo Province, Ethiopia) today would suggest, rather, that profitable prospects of 'improvement and better cultivation' induce big farmers to dispossess debtors and tenants, and to buy up 'other small occupiers of land'.

32 Smith, p. 350, in advocating that landlords should be encouraged to oversee part of their land directly and not let it all out.

33 Smaller farmers tend to obtain a given volume of calories for consumption (or a given worth of, say, fibres for sale) with different crops — those using less scarce land and more plentiful family labour. This only strengthens the argument.

34 Ricardo, p. 80.

35 R. D. C. Black, *Economic Thought and the Irish Question*, Cambridge, 1960, pp. 19, 29-30.

36 D. P. O'Brien, *J. R. McCulloch: a Study in Classical Economics*, Allen & Unwin, 1970, p. 375.

37 It is true that Smith, writing during the first stirrings of the British industrial revolution, sought to correct the pro-agricultural bias of the Physiocrats (Smith, pp. 275-86; Roll, *A History of Economic Thought*, pp. 148-9, 154), but it was not Smith but his successors who imported the reverse bias into political economy.

38 A distinguished exception is the last (1914) paper of the great Austrian economist, Böhm-Bawerk, 'Macht oder okonomisches Gesetz?' (in vol. 1 of his *Gesammelte Schriften*, ed. F. X. Weiss, Leipzig, 1924). He argues that the 'power' of economic agents — such as workers and employers — is used within discoverable boundaries, of what is profitable for each, set by the 'economic laws' of marginal-productivity and marginal-utility theory.

39 Marxists recognise the concentration of power among city-dwellers; marginalists, the disparity between the efficiency of capital in agriculture and in industry.

40 B. F. Hoselitz, in D. Wall, ed., *Chicago Essays in Economic Development*, Chicago, 1972.

41 That least dogmatic and most insightful of marginalists, Alfred Marshall, predicted — anticipating Myrdal's 'cumulative causation' by sixty years — the failure of this equilibriating system. Rural skill drain, Marshall argued, would persistently pull the ablest villagers towards urban opportunities, worsening inequality between village and town. See Marshall, pp. 165-7, 545, 649.

42 Similar objections apply to the view that — in poor countries with imperfect capital markets! — savings 'automatically' flow into rural areas if the return is higher, thus raising capital stock per worker, bidding up wages and eliminating urban bias.

43 While these afflict agriculture, they would, in any serious attempt to characterise agriculture even at a high level of economic abstraction, appear rather unimportant; compare, for instance, the importance of seasonality; of year-to-year output fluctuations and

their impact upon business risk; and of the tendency for the same agents, family farmers, to receive returns on labour, land and capital. See the debate between Pigou and Clapham on 'empty economic boxes': *Economic Journal* (hereafter cited as *EJ*), Cambridge, 1923 and 1924.

44 P. A. Samuelson, *Economics*, 6th ed., McGraw-Hill, 1964, p. 11.

45 Ingenious econometric manipulations of collinear sets of input data notwithstanding.

46 Marshall, p. 540. A fourth argument, that it is somehow more difficult for inefficient operators to be taken over by efficient ones in agriculture than in industry, is essentially a restatement of the classical case for static returns to scale diminishing in agriculture, increasing in industry: see above, pp. 96-7.

47 Output per unit of *all* inputs weighted at constant prices.

48 Compare H. G. Johnson's argument that 'infant industries', if they have the potential to become efficient, can borrow in early life and hence need no tariff protection. Here as there, artificial difficulties in borrowing money (because of undeveloped financial institutions, ignorance and risk) are relevant; but they are likelier in villages than in cities, and thus strengthen our case.

49 Samuelson, *Economics*, pp. 401, 763.

50 Since capital is generally worth more than market prices suggest (p. 303), this process would help to account for a more rapid increase in total factor productivity inside agriculture than outside it.

51 P. Dorner, *Land Reform and Economic Development*, Penguin, 1972; E. J. Long, 'The Economic Basis of Land Reform', *Land Economics*, March 1961, reprinted in T. Shukla, ed., *Economics of Underdeveloped Agriculture*, Vora, 1969 (hereafter cited as Shukla); M. Lipton, 'Towards a Theory of Land Reform', in D. Lehmann, ed., *Agrarian Reform and Agrarian Reformism*, Faber, 1974 (hereafter cited as Lehmann).

52 Similar arguments usually persuade smaller farmers to devote more of their land to 'labour-intensive' crops than do larger farmers.

53 Such redistribution could well ultimately *increase* the farmers' 'marketed surplus' of food to the towns (see Lehmann). But it is *instant* industrialisation that most urban elites want—and a marketed surplus to match.

54 This brief discussion is inevitably eclectic, drawing on Marx at various times in the development of his thought, and on a few key 'Marxists'. Nevertheless, I believe it accurately portrays the mainstreams of Marxist thought about the urban-rural divide. One must beware of 'reduc[ing] the Marxist theory of development to a rigid orthodoxy' (F. Engels, letter of 12 May 1894 to F. A. Sorge, in Engels p. 536). See also Engels' preface to vol. III of K. Marx, *Capital*, Foreign Language Publishing House, Moscow, 1959 (hereafter cited as *Capital*), *pp. 13-14.*

55 'Differentiation of the peasantry [is required to create] a home market for capitalism by converting the peasant into a farm labourer, on the one hand, and into a small-commodity producer, a petty-bourgeois, on the other.' These create a 'home market' for capitalist industry by demanding, respectively, wage goods and producer goods from it. V. I. Lenin, *The Development of Capitalism in Russia* (1899 and 1907), Progress Publishers, Moscow, 1964 (hereafter cited as Lenin), p. 155.

56 Plamenatz, *Man and Society*, pp. 293-4.

57 F. Engels, *The Peasant Question in France and Germany*, in *SW*, vol. 2, p. 381; K. Marx and F. Engels, *Manifesto of the Communist Party*, *SW*, vol. 1, p. 42.

58 Engels, prefatory note to *The Peasant War in Germany*, *SW*, vol. 1, p. 585; my italics.

59 Marx, *The Eighteenth Brumaire of Louis Bonaparte*, *SW*, vol. 1, p. 306; my italics.

60 F. Fanon, *The Wretched of the Earth*, MacGibbon & Kee, 1965, pp. 88-9, 95, 99 (hereafter cited as Fanon); my italics. On such 'making use' of people, see I. Kant, *The Moral Law*, tr. and ed. H. J. Paton, Hutchinson, 1948. Given their priorities, no wonder the socialist — and non-socialist — urban-based parties are early rendered 'suspicious and odious in the minds of the peasants' (Fanon).

61 See K. Marx, letter to V. I. Zasulic (Sassulitsch), 1881 (*Marx-Engels Werke*, vol. 35, pp. 266-7) — Marx's italics; *Capital*, p. 328. For early views, see Engels, pp. 36-8, a rural idyll to the point of self-caricature; and, more tough-mindedly but with no more real evidence, K. Marx, *Pre-Capitalist Formations* (1857-8), ed. E. Hobsbawm, Lawrence & Wishart, 1964, p. 96. See also N. Bukharin and E. Preobrazhensky, *The ABC of Communism*, Communist Party of Great Britain, 1922, p. 315, R. Luxemburg, *The Accumulation of Capital* (1914), Routledge, 1953 (hereafter cited as Luxemburg), p. 377)

62 Lenin, pp. 83-4, 119-20; P. Hill, 'The Myth of the Amorphous Peasantry: a Northern Nigerian Case Study', *Nigerian Journal of Economic and Social Studies*, July 1968, and *Studies in Rural Capitalism in West Africa*, Cambridge, 1970, pp. 153-6; D. Thorner, *Cooperative Farming in India*, Asia, 1965.

63 Lenin, pp. 71, 157, 177-8 and cf. p. 73.

64 Lenin (p. 182) concedes that there is no statistical evidence 'on the question of whether the differentiation of the peasantry is progressing, and if so at what rate'! Yet he concludes that — because his statistics prove that rural people are unequal at a point of time — 'the peasantry have been splitting up at enormous speed into a numerically small but economically strong rural bourgeoisie and a rural proletariat' (p. 310)!

65 Lenin, p. 148.

66 *Capital*, p. 787.

67 Engels, p. 309.

68 *Capital*, p. 103.

69 Respectively, horseless (cultivating on average 1.5 cropped acres, though they owned more) and with five or more horses (21.1 cropped acres): Lenin, pp. 157-8. See p. 112 and note 64.

70 For a discussion on the expansion of artificial fertiliser, rapidly accelerating after the introduction into Britain of Peruvian guano in 1839, see F. Dovring, in Habakkuk, p. 655.

71 Perhaps more effectively; small farmers are better placed to cope with an innovation that proves to place strains on labour requirements in unpredicted ways, as they have more cheap family labour per acre to supplement it with.

72 Lenin, and V. I. Lenin, *Capitalism in Agriculture* (1910), Little Lenin Library (New York), 1946.

73 Bukharin and Preobrazhensky, *The ABC of Communism*, p. 298; Engels, *The Peasant Question in France and Germany*, in *SW*, vol. 2, p. 394; V. I. Lenin, cited in D. Mitrany, *Marx against the Peasant*, Collier, 1961, p. 217.

74 *Capital*, p. 100; Lenin, p. 74.

75 Lenin, pp. 106, 110. The number of cartloads of manure used *per household* rises in the five groups with farm size (80-116-197-358-752), but use *per acre* shows an exactly opposite trend (47-25-22-20-19).

76 Kautsky. The unfortunate fact that this book is unavailable in English (while the French and Russian translations are hard to come by) has denied Kautsky much of the attention he deserves. So did his later 'conversion' to social-democracy, which made him *persona non grata* with the Communists.

77 Kautsky, pp. 7-10.

78 Kautsky, pp. 10-11; *Capital*, p. 603 (note).

79 Kautsky, pp. 11-12. 'The old harmony and community of interests' (p. 13) is thus destroyed in the family (Kautsky nowhere claims it ever existed in the village community, but one wonders whether, even in the family, patriarchy is not a somewhat enforced 'harmony').

80 Luxemburg, p. 371; P. J. Harding, cited in G. Ionescu and E. Gellner, *Populism: its Meanings and National Characteristics*, Weidenfeld, 1969, p. 140; Lenin, p. 256.

81 Kautsky, pp. 208-9.

82 R. M. Goodwin, 'The Multiplier as Matrix', *EJ*, 1949.

83 Kautsky, p. 209.

84 Kautsky, p. 220. Cf. Marshall, cited in n. 46; and see pp. 259-61 below. Kautsky, on p. 219, also points out the severe imbalance in the rural age structure caused by selective urbanisation in the young.

85 Cf. Engels, *The Peasant Question in France and Germany*, in *SW*, vol. 2, p. 391, who also saw that such measures helped mainly 'big landlords' and 'big landed estates'.

86 Kautsky, p. 221.

87 Marx, *Eighteenth Brumaire* . . ., in *SW*, vol. 1, pp. 305-6 (my italics),

but compare *Capital*, p. 787; Lenin, pp. 271 (my italics), 317; and cf. pp. 325-7.

88 Luxemburg, p. 368 (and cf. p. 467); M. Lewin, *Russian Peasants and Soviet Power*, Allen & Unwin, 1968, p. 154 (hereafter cited as Lewin), my italics; Mao Tse-tung, 'On Contradiction' (1937), in *Collected Works*, Foreign Languages Press (Peking), vol. 1, 1964, p. 345; Fanon, p. 95; J. Saul, in Gellner and Ionescu, *Populism*, p. 131; A. G. Frank, *Capitalism and Underdevelopment in Latin America*, Monthly Review Press, 1967, p. 12.

89 A. Maddison, *Economic Growth in Japan and the USSR*, Unwin University Books, 1969, p. 104.

90 T. H. von Laue, *Sergei Witte and the Industrialisation of Russia*, Atheneum (New York), 1969; see below, note 110.

91 Lenin.

92 E. Wolf, *Peasant Wars in the Twentieth Century* (1971), Faber Paperbacks, 1973 (hereafter cited as Wolf), pp. 95-8.

93 Maddison, *Economic Growth in Japan and the USSR*, p. 105; R. D. Davis, discussion with M. Lewin, Sussex Tapes no. R. 2026, cited in D. Yaffe, *Soviet Industrialisation: Planned Economic Development and the World Economy*, Institute of Development Studies (mimeo), Brighton, 1972 (hereafter cited as Yaffe), p. 43.

94 P. Bairoch, *The Economic Development of the Third World since 1900*, Methuen, 1975, p. 18.

95 C. K. Wilber, *The Soviet Model and Underdeveloped Countries*, Chapel Hill, 1969, pp. 14-15, adds Pakistan (before the secession of Bangladesh) and also the Philippines, Turkey, the Congo, Nigeria, Mexico and Argentina — all to my mind far too small for a Stalinist solution to be conceivable—and even Ghana, Colombia and Venezuela!

96 Lewin, p. 154, argues this case.

97 A. Nove, Introduction in Preobrazhensky, p. xi, citing Bukharin (my italics); Lenin ('Tax in kind'), Trotsky and Stalin are cited in A. Ehrlich, *The Soviet Industrialisation Debate*, Harvard, 1967, pp. 6, 96. On the 1923 peasant response, see Yaffe, p. 27, and A. Nove, *Economic History of the USSR*, Allen Lane, 1969, p. 112.

98 Yaffe, p. 31.

99 Lewin, pp. 127-35; Preobrazhensky, p. 82. (I am grateful to David Yaffe for these references, with which, unlike myself, he is in substantial agreement.)

100 Nove, in Preobrazhensky, pp. xi, xii.

101 For the role of the peasants as the vanguard of Russian radicalism— often dragging the urban radicals in their wake—see Wolf, pp. 69-70, 79, 86-8. Wolf shows how religious chiliasm, booming peasant education, and deep, lasting and bitter disappointment all helped radicalise the Russian peasantry. For the dismissal, by Vietnamese and Soviet critics of Fanon, of the peasantry in today's LDCs as a political vanguard in favour of 'the militant ... from the towns who must patiently ...educate them', see D. Caute, *Fanon*, Fontana/Collins, 1970, p. 72.

102 Nor are they in today's LDCs. In India's 1967 election, the proportion of owner-cultivator voters backing non-'reactionary' parties was
60.7%, of farmworkers (many of them small peasants 'on the side')
64.8%, and of the electorate as a whole 61.8% — negligible differences (R. Kothari, *Politics in India*, Little, Brown, 1970, pp. 202,
211). And India's most effective land reform was not legislated by
the urban 'vanguard'; it was the seizure, by Bengali peasants in
1968, of land above the ceiling, long retained illegally by big farmers in default of law enforcement by that 'vanguard'.

103 Mitrany, *Marx against the Peasant*, p. 232.

104 Preobrazhensky, pp. 88-9.

105 Lewin, p. 151; Preobrazhensky, p. 89.

106 Preobrazhensky, p. 84; cf. Zinoviev, cited in Mitrany, *Marx against
the Peasant*, p. 68.

107 O. Lange and F. W. Taylor, *Economic Theory and Socialism*,
Minnesota, 1938.

108 Preobrazhensky, p. 84; Lewin, p. 259. Compare the wishful thinking that Pakistan's urban capitalists, made stronger and richer by a
squeeze on the rural poor, would later share with them the fruits
of growth (pp. 33-4).

109 Preobrazhensky, pp. iii, 95-7; Lewin, p. 151.

110 Preobrazhensky, p. 89 (my italics).

111 Preobrazhensky, pp. 104-10; M. Dobb, *Soviet Economic Development Since 1917*, 6th ed., Routledge, 1966, p. 183.

112 L. Trotsky, *The Revolution Betrayed*, Faber, 1937, pp. 38-40. He
blames, also, the incapacity 'of the industries to furnish large-scale
agriculture with the necessary machinery': what is the evidence
that more machinery, without production incentives, would have
raised output or deliveries? Why should an urban state rush
machinery to help the dispersed rural sector?

113 Yaffe, pp. 25, 27; and chapter 13, notes 18, 66, 67 and 74.

114 Stalin, speech to the 1928 Central Committee of the CPSU, 'not
published until twenty years later' (Lewin, p. 258); and Lewin,
pp. 260-1.

115 See Haydn's *The Seasons* for a German equivalent of eighteenth-
century English pastoral attitudes; the text is based on von Swieten's
version of Thomson's poem.

116 E. Schumacher, *Small is Beautiful*, Blond & Briggs, 1973.

117 *As You Like It*, II. v.

118 Alexander Pope, *A Discourse on Pastoral Poetry* (1709), in W. Elwin,
ed., *The Works of Alexander Pope*, Murray, 1871, vol. 1, p. 266.

119 W. Wordsworth, *Prefaces to the 'Lyrical Ballads'*, etc. (1801),
Nelson, 1937, p. 15. Cf. J. S. Mill, *Principles of Political Economy*
(1871 ed.), bk. II, chapter 6, note 1.

120 W. Wordsworth, *Poetical Works*, Oxford Standard Authors, 1969,
p. 62. Cf. A. Chekhov, 'Peasants', in A. Yarmolinsky, ed., *The Unknown Chekhov*, Owen, 1959, p. 170: 'The dew was glistening on
the green shrubs that were mirrored in the water. Then the air grew

warmer. . . . What a glorious morning it was! and how glorious life would probably be in this world, were it not for want, terrible, inescapable want, from which you cannot hide anywhere!'

121 Cf. Chekhov, in Yarmolinsky, ed., *The Unknown Chekhov*, p. 201.

122 'I speak from personal knowledge of life in Kathiawad [Gujerat, India] over sixty years ago . . . there was more lustre in people's eyes, and more life in their limbs, than there is today.' M. K. Gandhi, *Harijan*, September 1940, cited in R. K. Prabhu, *Panchayati Raj* Navajivan (Ahmedabad), 1969, p. 3. Cf. Wordsworth, cited by Mill, note 119.

123 H. Maine, *Village Communities in East and West*, 7th ed., John Murray, 1895. Wordsworth, *Prose Works*, vol. II, Oxford, 1974, pp. 200-1, 206-7.

124 W. Empson, *Some Versions of Pastoral*, Chatto & Windus, 1935, p. 4.

125 Wordsworth, *Prefaces to the 'Lyrical Ballads'*, p. 18. See also Goldsmith, *The Deserted Village*, 'If to the city sped . . .'; Blake, 'London'; Arnold, *The Scholar Gipsy*, on the 'strange disease of modern life'; Housman, *A Shropshire Lad*, XLI; Eliot, *The Waste Land*, on the crowd, whom 'death had undone', on London Bridge; Rilke's sequence in *Stundenbuch* beginning *'Denn, Herr, die grossen Städte sind/Verlorene und aufgelöste'*; J. Ruskin, *Fors Clavigera* (1872), *passim*; and many other expressions of revulsion from the city.

126 See, for example, P. Toynbee, 'Pilgrimage to a modern prophet' (Ivan Illich), *Observer Magazine*, 24 February 1974.

127 V. L. Menon, *Ruskin and Gandhi*, Sava Seva Sangh Prakasan (Varanasi), 1965, p. 5.

128 G. Ashe, *Gandhi: A Study in Revolution*, Heinemann, 1968, p. 83. His vegetarian group in London 'carried on a tradition [of thinking] deriving from Shelley' (p. 33), behind whom stood Wordsworth, Clare, Goldsmith. . . . . 'Additional inspiration came from Thoreau, from Ruskin, and to a lesser extent from Whitman' (p. 33).

129 Gandhi, *Harijan*, in Prabhu, ed., *Panchayati Raj*, pp. 15-16.

130 H. Maine, *Lectures on the Early History of Institutions*, John Murray, 1874, gives a highly *narodnik* account of the 'natural communities' of rural Russia, with their 'peasants' practising 'co-operation'. Even Lenin does not challenge this, though his data do (pp. 111-12). R. Bendix, 'Tradition and modernity reconsidered', *Comparative Studies in Society and History*, 1966-7, p. 302, emphasises the similarity of avowedly 'conservative' and 'radical' critiques of modernisation, capitalism, industry and commerce.

131 The diversion towards issues of 'price policy versus physical controls', and of foreign-exchange management—as if they were causes rather than symptoms of urban bias—is a similar error; see pp. 76-7.

132 M. K. Gandhi, *Village Swaraj*, compiled by H. M. Vyas, Navajivan (Ahmedabad), 1962.

133 *Speeches of Jawaharlal Nehru*, Ministry of Information and Broadcasting, Delhi: vol. II (1949-53), pp. 93, 242; vol. V (1963-4), p. 82, 110-12. In Latin America, Celso Furtado reacts similarly; his main

case for rural outlays is that 'agricultural surpluses required to supply the cities will become available only if productivity increases in
the agricultural sector' (*Obstacles to Development in Latin America*,
Anchor, 1970, p. 173). This echoes Nehru's view that 'unless we
have surplus from agriculture, we cannot progress in our economy.'
134 Caute, *Fanon*, pp. 22, 25.
135 Fanon, pp. 88-9. Compare Lugard's 'indirect rule' through the religious dignitaries of Nigeria, and the British attempts to use the
Indian princes and to codify Brahminical law.
136 Fannon, p. 97. Marx's Eurocentric view of the proletariat as vanguard and the peasant as 'reactionary' is partly to blame. So is
Lenin's view of 'the Party as vanguard', dragging the people forward rather than learning from them.
137 Fanon, p. 9. Consider the expression 'Francophone Africa' — and
the fact that Nehru and his daughter (Mrs Gandhi) were more at
home in English than in any Indian language.
138 Fanon, pp. 95, 126, 138.
139 Fanon, pp. 152-4.

5   THE DISPARITY IN WELFARE AND EARNING

1 'Capital', in the rest of this book, means 'the value of fixed assets
yielding annual flows of income or welfare'— machines, factories,
barns, dams, wells, roads, houses, etc. These items are difficult to
add up, value and measure, but sensible attempts to allow for such
problems tend to increase the estimated rural-urban gaps (pp. 198-
201). Each year capital is reduced by 'depreciation'— wearing out
plus obsolescence— but increased by 'gross investment' or installation. Gross investment minus depreciation is 'net investment'. Any
nation's investment is made possible by, and is equal in each year
to the sum of, national and foreigners' savings. National savings
equals national output minus national consumption; foreigners
savings equals imports minus exports (that is, foreigners' output of
goods sold to the nation, minus their use of goods produced by it).
2 For the view that this widening is due to 'diminishing returns' in agriculture as against 'increasing returns' in other sectors, see pp. 95-7.
3 Any discussion of this topic owes deep, obvious debts to the pioneering studies of Simon Kuznets, most recently summarised in *Economic Growth of Nations*, Harvard, 1971. A further useful discussion
is J. R. Bellerby, *Industry and Agriculture*, Oxford, 1956.
4 G. S. Chatterjee and N. Bhattacharya, 'Rural-Urban Differences in
Consumer Prices', *EPW*, 17 May 1969, p. 850, and J. B. Knight,
'Measuring Rural-Urban Income Differentials', *Proceedings of a
Conference on Urban Unemployment in Africa*, Institute of Development Studies, mimeo, September 1971, p. 13.
5 As regards efficiency and equity, however, these differences reflect
a hidden drawback of urban allocations. *Efficiency:* Urban prices
somewhat exceed rural prices mainly because of the cost of trans-

porting food townwards for workers and their families. By increasing their numbers, an emphasis on urban development raises the real unit cost of consumable food, especially as its real value is reduced by losses in movement and storage. *Equity:* in rural areas *urban* goods, consumed mainly by the rich, are relatively dear; while in urban areas it is *rural* goods, especially food consumed mainly by the poor, that are costlier (T. N. Srinivasan and P. K. Bardhan, 'Resource Prospects from the Rural Sector: a Comment', *EPW*, 28 June 1969). Hence cost-of-living differences between country and town hurt the urban poor, but the rural rich. They increase urban inequality, but reduce rural. They thus increase the welfare loss from urban-oriented investments that encourage people to move from rural to urban areas. Hence towns are even more unequal, as compared with villages, than the data (p. 167) suggest; and allocations tempting people from village to town have another concealed equity drawback.

6 S. L. Shetty, 'An Inter-sectoral Analysis of Taxable Capacity and Tax Burden', *Indian Journal of Agricultural Economics*, July-September 1971, p. 222; UN (Bangkok). For a refutation of V. Gandhi's overestimate, see Shetty, 'An Inter-sectoral Analysis of Taxable Capacity and Tax Burden', *Indian Journal of Agricultural Economics*, pp. 229-30, and UN (Bangkok), para 18.

7 Where they are, they accentuate the hidden drawbacks of urban emphases; see note 5 above.

8 Of the twenty-six LDCs (excluding those with under one million population) having available data for the 1960s, nineteen had larger rural households, and two showed no difference in average household size between urban and rural areas. Unweighted average household size for the twenty-seven countries: urban, 4.90, rural 5.25. (Chile and Ecuador from *UND 1971*, Table 11; all others from *UND 1968*, Table 12.) The most populous country, India, however, showed no difference between urban and rural household size (5.2), and two other very big countries, Pakistan and Indonesia, featured larger urban households.

9 See ch. 11; health services, free in urban Colombia, are costly (and inferior) in rural areas.

10 Some of these costs, notably storage and water supply, cost *society* more per household in urban areas. But they are either shown in urban household budgets—as rates, or as part of normal outlays—or do not fall on the urban household at all. It is because many such rural costs are not monetised, but borne as unpaid *effort,* that survey data conceal them and thus overstate the welfare of rural households.

11 Remittances from migrants in towns (unlike these costs) are not concealed in rural income or expenditure surveys; they *are* concealed in earnings and output comparisons. However, urban-rural and rural-urban remittances are not vastly different in most LDCs (p. 236).

12 Including income in kind, if consumed. The terms 'spending', 'consumption' and 'outlay' are used interchangeably here.

13 See also note 12. The greater internal equality of the rural sector (p. 167) also probably induces a higher ratio of consumption to income. It is *not* true that rural people save less at given income levels than townspeople: rather the reverse. See pp. 246-8.

14 Including income in kind from work on the family farm.

15 P. Laslett, *The World we have Lost*, 2nd ed., Methuen, 1971, chapter 5, gives interesting historical analogies.

16 See the citation from Pye on p. 64.

17 It is ironic that these urban activities by rural residents create the illusion that the rural-urban gap is small; for such activities usually start off with urban reinvestment of surpluses from rural lending or renting. The urbanisation of rural surpluses not only impoverishes the village; it generates statistics that cause underestimation of rural poverty.

18 The impact on urban and rural inequality of reassigning 'quasi-rural' townsmen to the rural sector is unclear. As conventionally measured, urban areas of LDCs are usually more inegalitarian (p. 167). If some of the measured rural rich—some of the top 5%—are really urban, measured rural inequality is reduced, and measured urban inequality increased. If some of the measured urban poor—of the bottom 20% or so—are really rural, measured urban inequality is somewhat increased.

19 *Report of the Committee on Distribution of Income and Levels of Living*, Government of India, Planning Commission, Delhi, 1969, Tables B3, B4; Chatterjee and Bhattacharya, 'Rural-Urban Differences in Consumer Prices', *EPW*, p. 850; P. K. Bardhan, 'Green Revolution and Agricultural Labourers', *EPW*, 1973; S. Swamy, 'Structural Changes in the Distribution of Income: The Case of India', *Review of Income and Wealth*, June 1967, p. 172. I do *not* assert that rural labourers actually got poorer in 'Green-Revolution' areas (only that gains there failed to make up for losses elsewhere); still less that the 'Green Revolution' is bad, or bad for the poor. It is a convenient technological scapegoat for social and political ills.

20 P. K. Bardhan, 'The Pattern of Income Distribution in India: a Review', IBRD Development Research Centre, June 1973, p. 44. Meanwhile the urban proportion rose from 32% to 41%, but the latter figures may be too high: Bardhan's poverty minimum is set 20% higher in urban areas, though Chatterjee and Bhattacharya (*EPW*) suggest living costs only 11% higher.

21 S. R. Bose, 'Trend of Real Income of the Rural Poor in East Pakistan, 1949-66', *Pakistan Development Review*, vol. VII, no. 3, 1968. Patchy data on rural-urban income differentials exist for some other Asian countries. Particularly good data for Ceylon (now Sri Lanka) show how a surplus extracted from a (racially distinct and geographically immobile) plantation workforce permits most of the burden of urban bias to be taken off the shoulders of other rural workers: see Central Bank of Ceylon, *Surveys of Consumer Finances, 1963, 1972*.

22 Central Statistical Office of Pakistan, *National Sample Survey no. 6* (1967).

23 A. Fishlow, 'Brazilian Size Distribution of Income' in *American Economic Review*, May 1972 (Papers and Proceedings of the 84th Meeting of the AEA), p. 399.

24 Knight, 'Measuring Rural-Urban Income Differentials', *Proceedings of a Conference on Urban Unemployment in Africa*, pp. 18-20 and Tables 5 and 6.

25 UN (Bangkok).

26 In ten villages in Tamilnadu (Madras) State, South India, with considerable numbers of migrants, data for the 1950s and 1960s show that 1.4% of income was urban-rural remittances, but 0.8% comprised reverse remittances. If one village suffering from a flood in the previous year is excluded, the proportions are almost identical. Other evidence from elsewhere supports this. J. Connell, B. Dasgupta, R. Laishley and M. Lipton, *Migration from Rural Areas: the Evidence from Village Studies*, report submitted to ILO, 1975 (hereafter cited as Connell), Chapter 5.

27 Kuznets, p. 294.

28 The fact that farm families eat much of what they grow is irrelevant. For simplicity, suppose all families comprise two working parents and two children. Farm families produce food worth £250 at prevailing prices, selling half and eating half. Non-farm families produce £750 worth of output. The disparity is 3. Average farm output provides its beneficiary with the option of buying one-third of each and every bundle of products that can be bought by the beneficiary of average non-farm output (leaving aside the question of marketing costs). Hence the purchasing-power ratio is also 3. This is irrespective of the choice actually made by the farm sector — in effect, to market all its food and buy half back. The low population density of rural areas imposes extra marketing costs, raising the disparity.

29 It understates the *gap*, because on top of a 3 to 1 output-per-worker gap (say) there is a 1.1 or 1.2 to 1 leisure-per-person gap!

30 That is, than national income divided by the number of persons (or workers).

31 Miss Peter Ady suggested to me in an Oxford seminar that, because unemployment rates (that is, shares of involuntary non-workers in the adult population) are higher in urban than in rural areas, the disparity between output-per-worker ratios overstates the welfare gap. However, the surveys and censuses used here measure output per participant, even if he is out of work for most of the year, provided he is seeking work. Hence, if a given ratio of urban to rural income per participant involves less work in the urban sector as Miss Ady suggests, that would mean the disparity *understated* the welfare gap, though not the ratio (see n. 29).

32 *FAO/P, 1971*, pp. 21-3.

33 Domestic product includes 'factor incomes paid abroad' — for example, for India, remittances to the UK by ICI and Brooke Bond Tea

— and excludes 'factor incomes received from abroad', for example, earnings remitted to India from the UK by Indian citizens. 'National product' reverses this. Domestic product thus comprises goods and services produced within the 'domestic' boundaries of a country, whoever enjoys the income for producing them; national product is the value of incomes, for producing goods and services, accruing to 'nationals' of a country, wherever those goods and services are produced.

34 Less than 5% of India's capital was foreign-owned even at independence in 1947, and while most was in industry the proportion in tea plantations was substantial. Since capital receives about 20% of Indian GNP, the excess of domestic over national product can hardly have exceeded (20% of 5%), or 1%, of the latter, even if all profits on the 5% of foreign-owned capital had been repatriated. Even that 1% maximum 'loss' would have been shared between agriculture and the rest of the economy. (For Venezuela see UN, *Yearbook of National Accounts Statistics 1973* (hereafter cited as *UNA*), vol. II, pp. 745, 747: 8.2% in 1960, 7.5% in 1970. For India see M. Lipton and J. Firn, *The Erosion of A Relationship: India and Britain since 1960,* Oxford-Chatham House, 1975; foreign non-capital (that is, labour and land) incomes in India are negligible compared to her total output.)

35 For sources, see Table 5.4, note.

36 Sources as in Table 5.5, note.

37 Kuznets, p. 294.

38 Bellerby's ratios of agricultural to non-agricultural 'incentive income' in twenty-eight countries (*Industry and Agriculture,* p. 270) show roughly similar patterns for 1938. Three of his four countries with ratios below 1.33 were highly developed. All his five countries with ratios above 2.9 were very poor. See Kuznets, p. 209, for similar data for 1960; and FAO, *The State of Food and Agriculture 1967,* Rome, 1967 (hereafter cited as *FAO/S*), p. 52, for confirming evidance on a *national*-product basis for a few countries.

6   THE DISPARITY: EXPLANATIONS, EVALUATIONS, SIGNIFICANCE

1 To Guyana, Colombia, Trinidad-Tobago, Surinam, Costa Rica and Ceylon one might add Barbados, which has no output data for the late 1960s but showed the lowest disparity of all—0.95, i.e. output per person higher inside agriculture than outside—in 1965.

2 Myrdal, vol. I, chapter 14, pt. 5; Kuznets, pp. 304-5.

3 Kuznets, p. 295.

4 Seers, pp. 17-18, 32-3, and chapter 2; Myrdal, vol. I, chapter 14, esp. sections 4, 6 and 8.

5 Personal communication, July 1974. He describes his explanation, modestly but wrongly, as 'obvious' and 'simple-minded'!

6 A. Gerschenkron, *Economic Backwardness in Historical Perspec-*

tive, Harvard, 1962, pp. 343-4, and 'Agrarian Policies and Industrialisation: Russia 1861-1971', in Habbakuk, esp. pp. 711, 716-17 and 783; A. O. Hirschman, 'The Political Economy of Import-Substituting Industrialisation in Latin America', *Quarterly Journal of Economics,* 1968, reprinted in *A Bias for Hope,* Yale, 1971, esp. pp. 94-5.

7 Not 'because growing Western agriculture keeps food prices down': size and distance *partly* isolate many LDCs from the world grain markets; and they have not been loth to protect other sectors!

8 For conceptualisations of how people could in this matter give a disinterested view, see J. Rawls, *A Theory of Justice,* Belknap (Harvard), 1971; G. Runciman, *Relative Deprivation and Social Justice,* Routledge, 1966, pp. 260-74; Lipton, pp. 101-2.

9 E. Hobsbawm, 'Peasants and Politics', *Journal of Peasant Studies,* October 1973, pp. 3-21.

10 Rawls, *A Theory of Justice.*

11 This is in the short run; for long-run objections, see ch. 10. The *primary* impact on the poor is almost certain to be better, given the large disparity (ch. 5).

12 For India, see UN (Bangkok).

13 Chenery, p. 21. The seven include India, Pakistan, Chile and Mexico. The 'odd man out' is Thailand. A recent survey adds an eleventh set of reliable data—the Post-enumeration Survey for Malaysia—also showing greater intra-rural than intra-urban equality. See S. Anand, *The Size Distribution of Income in Malaysia,* pt. 3, Development Research Centre (IBRD), Washington, 1973, pp. 14-16. Moreover, urban inequality is increased because the urban rich enjoy major price advantages; and rural inequality reduced, because rural price advantages go to the poor (ch. 5, n. 5).

14 Real, though grossly exaggerated by some 'functionalist' sociologists.

15 Or income-like benefits for villagers building their own homes without monetary reward.

16 For evidence that LDCs show greater *overall* inequality than NRCs, see Chenery, pp. 6-10.

17 S. Anand, *The Size Distribution of Income in Malaysia,* pt. I, pp. 41, 74, 75a; M. Mangahas, 'Income Inequality in the Philippines: a Decomposition Analysis', ILO World Employment Programme Research, Population and Employment Working Paper no. 12, pp. 14, 19-22 (the 1971 data are not usable: see p. 12 and p. 19, note 2).

18 *All-India Rural Household Survey,* vol. II, NCAER, Delhi, 1965. p. 55, interpolating household size from Table 15 into Table 14; *Urban Income and Saving,* NCAER, Delhi, no date (both sets of data cover 1961-2), pp. 19, 22, interpolating household size from Table 19 into Table 22.

19 See Lehmann for some of the relevant points.

20 This outcome is implicit in M. Todaro and J. Harris, 'Migration, Unemployment and Development: a Two-Sector Analysis', *American Economic Review,* vol. 60, 1970, pp. 126-42. Such reverse migration

would raise the supply of rural labour, but reinforce its literate leadership; the net impact on its power, and hence on intra-rural inequality, is obscure.

21 Of course, the analysis into intersectoral and intrasectoral inequality is only one way of cutting the cake. Reductions in urban bias should, however, on balance reduce inequality linked to differences in age, sex, caste, etc. See pp. 72-4.

22 There is a fifth, definitional, sense. Assume rural inequality constant. Then a given disparity does not deprive an 'average' villager of welfare W. It deprives rich villagers of rather less — and poor ones of *much* more.

23 In Brazil in 1960-70, the agricultural sector contained about 46% of workforce (*FAO/P 1971*, p. 21) and about 16.1% of GDP (*UNA 1971*, New York 1973, p. 104). It raised its income per person by about 1.2% yearly in agriculture in 1960-70, as against over 3% for the rest of the economy (C. G. Langoni, *A Distribuição da Renda e o Desenvolvimento Econômico do Brasil*, ed. Expressão e Cultura, Rio, 1973). The poorest half of the total population experienced only 1% growth of income per head over the decade, as against well over 30% for the richer half.

24 2½% growth in the average urban $300 income is $7½, and ½% growth in the average rural $100 is $½; total $8 growth upon $400 for a pair of typical people, or 2%: nearer the urban rate, because the towns enjoy three-quarters of income and a larger proportion of the extra income, and thus have more weight than the rural sector in national growth of income per person.

25 While option *B* is better than option *A*, more radical options are better still. For example, if it were possible politically to keep the growth of the 'upper 50%' down to 1% yearly in income per person — and if this were economically compatible with a sustained 5.06% growth in total output and income — the 'poorer half' could raise income per person by over 4% yearly for several years.

26 This is true although earnings ratios reflect ratios between sectoral MPLs, not PAELs. There is no general reason why the ratio of PAEL to MPL in agriculture should systematically exceed that in non-agriculture.

27 This effect is weakened, however, to the extent that (1) governments cheapen imports and other heavy, labour-replacing capital as a favour to industry (pp. 296-304); (2) urban trade-union leaders campaign for techniques raising the wages of their current membership (and thus making capital-intensive innovation, raising PAEL relative to MPL, more attractive to employers) rather than trying to increase the size and power of their (unionised) workforces; (3) the spectrum of techniques available to businessmen in LDCs is restricted to capital-intensive devices because it was researched and developed to meet the needs of the scarce-labour, high-saving economies of the rich world.

28 It needs careful interpretation, given the historical alternatives. Dynamic factors probably push the PAEL above the true MPL in-

creasingly, as a sector gets more investment per unit of extra labour. If agriculture had received more investment historically, or were now to do so, its PAEL would be boosted. Non-agriculture's bigger PAEL-MPL gap is a consequence of its past over-allocations, not an argument for future ones.

29 Balassa, pp. 36-7; Little, p. 73. Col. 4 of Table 6.3 is, in effect, the Table 5.4 disparity revalued by multiplying the basic GDP share in agriculture, used in Table 5.4, by the ratio of agriculture's revalued share in GDP to its market-price share in the Balassa or Little data; and similarly for non-agriculture. For the 'superior' method of valuing non-tradeables, see I.M.D. Little and J. Mirrlees, *Manual of Industrial Cost-Benefit Analysis:* vol. 2, OECD, 1968; see also, however, pp. 199-200 for a reason why non-tradeables (which are produced largely outside agriculture) are 'really' less valuable than they seem (because their high price is due partly to the very unequal income distribution — which enriches those who buy them — rather than to their importance in satisfying needs).

7 UNBALANCED SHARES IN CAPITAL

1 Of course, agriculture needs much more land, per rupee of output, than do other activities, but here this hardly matters; see pp. 194-5.

2 If output from such activities is high, why does it not induce (and suffice to service) 'reasonable' foreign lending? Because the benefits accrue to many dispersed people, with high propensities to consume extra income, and are thus hard to extract for foreign repayments.

3 Where there is, agriculture seldom gets much consideration. In the otherwise comprehensive discussion by V. Prakash of the aims of urban land policies ('Land Policies for Urban Development', in Jakobson, esp. pp. 207-12), avoidance of impingement on good farmland is unmentioned, yet the major 'boundary expansion of existing cities' (T. McGee, 'Catalysts or Cancers? The Role of Cities' in Jakobson, p. 161) has in most LDCs been in equally total neglect of this criterion. This is partly because price twists against farm products (ch. 13) reduce the returns to agricultural uses of land.

4 World-wide, of course, allocation of extra land to agriculture affects output values elsewhere. More land for rice means more value added in the rice-milling industry. But in any particular LDC such transference, at least between big sectors, should be small: what would Thai millers gain, or lose, if they milled Burmese or Italian instead of Thai rice?

5 Savings caused by rising inventories are usually very short-lived. They do, however, use up *some* savings capacity, and this is why they are often counted as 'investment'. An agriculture that needs to carry far lower inventories than other sectors (for example, South Africa's) clearly scores over one where the reverse is true (for example, India's).

6 It is, however, quite correct to regard fertiliser factories as purely industrial capital. Fertilisers, unlike irrigation water, are importable;

the farmer gains little, and may lose, from the presence of domestic suppliers. See p. 204.

7 Reciprocal causation applies here: educated people are especially likely to seek urban work because their urban-rural wage differential is especially high (p. 263). At a seminar in Sri Lanka in 1973, participants estimated for me the differentials, in their home countries, between the pay of an agricultural extension officer (village-level) and the lowest grade of clerk in the government service in the capital city. For twelve LDCs the range varied from 2:1 to 5:1, in favour of the clerk! Plainly this cuts the effective quantity and quality of 'human capital' supporting unskilled rural labour.

8 There is some evidence from India that industry hires 'white-collar' employees until their contribution to output falls very low indeed.

9 See Tables 7.1 and 8.1. Economists concerned about 'indirect capital' are referred to pp. 204-5.

10 There are striking exceptions; but normally even very intensively farmed areas contain some lands that, for some or all of the year, can be used only for animals.

11 Just as outlay on land *improvement* is properly 'investment', and the value of such improvement is part of 'capital' and not of 'land'.

12 Moreover, while rural livestock (like rural lands) generally are assigned *in toto* to agriculture, much of the value of their output — dung for cooking fuel, draught for transport — accrues outside it.

13 Capital (or investment in extra capital) in schools, hospitals or government offices similarly (1) uses up allocable savings, and (2) yields income outside agriculture. This income is usually measured, rather artificially, by the value governments assign to the outputs and hence pay teachers, etc.; but income it certainly is, and in the non-farm sector.

14 J. R. Hicks, *Capital and Time*, Oxford, 1973, p. 11.

15 A. Ganz, 'Problems and Uses of Wealth Estimates in Latin America', in R. Goldsmith and C. Saunders, eds., *The Measurement of National Wealth* (Income and Wealth Series VIII), Bowes & Bowes, 1959, p. 231.

16 Little, pp. 38, 62, 223-4; G. Papanek, ed., *Development Policy: Theory and Practice*, Harvard, 1968, chapters 3 and 4.

17 Those who believe that this argument is unreal, that the farm is the only place in which small farmers *can* form productive capital, should read the accounts of their present productive diversification (into 'Z-goods') in S. Hymer and S. Resnick, 'A Model of an Agrarian Economy with Non-agricultural Activities', *American Economic Review*, September 1969, and E. Chuta and C. Liedholm, *A Progress Report on Research on Rural Small-scale Industry in Sierra Leone*, Working Paper no. 4, Departments of Agricultural Economics of Njala University and Michigan State University, Michigan, 1974.

18 The right balance is struck by Colin Clark, 'Capital Requirements in Agriculture: an International Comparison', *Review of Income and Wealth*, September 1967, who emphasises both agriculture's low

initial capital/output ratio, and *within* agriculture the high, though cheaply financed, capital/labour ratios of smaller farms. It is only because of cattle ownership that the latter point is valid; scarce capital, formed by the act of monetary saving, is normally worked more intensively by the small farmer.

19 The strange South African figures reflect (1) capital-using support and subsidy to the powerful White farmers, (2) a very high share of profits in agriculture, (3) probably relative overvaluation of livestock, (4) certainly—compare rows 9 and 10!—some curious inventory valuations, probably in gold-mining.

20 K. Ohkawa, 'Phases of agricultural development and economic growth', in K. Ohkawa, B. Johnston and H. Kaneda (eds.), *Agriculture and Economic Growth: Japan's Experience*, Princeton and Tokyo, 1970, pp. 21-2.

21 The apparent decline in money terms for India in row 10 of Table 7.1 is outweighed by the fact that a bundle of food output, in 1960-1, exchanged for 11% less of finished manufactures than in 1950-1 (*Statistical Abstracts of the Indian Union*, CSO, Delhi, 1958, p. 339, for 1950 and 1964; 1964, p. 225, for other years; '1950-1' price index $= \frac{3}{4}(1950) + \frac{1}{4}(1951)$ and similarly for 1960-1). The 'real quotient', in constant prices, thus rose. See also R. Krishna and S. S. Mehta, 'Productivity trends in large-scale industries', *EPW*, 16 October 1968; in India their average capital/output ratios were 1.8 in 1946-51, 2.2 in 1952-7 and 2.6 in 1958-63. (They have risen further since.)

22 Little, p. 73; not cited in Table 6.3 because Argentina is only marginally an LDC.

8   CAPITAL EFFICIENCY

1 This is sometimes misread as proving that agriculture has 'low absorptive capacity'. What it really suggests is that its share of administrative resources — people and cash — falls short of its share in investible resources. See Lipton/Streeten p. 86.

2 Taiwan, after similar correction, increases its quotient from 0.71 to 0.80, but remains unusual in having higher output per unit of capital outside agriculture than inside.

3 See below, note 17.

4 Balassa, pp. 281-2.

5 (1) Of the seven LDCs in Table 6.3, Little's data for the Philippines put the relative overvaluation of non-farm output lower than all but Malaya (it ties with Taiwan).
(2) The six LDCs for which Balassa (p. 60) estimates currency overvaluation for the mid-1960s are: Chile 68%, Pakistan 50%, Brazil 27%, Philippines 14.5%, Mexico 9%, Malaya 4%.

6 The quotients in Table 8.2 are the ratios of
$$\frac{\text{extra capital in non-agriculture}}{\text{extra capital in agriculture}} \text{ to } \frac{\text{extra output in non-agriculture}}{\text{extra output in agriculture}}$$
The repricings of Table 6.3 — averaging all seven countries and

taking the smaller of the Balassa and Little estimates where both exist — show that the value of the second bracketed component has to be cut by about 18%, to get from market prices to world prices in the average LDC. The above 'imported capital effect' normally requires a rise of 5 to 15% in the first component.

7 For 1960-5, the quotient (the last column of Table 8.2) was regressed on the ratio between agriculture's share in investment and in output (between the last and the last but one columns of Table 8.1). I excluded Malawi, Ethiopia, Syria and Cyprus, which all had very high quotients requiring special explanations (greater than 7; no other country was above 4.5). For the other thirteen countries, the quotient was related to 35% of variations in agriculture's relative 'investment endowment': the regression equation is $q = 3.43 - 2.12 \, x$ $(r^2 = 0.35)$.

8 W. Galenson and H. Leibenstein, 'Investment, Productivity and Economic Development', *Quarterly Journal of Economics*, 1955.

9 For a contrary view of bottlenecks, see A. O. Hirschman, 'Unbalanced Growth: an Espousal', in his *The Strategy of Economic Development*, Yale, 1958.

10 For instance the 'green revolution' requires capital in seed drills, in draught power for accelerated harvesting, in hand or power sprayers for pest control, and above all in tubewells or pumpsets for timely water application and in channels for both irrigation and drainage.

11 R. Evanson, in L. Reynolds, ed., *Theory of Agricultural Development*, Yale, 1975 (hereafter cited as Reynolds).

12 The medieval 'green revolution'—mouldboard ploughs and horse-shoes for stronger ploughing-horses, with oats in a three-crop, soil-restoring rotation—took six centuries to spread across Europe for lack of capital; yet for any village it was revolutionary indeed. See Lynn White, *Mediaeval Technology and Social Change*, Clarendon, 1962.

13 International free trade and negligible transport costs would *theoretically* remove these differences in relative prices.

14 Prices in an LDC are of course influenced by world prices. However, protection and transport costs (food especially has a high weight/value ratio) leave LDCs much leeway to influence the relative domestic prices of agricultural and other products.

15 Furthermore, an LDC is far likelier to import investment goods than consumer goods. The real cost to it of flour mills or sail-making equipment—their landed prices—would change very little, even if the LDC redistributed income so that the relative prices of yachts and bread on the home market changed a good deal.

16 The first and last of these causes are allowed for if, in calculating the quotient, we estimate each sector's output net of the cost of making good depreciation, but often such information is not available or not reliable.

17 Capital produced on the farm was 77% of all agricultural capital in

the Indian Punjab, 1950/1-1964/5; 33% in Taiwan, 1961-5; 36% in Colombia; 28% in Brazil, 1962-3. US Department of Agriculture, *Economic Progress of Agriculture in Developing Nations, 1950-68*, Foreign Agriculture Report no. 59, 1970, p. 36.

18　It does not follow, however, that a lack of systematic differences in returns to capital, as between farm and non-farm *projects*, would cast doubt on *sectoral k-disparities*. Agriculture has fewer, and more 'similarly produced', outputs than the rest of the economy. Hence its output response to a package of related investment projects is usually better. Thus, in an economy underinvesting in the farm *sector*, the return to particular *projects* — in irrigation in the North, in credit in the West, in pest-control in the South — is pulled down by the absence of complementary projects (for example, credit and pest-control in the North). The comparable effect outside agriculture is probably in most cases weaker.

19　D. Lall, *Wells and Welfare*, OECD Development Centre, 1972.

20　The IBRD's 'nine-volume survey' of land and water resources in Bangladesh, for example, showed that, among rural works, surfaced roads showed tiny rates of return, while returns on unsurfaced road-building and minor drainage and irrigation works were satisfactory or better.

21　For instance, the Kosi barrage in North Bihar owed its inception to Nehru's horror at flood damage in 1955; but the high-yielding wheat and rice varieties of 1965-75 have, after the event, made it a major contributor to farm output.

22　P. Hauser, cited in G. Breese, ed., *Urbanisation in Newly Developing Countries*, Prentice-Hall, 1966, p. 501 (hereafter cited as Breese). So why build? Because the share of profit is much higher in the $10-20 than the $40-50!

23　Also, a glance around any major African or Asian city will reveal major possibilities for alleviating its housing problem by property redistributions far less drastic than those (rightly) commended to, and sometimes imposed on, villagers in the name of land reform. Insofar as the poor could — if economies in urban housebuilding compelled it — be assigned housing in now-unused dwellings of the rich, the benefits of such housebuilding are even less!

24　S. H. Wellisz, 'Economic Development and Urbanisation', in Jakobson, p. 41.

25　*Ibid.*, p. 42.

26　This fact is perhaps overlooked because land and existing farm capital can usually be worked harder, to yield more output, if some new input (such as extra fertiliser) becomes available; while capital in the textile and other industries is believed to have a 'rated capacity' above which extra inputs (such as cotton for milling) cannot be handled. This 'rated capacity', however, is largely an engineering myth — consider the possibilities of extra shiftwork — and is anyhow seldom attained in LDC industries, not least because of low or late deliveries from an underendowed agriculture.

27 This is usually true, but not always: both construction periods and learning times are longer on a big and complex dam than on a small cotton-weaving plant.

28 Or (if it saves imports or is exported) might have released the foreign exchange to import.

29 L. Rosten, *The Joys of Yiddish*, Penguin, 1971, p. 94. It is the very incentive patterns, created by artificial favours to industry, that make it profitable for industrial entrepreneurs to use time in manoeuvring for investment licences rather than in raising levels of capacity use (Papanek, p. 62) and to keep down labour costs even if it implies excess capacity (G. C. Winston, 'Capital Utilisation in Economic Development', *EJ*, March 1971).

30 The irreversibility argument was first put forward, I believe, by J. Mirrlees at the May 1973 Bellagio Conference on the theory of agricultural development. The risk argument, discussed below, is due to T. N. Srinivasan, *Journal of Economic Literature*, vol. 8, 2, January 1970, pp. 456-8.

31 Countries, followed by the coefficient of variation of agricultural and non-agricultural output about the trend, were: Argentina, 3.8% and 13.8%; Philippines, 2.4% and 24.1%; South Korea, 0.1% and 24.6%; Syria, 19.1% and 26.7%; and Venezuela, 20.5% and 21.6%. *UNA 1960*, pp. 6, 175, 179; 1964, pp. 287, 325; 1967, pp. 5, 392, 539, 648, 734.

32 Streeten, pp. 71-116.

33 *Ibid.*, pp. 91-6, 109-16.

34 A. O. Hirschman, *A Bias for Hope*, Yale University Press, 1971, pp. 42-73.

35 D. Lall, 'Employment, Income Distribution and a Poverty Redressal Index', *World Development*, March/April 1973, pp. 121-5. See also the discussion in Chenery of 'poverty weights'.

36 It is true, and consistent, that (1) agriculture suffers from relative deprivation of, and shows the highest returns to extra, administrative resources; (2) it is in non-agriculture, especially infrastructure, that yield from *extra* investments — especially large, complex and integrated ones — is most cut back by administrative bottlenecks.

37 Hirschman considers, and rejects, assigning *more* capital to the power sector because there is a power shortage; this would be 'of little avail' where the low power output is due to 'dispersal of effort . . . [too low power] rates, the frequent changes in plans and personnel' (pp. 47-8). For me, if such factors are endemic in a sector and render its k chronically high, this argues for a *cut* in its capital assignments. Such 'power shortage' is clearly not due to demand that outruns installed capacity.

38 To bring about these 'marginal' equalities is no simple matter of evolutionary adjustments. It requires new motives, probably a new power structure, sometimes perhaps a 'cultural revolution'.

39 In a joint paper (1962) with Lindblom, also reprinted in *A Bias for Hope*, Hirschman sharpens this argument into what is surely total

unviability: 'To start by developing industry is likely to induce more compelling pressures (because of the resulting food shortages or, if food is imported, . . . balance-of-payments difficulties) than if the sequence is started by an expansion in agricultural output.' It is not unfair to read this as advice to do what is wrong, because it will 'induce more compelling pressures' to do what is right than if right had been done straight away.

40 L. and S. Rudolph, *The Modernity of Tradition*, University of Chicago Press, 1967; M. Lipton, 'The Theory of the Optimising Peasant', *JDS*, April 1968; and, for an account of the risks to the poor from transformations that relax social constraints without replacing associated social guarantees, Epstein.

9 THE MYTHS OF URBANISATION

1 M. Todaro and J. Harris, 'Migration, Unemployment and Development: a Two-Sector Analysis', *American Economic Review*, Vol. 60, 1970, pp. 126-42.

2 G. Becker, *The Economics of Discrimination*, 2nd ed., Chicago, 1971, esp. pp. 84-5.

3 *First Agricultural Labour Enquiry*, Ministry of Labour, Delhi, 1955, chart facing p. 19. In 1950, at the time of the enquiry, 30% of rural households depended mainly on performing 'agricultural labour' for others. Today the proportion is probably somewhat higher, but the share of 'attached' workers slightly lower.

4 For discussions of urban-rural and intra-rural literacy differentials, see pp. 261-3. High correlations between educational level and propensity to migrate are revealed for Taiwan (Y. C. Tsui and T. L. Lin, *Chinese-American Joint Series on Rural Reconstruction: Economic Digest Series No. 16*, May 1964, p. 19), Colombia (T. P. Schultz, *Population Growth and Internal Migration in Colombia*, RAND for AID, Washington, 1969, p. 63), Chile (B. M. Herrick, *Urban Migration and Economic Development in Chile*, MIT Press, 1965, 78-9) and Ghana (T. C. Caldwell, 'Determinants of Rural-Urban Migration in Ghana', *Population Studies*, 22, 3, November 1968). See also Connell.

5 It is in rural-to-*rural* movements that the very poor predominate (Connell). The poorest villagers often achieve, too, temporary transformation into jobhunting townsmen: 'The urban poor are only an overflow of the rural poor into urban areas' (V. M. Dandekar and N. Rath, 'Poverty in India', *EPW*, 21 January 1971).

6 Caldwell, 'Determinants of Rural-Urban Migration in Ghana', *Population Studies*. For the possibility that migration may nevertheless help the remaining villagers, see p. 221.

7 A. Gerschenkron, 'Agrarian Policies and Industrialisation: Russia 1871-1917', in Habakkuk. It is of course not contended that white farmers' pressure is the *only* reason for restrictions on non-white urbanisation by the white-minority government in South Africa.

8   S. H. Wellisz, 'Economic Development and Urbanisation', in Jakob-
    son, pp. 45-6.
9   Compare the response, to a growing world energy shortage, that
    would deny the world's poor countries the chance of energy-intensive
    modernisation—even where such a path was efficient.
10 N. V. Sovani, 'The Analysis of "Over-Urbanisation"', in Breese, p. 324.
11 Nor do I argue that reductions in urban bias would, of themselves,
    necessarily apply a squeeze so selective as to make cities more
    genuinely 'industrial'.
12 Laquian, in Jakobson, p. 201; McGee, in Jakobson, p. 159.
13 A. R. Jolly, 'Rural-Urban Migration: Dimensions, Causes, Issues and
    Policies', in *Prospects for Employment Opportunities in the 1970s*
    (Report of the 1970 Cambridge Employment Conference), HMSO,
    1971, p. 119.
14 A. Dotson, 'Urbanisation, Administration and National Development:
    a Prolegomenon to Theory', SE Asia Development Advisory Group
    Paper No. 60, Asia Society (New York), 1969, pp. 7, 11.
15 Breese, p. 135.
16 Why are the miseries of the urban black in South Africa so well arti-
    culated, and the far deeper miseries of his rural brother (or, usually,
    sister) so generally ignored?
17 The employer's choice of capital-intensive urban techniques—while
    assisted by import policies to cheapen them, and goaded by trade
    unions that raise the price of already urbanised labour—is partly
    a response to bias against new migrants from the villages. The last
    group of immigrants is often the most hostile to any new group, be-
    cause of its insecurity, its residence in the area of competition—and
    in part because recent migrants are often 'upwardly mobile' socially
    and hence less tolerant of the next competitors to 'arrive'. See, for
    example, E. J. B. Rose et al., *Colour and Citizenship*, Oxford, 1969,
    p. 561. The observation that more urban jobs will only swell the
    number of job-seekers, and thus do nothing to lower urban (!) un-
    employment rates (Todaro and Harris, 'Migration, Unemployment
    and Development: a Two-Sector Analysis') also manifests urban bias.
18 A strange distinction anyway; if I move from A to B, I do so because
    I prefer B to A. If A is a house on fire, or B a gold-mine, the causality
    is clear: but if on balance I prefer B to A, it makes little sense to ask,
    'Do you prefer it because of B or because of A?' Most migration—
    except for disaster treks—is just such 'preference on balance'. It
    does make sense to ask what *changes* the balance: more urban appeal
    than before, or less rural.
19 Kuznets, p. 313.
20 West Asia, nine rises, two falls, four static; Latin America, nineteen
    rises, seven falls, eleven static (*FAO/S 1970*, pp. 228-9, 238, 247,
    256-7). We define 'static' to include rises or falls of up to 1%, in partial
    deference to the inaccuracy of the basic data. Predictions that the
    share of people in agriculture will fall in 1962-85 from 70 to 60% in
    Asia and the Far East, and from 82 to 70% in Africa south of the

Sahara (FAO, *Provisional Indicative World Plan*, vol. 1, p. 23), thus seem out of line with the facts of recent development.

21 J. Krishnamurty, 'Working Force in 1971 Census', *EPW*, 15 January 1972, p. 117.

22 Jolly, 'Rural-Urban Migration: Dimensions, Causes, Issues and Policies', in *Prospects for Employment Opportunities in the 1970s.*

23 H. Lubell, 'Urban development and unemployment in Calcutta', *International Labour Review*, July 1973, p. 30; *Current Digest*, Hong Kong, June 1971, summarised in 'Balancing Population and Food', in P. Piotrow, ed., *Population and Family Planning in the People's Republic of China*, Victor-Bostrom Fund (New York), 1971, p. 14; UN, *Growth of the World's Urban and Rural Population 1920-2000*, UN/ST/SOA/SER.A/44 (New York), 1969, pp. 12, 24.

24 *Growth of the World's Urban and Rural Population 1920-2000*, p. 64. From 1940 to 1960 'agglomerated' population grew by 4.2% yearly in poor countries, as against 1.2% in rural areas and small towns. For 1960-80, the projections are respectively down to 3.9% and up to 1.7%. Such a decline was already observed in India in 1951-61 : 'Rural-urban [population] redistribution showed a general upward trend until 1941-51; [reversed] during 1951-61', partly because natural increase was higher in rural areas. K. C. Zachariah and J. Ambannavar, 'Population Redistribution in India', in A. Bose, ed., *Patterns of Population Change in India*, Allied (Bombay), 1967, p. 102.

25 A. Bose, 'Migration Streams in India', in *International Union for the Scientific Study of Population, Sydney Conference, August 1967*, esp. pp. 598-9, 602-5. Similarly small movements in Pakistan are suggested by M. Afzal, *ibid.*, esp. pp. 692-3; see also Bose's paper in Jakobson, p. 98.

26 McGee, in Jakobson, pp. 161-2.

27 Notably in Nigeria (1953-63), Sudan (1956-64/5), UAR (1960-6), Honduras (1950-61), Mexico (1950-60-70, with reclassification accounting for a huge part of apparent urbanisation), Brazil (where there were eleven localities over 100,000 in 1950 but thirty-one in 1960), Colombia (1951-64), Venezuela (1950-61-69), India (1951-61) and Pakistan (1951-61-70): *UND*, 1963, 1970, 1971. Detailed country data calculated from W. D. Harris, Jr., *The Growth of Latin American Cities*, Ohio, 1971, pp. 87, 96, 112; H. T. Khazaneh, in *Proceedings of 1969 Sydney Conference*, International Union for the Scientific Study of Population, p. 756; J. B. Knight, 'Rural-urban Income Comparisons and Migration in Ghana', *Bulletin of the Oxford University Institute of Economics and Statistics,* 1972, pp. 203-4. A remedy would be to raise the 'borderline' by the intercensal rate of natural increase: thus in India, where villages stopped at 5,000 in 1951, they would stop in 1971, not at 5,000 as they did, but at (5000 x $\frac{550}{356}$ million); that is, 5,000 times the ratio of the 1971 to the 1951 population, or about 8,000.

28 Connell.

29 For the historical context, see J. F. I. Turner, 'Uncontrolled Urban Settlement: Problems and Policies', in Breese, pp. 512-13.

30 K. C. Zachariah, 'Bombay Migration Study: A Pilot Analysis of Migration to an "Indian Metropolis",' in Breese, p. 362.

31 Connell.

32 *UND 1970*, Table 6, and corresponding Tables in other issues.

33 There may be none, because typically more boys are born (105 to 110 per 100 girls) and the higher male death-rate has its main impact after childbearing age; and perhaps because girls, being less sought after, receive less care from their families and thus show higher early death rates, relative to boys, than in the West.

34 The fact that some village females later follow male migrants is hardly relevant, since the delay suffices to create the unbalanced urban sex ratio, and hence to drive down urban birth rates. It should be noted that the excess of 'men without women' increases the crime rate and the incidence of prostitution and VD, and hence the external cost of migration (pp. 229-30) and also makes people miserable; all this must help to put off future migrants.

35 Wellisz, 'Economic Development and Urbanisation', in Jakobson, pp. 41, 50; B. J. L. Berry, 'City Size and Economic Development', in Jakobson, p. 141.

36 C. Furtado, cited in Breese, p. 483.

37 ILO, *Matching Employment Opportunities and Expectations: a Programme of Action for Ceylon*, Geneva, 1971, pp. 24, 31-6, 117-20 (hereafter cited as *Ceylon Report*).

38 See also Connell; Knight, 'Rural-urban Income Comparisons and Migration in Ghana', *Bulletin of the Oxford University Institute of Economics and Statistics*, 1972, p. 224.

39 Knight, *ibid.*, p. 224; S. N. Agarwala, 'Socio-economic and Demographic characteristics of the Rural Migrants and the Non-Migrants', *Journal of the Institute of Economic Research*, vol. 3, 1968, pp. 1-15; Connell.

40 Zachariah, in Breese, p. 363.

41 L. P. Vidyarthi, *Cultural Configuration of Ranchi*, Planning Commission, Delhi, 1969, p. 92.

42 Bose, in Jakobson, p. 100.

43 Breese, p. 82, citing D. J. Bogue and K. I. Zachariah (1962), on India.

44 Knight, 'Rural-urban Comparisons and Migration in Ghana', pp. 216-17; Connell.

45 J. Abu-Lughod (on Cairo), in Breese, p. 378. Her research was first published in 1960. Since then declining job chances (and rising standards of paper qualifications for jobs) have in many Third World cities pushed large proportions even of 'bright youths' into the informal sector (which to some extent, as suggested, replicates rural culture).

46 The fact that immigrants to the town—because willing to take temporary work while they look for something more settled—often have lower unemployment rates than settled urban populations (with

higher levels of education and expectations) in no way refutes this. If such immigrants merely drift among low-paid 'informal' work, will they stay in the town for long? See Connell.

47 Zachariah, in Breese, p. 365. My italics.

48 In countries now developed, the fact that trade unions grew up last among farm labourers (and are still weakest there) probably owes much to the 'brain drain' of potential union leaders through townward migration.

49 L. P. Vidyarthi, *Cultural Configuration of Ranchi*, p. 92; Connell. The myth of huge urban-rural remittances, even net of reverse flows, may stem from false analogies with work-seeking *international* migration. Turkish workers in Germany, Indians and Pakistanis in Britain and Algerians in France indeed remit huge sums to their families in the country of origin—but mainly to urban areas. For migrants to cities *within* LDCs, wages and job chances (and hence capacity to remit) are much lower.

10 THE NEED FOR SAVINGS

1 In rich countries with unemployment problems, Keynes argued that *inequality was a bad thing because savings are a bad thing*: redistribute income from savers to spenders, and both demand and employment will rise (J. M. Keynes, *General Theory of Employment, Interest and Money*, Macmillan, 1936, pp. 372-3). This argument will not do in LDCs, where unemployment has different causes, so that simply boosting demand will raise prices rather than output, especially for food (M. Lipton, 'Financing Economic Development' in Seers, pp. 241-6). Here the case is that *savings are a good thing but inequality does not help them much.*

2 Whether these are private individuals or the state does not affect the argument.

3 The main reason why a unit of investment usually yields more output in agriculture and in rural areas—that it is associated with more human effort—is the same as the reason why a larger part of that yield goes to non-savers, to workers rather than capital-owners.

4 This argument implies more than downgrading agriculture: that wages are 'worse' than profits, that inequality is 'good for growth' —and that benefit/cost analysis and project-evaluation must echo these values. Costs are downvalued—while benefits get a premium —if they comprise income for industrialists who build the project but are likely to save their earnings. (A. K. Sen et al., *Guidelines for Project Evaluation*, UNIDO, Vienna, 1972, pp. 67-70; I. M. D. Little and J. Mirrlees, *Manual of Industrial Project Evaluation in Developing Countries*, vol. II, OECD, 1969, esp. pp. 161-2.) The push given to non-agricultural, anti-egalitarian investment is clear.

5 The idea that only extra *physical* capital is investment—and that only finance of such capital is saving—will one day be as antiquated as the parallel view that only goods, but not services, are part of the

value of national output. This is a view originally, and unfairly, associated with the eighteenth-century French 'Physiocrats'; specifically rejected as a principle of social accounting by Marx; yet incorporated in his name into the 'net material product' of East European statistics.

6 Temporarily one can pay the doctor, engineer or builder's labourer by running an import surplus, or by just printing the money. The former cannot go on forever; the latter means the money is spent to bid up the prices of consumer goods, so there is still 'forced saving' at the cost of consumption, just as if (but less equitably or predictably than if) the doctor, etc., had been paid by cutting consumption directly in the first place.

7 People are loth to believe that by hiding my income under the bed I 'save' and thus pay a doctor, or a builder's labourer, to produce non-consumption goods; but it is perfectly true. I have been paid income for producing a certain addition to output of goods and services. By not requiring as much in current consumption as I have earned and produced, I free the balance for non-consumption uses.

8 M. Blaug, *Economic Theory in Retrospect*, 2nd ed., Heinemann, 1968, pp. 190, 280.

9 Both urban and rural 'diversion from consumption to finance economic surplus for future production' are underestimated by the ratio of savings to income, because private outlays on health, education, etc., are not counted as savings in the statistics from which such ratios are calculated. The underestimation is perhaps relatively more important in rural areas, because access to free or subsidised health and education is so much worse than in the cities (ch. 11), so that a larger share of income has to be used (officially 'spent', conceptually 'saved') on buying them privately.

10 S. Freud, *The Interpretation of Dreams* (1900) Hogarth Press, 1953, pt. I, pp. 119-20.

11 Freedom from Hunger Campaign, Basic Documents: No. 5, *Nutrition and Working Efficiency*, Rome, 1962.

12 Sue Schofield, 'Seasonal Factors affecting Nutrition in Different Age Groups', JDS, October 1974.

13 This is logically quite distinct from the last argument—that *income from producing* output, insofar as it is steered to poor rural people, is (albeit perhaps saved to a lesser extent) likelier to be spent on consumption of food, and hence to raise production later.

14 F. G. Bailey, in M. N. Srinivas, ed., *India's Villages*, Asia, 1960, pp. 135-9.

15 Or even if the food is eaten directly by the families that grow it.

16 Also in some cases by eating up so much imports, for heavy industrial investment, that more and more *existing* industrial capacity stands idle for want of imported raw materials.

17 Suppose we maximise saving out of a given income Y by maximising the share of profits. Income consists of profits and wages: $Y = P + W$. Profits equal the profit rate, times the number of units of capital;

wages equal the wage rate, times the number of workers; thus $Y = pK + wL$, and to maximise the savings ratio S/Y we must (since much more profits than wages are saved) maximise $pK/(pK + wL)$. The savings argument rightly points out that an industrial concentration of investment will raise K relative to L and—other things being equal—help maximise S/Y. We here object that the other things are systematically not equal: that raising K relative to L involves raising w (by improving industrial workers' bargaining power—especially if, as is normally the case, there is no *absolute* fall in L) and lowering p (because of diminishing returns to capital). The maximum profit share, even if desirable (and we have ignored the obvious damage to today's poor), cannot be achieved by allocating investment to maximise the capital/labour ratio (which would indeed involve a very high concentration upon urban industry).

18 Certainly *some* of the apparent disparity in marginal capital/output ratios between agriculture and industry, revealed in Table 8.2, is due to the greater concealment in agriculture of such capital formation. However, this does not seriously weaken the force of the argument presented by this disparity for raising the share of allocable investment that goes to farming. Investment put there by the farmer's own hands, in his spare time, is not a scarce (or even allocable) resource; what counts is the extra output associated with extra scarce, allocable capital, whether imported or made by domestic investment-goods industries.

19 P. Eklund, 'An Analysis of Capital Flows between the Agricultural and Non-agricultural Sectors of West Pakistan', *Economics Department Working Paper no. 41*, IBRD, Washington, 1969.

20 Comment by Anisur Rahman, in E. A. G. Robinson and M. Kidron, eds., *Economic Development in South Asia*, IEA/Macmillan, 1970 (hereafter cited as Robinson), p. 521. The general issue of concealed rural saving is dealt with by K. N. Raj, in Robinson, pp. 278-87, in an Indian context.

21 A. A. Rozental, 'A Note on the Sources and Uses of Funds in Thai Agriculture', *Economic Development and Cultural Change*, vol. 18, no. 3, 1970.

22 E. H. Schebeck, 'An Analysis of Capital Flows between the Agricultural and Non-agricultural Sectors in India', *Economics Department Working Paper no. 42*, IBRD, Washington, 1969, p. 12.

23 P. G. K. Panikar, 'An Essay on Rural Savings in India', in Shukla.

24 C. Clark, 'Capital Requirements in Agriculture: an International Comparison', *Review of Income and Wealth*, September 1967. This is, however, oddly interpreted as 'relative wastefulness of capital requirements on the small farms' (p. 211); in fact, the small farms in his data (for Uttar Pradesh, India) use half the implements, by value, per unit of product used by the big ones, but considerably more livestock (p. 210) and, probably, more home-made, on-farm bunds and other structures.

25 National Council of Applied Economic Research, *Urban Income and*

Saving, Delhi, 1963, p. 78; *All-India Rural Household Survey*, vol. II, Delhi, 1965, p. 96. (The latter survey was slightly later, prices slightly higher, and rupees thus worth slightly less, strengthening the argument.) See chapter 12, note 23, for similar evidence for Pakistan. In the USA, the proportion of a given income saved goes up so sharply, as the size of a community falls, that small farming villages save as much per person as richer urban centres. R. T. Norris, *Theory of Consumers' Demand*, Yale, 1952.

26 See J. Locke, 'Some Considerations of the Consequences of Lowering the Interest and Raising the Value of Money' (1961), in *Works*, 1963, Scientia (Darmstadt), vol. V, esp. pp. 7-9.

27 It is notable that total credit goes *up* when rural communities get richer. The extra demand for producer credit—and the growing willingness to supply it, as borrowers become more creditworthy—outweighs the reduced demand for consumer credit.

28 D. Thorner, *Agricultural Co-operatives in India*, Asia, 1965.

29 It is notable that the parts of India where rural-cooperative credit societies do relatively well, such as Maharashtra, feature less inequitable land tenure than other parts of the country—so a small farmer is 'less unequal' to his bigger neighbour.

30 Indeed so-called 'producer credit' will always be diverted from its intended purpose to a great extent, so long as the highest-yielding use of such credit for the small borrower is not to invest but to repay part of a usurious consumption loan—thus shedding a burden of perhaps 35 to 50% a year, more than almost any investment could yield, and without risk!

31 K. Krishnamurthy, 'International Comparisons of Savings Rates: A Review', IBRD Working Paper, 1968; S. Kuznets, *Modern Economic Growth: Rate, Structure, Spread*, Yale, 1966, p. 245.

32 R. P. Dore, *Tokugawa Education*, Routledge, 1965, chapter VII, esp. p. 261. See also Kuznets, p. 111, rows 10-14, col. 5.

33 For 1950-1 to 1958-9 the regression of total Indian savings on agricultural income was—
$$S = -0.2137 + 0.1501\ A \qquad (r^2 = 0.22);$$
on non-agricultural income—
$$S = -0.6685 + 0.2605\ N;$$
and for both together—
$$S = -6.05 + 0.2897\ A - 0.0435\ N \qquad (r^2 = 0.66)$$
For 1960-1 to 1969-70 the corresponding equations were
$$S = -0.8162 + 0.2259\ A \qquad (r^2 = 0.90);$$
$$S = -362.99 + 0.2520\ N \qquad (r^2 = 0); \text{ and}$$
$$S = -424.49 + 0.3678\ A - 0.11\ N \qquad (r^2 = 0.98)$$
Standard errors have not been calculated, lest these results be taken too seriously; they serve only to refute any claim that extra farm income is clearly less important than extra non-farm income in generating extra total saving. Central Statistical Office, *Estimates of National Income*, January 1963, May 1971; Reserve Bank of India *Bulletins*, August 1961, May 1971, July 1974.

34 We leave aside, for the moment, the important issue of 'complementarity' — A low v investment in one sector might score globally by improving the performance of capital (and thus raising v) in another part of the economy. For various reasons this is not, on balance, likely to tilt the argument against farm investment. See pp. 204-5.

35 Alan S. Manne, ed., *Investments for Capacity Expansion: Size, Location and Time Phasing*, MIT Press, 1967, esp. pp. 141-3.

36 K. Wicksell, *Selected Papers on Economic Theory*, Allen & Unwin, 1948, p. 183; cited and discussed by Streeten, pp. 88-9.

37 Not of course, that high yield and social efficiency always go hand in hand, especially in the presence of price distortions (ch. 13); but they are likely to be related positively most of the time.

38 R. I. McKinnon, *Money and Capital in Economic Development*, Brookings, 1973; E. S. Shaw, *Financial Deepening in Economic Development*, Oxford (New York), 1973.

39 Not normally as a corrupt practice at all; it is after all about these firms that the board knows most. A manager of a big branch of a Maharashtra bank told me about this practice of credit rationing by interlocking directorships in 1965, before India nationalised the banks; but, irrespective of bank ownership, it is likely to prevail wherever bank credit is artificially cheap.

40 R. Firth and B. S. Yamey, eds., *Capital, Saving and Credit in Peasant Societies*, Allen & Unwin, 1964, esp. pp. 27-8, 31-2, 49-51, 117-18. The contributors of course also show how traders, brokers and relatives in the city can ease 'lock-in'; the point is that such a problem exists, as it hardly does in a developed country.

41 It is true that 'lock-in' to the non-farm sector means high s for future reinvestment there, as well as low v. However (1) development could well ease intersectoral capital flows, (2) growth of farm income should raise the farm s, (3) the evidence does not, conversely, suggest a convergence between the farm and non-farm sectors as regards the value of v.

42 It gets there pretty fast. Even if we assume that it takes the average income receiver a week to spend such weekly income as is not to be saved, within seventeen weeks £972 will have 'leaked' into savings in this example.

43 Strictly, the requirement is even more extreme: there has to be a group of sectors that (1) save nothing and (2) spend all extra income only on products of other sectors in the group. Incidentally, it does not affect the argument if the savings ratio of a sector changes during the circulation of income; if it rises, the total of savings is achieved faster, but it does not increase.

44 Note for neo-classical economists: if the exchange rate does not overvalue the domestic currency, and if the interest rates in local markets do not impede investment desired by the planners, and if there is neither a foreign-exchange shortage nor a savings-finance constraint on investment, this does not matter!

45 Can one object that the total effects of all the rounds of spending on

foreign exchange, not just on imports, determine its availability to support investment? If so, it is the balance between the impact of investment upon a sector's output of 'tradeables' and upon total demand for 'tradeables' that decides these effects; and agriculture scores high because of its high yields on extra capital.

46 This is also true of industrial investment, though for a different reason: the time-lag between investment and 'full-stream' output, the 'gestation period', is longer than in agriculture.

47 Of course this is only one of the two abysses that are separated by the price-policy tightrope. The other is that of excessive inflation of consumer necessities—kerosene, coarse grains, cotton cloth. Neither equitably nor, in a political sense, viably can these be made the 'transferees' in a process of keeping inflation off investment goods.

48 If C is singular, each sector (row and column) depends linearly on others; e.g. if each sector buys 50 gm. more tea (T) if and only if it also buys 80 gm. more milk (M) and 90 gm. more sugar (S). We then *reduce* C by one row and column. The T, M, and S rows and columns give way to two rows and two columns of composite TMS-sectors. (Each of the four new lines has fixed, normally different, ratios of T to M and S.) If need be, repeat the process until a non-singular matrix results. The proof in the text, for this matrix, implies the key statement (p. 253, para, 3) for C.

49 The 'ultimately' shows that this has nothing to do with the 'Keynesian' or accounting identity of savings and investment, which holds in any period however short. Initial-plus-multiplier savings (which, in Keynesian fashion, equals initial-plus-multiplier investment) is *exactly double* the initial investment (which, in Keynesian fashion, equals the initial saving).

50 If this is possible, then there will be within C one block (say n by n, $0 < n < m$), C_N, for which the step from equation (3) to equation (4) is invalid; for $D_N = C_N D_N$ (where D_N is the subvector of D feeding initial investment demands into the n sectors comprising the submatrix C_N). Hence (4) must in this case read $S = 0$. We can get to the same answer by observing that $C_N = I_N$

11 THE RURAL SKILL DRAIN

1 For evidence that it is the better-educated villager who migrates to the city see chapter 9, note 4. Moreover, migrants are concentrated among men aged 15-25—a group responsible for agricultural innovation out of all proportion to its share in farm management. (E. Rogers and L. Svenning, *Modernisation among Peasants*, Rinehart & Winston, 1969, pp. 302-3; E. Rogers, *Characteristics of Agricultural Innovators and Other Adopter Categories*, Ohio Agricultural Experiment Station, 1961, pp. 14-15.) Rural skill drain has been spotlit as a source of poverty by men as diverse as Marshall, Kautsky and Gandhi (ch. 4, notes 46 and 84).

2 See Table 11.1 Since rural persons comprise 79.6% of the 19-22 age-group but receive only 34.1% of university and college places, their chances of such places relate to urban chances as $\frac{34.1}{79.6}$ to $\frac{100-34.1}{100-79.6}$ or about 1 to $7\frac{1}{2}$.

3 Or even more 'her'; the disparity in prospects of schooling between city and village is even greater for girls than for boys, and the prospect of improvement by migration is even smaller. In Nigeria in 1961-6, 50% of boys and 53% of girls aged 6-12 were enrolled for primary education in Lagos City; in the district including Ibadan City the proportions were 51% and 38% respectively; in rural districts the differential was bigger—Oshun 26% and 15%, Oyo 28% and 17%. *Interim Report of ILO Mission to Study Education in a Rural Area of Western Nigeria,* Ministry of Planning and Social Development (Lagos), 1967, p. 38.

4 Even more than appears from Table 11.1, because we shall see that the *calibre* of educands is also less in rural areas; and because most poor countries feature an even greater degree of urban grab of rural ex-educands than does India.

5 If the latter is omitted, regressive income redistribution towards educated persons is implied. Given the political realities, the policy outlined here would mean, at best, allotting most of the fruits of *growth* in educated persons' incomes to those working in the rural sector.

6 Three sources of earning capacity are transferred to the town when an educated villager migrates thither: not just his training, but also his ability and the prestige attached to his qualification. Hence one cannot measure the 'returns to education' by the extra income earned by educated persons, because such extra earnings also reflect their greater native wit and/or society's regard for certificates. This objection, while valid, does not vitiate the measure of *transfer* used here.

7 This is simply the extra yearly income associated with each type of education (from M. Blaug, R. Layard and M. Woodhall, *The Causes of Graduate Unemployment in India,* Allen Lane, 1969, p. 212-34 — hereafter cited as Blaug), multiplied by the Table 11.1 figures of numbers of each type of ex-educand transferred from village to town. Extra remittances to the village due to the fact that migrants are educated should really be deducted from this figure; conversely, one should add support costs to village families of educating those who later urbanise, plus costs of supporting educated migrant jobless (boosted by forward discounting, because rural families incur these costs *before* receiving any remittances). Few usable data exist, but unpublished estimates by the Agro-economic Research Centre, Madras University, from ten Tamilnadu village studies for all migrants from village to town, indicate that urban-rural and rural-urban cash flows were about equal. Indeed annual village-to-town remittances in the mid-1950s exceeded reverse flows by (Rs. 1,850 —

Rs. 1,290), or Rs. 570, per village, if we exclude one village, Rija-gambiram, with large-scale emigration to the city in the wake of successive droughts followed by a cyclone. The separate issue of urban-rural allocation of costs and in-school benefits of state educa-tion is dealt with in UN (Bangkok).

8 A. K. Sen, 'Aspects of Indian Education', in P. Chaudhuri, ed., *Aspects of Indian Economic Development,* Allen & Unwin, 1971, pp. 152-5, and the work of D. Chaudhuri cited therein; for a dif-ferent approach to related evidence, see Rogers, *Characteristics of Agricultural Innovators and Other Adopter Categories.*

9 A. M. Khusro, *A Survey of Living and Working Conditions of Stu-dents of the University of Delhi,* Asia, London, 1967, pp. 31, 72, 77.

10 V. K. R. V. Rao, *University Education and Employment,* Institute of Economic Growth, Delhi, 1961, pp. 10-11.

11 *Fact Book on Manpower—Pt. III—Scientific and Technical Person-nel,* 2nd ed., Institute for Applied Manpower Research, New Delhi, 1970, p. 259, for numbers of teachers; we assume that at each level of education eight out of ten persons of teachable age live in rural areas.

12 Furthermore, rural teachers were somewhat less likely to be proper-ly qualified, even at any given level; in primary schools, the propor-tion of trained teachers in urban areas was 97,457/130,822 or 75%, but in rural areas 679,979/930,770 or 73% (Blaug).

13 *Education, Human Resources and Development in Argentina,* OECD, Paris, 1967, pp. 146, 148.

14 Excellent evidence appears in *Interim Report of ILO Mission to Study Education in a Rural Area of Western Nigeria,* Ministry of Planning and Social Development, 1967. In villages, 57% of teachers said they would prefer some other job at the same salary; in towns, it was 'only' 34%. In the village primary schools, 56.3% of classrooms had no ceilings (towns 17.4%) and the effect of unshielded heat 'was not conducive to alert mental activity'. In schools serving villages with under seven hundred inhabitants, student wastage was a stag-gering 85% (rural towns 47%, Ibadan City 20%). *Interim Report,* pp. 13-14, 19, 47.

15 Sen, 'Aspects of Indian Education', in Chaudhuri, ed., *Aspects of Indian Economic Development,* p. 157.

16 Blaug, pp. 69-70. Similar disparities exist elsewhere; for Sri Lanka, see *Ceylon Report,* pp. 27-8.

17 Blaug, p. 178; G. S. Chatterjee and N. Bhattacharya, 'Rural-Urban Differences in Consumer Prices', *EPW,* 17 May 1969, p. 852.

18 Central Bank of Ceylon, *Survey of Consumer Finances,* 1963. The 'median' is the one in the middle, with as many better off as are worse off in the category; where available it is a better guide to the typical situation than a simple average.

19 J. B. Knight, *Measuring Urban-Rural Income Differentials,* paper to Conference on Urban Unemployment in Africa, (mimeo), Insti-tute of Development Studies, Brighton, September 1971.

20 *Education, Human Resources and Development in Argentina,* OECD, p. 279.

21 The urban agricultural workforce is substantial in India (about 10% of urban workers).

22 T. Burgess, R. Layard and P. Pant, *Manpower and Educational Development in India 1961-1986,* Oliver & Boyd, 1968, pp. 3, 66.

23 UNESCO, *Statistical Yearbook 1969,* Paris, 1970, Tables 2.13, 2.15. There were still no *agricultural* scientists or other specialists graduating, in the latest year for which by 1974 data were available, in the Congo, Dahomey, Ivory Coast, Mozambique, Rwanda, Senegal, Tanzania, Togo, Zambia, Guyana or Laos: UNESCO, *Statistical Yearbook 1973,* Paris, 1974, Table 4.4

24 OECD, *Statistics of the Labour Force in 53 Countries,* Paris, 1969, and *Education, Human Resources and Development in Argentina,* Paris, 1967.

25 *Nigeria's Professional Manpower in Selected Occupations,* National Manpower Board, Lagos, 1967, p. 22. Agricultural specialists are slightly younger on average, but this is too small a difference to account for much of the pay gap.

26 *Census of India 1961: Monograph Series no. 1: Scientific and Technical Personnel,* New Delhi, 1965, pp. 26, 28.

27 One of Tom Lehrer's grimly realistic jokes concerns a student who took to medicine, 'specialising in the diseases of the rich'.

28 J. Bryant, *Health and the Developing World,* Cornell, 1969, p. 52.

29 *Fact Book on Manpower—Pt. III—Scientific and Technical personnel,* 2nd edn., Institute for Applied Manpower Research, Delhi, 1970, p. 167. Doctors in the scientific sense of the word ('allopathic') were only 18% of all physicians working in rural areas, as against 43% in urban areas.

30 *Manpower Survey: Health and Medical Manpower,* National Institute of Health Administration and Education and Institute of Applied Manpower Research, Delhi, 1966, pp. 19-25; rural areas (with about 80% of India's population) were served by 35% of India's male doctors, but by under 13% of her female doctors.

31 O. Gish, *Doctor Migration and World Health,* Bell, 1971, pp. 66, 77-8, 101 (hereafter cited as Gish).

32 The concept of the 'patient gradient' is due to Richard Jolly and Maurice King; see their paper, 'The Organisation of Health Services', in M. King, ed., *Medical Care in Developing Countries,* OUP (Nairobi), 1966, sections 2.9 to 2.11.

33 *UND 1970,* p. 137; M. Sharpston, 'Uneven Geographical Distribution of Medical Care; a Ghanaian Case Study', *JDS,* January 1972, pp. 211-12. See also Bryant, *Health and the Developing World,* p. 52.

34 In 1968, in the two weeks preceding a survey in Colombia (where urban health bias is not extreme — p. 448), 31 rural persons per 10,000 inhabitants received consultations, as against 100 per 10,000 from big towns. ILO, *Towards Full Employment in Colombia,* Geneva, 1970, p. 252 (hereafter cited as *Colombia Report*).

35 In Colombia, village women received medical attention in 18% of pregnancies (women from big towns, 73%) and were attended by doctors in 16% of deliveries (76%): *Colombia Report*, p. 253.

36 In Western countries many comparable conditions are treated by self-medication. So again *appropriate* rural education could help

37 In Colombia, 63% of all rural consultations were paid for by the patients in full, as against 46% of consultations by the patients in big towns (*Colombia Report*, p. 254). Yet the latter patients are both wealthier and getting better medicine.

38 M. Lipton and J. Firn, *The Erosion of a Relationship: Indo-British Relations since 1962*, Oxford (for Royal Institute of International Affairs), 1975, chapter 7.

39 Gish, pp. 87, 107, 111, 113.

40 A few half-hearted efforts have been made: see *Ceylon Report*, pp. 226-7.

41 This argument is forcefully advanced by Gish, especially in explanation of the fact that urban health bias is so much worse in Pakistan than in India.

42 Gish; Sharpston, 'Uneven Geographical Distribution of Medical Care: a Ghanaian Case Study', *JDS*.

43 P. Piotrow, ed., *Population and Family Planning in the People's Republic of China*, Victor Bostrom Fund (New York), 1971.

44 Information from discussion with M. Sharpston. The essence of the complaints — among urban specialists, not among ill people — in India is expressed by a doctor writing in *The Times of India*, 9 November 1969: 'only one hospital in the whole of Bombay . . . possesses an artificial kidney'.

45 K. Marx and F. Engels, *Communist Manifesto*, in *SW*, vol. 1, p. 36.

46 We have concentrated on the maldistribution and mistraining of doctors, because the data are available and the effects on rural life dramatic. Scattered evidence of the scale of urban bias, however, does exist for other forms of expertise: engineers, born in rural areas, improve city tapwater supplies rather than village irrigation, or are trained to build bridges rather than to manage water; accountants proliferate, half-employed, in electronics factories, while few are available for rural cooperative credit societies; the vital crop research institutes of Sri Lanka cannot retain their cadre economists because they are outbid by the Central Bank and the Planning Ministry in Colombo.

12 TAX POLICY TOWARDS THE RURAL SECTOR

1 S. R. Lewis, 'Agricultural Taxation and Intersectoral Resource Transfers', Discussion Paper 134, IDS, Nairobi, 1971. In Thailand, the rice export premium tax alone removes 11% of farm incomes (Ngo Van Lam, 'Incidence of the Rice Export Premium in Thailand', Sydney U., Dept of Econ, Working Paper no. 6, p. 11.

2 Measured at world prices.

3 Smaller, both because of the inefficiencies of the process (discourage-ment of efficient farm activities, encouragement of high-cost indu-stries) and because of its administrative costs.

4 K. Krishnaswamy, in A. Peacock and G. Hauser, eds., *Government Finance and Economic Development*, OECD, 1963 (hereafter cited as Krishnaswamy).

5 Indeed the arguments about whether Indian tax policy has raised or lowered agricultural income, at the cost (or to the gain) of other sectors, are well within the range of a 5% impact either way. V. Gandhi, *Tax Burden on Indian Agriculture*, Harvard, 1966 (here-after cited as V. Gandhi); E. T. Mathew, *Agricultural Taxation and Economic Development in India*, Asia, 1968; UN (Bangkok).

6 S. R. Lewis, 'Agricultural Taxation in a Developing Economy', in H. M. Southworth and B. F. Johnston, eds, *Agricultural Develop-ment and Economic Growth*, Cornell 1967 (hereafter cited as Southworth), p. 453. Both Lewis's observation and my comment apply whether 'enough' means enough for efficiency, for fairness or for rapid growth.

7 N. Kaldor, 'Taxation for Economic Development', *Journal of Modern African Studies*, 1963, reprinted in M. C. Taylor, ed., *Taxation for African Economic Development*, Hutchinson, 1970 (hereafter cited as Taylor), p. 165.

8 V. Gandhi; criticised by Lewis in Southworth, p. 482; recalculations make matters worse in Gandhi,'Agricultural Tax Policy: Search for a Direction', *Artha-Vikas*, July 1969, pp. 3-49.

9 T. H. Silcock, 'Thailand', in R. T. Shand, ed., *Agricultural Develop-ment in Asia*, Australian National University Press and Allen & Unwin, 1969, p. 110.

10 The yield of tax is the result of multiplying the number of people who pay it (the tax base) by the average rate each person pays (the tax rate). Both base and rate, to assist forward planning, should be immune from major fluctuations.

11 Corresponding criteria apply to public *expenditure*: that it should involve relatively low administrative and political costs; that it sti-mulate growth, by being embodied in efficient uses and by promot-ing savings; that it generate total private incomes which are plan-nable and stable; and that its impact be horizontally and vertically equitable. Because the impact of public expenditure, along these dimensions, is dealt with elsewhere in the book, this chapter con-centrates on the tax side of the government accounts. However, these four criteria are really best applied to the total impact of taxation and outlays together (because items on one side of the account can be turned from errors into virtues by items on the other side).

12 R. M. Bird, *Taxation and Development: Lessons from Colombian Experience*, Harvard, 1970, p. 88.

13 Neither this nor any other remark in this book should be taken to imply that the rural sector (even less that the rural rich) should pay

less tax: only that they should pay a smaller *share* of total tax collected. That total should in most poor countries be much higher. See below, pp. 285-6.

14 Of course the rich would pay higher *proportions* of income as tax than the pooi. The burden of a given payment — and even of a given proportionate payment — is greater for the poor.

15 For data relating tax/income ratios to income per person, see Krishnaswamy.

16 An excellent discussion is D. P. Ghai, *Taxation for Development: a Case Study of Uganda*, East African Publishing House, 1966, pp. 2-17. The proposition in the next sentence of the text is proved by Ghai on p. 2, note 3.

17 Land taxation is perhaps the best form of tax on agriculture; but it is notoriously static when income grows. Progressive land taxation — set higher on larger or more fertile holdings, or raised when income per acre rises — is a popular theoretical remedy, but notoriously hard to implement. H. P. Wald, 'Basic Design for More Effective Land Taxation' (1959), reprinted in Taylor, pp. 320-31; Lewis, 'Agricultural Taxation in a Developing Economy', in Southworth, esp. p. 466.

18 This is also true of most indirect taxes, on consumer goods. These tend to take a larger share of income from farmers and villagers because — being very poor — they consume a bigger share of their incomes; but as they get richer they raise the proportion of income saved and cut the share of spending. Direct taxes, especially progressive ones, are likelier to be income-elastic in yield; but townsmen pay a larger share of direct than of indirect taxes.

19 Kaldor, 'Taxation for Economic Development' (1963), in Taylor, pp. 158, 167; but see E. Dean, *The Supply Response of African Farmers*, North-Holland, 1966, esp. Chapter 4; G. Helleiner, 'Smallholder Decision-making: Tropical African Evidence', in Reynolds; R. Krishna, 'Farm Supply Response in India-Pakistan: A Case Study of the Punjab', *EJ*, September 1963, and 'Agricultural Price Policy and Economic Development' in Southworth; P. and K. Bardhan, 'Price Response of Marketed Surplus of Foodgrains', *Oxford Economic Papers*, July 1971, p. 262; and Chapter 13, notes 84 and 85, below.

20 Papanek, p. 62.

21 It is a weakness of this argument that the rural poor can respond to extra tax burdens by borrowing to meet the tax. This will largely be from rural moneylenders, and will bid up interest rates. Money-lenders will therefore find lending (to sustain rural consumption in face of higher taxes) even more profitable, as compared with financing their own (or other people's) productive investment. See p. 248.

22 G. K. Helleiner, 'The Fiscal Role of Marketing Boards in Nigerian Economic Development', *EJ*, September 1964, reprinted in Taylor, p. 443.

23 W. Tims, *Analytical Techniques for Development Planning: a Case Study of Pakistan's Third Five Year Plan*, Pakistan Institute of Development Economics, 1968, p. 52.

24 Lewis, 'Agricultural Taxation in a Developing Economy', in Southworth, p. 460.

25 J. F. Due (1963), reprinted as 'Tax Policy and Economic Development', in Taylor, p. 186.

26 If 'subsistence' farmers are already substantial marketers, such actions may leave them less able to pay the extra tax (if the price falls more than in proportion to their rise in marketings).

27 For example, irrigation canals also irrigate weeds. A 2-acre farmer's family often has little to do except dig them up. A big farmer must hire weeding labourers — and, if he is a major local employer, bid up wages in the process.

28 *Interim Report,* Pakistan Taxation Commission, Karachi, 1971, p. 6; *UNA 1973*, p. 119 (figures are for GDP, not GNP, but this makes little difference); ILO, *Yearbook of Labour Statistics 1970*, p. 119.

29 Furthermore, the richest households — where much taxable capacity is concentrated (n. 31) — are more burdened by populousness in rural than in urban sectors. In India in 1961-2, the richest 4% of urban households averaged 7.5 members, as against 8.5 for the richest 4.4% of rural households, and probably about 8.7 for the richest 4%. National Council for Applied Economic Research, *Urban Income and Saving,* Delhi, 1963, p. 42; *All India Rural Household Survey,* vol. II, Delhi, 1965, pp. 52, 55.

30 Nor does a tax on moneylenders — highly desirable on other grounds — help here; by reducing their capacity to supply rural credit, such a tax makes credit scarcer, and rural interest rates rise higher still.

31 UN (Bangkok), Tables 4a, 4b.

32 T. N. Srinivasan and P. K. Bardhan, 'Resource Prospects from the Rural Sector: A Comment', *EPW*, 28 June 1969.

33 UN (Bangkok), which drew on V. Gandhi, but corrected some of his assumptions (for example, that urban land confers no taxable capacity) and incorporated new data.

34 Assumed 40% higher in towns than in villages — despite the previous paragraph!

35 Proportional taxation — everyone paying the same proportion of taxable capacity (say, of income *plus* 10% wealth *minus* subsistence) — is generally considered too hard on the poor. Constant progressiveness — which can be shown to imply that everyone pays the same proportion of the *square* of his taxable capacity — is usually considered too severe on the rich to be acceptable politically. A common compromise goal is to seek to design a tax system so that each person pays in proportion to taxable capacity (T) raised to the power of 1.5.

36 This is partly because of profits-tax evasion; partly because rural taxes are mainly indirect and thus harder to evade; and partly because much evasion of a variety of taxes is due to personal mobility, which is greater in urban areas. G. Oda Orewa, *Taxation in Western Nigeria*, Oxford, for Nigerian Institute of Economic and Social Research, 1962, p. 22 and Table 5. Kaldor, *Indian Tax Reform*, Department of Economic Affairs, Ministry of Finance, New Delhi, 1956,

p. 104, estimates that in 1953-4 there were Rs. 2,850 million of agricultural income, but Rs. 5,700 million of non-agricultural income, that should have been assessed for income tax but evaded assessment (the shares in GNP were about fifty-fifty).

37   *FAO/S*, 1970.

38   See ch. 3, n. 5. The true share may well be lower—2% for UK aid (1st Report, H. of C. Select Cttee on Overseas Devel., HMSO, 1976, pp. xxiv-xxv.

39   R. S. McNamara, *Address to the Board of Governors at the Nairobi Meeting*, IBRD, Washington, 1973, pp. 13, 17, and esp. p. 23.

40   (1) Equity arguments could well be taken to suggest that rural people, being poorer, should receive a *larger* share of public-sector benefits — whether from domestic or from aid outlay — than the share of taxation that they contribute. (2) Yet even the 12% figure overstates the share of aid that has benefited agriculture; first, because some contracts (especially in irrigation) went to urban firms; second, because one should really *deduct* part of food aid, which is 'aid against agriculture' to the extent that it cuts farm incomes by driving down the price of farmers' surpluses (pp. 293-4).

41   UN (Bangkok), para. 28.

42   *Interim Report*, Pakistan Taxation Commission, p. 6.

43   In India during the same period, the latter share was estimated (liberally) in the 1968 draft of the Fourth Plan at one-third for the entire rural sector, including agriculture; almost certainly the share in Pakistan was smaller. For evidence of the great urban concentration of infrastructural outlays in Pakistan, see S. H. Wellisz, in Breese.

44   R. H. Sabot, *Economic Development, Structural Change and Urban Migration: a Study of Tanzania*, forthcoming.

45   This chapter has largely ignored the problem that, by passing indirect (and perhaps even direct) taxes back to suppliers, or on to buyers, people can prevent the impact of a tax from falling wholly in the same sector as its apparent, legislated incidence. As agriculture emerges from subsistence and deals more with the rest of the economy, this problem grows. However, there is no evidence of the size, or even direction, of these gaps between the sectoral impact and incidence of taxes in LDCs, and with big sectors there are some *a priori* reasons to expect a small net gap. The assumption that 'incidence equals impact', for rural or urban sector as a whole, may not be too unreasonable.

13   PRICE TWISTS

1   All production creates net output, by transforming inputs into gross outputs. The value of output provides, and equals, wages plus profits plus (sometimes) rent, to pay factor inputs — services of labour, capital and land respectively. In value, gross output equals net output (payment of factor inputs) plus *current inputs* — on the farm, such items as fertilisers, seeds, water, manure, draught power, etc. It is possible to subsidise current inputs only if they are purchased:

fertilisers can be subsidised, or cattle-cake, but not the manure or draught power of the farmer's animals.

2 If the small farmer does manage to get hold of some, these same considerations encourage him to sell them to the big farmer. This is notably the case with subsidised fertilisers, especially where smallholders can easily sell them to a nearby plantation.

3 Indeed, subsidies, if absent or smaller in a nearby country, can well cause fertilisers to be smuggled out thither. Subsidised fertilisers in Bangladesh in 1972-3 were often resold, at full price, to India.

4 More accurately, if agriculture receives a 10% 'subsidy' on all current inputs while the rest of the economy receives 20%, agriculture is really suffering an input tax, to permit the rest of the economy to enjoy an input subsidy. Even if both sectors receive an identical rate of input 'subsidy', the sector with a lower ratio of purchased inputs to net output — invariably agriculture — is in effect taxed.

5 FAO, *Provisional Indicative World Plan for Agricultural Development*, Rome, 1969, vol. 1, pp. 199-200, 216. Oil price inflation has since inflated costs — and food price inflation, benefits.

6 USDA Economic Research Service, *Economic Progress of Agriculture in Developing Nations 1950-68*, Foreign Agricultural Economic Report no. 59, pp. 40-1. See also, E. Mason, *Economic Development in India and Pakistan*, Harvard, 1966; V. M. Dandekar, 'Agricultural Price Policy: A Critique of Dantwala', *EPW*, 16 March 1968.

7 Mellor, p. 274. Unpublished work by G. R. Allen suggests this is no longer true in 1974-5.

8 W. F. Falcon and C. P. Timmer, 'The Political Economy of Rice, Rice Production and Trade in Asia', in Reynolds.

9 FAO/P *1972*, Tables 129, 134B, for prices; *UNA 1971*, vol. 3, for national income per person (1970 data used only when 1971 not available). The 'three poor countries' are Korea, Algeria and Egypt. (The chance that 3 items of 17 fall into the bottom 8 is below 1 in 12). Huge foodgrain losses from overpriced protected fertiliser are proved for India, 1961-71, by T. W. Schultz (citing M. S. Rao) in C. N. Vakil and C. H. Shah (eds), *Agricultural Development of India*, Bombay U., 1976.

10 Agricultural Prices Commission, *Annual Report 1967-68*, Delhi, p. 3.

11 See pp. 123-30 above on the USSR, 1920-33; pp. 93-4 above, and M. Tracy, *Agriculture in Western Europe*, Cape, 1964, on the aims of the British free traders, 1815-64; S. M. Eddie, *Terms of Trade Change and Income Transfer from Agriculture*, Williams College, CDERM 35, 1970, on Austria-Hungary.

12 Unless, if they were rejected, equivalent aid (or other advantages) would be offered instead. This is very unlikely, because the cost of PL480 food aid to the USA — overwhelmingly the main donor — has been almost nil: the reserves already existed in the USA, built up as part of a farm support policy, so that the production costs had already been incurred irrespective of whether the food was given away or not; had it been sold on world markets instead, the downward pressure on wheat prices could well have destroyed all the gains to the USA, which is the main commercial exporter of wheat as well as the

main donor. T. W. Schultz, 'Value of US farm surpluses to under-developed countries', *Journal of Farm Economics,* 1960.

13 Some of the PL480 farm products would have been imported even if no PL480 aid had been given. The cash thus saved, in part, can be used for non-farm imports. But PL480 raises the supply of farm products more than that of non-farm products, and worsens the farm sector's internal terms of trade accordingly.

14 R. Krishna, 'Agricultural Price Policy and Economic Development' in Southworth; Streeten/Lipton, pp. 101-2; R. Hill, 'Aid to India', in Streeten/Lipton, pp. 341-6.

15 UN (Bangkok).

16 J. S. Mann, 'Impact of PL480 Imports on Prices and Domestic Supply of Cereals in India', *Journal of Farm Economics,* February 1967.

17 Even before allowing for the fact that, by switching from (PL480-affected) wheat sales to — say — potato cultivation and sales, the farmer pulls down potato prices!

18 Krishna, 'Agricultural Price Policy and Economic Development', in Southworth, pp. 512-17.

19 Lewis, 'Agricultural Taxation in a Developing Economy', in Southworth, p. 480.

20 D. H. Penny, 'Indonesia', in Shand, p. 269. See also ch. 12, n. 1.

21 Dandekar, 'Agricultural Price Policy: A Critique of Dantwala', *EPW.*

22 In 1958, all eleven surveyed South Asian countries cited 'stabilisation of the cost of living' as an aim of food price policy. Only one (Ceylon) cited 'producer incentive'. FAO, *Agricultural Price Policies in Asia and the Far East,* UN/CN. 11/484, FAO, Rome, 1958, p. 1.

23 K. Rafferty, *FT,* 10 April 1974, p. 33.

24 FAO, *Agricultural Price Policies in Asia and the Far East,* p. 8.

25 *Ibid.,* p. 9.

26 H. V. Richter, 'The Union of Burma', in Shand, p. 163.

27 A useful summary, with references, appears in Lewis, 'Agricultural Taxation in a Developing Economy', in Southworth, p. 469.

28 On pp. 315-19 we consider whether the benefits to non-farmers can in any sense compensate for the damage to farmers.

29 Mellor, p. 311, provides a fascinating month-by-month record (originally due to Dr B. L. Agrawal) of costs and outlays for a set of farm families in the Indian Punjab.

30 Robert S. McNamara, *Address to the Board of Governors at the Nairobi Meeting,* IBRD, 1973, p. 20, and *FAO/S 1972,* Table 5; E. Szczepanik, *Agricultural Policies at Different Levels of Development,* FAO mimeo draft, April 1973, Table 4.3, pp. 4.20-4.23; J. Burrows et al., *The Second Decade: a Basic Economic Report on Kenya,* Report no. 201-KE, Annex 3 (vol. 4), 'Key Issues in the Private Sector', IBRD, Washington, 1974 (hereafter cited as Burrows), pp. 26, 42.

31 Because a bad local harvest, or a low price for the main local cash crop, will lead to defaults that cannot be offset against good results elsewhere.

32 Mellor, p. 320: 'Co-operative credit agencies . . . are basically competing with the moneylenders in offering consumption credit, even though the tying of loans to production instruments may give the appearance of producer credit.'

33 Agencies (unlike moneylenders) do need to see that loans are not used to increase the lavishness of weddings and funerals. However, loans for these purposes form a surprisingly small proportion of most rural credit, and such outlays are probably too influenced by social pressures to be very responsive to credit availability.

34 The rural sector loses on balance, and the urban sector gains, because these 'gifts' are exceeded by the induced transfer of rural funds to urbanising (pp. 117-21) moneylenders, through the failures of rural agency credit to replace them.

35 Low agency interest rates are due partly to overoptimism, caused by underestimating the part of moneylender interest corresponding to administrative costs that remain even if risks can be spread by lending in many villages (A. Bottomley, 'The Cost of Administering Private Loans in Underdeveloped Rural Areas', *Oxford Economic Papers,* June 1963), though the credibility of such underestimation as an excuse diminishes with experience!

36 *Ceylon Report,* p. 98, para. 331.

37 U. J. Lele, 'The roles of credit and marketing in agricultural development', in Nurul Islam, ed., *Agricultural Policy in Developing Countries,* Macmillan 1974, pp. 421-23.

38 The criterion for success is different — profit for the moneylender, the support of activities with high social benefit/cost ratios for the institutions; but the rules apply in both cases.

39 A sympathetic reader describes this paragraph as 'conspiracy theory'; I feel strongly that it is not. It has been left substantially unamended, so that the reader may judge for himself.

40 I. Adelman and G. Dalton, 'A Factor Analysis of Modernisation in village India', *EJ* 1971. See also the evidence in the IBRD's nine-volume *Survey of Land and Water Resources in Bangladesh,* Washington, 1972.

41 Profit rates for traders and merchants are often kept low by competition: see U. J. Lele, 'The Traders of Sholapur', in J. W. Mellor, T. F. Weaver, U. J. Lele and S. R. Simon, eds., *Developing Rural India: Plan and Practice,* Cornell, 1968.

42 Since most agricultural (and rural consumer) credit is short-term, policies discriminating against short-term credit would indirectly have a similar effect; certainly governmental support of heavy industrialisation tends to make lenders more favourable to projects with distant yield as against those requiring shorter-term credit.

43 For this reason, and because agriculture enjoys relatively little protection against competing imports, almost all post-war private foreign investment has gone into urban activities. The sort of exception welcomed by some poor countries illuminates their view of agriculture; for example, Mr Robert Vesco, whom the US authorities

sought to extradite on grounds of alleged massive frauds, was for some time allowed to invest in his new home country of Costa Rica only in agriculture and tourism, where his influence was considered acceptable! *FT*, 18 February 1975.

44 F. Kahnert et al., *Agriculture and Related Activities in Pakistan*, OECD, 1970, p. 63.

45 The official rate stayed at $1 – Rs. 4.76 from 1964-5 to 1970, while market rates ranged from Rs. 8.50 to Rs. 11.15. (The latter rates, however, were probably pushed up by the Government's need to 'ration' the supply of foreign currency at the cheap official rate.) *Pick's Currency Guide*, annual issues, *passim*.

46 Little.

47 Lewis, p. 148.

48 M. L. Dantwala, 'From Stagnation to Growth', *Indian Economic Journal*, October-December 1970, p. 189.

49 *Pick's Currency Guide*, 1962-8, annual. The proportions ranged from 68.1% in 1964 and 1965 to 31.3% in 1963. See, however, note 45 above.

50 Of course, if food aid were offloaded onto commercial markets, grain prices would fall (n. 16). But if exporters had no outlet for food now going as aid and withdrew it from international dealings, prices would rise.

51 Just as with 'internal' (agriculture/non-agriculture) terms of trade, these statements relate to the relative prices of farm and non-farm products (this time on world markets) at each point of time and do not imply that there is a discernible trend in such prices over time; there probably is not. Streeten, pp. 460-7.

52 None of the above paragraphs should be taken to accept, reject or require the belief that, in project evaluation, inputs and outputs *should* be valued at 'world prices'.

53 Notice, however, that the rising urban share of population, the concentration of farm holdings and (see above, pp. 115-16) the process of monetisation and economic integration combine to push up the marketed share of farm production, and hence the cost to the farm sector of any *given* degree of underpricing of its output. This important trend is totally obscured by data purporting to show how that degree has changed over time (changing agricultural 'terms of trade'). Note that subsistence farmers do suffer indirectly from bad (as opposed to changing) terms of trade, as Lenin observed (ch. 4, n. 80).

54 Lewis, pp. 149-50, and *UNA 1965*, p. 279, using $1= Rs. 4.76; Burrows, p. 35; and see below, note 99.

55 UN (Bangkok); V, Sukhatme, Ph.D. Chicago U., work in progress.

56 C. E. Young, 'Rural-urban terms of trade', *African Social Research*, December 1971. For Japan, see K. Ohkawa, 'Phases of agricultural development and economic growth', in K. Ohkawa, B. Johnston and H. Kaneda (eds.), *Agriculture and Economic Growth: Japan's Experience*, Princeton and Tokyo, 1970, p. 29. From 1877 to 1919,

agricultural output prices (relative to prices of non-farm inputs to agriculture) rose by 97 per cent!

57 Rong I-Wu, *The Strategy of Economic Development: A Case Study of Taiwan*, Vander (Louvain), 1971.

58 Mellor, p. 206. He even regards the 'arguments against . . . a relative increase in agricultural prices' as 'clear' and 'not . . . controversial' (p. 208)!

59 FAO, *Agricultural Price Policies in Asia and the Far East*, p. 1. Only one of the eleven (Ceylon) mentioned producer incentive as an objective of farm price policy.

60 Lewis, 'Agricultural Taxation in a Developing Economy', in Southworth, p. 484.

61 Rong I-Wu, *The Strategy of Economic Development: A Case study of Taiwan*, p. 166.

62 R. Krishna, 'Agricultural Price Policy and Economic Development', in Southworth, pp. 498-502.

63 O. Lange and F. W. Taylor, *On Economic Theory and Socialism*, Minnesota, 1938. I am aware that 'second-best theory' generates logically consistent, but not plausible, objections to this.

64 The many commentators espousing this view are sampled in Raj Krishna, 'Farm Supply Response in India-Pakistan: A Case Study of the Punjab Region', *EJ*, 1963, pp. 477-8, note (reprinted in Shukla, pp. 193-4, note 3). See 'The Spectre of Pricism in the Third World', *Times Literary Supplement*, 13 September 1972, p. 1056, col. 3, for more recent instances.

65 E. K. Fisk, in Reynolds.

66 This certainly works for specific crops. Responsiveness to price rises seems higher in India than in the USA (Krishna, 'Farm Supply Response in India-Pakistan: A Case Study of the Punjab Region', in Shukla).

67 In Southworth, pp. 512-15. See also G. Helleiner, in Reynolds; and UNCTAD Research Memo no. 68, Geneva, 1974.

68 Mellor, pp. 203-4, for citations in this paragraph.

69 Connell.

70 S. Hymer and S. Resnick, 'A model of an agrarian economy with non-agricultural activities', *American Economic Review*, Sept. 1969.

71 Why didn't I borrow against the security of yield from such investment before crop prices rose? Well, look at rural interest rates in poor countries for small farmers. Capital markets are neither perfect nor unbiased.

72 That is why, from UK figures, long-run price responsiveness exceeds short-run by more for 'all grains' than for specific grains. A model for Mexico cunningly suggests very high *long-run* price response for total.farm output: L. Goreux and A. Manne, *Multi-level Planning*, North Holland, 1973.

73 M. Lipton, 'Should Rational Farmers Respond to Price Changes?', *Modern Asian Studies*, 1 January 1966, pp. 95-9.

74 Apart from the papers by Krishna and Helleiner already cited, see E. Dean, *The Supply Response of African Farmers: Theory and*

Measurement, Amsterdam, 1966, chapter 4; and D. Narain, *The Impact of Price Movements on Areas under Selected Crops in India, 1900-39*, Cambridge University Press, 1965.

75 Mellor, p. 198.

76 Krishna does not mention (perhaps because it is 'obvious') this key explanation of differences in response as measured by price elasticity: see Shukla, p. 208, and Southworth, p. 504. This is why, in Bangladesh, rice (grown on perhaps 90% of the relevant land) has low price-elasticity, but jute (on 10%) high.

77 Krishna, 'Agricultural Price Policy and Economic Development', in Southworth, especially the data for Malayan rubber cited on p. 507.

78 G. D. Gwyer, *Perennial Crop Supply Response: The case of Tanzanian Sisal*, School of Rural Economics and Related Studies, Wye College, 1971; M. Arak, *Supply of Brazilian Coffee*, Ph.D. thesis (Economics), Massachusetts Institute of Technology, 1967.

79 In Bangladesh in early 1973, high rice prices, plus a jute price that was too low and whose announcement by the procuring authority was too long delayed, led to very serious cutbacks in jute planting; hence specific incentives to land use worked, but at a social cost much higher than predicted. See note 76 above.

80 A similar analysis applies to marketing of raw materials.

81 Further empirical facts (strengthening the impact of improvements in agriculture's terms of trade on sustainable urban workforce, inferrable from these 'logical facts') are that such improvements also (1) probably increase the volume of net townward marketings (see below), and (2) almost certainly lead to reductions in the share of urban wage income spent on food (see Mellor, p. 72; R. Sinha and F. Hay, 'Analysis of Food Expenditure Pattern of Industrial Workers', *JDS*, July 1972).

82 This includes some work of great intrinsic interest, such as D. Narain, *Distribution of the Marketed Surplus of Agricultural Produce by Size-Level of Holding in India, 1950-51*, Institute of Economic Growth (Delhi), Occasional Paper, Asia (Bombay), 1971, and U. Patnaik, *Capitalism in Indian Agriculture*, Ph.D. (Oxford), 1972. For a useful discussion, see C. Bell, 'A Note on "Perverse" Producer Response to Changes in Prices', in Lehmann.

83 They make up the farm deficit by work for others, usually commercial farmers. It should be added that the great mass of such 'distress sales' are in local *rural* markets; there is not even much *temporary* townward movement of these marketings, except for fruit, vegetables and dairy products.

84 Narain, *Distribution of the Marketed Surplus of Agricultural Produce by Size-Level of Holding in India, 1950-51*.

85 Krishna, 'Agricultural Price Policy and Economic Development', in Southworth, pp. 511-12, and A. R. Khan and A. H. M. N. Chowdury, 'Marketable surplus function: a study of the behaviour of West Pakistani farmers', in Shukla, pp. 220-3.

86 P. and K. Bardhan, 'Price response of marketed surplus of food-

grains', *Oxford Economic Papers*, July, 1971, p. 262; S. Ghatak, 'Marketed surplus in Indian agriculture: theory and practice', mimeo, pending publication; S. K. Qureshi, 'Price responsiveness of marketed surplus of wheat in Pakistan', *Pakistan Development Review*, summer 1974, p. 120; M. Raqibuzzaman, 'Marketable surplus function of major agricultural commodities in Pakistan', *Pakistan Development Review*, Autumn 1966, p. 380; International Rice Research Institute, *Annual Report 1966*, Los Baños, 1967, p. 248.

87 Agriculture gets many inputs from other parts of agriculture, but in poor countries they are seldom purchased. Seed, feed and manure tend to come from the family enterprise itself, so that there is little dilution, through higher costs of purchased inputs, of the gains to farmers from rising farm prices.

88 Even the Indian Agricultural Prices Commission, set up in the 'green-revolutionary' wake of the 1965-6 food shortages and operating in a climate nominally very favourable to farm incentives, has terms of reference emphasising restraint on living costs: *1968-9 Report*, p. 3.

89 Such contracts in kind (for example, payment of harvest wages in the Punjab) are convenient—that is, reduce transaction costs—for both sides, and reduce the uncertainty associated with price fluctuations. They have therefore proved surprisingly robust in face of rural modernisation.

90 M. Lipton, 'Farm price stabilisation in less developed countries: some effects on income stability and income distribution', in P. Streeten, ed., *Unfashionable Economics: Essays in Honour of Lord Balogh*, Weidenfeld & Nicolson, 1970, spells out the exact—and rare—conditions under which price stabilisation can stabilise farm incomes.

91 This statement remains true, despite the problems (which economists will recognise) about assuming that the *incidence* falls largely on the farmer rather than the consumer.

92 These are governmental purchases for stock to bid up prices when they are low, and sales from stock to push prices down when they are high.

93 P. Bauer and F. W. Paish, 'The reduction of fluctuations in the income of primary producers', *EJ*, 1952, correctly analyse the damage, but seem to attribute it, mistakenly, to state trading as such, not to urban bias operating on pricing. A similar irrelevant ideological polarisation marked the debate on grain wholesaling in India in 1972-4; it was about the size of the state's role, not about the prices it should pay (or cause to be paid) to farmers.

94 Krishna, 'Agricultural Price Policy and Economic Development', in Southworth, p. 518.

95 Mellor, pp. 204-5; Agricultural Prices Commission (India), *Annual Report 1967-8*, para 2.21; Krishna, 'Agricultural Price Policy and Economic Development', in Southworth, p. 518.

96 This is a condensed and oversimplified account. Interested readers should consult Balassa and Little. For a good illustration, see Bur-

rows, esp. p. 37: 'the foreign-exchange management system benefit[s] the foreign capitalist most, and then the local capitalist, and wage-earner in manufacturing, all at the expense of agricultural producers'.

97 Streeten, p. 461.

98 See G. F. Papanek, ed., *Development Policy: Theory and Practice,* especially Felix's chapter 3; and Burrows, p. 12 (note the wording of the 1970-4 Plan as cited in para. 3.04). Of course, many LDCs have talked of seeking self-sufficiency in foodgrains, but their policies have usually encouraged 'self-sufficiency' only in such lines as steel, fertiliser production and vehicle assembly.

99 Little.

100 A. Ferrer, 'Income Distribution', in W. Baer and I. Kerstenetzky, eds., *Inflation and Growth in Latin America,* Irwin, 1964. In 1958, agriculture contributed 15.6% of GDP, which was worth about $10,892 million. *UNA 1965,* pp. 5, 494.

101 Though, because protection is at work, the outputs he competes with are generally overpriced — a combination logically impossible in large, integrated, developed economies, where protection that raises one firm's output price *ipso facto* raises the costs of any other domestic firm using that output as an input.

102 Protection rates are usually calculated as proportions of the price of an item; properly calculated, as proportions of domestic value added, they are far higher. Balassa, pp. 3-26, 49-70, 315-40.

103 B. R. Shenoy, *Indian Planning and Economic Development,* Asia, 1963, pp. 8-9.

104 G. Bueno, 'The structure of protection in Mexico', in Balassa.

105 In Kenya, income has been shifted from relatively poor rural producers to better-off urban consumers by price policies in beef, maize, wheat, sugar and milk. L. D. Smith, *Resource Allocation, Income Redistribution and Agricultural Planning Policies in Kenya,* IDS, University College of Nairobi, Discussion Paper no. 85, 1969.

106 This is not to deny the powerful case for subsidising really poor men's food — coarse grains, some pulses, *not* milk — out of general taxation (not by pushing farm prices down).

107 The lack of serious effort to implement land reform in most poor countries illustrates this.

14 WHAT CAN BE DONE?

1 Cash is the best cure for low rural absorptive or administrative capacity in most cases; see pp. 195-8.

2 S. L. Barraclough and A. L. Domike, 'Agrarian Structure in Seven Latin American Countries', in R. Stavenhagen, ed., *Agrarian Problems and Peasant Movements in Latin America,* Anchor, 1970, chapter 2, quantify this extreme case.

3 *Ceylon Report,* pp. 92-6, 182-4, and *Technical Papers,* p. 117; Lehmann, pp. 285-6.

4 Wolf, esp. pp. 3-48.
5 For a relevant commentary, see P. Freire, *Pedagogy of the Oppressed,* Penguin Education, 1972, esp. pp. 60-9.
6 A welcoming attitude to multi-shift working of plant, perhaps, is the acid test of whether such a strategy has been adopted.
7 Once agriculture starts moving, all sorts of localised activities providing and processing its inputs and outputs, and meeting the demands of its workers, become profitable too, and often in rural areas.
8 This is analogous to the need for scholarships to help 'Third Worlders' research the problems of their countries, and not principally those of the USA, USSR or UK.
9 Many more proposals are possible along these lines, each implicit in an obvious misincentive. For instance, the entire education of most potential businessmen, in almost all poor countries whether socialist or capitalist, takes place in towns; its values, textbooks and vocational directions are largely urban. For both businessmen and employees, the whole structure of support and subsidy, from houses and health to transport, parks and roads, encourages urban living.
10 Notably the exception to both rules—the USSR in 1925-39—was an extreme, pioneering case of urban bias.
11 One-day stays, or one-week whistle-stop tours, are at best useless.
12 In one poor country, a very senior official in the Ministry of Agriculture objected, in some distress, to my suggestion of composting as a means to improve the nitrogen content of the soil: 'But won't that need big machines?' (He was quite serious—not the joking type.)
13 The investment emphasis on agriculture (including major and medium irrigation) in India's Draft Fifth Plan (1974-8) is even smaller than in the Third and Fourth Plans. 'Rather than growing at home adequate amounts of food . . . we took the easy way out, and accepted large amounts of food aid. Our perception of the role of agriculture in our development strategy continues to be just as defective today as it was during the Second and Third Plans,' according to Dr B. S. Minhas, perhaps India's most distinguished applied economist, who resigned in desperation from the Planning Commission at the end of 1973. (*Whither Indian Planning?*, Indian Renaissance Institute, 1974, pp. 4, 22.)
14 See Fanon, cited on p. 140-1. In a poor country, that would have to be at the expense of further improvements in urban public servants' access to such facilities as subsidised housing, food, transport and medicine.
15 Usually, extreme shortages of appropriate skills hamper this task. One team, however, can provide 'pool' services for many local authorities. And shortages can be eased by reducing the pull to the capital city. (Ceylon's commodity research institutes, like Bangladesh's, persistently lose cadre economists to higher-paid jobs in the capital city.) Often planning exercises are worthless because the pull has left hardly anyone in the field to fill the plan out with feasible local projects.

16 The Indian situation typifies the problem. A really able executive civil servant can easily become a rural Block Development Officer — in administrative control of about fifty to sixty villages, or thirty to forty thousand people — in his mid-thirties. He can seldom go higher (though marginal improvements have recently been made) because the 'administrative' grades are normally entered by examination at age nineteen to twenty-four. This career structure offers him little incentive — especially as he seldom stays 'in place' for more than two years.

17 S. J. Simon, *Why you Lose at Bridge* (1945), Pelham Books, 1970.

18 Not usually protein yield: the most efficient way to beat shortages of specific proteins is usually to raise total calorie intake, freeing existing protein eaten from 'burning-up' (caloric) uses for protective and tissue-building uses. A. Berg, *The Nutrition Factor,* Brookings Institution, 1973.

19 H. H. Mann, 'Millets in the Middle East', in *The Social Framework of Agriculture,* Cass, 1968, esp. p. 379.

20 Personal communication from R. P. Dore.

21 Personal communication from D. Newbery.

22 On this model, the public sector's share in rural activity would rise, in urban activity fall (unless *existing* private capital were taken over), and in total activity either rise or fall, according to political preference.

23 See N. S. Jodha's 'Special Programmes for the Rural Poor: the Constraining Framework' in *EPW,* 31 March 1973. A forthcoming paper by Dr G. R. Mulla in *JDS* shows that near Bombay even land 'for the landless' drifted to larger farmers. See also Epstein, pp. 54-6. I have seen a similar drift with the 'settlement schemes' in Sri Lanka.

24 R. Evanson, in Reynolds. In conjunction with extension — even bad, mis-staffed, undertrained extension — the returns were higher still. See also Y. Hayami and V. W. Ruttan, *Agricultural Development: an International Perspective,* Johns Hopkins, 1971, pt. IV.

25 Persuading him to reject an urban-biased structure of rural benefit from innovation — a structure poised top-heavily on a few big surplus farmers — is another matter.

26 The growing share of trade that industrialised countries do with each other means that even those of their firms that are mainly exporters tend increasingly to specialise in products meeting the needs of modern industry, and to wish to sell such products to poor countries.

27 The same applies to shipping, packing, processing and handling. Where charges for these are set by Western cartels, the latter can profitably push such charges up, although the demand (as for tropical beverages) may be slightly reduced.

28 H. W. Singer, F. Ellis et al. *Trade Liberalisation, Employment and Income Distribution,* IDS Discussion Paper no. 31, Brighton, 1974, is a first shot at this.

Tables

Table 1.1 Yearly average growth (compound) of real gross domestic product per person, 1950-70 (%)

	1950-55	1955-60	1960-65	1965-70	1950-60	1960-70	1950-70
All less-developed countries covered: total	2.8	2.4	2.8	3.3	2.6	3.0	2.8
Latin America[a]	1.9	2.1	2.3	2.7	2.0	2.4	2.2
Asia[b]	2.5	2.1	2.3	3.6	2.3	3.0	2.7
Middle East	.	.	5.4	5.0	4.3	5.3	4.8
South Asia[b]	.	.	1.0	2.3	1.6	1.7	1.6
Far East[b]	.	.	2.6	4.5	2.2	3.5	2.8
Africa[c]	2.2	2.4	1.9	2.2	2.3	2.1	2.1
Europe (LDCs)[d]	5.5	3.8	5.8	5.0	4.6	5.3	5.0
Developed countries: total	.	.	4.0	3.5	.	3.8	.
Brazil[e]	2.7	2.8	1.2	4.2	2.7	2.7	2.7
India	1.8	2.0	0.5	2.5	1.9	1.5	1.7
Indonesia	.	.	0.1	1.5	.	0.8	.
Mexico	4.0	4.1	2.5	4.7	4.0	3.6	3.8
Nigeria	3.3	0.6	2.1	2.1	1.9	0.0	0.9
Pakistan	−0.4	1.2	2.6	2.4	0.4	2.5	1.4
Philippines	3.7	1.5	1.4	3.2	2.6	2.3	2.4
South Korea	5.7	1.3	3.6	9.5	3.5	6.5	5.0
Spain	7.5	2.7	7.4	5.8	5.1	6.6	5.8
Thailand	3.4	3.0	3.6	6.0	3.2	4.8	4.0

ª Excludes Cuba and (because 'developed') Uruguay and Argentina
ᵇ Excludes China, Turkey, Cyprus and (for 1950-60 only) Indonesia, and (because it is 'developed') Japan
ᶜ Excludes South Africa and (1950-60 only) Congo (Leopoldville)
ᵈ Spain, Turkey, Yugoslavia, Greece, Cyprus and Malta
ᵉ Named countries include over 70% of LDC populations, outside China

Sources: For 1950-60 except for intra-Asian *regions* (where data are calculated directly from OECD Development Centre, *National Accounts of Developing Countries*, Paris, 1968), we take the growth of total real GDP from OECD (DAC), *Development Assistance 1966*, Paris, 1966, pp. 20-1. Populations in 1950, 1955 and 1960 from UN, *Demographic Yearbook 1970*, New York, 1971, pp. 105, 126-32, adjusting regional populations to correspond to those used for OECD income calculations. Data for 1960-70 are from OECD (DAC), *Development Assistance 1971*, Paris, 1971, p. 116 and *ibid.*, 1969, p. 314.

Table 1.2 Physical measures of 'development'

	(2a) Nitrogenous fertiliser consumption (hundred metric tons)			(2b) Thousands of inhabitants per physician		(2c) Primary and secondary school enrolments (% of age-group)		
	1950	1960	1970	1960	1966	1950	1960	1967/8
Brazil	110	578	1443	3.6	2.1	31	47	65
India	631	4293	12439	5.8	4.8	19	31	41[a]
Indonesia	126	839	1650			(25)	37	44
Mexico	104	2243	3780	1.7	1.8	37	49	67
Nigeria				33.0	27.9	9	21	19[b]
Pakistan	50	950	3200	11.0	6.0	24	26	32
Philippines	181	493	709	1.6	1.4	68[c]	68	87
South Korea	722	1976	3202			52	65	75
Spain	799	3509	6042			43	50[d]	81
Thailand	15	179	737	7.8	8.8	43	56[a]	57
Turkey	54	537	2311			28	37	55
UAR	804	2322	2881	2.6	2.2	(28)	43	52

(a) 1965. (b) 1966; reduced by internal disturbances. (c) 1955. (d) 1961.

Source: FAO, *Production Yearbook 1970,* Rome, 1971. The 1970 figures are for the crop year 1969-70.

Source: UN, *World Economic Survey 1969-70,* New York, 1971.

Source: UNESCO, *Statistical Yearbook 1970,* Paris, 1971, Tables 2.5 and 2.6.

(2d) Illiteracy (% of persons over 15)

	Early year	percentage illiterate	Late year	percentage illiterate
Algeria[a]	1954	81	1966	81
Ceylon	1953	32	1963	25
El Salvador	1950	60	1961	51
Iran	1956	87	1966	77
Turkey	1960	62	1965	54
Venezuela	1950	48	1961	37

(a) 1954, Moslems only: 92%. Since there was large-scale emigration to France by (almost universally literate) adult non-Moslems, between 1954 and 1966, the figures imply a substantial fall in true illiteracy.

Source: UNESCO, *Statistical Yearbook 1970*, Paris, 1971, Table 1.3.

Table 5.1   Survey data on rural-urban differentials

	Urban-to-rural ratio of per head:		Date	Source
	Expenditure	Income (personal disposable)		
Asia				
Bangladesh		2.7	1963-4	Bose
Ceylon (Sri Lanka)	1.76[a]	2.07[a]		CB
India	1.43	1.67[b]	1950-9	PC
Pakistan (West)	1.14	1.27	1963-4	CSO
Philippines	2.23	1.92[c]	1965	BCS
Thailand	1.34-2.0[d]	1.55-2.05[d]	1963	NSO
Africa				
Ghana	(1.5)		1960-3	Knight
Tunisia	1.91[e]			
Uganda		3.24[h]	1964	Knight
UAR	1.60[f]		1965	NBE
Zambia		9.38[g]	1966	Knight
South America				
Brazil		2.73[j]	1970	Langoni

(a) Rural and estate incomes are added, and divided by total rural and estate population; similarly with expenditure.

(b) 1959-60.

(c) *BCS*, p. 13, assuming 'families with 10 or more members' average 12 members in rural and urban areas alike.

(d) Expenditure (income) disparity in Central Region, 1.34 (1.55); Eastern, 1.50 (1.75); Northern, 2.00 (2.05); and Southern, 1.60 (1.71).

(e) Per-household data; no household size estimates are available. If Tunisia features Moroccan ratios between urban and rural average household sizes, which were respectively 4.3 and 5.1 in 1960 (UN, *Demographic Yearbook 1968*, Table 12), the sectoral ratio between expenditure per person rises to 2.27.

(f) Expenditure per household (p. 252) was divided by persons per household from UN, *ibid.*, Table 12, because of apparent inconsistencies in the survey's method of estimating per-person data; rural households are clearly bigger (p. 252), yet the National Bank's conversion from per-household data (p. 252) to per-head data (p. 253) *lowers* the rural-urban disparity.

(g) Ratio between average earnings per African urban *employee* and total income per rural *household.*

(h) Ratio between wage income per urban employee and total income per active working peasant.

(i) Census-based estimate of urban percentages of income and population.

Sources: S. R. Bose, 'Trend of Real Income of the Rural Poor in East Pakistan 1949-66', *Pakistan Development Review,* vol. VIII, no. 3, 1968; J. B. Knight, 'Measuring Urban Rural Income Differentials', in *Proceedings of a Conference on Urban Unemployment in Africa,* mimeo, IDS, 1972; C. G. Langoni, A *Distribuição da Renda e o Desenvolvimento Econômico do Brasil,* ed. Expressão e Cultura, Rio, 1973. CB = Central Bank of Ceylon, Department of Economic Research, *Report on the Survey of Ceylon's Consumer Finances 1963,* Colombo, 1964, pp. 1, 3, 251, 265. PC = Planning Commission, Government of India, *Report of the Committee on Distribution of Income,* Delhi, 1969, Tables B3, B4. CSO = Central Statistical Office, National Sample Survey no. 6, 1967. BCS = Bureau of the Census and Statistics, *Survey of Households Bulletin: Family Income and Expenditure 1965,* Manila, 1968. NSO = National Statistical Office, *Household Expenditure Survey: Advance Report,* 4 vols. Bangkok, 1954. NBE = National Bank of Egypt, *Economic Bulletin,* vol. 20, no. 3, 1967.

Table 5.2   Earnings per employee: farm-nonfarm ratio

				Non-agricultural earnings as multiple of agricultural earnings	Types of employee: agricultural	Types of employee: non-agricultural	Type of farm payments covered
Ghana		1970	month	2.28	all	all + salariat	completely cash only
Kenya:	men	1966	month	2.63	regular	manufacturing; inc. salariat	cash and kind
	women	1966	month	3.73	regular	manufacturing; inc. salariat	cash and kind
Malawi		1971	month	4.02	all+salariat	all+salariat	cash and some kind
Mauritius		1971	day	1.16	plantations (sugar, tea, tobacco)	all	completely cash only
Tanzania		1971	month	2.23	men	adult men	cash components only
Zambia		1971	month	2.93	Africans: all+salariat	Africans: all + salariat unskilled construction	cash components only
British Honduras		1970	day	0.97	day casuals, on plantations		completely cash only

Colombia						
Ceylon (Sri Lanka)	1971	day	2.70	tea plantations	exc. services	completely cash only
India	1970	month[a]	2.89	all	manufacturing	cash components only
South Vietnam: men	1970	day	2.89	unskilled on plantations	unskilled; exc. mining and quarrying	cash and kind
women		day	2.46	unskilled on plantations	unskilled; exc. mining and quarrying	cash and kind

[a] Daily earnings, Maharashtra only, for agriculture; here used for all-India, assuming 24 working days per month.

Source: ILO, *Yearbook of Labour Statistics,* 1972. For Ghana, Ceylon and India, separate data for male and female workers in agriculture were weighted by the proportions of agricultural *employees* of each sex shown in *ibid.*

Table 5.3   Earnings data: Trends in farm-non-farm gap

			Non-agricultural agricultural ratio, end-period (start-period =100)
Ghana		1962-70	126.7
Kenya:	men	1962-66	103.5
	women	1962-66	108.4
Malawi		1968-71	97.3
Mauritius		1966-71	107.4
Tanzania[a]		1962-71	116.1
Zambia[b]		1962-71	111.0
British Honduras		1962-70	97.0
Colombia			
Ceylon (Sri Lanka)		1962-71	104.7
India		1962-70	130.1
South Vietnam:	men	1962-70	187.7
	women	1962-70	160.8

(a) Base of index changed between 1964 and 1965. For 1962 = 100, 1964 = 97.9; for 1965 = 100, 1971 = 108.3.
(b) Earnings in kind included to 1969 only in both sectors. For 1962 = 100, 1969 = 90.9; for 1970 = 100, 1971 = 101.7.

Note: Survey data for rural and urban income per person are available for 1961 and 1965 for the Philippines (source as in Table 1.1) and for several dates in the 1960s for India (National Sample Survey). Slight uptrends in the ratio of urban to rural incomes are suggested in both sources.

Source: As Table 5.2; periods of payment, types of employee and types of farm payment covered are as listed there.

10 to 30 years after growth accelerated

Africa 1970		Asia 1970		Latin America 1970	
Zaire	40.8				
Zambia	34.9				
Libya	24.4	Saudi Arabia	23.5		
Malagasy	14.3				
Tanzania	10.9				
Upper Volta	10.3				
Niger	9.7				
Liberia	9.5				
Ivory Coast	9.5				
Rhodesia	8.9				
Kenya	8.9				
Gabon	8.1	Lebanon	8.0		
Sudan	7.8			Mexico	7.2
Malawi	7.3				
		Thailand	6.7		
		South Vietnam	6.6		
Sierra Leone	6.0	Turkey	6.0		
Tunisia	5.7			Bolivia	5.9
Uganda	5.5				

(table continues overleaf)

Table 5.4:   Output-per-person disparity: LDCs and NRCs *(contd.)*

Africa 1970		Asia 1970		Caribbean and Latin America 1970		Historical development 10 to 30 years after growth accelerated	
		Philippines	5.4	Puerto Rico	5.3		
		Nepal	5.2	Dominican Republic	5.2		
Cameroons	4.7						
Ethiopia	4.6	Khmer	4.6	Chile	4.4		
				Jamaica	4.2		
				Honduras	4.1		
		Iraq	4.0	Venezuela	4.0		
				Brazil	3.9		
South Africa	3.8	Malaysia	3.8	Nicaragua	3.8		
		Syria	3.7				
		Burma	3.6	Haiti	3.6		
Togoland	3.5	South Korea	3.5	El Salvador	3.5		
Morocco	3.5						
		Pakistan	3.2				
		India	3.1				
		Jordan	3.1				
		Taiwan	3.0			Norway 1865	3.4
		Iran	2.8				

Country	Year	Value
Nigeria		2.0
Indonesia		2.4
Ceylon		2.2
Dahomey		1.6
Costa Rica		2.6
Panama		2.5
Surinam		2.5
Paraguay		2.4
Trinidad/Tobago		2.4
Colombia		2.2
Guyana		1.8
Japan	1880	2.7
Sweden	1863	2.7
Netherlands	1860	1.7
Germany	1857	1.7
Italy	1898	1.6
Great Britain	1801	1.1
Denmark	1972	1.1
France	1830	1.1

Sources: *1970 data*: Sectoral populations from FAO, *Production Yearbook*, 1971, pp. 21-3. Sectoral GDP from UN, *Yearbook of National Accounts Statistics 1972*, vol. 2. Where 1970 was clearly abnormal climatically, or where data for 1970 were not yet available, the closest year that seemed climatically typical was used. *Historical data*: S. Kuznets, *Modern Economic Growth*, Harvard, 1964, pp. 89-91, and *Economic Growth of Nations*, Harvard, 1971, pp. 140-6. 250-1; P. Bairoch, *International Historical Statistics*; vol. 1: Workforce, Brussels, 1968, extrapolated in some cases; W. C. Hoffmann, *Das Wachstum der Deutschen Wirtschaft*, Springer (Berlin), 1965, pp. 454-5, 506-9; P. Deane and W. Cole, *British Economic Growth 1688-1959*, 2nd ed., Cambridge, 1967, pp. 142, 166, 175; O. Johnson, *The Gross Domestic Product of Sweden*, Stockholm, 1967, pp. 150-9; Norwegian Central Bureau of Statistics, *Trends in the Norwegian Economy 1865-1960*, no. 16 *Samfunnsøkonomiske Studier*, Oslo, 1960, pp. 53-4; Instituto Centrale di Statistica (Rome), *Indagine Stat.*, Table 35.6.

Table 5.5   Trends in output-per-person disparity, 1960-70

Sectoral disparity over time		*African LDCs*	*Asian LDCs*	*Latin American and Caribbean LDCs*
1970 > 1965 > 1960		1	6	9
1970 < 1965 < 1960		2	2	4
1970 > 1960		2	11	12
1970 < 1960		4	4	7
if 1960, 1970 available:	otherwise:			
1970 > 1965 or 1965 > 1960		8	12	14
1970 < 1965 or 1965 < 1960		15	7	8

Sources: Latest available estimates of GDP in 1960, 1965 and 1970 (or nearest available years) from UN *Yearbooks of National Accounts Statistic*, and of sectoral populations from FAO *Production Yearbooks*.

Table 6.1 The welfare inefficiency of increasing inequity

Affected sector	Population (m)		Total income ($m)	Income per head ($)	Option A: continue increasing inequity				Option B: distribute growth equally			
					Total income		Income per head		Total income		Income per head	
	1974	1975	1974	1974	($m) 1975	(Growth %) 1974-5	($)	(Growth %) 1974-5	($m) 1974	(Growth %) 1974-5	($) 1974	(Growth %) 1974-5
Richer (urban) half	10	10.3	3000	300	3167.25	5.575	307.5	2.5	3151.80	5.06	306	2.0
Poorer (rural) half	10	10.3	1000	100	1035.15	3.515	100.5	0.5	1050.60	5.06	102	2.0
All	20	20.6	4000	200	4202.40	5.06	204	2.0	4202.40	5.06	204	2.0

Table 6.2 Product associated with extra labour (PAEL):
agriculture and non-agriculture

	Period between censuses/ labour-force surveys	*Constant prices for GDP of:*	*Extra GDP in constant prices per extra worker: non-agriculture as multiple of agriculture*
Dominican Republic	1960-70	1962	3.43
Ecuador	1950-60	1950	2.72
El Salvador	1961-71	1962	4.11
Morocco	1960-71	1960	0.99
Panama	1960-70	1960	1.69
Philippines	1960-70	1967	0.99
South Korea	1960-70	1970	0.88
Sri Lanka	1963-71	1963	3.23
Syria	1960-70	1963	3.26
Thailand	1960-70	1962	5.62

Notes: Figures for workers exclude recorded numbers of unemployed; of persons seeking work for the first time; of persons in 'activities not adequately described'; and in Panama of persons working in the Canal Zone. Figures for GDP (gross domestic product) exclude import duties and 'statistical discrepancy' (both always positive) from both agricultural and non-agricultural GDP. For Morocco the original UN *constant-price* series for GDP by industrial origin excluded 'product originating in government agencies and in public establishments of an administrative nature'. To allow for this, the ratio at *current* prices between GDP with and without 'government consumption' was multiplied by constant-price figures for non-agricultural GDP for 1960 and 1971.

Sources: GNP from UN, *Yearbook of National Accounts Statistics 1973*, vol. I, pp. 269, 293, 717; vol. II, pp. 241, 281, 454, 559, 570; and *1972*, vol. II, p. 115 (Morocco), *1957*, p. 66, and *1960*, p. 83 (Ecuador). Labour force from ILO, *Yearbook of Labour Statistics 1974*, pp. 50-1, 67, 73, 91, 99, 101, 103, for 1970 and 1971 data; for 1960-3, *1969*, pp. 71, 91, 107; *1968*, pp. 69, 77, 99, 105, 109, 111; and *1966*, pp. 48-9; Ecuador 1950 from *1960*, p. 25.

Table 6.3 Real and apparent outputs and disparities

		Share of output in agriculture (%)		Productivity disparity for labour (1970)	
		At market prices	Revalued	As per Table 5.4	Revalued
	Year	1	2	3	4
Source					
Brazil					
Balassa	1965	29.6	36.1	3.9	2.92
Little	1966	(29.6)	38.9	3.9	2.57
Chile					
Balassa	1967	9.1	10.3	4.4	3.86
Mexico					
Balassa	1967	12.8	14.1	7.2	6.42
Little	1960	15.8	17.4	7.2	6.39
Malaya					
Balassa	1966	29.2	28.1	3.8	4.03
Pakistan					
Balassa	1967	46.1	58.0	3.2	2.00
Little	1963–4	46.4	53.0	3.2	1.70
Philippines					
Balassa	1967	31.0	34.9	5.4	4.56
Little	1965	31.9	35.4	5.4	4.63
Taiwan					
Little	1965	25.1	27.5	3.0	2.65

Note: Col. 4 is derived from col. 3 by multiplication by [(col. 1) (100 − col. 2)] ÷ [(col. 2) (100 − col. 1)].

Table 7.1 Capital stock: average allocation, productivity, endowment

1. Country	Argentina		Colombia	India		Japan	Mexico	South Africa	Yugoslavia
2 Year	1950	1955	1953	1950	1960-1	1955	1950	1955	1953
Percentage in Agriculture									
3 DRAC	10.1	9.6	25.2	23.6	—	4.2	7.8	13.8	13.0
4 DRAC + livestock	—	—	35.6	36.4	—	5.6	12.7	20.1	17.4
5 DRAC + livestock +inventories ('capital')	—	—	—	30.7	27.4	6.0	13.3	6.2	19.2
6 GDP (current factor cost)	15.6	17.1	37.9	51.2	45.7	23.0	22.4	15.2	31.5
7 Labour force	21.6	19.4	52.5	70.6	73.0	40.4	57.9	33.0	66.8
Agricultural/non-agricultural ratios: productivity									
8 DRAC	1.65	1.94	1.81	3.40	—	6.81	3.41	1.12	3.08
9 DRAC + livestock	—	—	1.10	1.83	—	5.04	1.98	0.71	2.18
10 'Capital'	—	—	—	2.37	2.23	4.68	1.88	2.71	1.94
Agricultural/non-agricultural ratios: endowment per worker									
11 DRAC	0.41	0.44	0.30	0.13	—	0.06	0.06	0.33	0.08
12 DRAC + livestock	—	—	0.50	0.24	—	0.09	0.11	0.51	0.10
13 'Capital'	—	—	—	0.18	0.14	0.10	0.11	0.13	0.12

Notes:

Row 8 is $\dfrac{\text{row 6}}{\text{row 3}} \cdot \dfrac{(100-\text{row 3})}{(100-\text{row 6})}$; row 9 is $\dfrac{\text{row 6}}{\text{row 4}} \cdot \dfrac{(100-\text{row 4})}{(100-\text{row 6})}$; row 10 is $\dfrac{\text{row 6}}{\text{row 5}} \cdot \dfrac{(100-\text{row 5})}{(100-\text{row 6})}$.

These rows show the ratio, agriculture to non-agriculture, of output per unit of DRAC, Drac+livestock, and total 'capital' respectively.

Row 11 is $\dfrac{\text{row 3}}{\text{row 7}} \cdot \dfrac{(100-\text{row 7})}{(100-\text{row 3})}$; row 12 is $\dfrac{\text{row 4}}{\text{row 7}} \cdot \dfrac{(100-\text{col. 7})}{(100-\text{col. 4})}$; row 13 is $\dfrac{\text{row 5}}{\text{row 7}} \cdot \dfrac{(100-\text{row 7})}{(100-\text{row 5})}$.

These rows show the ratio, agriculture to non-agriculture, of per-worker DRAC, DRAC+livestock, and total 'capital', respectively. For earlier analogues to rows 9 and 10, see C. Clark, *The Conditions of Economic Progress*, 3rd ed. Macmillan, 1960, pp. 527-9.

Sources: GDP and labour force data are latest available from UN, *Yearbook of National Accounts Statistics* and ILO, *Yearbook of Labour Statistics*, respectively. Capital stocks from R. Goldsmith and C. Saunders, eds., *The Measurement of National Wealth*, Income and Wealth Series VIII, Bowes & Bowes, especially Th.D. van der Velde, pp. 9-11, 15-16, 18, and papers in text. (I have corrected some small errors in pp. 8-10, such as item A.I.1 (b) for S. Africa and A.I.3 (a) for India; and for India I have shifted half the value of capital from agriculture to industry for tea plantations, and vice versa for other plantations.) Capital stock for India, 1960-1, from *Report of the Committee on Distribution of Income and Levels of Living*, pt. 1, Planning Commission, Delhi, 1964, p. 79.

Table 8.1 Shares of agriculture (per cent)

	Output (GDP)	Invest-ment	Employ-ment	Output	Invest-ment
	1950-60	1950-60	*c.* 1965	1960-5	1960-5
Bolivia	—	—	63	26.0	3.2
Cyprus	24.0	8.5	39	19.0	12.0
Ethiopia	—	—	89	66.1	4.0
Jamaica	15.7	9.9	44	12.3	10.9
Malawi	—	—	80	54.2	12.0
Philippines	37.8	5.2	58	34.0	5.7
South Korea	43.0	12.4	55	40.7	10.5
Sudan	59.0	22.9	77	54.0	23.3
Syria	—	—	55	32.8	19.1
Taiwan	33.0	24.5	47	27.7	18.3
Tanzania	61.8	8.4	95	59.0	18.2
Thailand	43.3	18.4	78	36.0	17.4
Trinidad & Tobago	14.0	2.5	20	10.6	2.1
Tunisia	—	—	60	23.7	19.9
UAR	—	—	55	30.6	16.2
Uruguay	16.3	8.4	17	16.7	11.9
Venezuela	7.0	8.1	29	7.5	12.8

Sources: E. F. Szczepanik, 'The Size and Efficiency of Agricultural Investment in Selected Developing Countries', in FAO, *Monthly Bulletin of Agricultural Economics and Statistics,* December 1969, FAO, *Production Yearbook 1968,* Table 5.

	1950-60				1960-5			
	Agriculture	Non-agriculture	Overall	Quotient	Agriculture	Non-agriculture	Overall	Quotient
Bolivia	–	–	–	–	0.7	3.3	2.9	4.71
Cyprus	3.5	3.3	3.3	0.94	1.0	7.5	4.1	7.50
Ethiopia	–	–	–	–	0.3	6.1	3.0	20.33
Jamaica	3.2	3.1	3.1	0.97	6.8	3.2	3.4	0.47
Malawi	–	–	–	–	1.3	64.0	10.7	49.23
Philippines	0.3	1.7	1.4	5.67	0.7	2.5	2.2	3.57
South Korea	1.4	2.9	2.5	2.07	0.7	2.8	2.1	4.00
Sudan	1.2	3.1	2.3	2.58	1.3	3.3	2.5	2.54
Syria	–	–	–	–	0.6	4.3	2.0	7.17
Taiwan	2.3	1.7	2.1	0.74	2.8	2.0	1.8	0.71
Tanzania	0.4	–	–	–	1.9	4.0	3.3	2.11
Thailand	1.5	2.5	2.2	1.67	2.1	3.2	2.5	1.52
Trinidad & Tobago	1.5	9.2	8.4	6.13	3.3	9.4	8.9	2.85
Tunisia	–	–	–	–	4.7	3.4	3.6	0.72
UAR	–	–	–	–	3.4	2.6	2.6	0.76
Uruguay	–	–	6.8	–	3.1	13.3	11.6	4.29
Venezuela	3.7	3.2	3.3	3.70	3.9	3.5	3.7	0.90
Total with data	1.78	3.7	2.7	2.08	1.73	3.9	3.2	2.25

Source: E. F. Szczepanik, 'The Size and Efficiency of Agriculture Investment in Selected Developing Countries', in FAO, *Monthly Bulletin of Agricultural Economics and Statistics*, December 1969, p. 2. The data for 'non-agriculture' are calculated by dividing (col. 5 – col. 8) of Szczepanik's table by $\frac{\text{col. 5}}{\text{col. 4}}$ – (col. 6)(col. 1), converting percentages into ratios beforehand.

Table 11.1 Rural skill drain, India, about 1965

Group of educands	Approx. age-group	Rural persons as percentage of all persons in age-group (1961)	Rural educands in group as percentage of all educands in group	Ex-educands working in rural areas as percentage of all ex-educand from group (1961)
Primary and pre-primary	7-12	82.5	69.7[a]	53-65[b]
Secondary and middle school	13-18	80.7	75.9[a]	30-32[c]
University and college	19-22	79.6	34.1[d]	26.9

[a] 1967-8.
[b] Literates 65.3; Primary or Junior Basic course graduates, 53.0.
[c] 30.3 (IAMR), 32.1 (Burgess et al.).
[d] 1957-8.

Sources: Institute of Applied Manpower Research, *Fact Book on Manpower,* Delhi, 1963, pp. 6, 85; E. T. Mathew, *Agricultural Taxation and Economic Development in India,* Asia (London), 1968, p. 47; T. Burgess, R. Layard and P. Pant, *Manpower and Educational Development in India 1961-1986,* p. 3; UN *Demographic Yearbook 1967,* p. 172 (after slight adjustments to allow for estimated differences in age-group boundaries).

Table 11.2   Employment of various groups in agriculture, 1960-5

Percentage of each group that is employed in agriculture

	Illiterate no schooling, no grade	Literate or primary only	Secondary matriculate	Graduate	Total work force	Total population
Argentina	45	18		3	18	20
Egypt	70	40[a]	11[b]	6	55	55
India	77	53[c]	11[d]	6	70	70
Jamaica	58[e]	26[f]		5	34	44
Panama	89	53		6	43	43
Peru	77	46		14	47	50
Philippines	76	66		17	59	58
Syria	65	38	4	2	50	55
Thailand	86	81	67	26	78	78

(a) Including semi-literates (able to read only).
(b) Certificate below Intermediate.
(c) Includes Junior Basic.
(d) Certificate up to Intermediate.
(e) Less than six years' primary.
(f) Six or more years' primary only.

Sources: OECD, *Statistics of the Occupational and Educational Structure of the Labour Force in 53 Countries,* Paris, 1969; FAO, *Production Yearbook 1970,* Rome, 1971, pp. 21-3.

Table 11.3 Distribution of physicians:

	physicians per 10,000 population, around 1964	
	Capital and large cities	Rural areas
Argentina[a]	28.8	8.0
Bolivia[b]	9.7	1.8
Brazil[c]	13.9	2.6
Chile[b]	10.6	3.4
Colombia[a]	7.4	3.8
Costa Rica[b]	9.3	2.0
Cuba[d]	22.8	5.3
Dominican Republic[b]	28.5	2.2
Ecuador[b]	7.2	2.3
El Salvador[b]	7.0	1.0
Ethiopia[c]	3.3	0.1
Ghana[e]	2.3	0.2
Honduras[b]	5.8	0.8
India[b]	8.3	0.9
Indonesia[g]	5.3	0.5
Iran[f]	6.8	0.5
Jamaica[g]	11.9	1.8
Kenya[g]	4.6	0.5
Korea[g]	10.0	1.0
Mexico[c]	14.9	3.1
Panama[d]	7.1	1.6
Paraguay[d]	24.2	1.6
Peru[d]	17.1	2.0
Philippines[f]	12.5	1.7
Senegal[g]	2.3	0.2
Sudan[g]	3.6	0.3
Thailand[g]	10.6	0.6
Trinidad[g]	5.0	2.4
Uruguay[b]	19.5	4.5
Venezuela[d]	17.6	5.3

(a) Federal districts and departments: or provinces with cities of over 500,000 population, and rest of country.
(b) Department or province with capital city, and rest of country.
(c) Federal district and cities of over 500,000, and rest of country.
(d) Metropolitan area of capital city, and rest of country.
(e) Three major urban centres (Accra/Tema, Kumasi and Sekondi/Takoradi), and rest of country.
(f) Urban, and rural; 'urban' communities generally mean those with over 5,000 inhabitants.
(g) Capital city only, and rest of country.

Sources: Latin American countries from WHO, Pan-American Organization, *Health Conditions in the Americas, 1961-4,* Washington, 1966. Jamaica, Senegal, Thailand and Kenya from J. Bryant, *Health and the Developing World,* Cornell, 1969. India from *Manpower Survey: Health and Medical Manpower,* National Institute of Health Administration and Education and Institute of Applied Manpower Research, Delhi, 1966, pp. 18, 25. Korea from 'medical Education and Medical Practice in Korea', W. C. Lee, *Journal of Medical Education,* vol. 45, no. 5, 1970. Ghana from 'Uneven Geographical Distribution of Medical Care: A Ghanaian Case Study', M. Sharpston, *Journal of Development Studies,* vol. 8, no. 2, January 1972, p. 210. Other countries from O. Gish, *Doctor Migration and World Health,* Bell, 1971, pp. 77-106.

Index

72, 122; fluctuations, agricultural and non-agricultural, 208; comparison of value now and later, 50-3; response of farm and other output to price, 311-2; 315-8; undervaluing of agricultural output, 176-9; extra capital produces more in agricultural than in non-agricultural sectors in LDCs, 178-9; agricultural output reduced by compulsory levies, 275; table of real and apparent outputs, 441; table of gross marginal capital/output ratios, 445. *See also* Agricultural sector, Growth, Industry, Rural sector, Urban sector

Oyo (Nigeria), 406 n.3

Paish, F.W., 420 n.93
Pakistan, 29, 72, 79, 81, 150-1, 178, 203, 228, 247, 264, 266, 275, 277, 283-4, 304, 306, 315, 318, 338, 366 n.15, 369 n.44, 370 n.1, 380 n.95, 381 n.108, 384 n.8, 386 n.22, 388 n.13, 392 n.5, 398 nn.25, 27, 402 n.19, 409 n.41, 411 nn.23, 28, 413 nn.42-3, 414 n.6, 417 n.44, 419 n.85, 420 n.86; decline in real income, 1949-54, 1959-64, 31; planners relied on analogy of earlier European development, 33-4; attack on terms of trade of farm sector, 68; overtaxation of agriculturalists, 280; GDP, 426; & physical measures of 'development', 428; rural/urban differentials, 430; disparity, 436; real and apparent outputs and disparities, 441; East Pakistan, 371 n.24, 385 n.21. *See also* Bangladesh
Panama, 368 n.24; disparity, 436; product associated with extra labour 440; educational standards in agriculture, 447; distribution of physicians in, 448
Panikar, P.G.K., 402 n.23
Pant, P., 408 n.22
Papanek, G.F., 64, (356), 360 n.4, 362 n.26, 391 n.16, 395 n.29, 411 n.20, 421 n.98
Papua, 219
Paraguay, 264; disparity, 436; distribution of physicians in, 448
Pareto V., definition of efficiency, adjusted, 49-50

Pastoral, 130-8, 166, cf. 233, 333; and exploitation, 42
Patel, S.J., 361 n.10
Patnaik, U., 370 n.7, 375 n.30, 419 n.82
Peasants *see* Farmers (small), Agricultural sector
Peasant movements, misdirection, 330
Pen, J., 366 n.12
Penny, D.H., 415 n.20
Perm (Russia), 115
Peru, 225; education and agriculture, 447; distribution of physicians in, 448
Petty, Sir William, 58
Philippines, 81, 169, 189-90, 225, 264, 298, 315, 361 n.10, 362 n.19, 380 n.95, 388 n.17, 392 n.5, 395 n.31, 434; growing inequality, 32, 361 n.16; growth, 426; physical measures of 'development', 428; rural/urban differentials, 430; disparity, 436; product associated with extra labour, 440; real and apparent outputs and disparities, 441; shares of agriculture, 444; & gross marginal capital/output ratios, 445; education agriculture, 447; distribution of physicians in, 448
Physiocrats, the 376 n.37, 401 n.5
Pick's Currency Guide, 417 nn.45, 49
Pigou, A.C., 102, 366 n.14, 375 n.27, 377 n.43
Piotrow, P., 409 n.43
Plamenatz, J., 373 n.6, 378 n.56
Planners, 13, 20-1, 33-4, 51, 66, 69-70, 146, 184, 199, 208-10, 212, 219, 237, 240-1, 293, 312, 329, 338-9, 342; cf. 126
Pollution, and poverty, 138
Poor people, 14-6, 36-8, 42-3, 53-4, 199, 213, 217, 238, 267, 328, 359 n.2, 361 n.12, 374 n.18, 388 n.13, 389 n.23, 394 n.23, 396 n.5; failure to benefit from growth in LDCs, 27-8, 72; average 1970 income below $50 per head for half of world's poor, 29; food consumption as index of low share in growth, 31-2; anger, 165-6; rural poor gain more than urban poor from extra expenditure in their sector, 167-8; misery and inequality, 172; and